RIVERS

OF

EMPIRE

RIVERS

OF

EMPIRE

*Water, Aridity, and the Growth of
the American West*

DONALD WORSTER

OXFORD UNIVERSITY PRESS
New York   Oxford

Oxford University Press

Oxford   New York   Toronto
Delhi   Bombay   Calcutta   Madras   Karachi
Petaling Jaya   Singapore   Hong Kong   Tokyo
Nairobi   Dar es Salaam   Cape Town
Melbourne   Auckland

and associated companies in
Berlin   Ibadan

Library of Congress Cataloging-in-Publication Data
Worster, Donald, 1941–
Rivers of empire : water, aridity, and the growth of the American
West / Donald Worster.
p.   cm.
Reprint. Originally published: New York : Pantheon, 1985.
Includes bibliographical references and index.
1. Water-supply—Political aspects—West (U.S.)—History—20th
century. 2. Irrigation—Economic aspects—West (U.S.)—
History—20th century. 3. Rivers—West (U.S.)—History—20th
century. 4. West (U.S.)—History. I. Title.
HD1695.A17W67   1992   91-46685
338.91′00978—dc20   CIP
ISBN 0-19-507806-3 (PBK.)

6 8 10 9 7 5
Printed in the United States of America

For William and Catherine

CONTENTS

ACKNOWLEDGMENTS

The help I have received in the writing of this book goes back many years, and some of it has undoubtedly been forgotten or overlooked. Near the top of my remembered list are the libraries and their staffs whose resources and services I have used: the Bancroft Library and Water Resources Center at the University of California at Berkeley, the Huntington in San Marino, the California State Library at Sacramento, the libraries at the University of California at Los Angeles and at Davis, as well as at the Claremont colleges, the Forest History Society archives, the National Archives, and the Library of Congress, among others. I would also like to thank the John Simon Guggenheim Memorial Foundation for their fellowship support, and the University of Hawaii, which provided sabbatical leave and travel funds for this project. The latter institution's Cartography Laboratory (and Lyn Lawrence in particular) provided the maps included here.

Portions of this book have been given as papers before groups scattered all over the American West, though predominately in California, and I have profited greatly from their reactions. I have also drawn on essays I have published in *Agricultural History, Pacific Historical Review,* and *Pacific Historian,* and appreciate their editors' and readers' good suggestions. Daniel Rodgers, John Rodman, Carolyn Merchant, and Mark Helbling have all read portions of the manuscript, furnished useful comments, and encouraged the project. Others who have given help in one form or another include: Judith Austin, Peter Berg, Brent Blackwelder, Lawrence Fuchs, Lewis Gould, David Hall, Richard Hart, Robert Hunt, Irving and Ada Helbling, Wes Jackson, Gary Nabhan, Howard Lamar, Phillip Leveen, Patricia Nelson Limerick, Daniel Luten, Gerard McCauley, Richard Orsi, William Robbins, Morgan Sherwood, Charles Wilkinson, and Langdon Winner. Dan Cullen of Pantheon Books has given this manuscript his sensitive and careful attention, and the final version owes much to him. A warm, affectionate acknowledgment is due my former colleagues and students in American Studies at the University of Hawaii, who generously gave me the time to do much of the writing, and who for many years provided me a most congenial, stimulating, and supportive environment.

This work has obvious links to that of some older historians of the American West, who have meant much to me as inspiration and model: Wallace Stegner, Bernard DeVoto, Walter Prescott Webb, James Malin, and Henry Nash Smith. Another small but distinguished group of historians have preceded me in the study of water in the West, and I have gained much from their ideas and research too, and in some cases, from their comments on my own efforts. They include Gordon Dodd, Robert Dunbar, Norris Hundley, Lawrence Lee, Donald Pisani, and William Kahrl.

The southwestern world of the Colorado River where it edges the Mohave Desert, a world of date palms, dusty railroad stations, and, when the air was right, the powerful smell of nearby water, muddy, pungent, and alive, was my first home and is still deeply imprinted on my memory. This book has in it much of that place of personal beginnings and, of course, of my parents who, though more by hard economic circumstances than by deliberate choice, brought me into it. Those debts to the past are not easy to specify or, at times, even to understand, but are all too easy to leave out of the reckoning. So are others that I owe, and they are the most important of all —to Bev, Katie, and Will, who have given much to me during the writing of this book. Largely because of them, I live, and live gratefully, in a more green, settled, and easy world now. That hard desert world, however, as these pages have argued, had its value too.

Concord, Massachusetts

I have no fear that America will grow too big. A hundred years hence these United States will be an empire, and such as the world never before saw, and such as will exist nowhere else upon the globe. In my opinion the richest portion of it, and a section fully as populous as the East, will be in the region beyond the Mississippi. All through that region, much of which is now arid and not populated, will be a population as dense as the Aztecs ever had in their palmiest days in Mexico and Central America. Irrigation is the magic wand which is to bring about these great changes.

—John W. Noble, Secretary of Interior, quoted in
The Independent (1893)

The ideal scheme is ever beckoning from the West; but the scheme with an ideal record is yet to find—the scheme that shall breed no murmurers, and see no miscreants; that shall avoid envy, hatred, malice, and all uncharitableness; that shall fulfill its promises, and pay its debts, and remember its friends, and keep itself unspotted from the world. Over the graves of the dead, and over the hearts of the living, presses the cruel expansion of our country's material progress: the prophets are confounded, the promises withdrawn, the people imagine a vain thing. Men shall go down, the deed arrives; not unimpeachable, as the first proud word went forth, but mishandled, shorn, and stained with obloquy, and dragged through crushing strains. And those that are with it in its latter days are not those who set out in the beginning. And victory, if it come, shall border hard upon defeat.

—Mary Hallock Foote, *The Chosen Valley* (1892)

O N E

INTRODUCTION

Reflections in a Ditch

The problem of the West is nothing less than the problem of American development.

—*Frederick Jackson Turner, "The Problem of the West" (1896)*

In his 1862 essay "Walking," Henry David Thoreau described a daily ritual that was characteristically American in his time. Coming out of his house on Main Street in Concord, Massachusetts, he would pause for a moment to consult his instincts. Which way should he go for his ramble into the countryside? Generally the needle of his inner compass would settle west or southwest, and he would head off in that direction, just as thousands of pioneers were doing, had done, and would go on doing for a long time to come. "The future lies that way to me," he wrote, "and the earth seems more unexhausted and richer on that side." Going west, he anticipated finding a wilder America where the trees grew taller, the sun shone brighter, and the field of action was still open to fresh heroic deeds. That way the landscape was not yet owned as private property, and the walker could still enjoy a comparative freedom. As he set off in a long, springing stride, he soon left behind him the settled parts of Concord, the constraining fences, the narrow house lots, the clamoring institutions, the dead hand of tradition, the old closed world of diminished opportunity, left them at least for an hour or two, partaking temporarily of the migratory impulse, the spirit of adventure, that had seized so many of his countrymen. "Eastward I go only by force; but westward I go free."[1]

Had Thoreau kept on walking toward the west, traveling well beyond the outskirts of Concord clear to the Pacific shore, had he walked on and on through time into the late twentieth century, what would he have discovered? Would he have come upon a West that had delivered on its promise to him and the nation? Would he have found there in fact a greater scope for individuality, for innovation, for the creative mind, than existed in the East? A people who put less emphasis on the accumulation of property, who practiced less stratification in their society? Would he have found a more perfect democracy? A flourishing of personal freedom? A vindication of the idea of progress?

Thoreau died in the year his essay appeared in print and thus he could not have seen, could not even have anticipated, the real West as it has

3

evolved. For that matter, many who have lived out their lives in the region during more recent times have not seen it either, or at least have not seen some of its more telling outcomes. Even now, a century and more past Thoreau's age of romantic optimism, many westerners—not to mention millions living elsewhere—remain confused by idealizing myths and ritualistic incantations of the old slogans. The West is still supposed, in popular thinking, to be a land of untrammeled freedom, and in some of its corners it may be just that. However, that is not all it is, is not even the more important part of what it is. The American West is also more consistently, and more decisively, a land of authority and restraint, of class and exploitation, and ultimately of imperial power. The time has come to brush away the obscuring mythologies and the old lost ideals and to concentrate on that achieved reality. In 1862, Thoreau was writing about a vaguely located, unrealized, unsettled West still to be experienced, to be made. We, on the other hand, have to come to terms with an established West that now has a long history. To understand that history, to probe the meaning of that region, its dynamics, it contradictions, its dreams and realizations, is to understand better some broader American aspirations and, it may be, something of the aspirations and fates of modern people everywhere.

Perhaps the best place to begin that reexamination of the West is by sauntering along one of its irrigation ditches. In it are important, neglected clues to the meaning of freedom and autonomy, of democratic self-determination and openness, in the historical as opposed to the mythical West. One might choose, for example, the Friant-Kern Canal coming down from the Sierra foothills to the desert lands around Bakersfield in the Great Central Valley of California. It is a vastly different stream of water from the Sudbury and Concord rivers on which Thoreau paddled his boat: those were, in Thoreau's time as they still are today, grass-and-tree-edged rivers moving sluggishly to the sea and required to do little work en route. After 350 years of white settlement, they remain more or less natural flows draining their natural watersheds. Friant-Kern, in contrast, is a work of advanced artifice, a piece not of nature but of technology. It has no watershed of its own but rather draws off water from a reservoir and transports it briskly to deficient areas to raise a cash crop. It means business. For long sections it runs straight as an arrow over the land, cutting across the terrain with a devastating efficiency. Engineers report that it carries, at maximum, 5,000 cubic feet of water per second. In that method of precise calculation is hinted the determination on the part of engineers, farmers, and other modern westerners to wrest every possible return from the canal and its flow. The American West literally lives today by that determination. Though its importance has seldom been well understood, more than any other single element, it has been the shaping force in the region's history. In that determination to exploit to the uttermost, there is little of Thoreau's ideal of freedom sought or expressed or possible. There is no freedom for nature itself, for natural rivers as free-flowing entities with their own integrity and order, and there is very little of the social freedom Thoreau expected humans to enjoy in the West. Friant-Kern offers a study in ecological and social regimentation.

Here then is the true West which we see reflected in the waters of the modern irrigation ditch. It is, first and most basically, a culture and society built on, and absolutely dependent on, a sharply alienating, intensely managerial relationship with nature. Were Thoreau to stroll along such a ditch today, he would find it a sterile place for living things. The modern ditch is lined along its entire length with concrete to prevent the seepage of water into the soil; consequently, nothing green can take root along its banks, no trees, no sedges and reeds, no grassy meadows, no seeds or blossoms dropping lazily into a side-eddy. Nor can one find here an egret stalking frogs and salamanders, or a red-winged blackbird swaying on a stem, or a muskrat burrowing into the mud. Quite simply, the modern canal, unlike a river, is not an ecosystem. It is simplified, abstracted Water, rigidly separated from the earth and firmly directed to raise food, fill pipes, and make money. Along the Friant-Kern Canal, as along many others like it, tall chain-link fences run on either side, sealing the ditch off from stray dogs, children, fishermen (there are no fish anyway), solitary thinkers, lovers, swimmers, loping hungry coyotes, migrating turtles, indeed from all of nature and of human life except the official managerial staff of the federal Bureau of Reclamation. Where the canal passes under highways large, ominous signs are posted: "Stay alive by staying out." The intention of the signs, of course, is to promote public safety by warning the innocent of the dangers of drowning, of being sucked into siphons by the swift current. However, their darker effect is to suggest that the contrived world of the irrigation canal is not a place where living things, including humans, are welcome.

And what of the social order, the shape of western community, which is reflected in the waters of the ditch? That matter is to be the burden of this book, but a few preliminary suggestions may be made here. Exploring the settlements in the vicinity of the Friant-Kern Canal yields at first a sense of social chaos, of a bewildering disorder of people and their daily lives, contrasting markedly with the rigid, clean geometry of their water system. Here, for example, sits in isolation an old black woman in the scanty shade of a peach tree, her chickens scratching in the dust, a hand-lettered advertisement, "Okra for sale," dangling from a stick. Across the road a noisy gang of white children are splashing in a galvanized horse-tank outside their

5

mobile home. Next-door to them is a desolate brown field with rusted irrigation equipment stacked to one side, growing nothing now, as devoid of vegetation and interest as a parking lot, totally divorced from the lives of the children or the woman. Farther down the same road is a new suburban hacienda, separated from the neighbors by an ornate wrought-iron gate and brick wall. This home of a wealthy agribusinessman is resplendent in its brilliant sea of green lawn, the ignored roadside in front of it littered with empty beer cans. Beyond the house, at the end of rows of grapevines ready for harvest, are stacks and stacks of boxes piled by the road. "Malanco of Visalia" is printed on their wooden sides—they are not the property of the hacienda. The smell of oil wells rises incongruously out of alfalfa fields, and silver tanker trucks rumble along the country high-ways, past olive and almond groves. Intermixed are expanses of sugar beets, lying like rows of brown rocks in a field. The cacophonous sounds of machinery are everywhere in the rural air: irrigation pumps, tractors, tomato harvesters, helicopters spraying herbicides, the roar of a cotton gin, the scream of a black supercharged Chevy painted with red swirling flames, carrying migrant workers on to their next job. On every hand one finds a loose miscellany of buildings, crops, and other artifacts scattered across the landscape. The Vineyard Chapel of the Pentacostal Church of God. Our Lady of Guadaloupe. Rose of Sharon and True Light Gospel. Trinity Episcopal. Iglesia Bautista Mexicana. Corterisan Farms. Tenneco Farms. Zaragoza Market. Safeway Incorporated. The blue-green stucco Moctezuma Cafe. The drab pink Pioneer Club. Los 3 Aces Club. Progress Road. Seventh Standard Road. Brown and Bryant Agricultural Chemicals plant. DiGiorgio Park in the town of Arvin, where old Mexican men sit and talk softly in the late afternoons. The defiant words "Fight for Socialism—Power to the Workers" painted on a new wooden stockade surrounding a housing development. A billboard touting a pesticide: "We kill to live." There is nothing harmonious, nothing picturesque about the western world that has developed beside the irrigation ditch. There is little peace or tidiness or care, little sense of a rooted community. There is no equitable sharing of prosperity. The human presence here often seems very much like the tumbleweeds that have been caught in the barbed-wire fences: impermanent, drifting, snagged for a while, drifting again, without grace or character, liable to blow away with a blast of hot desert wind.

There is, however, if one looks carefully, a kind of order underlying this jumbled, discordant West, though it is not in the main the order of nature or of landscape aesthetics or of closely integrated community life. It is a techno-economic order imposed for the purpose of mastering a difficult environment. People here have been organized and induced to run, as the water in the canal does, in a straight line toward maximum yield, maximum profit. This American West can best be described as a modern *hydraulic society,* which is to say, a social order based on the intensive, large-scale manipulation of water and its products in an arid setting. That order is not at all what Thoreau had in mind for the region. What he desired was a society of free association, of self-defining and self-managing individuals and communities, more or less equal to one another in power and authority. The hydraulic society of the West, in contrast, is increasingly a coercive, monolithic, and hierarchical system, ruled by a power elite based on the ownership of capital and expertise. Its face is reflected in every mile of the irrigation canal. One might see in that reflection the qualities of concentrated wealth, technical virtuosity, discipline, hard work, popular acquiescence, a feeling of resignation and necessity—but one cannot find in it much of what Thoreau conceived as freedom.

Few parts of the American West, or for that matter of the world, have been changed so thoroughly as the Great Valley of California. Already at the time Thoreau wrote of walking west, the valley was beginning to undergo an ecological revolution. In turn, that upheaval brought about a social transformation of extraordinary proportions. In both respects, the valley can be seen as representative of an emerging West and its sudden transition, more sudden than in any other region, from wilderness to technological dominance.

The Great Valley is an immense trough extending four hundred miles from north to south. It is hedged about by mountain barriers, the Sierra Nevada to the east, rising to over 14,000 feet in elevation, and the Coast Ranges to the west, not nearly so lofty. In recent geological times (the past million years or so), the floor of the valley has become a poorly drained alluvial plain. Its sandy soils derive from the granite and shale peaks on either side. A cross-section of the pristine natural valley in, say, the Friant-Kern area would show a number of distinct ecological communities, arranged largely by elevation. In the foothills were originally found rolling savannahs dotted with magnificent oaks (the valley oak, *Quercus lobata,* mixed with the blue and live oak). At the low-lying extreme in the river bottoms, other trees, including the box elder, Oregon ash, Fremont poplar, walnut, alder, willow, and cottonwood (not to mention the wild grapes and blackberry vines), joined the oaks to form dense riparian jungles. Otter and beaver swam in the rivers, as did salmon, rainbow trout, perch, and sturgeon. In the southern portion of the valley, south of what is now the city of Fresno, the runoff from the Sierras had great difficulty finding an outlet to the ocean. In fact, several of the rivers there emptied into landlocked

7

lakes—Tulare and Buena Vista were the largest of them—and in flood season they created shallow marshes covering millions of acres. Elsewhere the periodic overflow of the San Joaquin and Sacramento rivers obliterated their edges, making sloughs and wetlands all the way to the delta. Here grew the tules, or bulrushes, reaching as high as eight feet. For several months each year the tule marshes became a wintering ground for migratory waterfowl, including Canada geese, pintails, cinnamon teal, whistling swan, and others. Finally, among the major ecological communities were the flat dry grasslands, making up the largest portion of the valley. The perennial bunch grass was a dominant species there, and on it subsisted the prong-horn antelope and the uniquely Californian herbivore, the tule elk, which ranged in herds of one to two thousand individuals.[2]

When Thoreau was coming of age in Concord, a town already two hundred years old in his lifetime, the Great Valley was still an environment virtually untouched by the white man. It was the undisputed province of those wild creatures and of several Indian peoples. The latter were the Wintun, Patwin, Valley Maidu, Valley or Plains Miwok, and, most numerous, the Valley Yokut tribes, of which there were fifty, each with its own name, dialect, and territory. All of the native peoples were lumped together by the invading white Americans under the contemptuous term "Diggers." These native peoples lived in large villages on the riverbanks or on the borders of seasonal lakes. Although they drew on a variety of food sources —fish, shellfish, game, waterfowl, insects, roots and seeds—their most important staple was the acorn from the valley oaks. Acorns were collected in the fall and stored through the winter in granaries or ground into meal that could be eaten as mush or cake. There was such a plentitude of the food that some 70,000 Yokut, along with the other groups, could subsist in the valley, forming one of the densest concentrations of natives found in North America. Unquestionably, they influenced the pristine ecological communities there, mainly through their use of fire to encourage the plants they wanted to see growing for food and game forage. But because the valley tribes were not agricultural and did not interfere at all with the river flow, their impact was insignificant compared to what came later. There was enough naturally produced food for them to hunt and gather in this place to support their numbers. More than that they did not need nor see any point in acquiring. After several thousand years of their habitation, the valley's ecological order was still more or less intact.[3]

The Spanish rarely ventured into the valley, and when they did, they were repelled by the prospect. It was too hot, dry, and bleak, or alternately too swampy, to attract them away from their coastal missions. The American fur trapper and explorer Jedediah Smith passed through in 1827, and then in 1849 came a voracious horde from the east, from all over the world, looking for gold. To protect the gold seekers from the Indians and make maps of the valley, the American government dispatched Lieutenant George Derby in 1849 and 1850. Derby was a twenty-six-year-old topographical engineer, about Thoreau's age and from his part of the country, but he had received an education in the sciences at West Point and become a wide-ranging traveler with a practical mission. Derby made the first thorough, systematic survey of the valley's agricultural potential. Of the possibilities for white settlers where the San Joaquin and Merced rivers converge, he wrote this: "Exceedingly barren, and singularly destitute of resources, except a narrow strip on the borders of the stream; it was without timber and grass, and can never, in my estimation, be brought into requisition for agricultural purposes." When he moved on south toward Tulare Lake (he called it Taché Lake), he became even more pessimistic about the opportunities. The country was "a perfect desert" and there was "no forage for the animals but wire grass, the water standing in the tulé marshes brackish, and no wood at all." Near the present site of Bakersfield he came upon "the most miserable country that I ever beheld. The soil was not only of the most wretched description, dry, powdery and decomposed, but everywhere burrowed by gophers, and a small animal resembling a common house rat. . . . The country presents the appearance of a large city which has been partially overwhelmed by the ashes of volcanic eruptions." Indeed, from the perspective of traditional humid-land farming, the valley was, over most of its acreage, an uninviting place to settle, and that was Derby's perspective. Consequently, it was for him an ugly, deficient land.[4]

A very different view of the Great Valley, with different implications for white settlement, was taken by another early American traveler, one with more of the wilderness-loving spirit of Thoreau in him than Lieutenant Derby. In 1868, John Muir, a native of Scotland and Wisconsin, came plunging ecstatically down the eastern slope of the Diablo Mountains into what he described as "all one sheet of plant gold, hazy and vanishing in the distance, distinct as a new map along the foot-hills at my feet." It was spring when he arrived, and the rains had produced a radiant world of flowers: gilias, lupines, chrysopsis, clarkia, pentstemons, mint, nemophilas —the species ran on and on, forming "one smooth, continuous bed of honey-bloom." Muir called the valley one of the great "bee-gardens" of California. He waded ankle-deep through the blooms, lay at night on them for a bed, shared their fragrance with the larks, antelopes, hares, and bees. Even then, however, destructive forces were at work in the valley, as he observed while working at a ranch there in the autumn of that year. With the gold seekers "a wild, restless agriculture" had come to the state. These new farmers were destroying the wild flora wholesale with their plows, and, worse, there were sheepmen now in the valley, with their "flocks of hoofed locusts, sweeping over the ground like a fire, and trampling down every rod that escapes the plow as completely as if the whole plain were a cottage garden-plot without a fence." Someday, Muir supposed, the destruction would be at an end, and a more careful set of agriculturists would supplant that generation of exploiters and wasters. The entire valley would then be irrigated from end to end and carefully managed. At that future point, he feared, Americans, surrounded by an artificial world of their own making, would no longer remember the vanished splendor of an awakening prairie spring, when the primeval valley had been at its most magnificent.[5]

In the period from 1850 to 1910, writes ecologist Raymond Dasmann, the state of California experienced a series of massive environmental changes, and nowhere more so than in the Great Valley.[6] During those few decades, the fauna and flora went through an upheaval comparable only to the cataclysmic postglacial extinctions. However, in this later case, the changes were not the work of blind forces of nature but rather of conscious, rational men. Those men, driven by a vision of the valley's potential wealth and by a passion to possess it, shot out the waterfowl. They trapped out the furbearers. They cut down large numbers of the great spreading oaks, burned away the saltbush, the chaparral, the blackberry and willow thickets, and drained the tule marshes. They decimated the large grazing herds, until only a tiny remnant of the elk remained in a wildlife preserve. As their food and habitat disappeared, so did the grizzly, the condor, and the wolf. And so did the aboriginal human settlers, the Yokut and the rest, who became the victims of disease, of superior force, of land hunger. In their place developed the wealthiest agricultural operation in the United States. It was described in 1939 by John Steinbeck in *The Grapes of Wrath,* and since then has been observed by a succession of writers, some of them marveling over its output, some of them critical of its human and environmental costs. All of them would agree that Lieutenant Derby had been hopelessly wrong about the potential of the valley to produce crops and money. All that was required to make the "miserable country" over was the management of water, and by the twentieth century the valley had set up one of the most advanced hydraulic systems in the world, a system that has become more and more elaborate down to the present. The technological control of water was the basis of a new West. It made possible not only the evolution of a prosperous agriculture but also, to a great extent, the growth of coastal cities like Los Angeles and San Francisco. It eventually made California the leading state in America, and perhaps the single most influential and powerful area in the world for its size.

This ecological and social transformation of the Great Valley is one of the most spectacular, and most revealing, episodes of the American West. The point of this book is to explore the implications of that episode and others like it in the region, and to counterpose them to the mythic imaginings of Thoreau, standing at his gate, dreaming beautifully of the wild, the free, the democratic, the individual.

So far, this hydraulic perspective on the West, the view that the society in the region has been shaped by its advanced technological mastery of water, has not received adequate attention. Many books and articles have been written about the arid West and its search for water, and they are good, scholarly books, but they remain on the periphery; they have not yet penetrated very far the thinking of most generalizers and theorists of the region's character. In those generalizers' hands the history of the West has tended to remain, against all evidence to the contrary, what it was in Thoreau's time: a saga of individual enterprise, of men and women going out from civilization to carve with their own hands a livelihood from nature, a tale of release (or attempted release) from eastern form, tradition, and control. To be sure, the West was all of that at times, but for most of its history and for most of its people the region has had a very different story to tell: one of people encountering difficult environments, of driving to overcome them through technological means, of creating the necessary social organization to do so, of leading on and on to indigenous bureaucracy and corporatism. It is time that this emergent technological West, the West of the hydraulic society, the West as seen in the Great Valley of California, be put beside the storybook West of fur trappers, cowboys, sodbusters, and intrepid adventurers.[7]

What I mean to suggest here, then, is a radically new angle of vision on the region and its historical significance. To do that some prevailing ideas must first be cleared out of the way, and that will not be easy. Even though there have been other, challenging voices asking for new departures, the standard interpretation of the West still begins with the old, much-handled frontier theory of Frederick Jackson Turner, a theory that has no water, no aridity, no technical dominance in it, that indeed has very little in it of the West as it is geographically defined today. Turner's views, first expressed in his celebrated essay "The Significance of the Frontier in American History" (1893), were shaped by the early period of the agricultural settlement of Wisconsin. That experience was one of dispersed occupation of a humid forest and prairie environment, and out of it came, so Turner maintained, a culture of individualism, self-reliance, and diffused power—the culture of American democracy. For all of its shortcomings the theory still

11

remains plausible for the history of Wisconsin or Ohio. But it is not a theory that is readily applicable to the West that lies beyond the Mississippi River, especially the West of deserts, semideserts, and dry crackling plains, of dust storms, cactus, alkaline wells, and bunch grass, the West of California, Idaho, Utah, and New Mexico—in other words, the West as we commonly locate it today. Turner himself had little direct experience of that West, so it is not surprising that it scarcely entered into his thinking.[8]

Turner was aware, nonetheless, that the western half of the United States would work a few changes in his theory of frontier culture and society. In an *Atlantic Monthly* article of 1903, he noted that in the preceding fifteen years western settlement had reached the Great Plains, where "new physical conditions have . . . accelerated the social tendency of Western democracy." The conquest of that country would be impossible, he went on, "by the old individual pioneer methods." The new frontier required "expensive irrigation works," "cooperative activity," and "capital beyond the reach of the small farmer." What Turner called "the physiographic province," that is, the condition of water scarcity, "decreed that the destiny of this new frontier should be social rather than individual." He compared it to the changes in social structure going on elsewhere in America: this West would be from the outset an "industrial" order, giving rise to "captains of industry," home-grown or imported versions of men like Andrew Carnegie, who were taking charge of the country generally. The task of settling the arid West, like that of creating a technological society, was too awesome for ordinary people using ordinary skills to carry out; they must therefore "combine under the leadership of the strongest." They would also be forced to rely on the federal government to build for them huge dams, reservoirs, and canals as well as show them "what and when and how to plant." "The pioneer of the arid regions," he concluded, "must be both a capitalist and the protégé of the government." That these were fundamental differences from the requirements of the old eastern frontiers, Turner clearly understood, yet strangely he assumed that his American democracy would be unaffected by them. The region would become a "social" rather than an "individual" democracy, but all the same it would be a democracy, freedom-loving and self-governing. To see matters otherwise would have shattered the hopeful, nationalistic pride that Turner felt in the westward movement.[9]

After Turner's theory of the frontier, the most influential interpretation of western American history has been that of Walter Prescott Webb, first developed in his book *The Great Plains*, published in 1931. It too has to be heavily revised to account for the West reflected in the waters of the Friant-Kern Canal. Professor Webb grew up in a milieu of dispersed small farmers trying to survive in droughty Texas. From that vantage, he sought to correct Turner by maintaining that there had not been a single process of frontier settlement, but two distinctly different processes, one involving an adaptation to the humid, forested landscape of the eastern states, the other an adaptation to the dry, treeless ecology found on the plains and westward. In the latter situation, settlers had to devise altogether new technologies and institutions or they would lose out. They had to begin using barbed wire instead of rail fencing, windmills and underground aquifers instead of springs and brooks, had to adopt new weapons, new water laws, and new housing materials. The American pioneers had come to "an institutional *fault* (comparable to a geological fault) running from middle Texas to Illinois or Dakota, roughly following the ninety-eighth meridian. At this *fault* the ways of life and living changed." This latest and last West must therefore become a unique region of the United States, one that could be understood only in terms of its own arid environment and of its people's ingenuity in meeting that condition.[10]

So far, Webb was perspicacious and on his way to a profound historical insight. A problem in developing this interpretation appeared, however, when he became caught in a misleading comparison of the West to the American South, making both regions weak, exploited dependencies of the main national power centers. At first the West was supposed by him to be innovative, unique, clearly set apart from the country east of his dividing meridian. However, he then went on to admit that all of the technical innovations in his region were mass-produced and marketed by easterners as part of what he called the "Industrial Revolution." It was through this dependence, he feared, that westerners had eventually come into bondage to eastern, metropolitan centers of capital. Their predicament, he pointed out, had been precisely the fate of the South: it too was an outlying region brought under domination, in this case by the cotton gin and the textile factory invented in the North.

> Both kingdoms [West and South] became tributary to the masters of the Industrial Revolution. Both kingdoms produced what promised to be a distinctive civilization, a thing apart in American life. Both kingdoms were pioneers in their character, the first occupants and users of the soil. And in time both were completely altered by the force that had developed them.[11]

The analogy between the two regions, Webb knew, broke down at points, but he never quite realized how badly it broke down. For one thing, the West was from its beginning far more adept than the South at learning the

13

methods of the modern technological domination of nature. In its condition of aridity, it had a powerful environmental force to make those lessons compelling. Hence it would not remain for long in a state of subordination, would not fight a losing, dispiriting war for independence; it would discover how to compel the rest of the nation to help finance its environmental conquest, and thus would emerge as a far more serious rival to the north-eastern hegemony than the South had ever been. Had Webb looked closely at California as well as at backwoods Texas, had he focused on the dams and canals of the West rather than on windmills, had he seen the entire region as an emergent hydraulic society, his interpretation might have stood up better over time.

What Webb was getting at was a view of the West as a colony of the American Empire, an empire centered in eastern metropolises. What he wanted was a regional declaration of independence from that empire. Already when he wrote, the idea of the West as a colony was a well-established one, having its roots in the Populist revolt against bankers and railroads in the 1890s, and it continued to draw support for a long while thereafter, so much so that it has become, along with Turner's theory, a major generalization for dealing with the western experience. In 1934, for example, just three years after Webb's work on the plains, Bernard DeVoto described the region as "a plundered province," and the plunderers he had in mind were easterners.[12] More recently, the colonial image of the West has resurfaced in the so-called Sagebrush Rebellion, in which many westerners have complained that the federal government imperiously controls their destiny through ownership of the public lands—the implication generally being that the government should turn over those lands to western entrepreneurs to exploit as rapidly as possible. A more thoughtful expression of that stance has appeared in the book *The Angry West,* written by the Colorado governor Richard Lamm and the historian Michael McCarthy. In their words, "the dark riders are at the gates," once more threatening western freedom. Those riders are all outsiders, all vaguely easterners—the private energy companies mining coal and oil shale, the Defense Department looking for missile sites, the Bureau of Land Management, the environmentalists, and President Carter, who, far away in Washington, wanted to cut back on western water projects.[13]

The trouble with such colonialist arguments, from Webb on down, is not that they are wholly false; they do point to a certain reality that has long been familiar to many westerners, particularly those living in the hinterland of the plains and Rockies. But they leave much out of the discussion, and what they leave out is the larger, more comprehensive truth about the region. The American West is not so much a colony as it is an empire; for a long time it was an empire in intention only, then after World War Two it became one in fact. Indeed, since the war it has become a principal seat of the world-circling American Empire. That is the interpretation I intend to develop here. How that imperial West arose out of the desert and near-desert, what it had to do with the command over nature there, what it has meant for Thoreau's mythic search for freedom—these are the leading themes of this book. And they all begin and end with water.

TWO

TAXONOMY

The Flow of Power in History

All thinking worthy of the name must now be ecological.

> —Lewis Mumford, The Pentagon of Power
> *(1970)*

There once were men capable of inhabiting a river without disrupting the harmony of its life.

> —Aldo Leopold, "Song of the Gavilan" *(1940)*

E arth has been variously called the planet of water and the planet of life, the connection between the two attributes being by no means casual. Without water, there simply can be no life. Water flows in the veins and roots of all living organisms, as precious to them as the air they breathe and the food they eat. It is the lifeblood of their collective body.

Water has been critical to the making of human history. It has shaped institutions, destroyed cities, set limits to expansion, brought feast and famine, carried goods to market, washed away sickness, divided nations, inspired the worship and beseeching of gods, given philosophers a metaphor for existence, and disposed of garbage. To write history without putting any water in it is to leave out a large part of the story. Human experience has not been so dry as that.

The power of water over history is a very old discovery. The earliest map of the Middle East, dating from the eighteenth century B.C., shows the River Euphrates dividing the lands of the earth into two islands. Around the perimeter of the map flows the vast circling sea, Oceanus, the ultimate river from which all lesser rivers come, at once the source and the destination of Euphrates. Human existence must be carried on, the map indicates, within that watery loop and along its pathways. It is easy to see how such a view of the earth could lead to the Bible story of a great deluge, leaving Noah, his family, and the animals resting precariously on a mountaintop in the aftermath. Too much water, that story tells us, has been one of the oldest plagues visited on the human species, wiping out life and property with such completeness that it has seemed like divine retribution for some monumental evil people have committed.

In other situations, however, it was the scarcity of water, not its excess, the potential to desiccate and shrivel, not the potential to surround and flood, that made people aware of the significance this element holds for living. "Water is important to people who do not have it," writes Joan Didion, "and the same is true of control." The fear of going dry has driven many communities to extraordinary efforts, provoking in them the deepest anxiety, the sorriest desperation, forcing them to make radical changes in their behavior and institutions. It has stirred them out of lethargy to undertake the most difficult labors: building enormous engineering works to bring water from distant places and stave off their thirst. That reaching out to establish control over a river, often driven by the raw instinct to survive, has had profound implications for the course of history. In light of such human endeavor, history has become no longer a matter of Euphrates dominating people, but of people bent on dominating Euphrates.

Control over water has again and again provided an effective means of consolidating power within human groups—led, that is, to the assertion by some people of power over others. Sometimes that outcome was unforeseen, a result no one really sought but dire necessity seemed to require. In other places and times, the concentration of power within human society that comes from controlling water was a deliberate goal of ambitious individuals, one they pursued even in the face of protest and resistance.

The history of providing protection for humans against rampaging floods undoubtedly furnishes some examples of how this process of power consolidation works. It is the nature of floods, however, to be sporadic and unpredictable; therefore, flood protection by itself has usually had a limited, ambiguous impact on the structure of society and power. Irrigation, on the other hand, is a type of water control that is constant, pervasive, and more socially demanding. Unlike flood protection, it leads in all cases to communal reorganization, to new patterns of human interaction, to new forms of discipline and authority. The difference is between holding an umbrella over your head when it rains and making the rain go somewhere else. The first is a momentary defense, the second a concerted attempt to control and defeat a threat once and for all. Consequently, nothing suggests more clearly than the study of irrigation in history how dependent societies may become, not merely on water, but on their manipulations of its flow. And nothing makes more clear the link between water control and the social orders humans have created than irrigation history.

The American West is only the latest in a long series of experiments in building an irrigation society. Unfortunately it has never been studied in the context of that larger world experience. As a result, the connections between aridity, human thirst, water control, and social power have not been obvious to the region or its historians. To remedy that failure—and it is an immense one, with immense implications—we must make a long, wide-ranging excursion outside the borders of the United States to the farthest points of the earth, wherever other people have also encountered dry places and tried to overcome their natural limits. We must ask what have been the main modes of water control that have evolved in those places, where the case of the West fits into that taxonomy, and where it compares to and where it differs from the other modes. Then we may be able to say more precisely what the western manipulation of rivers has produced in social terms—what the flow of power in this region has been and is today.

Much more is needed, however, than a mere catalogue of the varieties of river manipulation in history. By itself that would lead to a few superficial conclusions about the American West and its differences from other irrigation societies. It would not lead us into deeper waters. It would not tell us much about questions that transcend the region and its idiosyncrasies, that have to do with fundamental issues facing humans in their dealings with technology and the environment everywhere. The West offers that larger resonance. In particular it has much to tell us about the social implications embedded in our various ways of dealing with nature. But to catch those larger tones the historian must move beyond typology to the realm of theory, beyond making comparisons to drawing out general ideas. A history of water use without any theory in it becomes a mere massing of details—specifics without conclusions, data without consequences.

The theory that underlies the specific problem of water and society in history comes out of the interdisciplinary study of culture and ecology. This chapter will undertake to tap some of that ecological work, lying as it does for the historian like a great hidden, unutilized aquifer, concealing in its depths many important suggestions for understanding the relationship humans have worked out with nature, in the past and today, and the consequences of that relationship. The man who first began pumping in earnest from that aquifer was a German immigrant to America, the historian Karl Wittfogel, a sometime student of Karl Marx. It is to his work, therefore, that we must first turn to gain some larger understanding of the issues involved in irrigation. Then it will be time to look at those several modes of water-controlling societies and to find a place among them for the western American experience.

WITTFOGEL, MARX,
AND THE ECOLOGY
OF POWER

The idea that nature has had something to do with the shaping of cultures and history is an idea that is both obviously true and persistently neglected. Maybe that is because there have been so many absurd versions of it, so many laughable claims: for instance, hot weather has been supposed to make peoples passionate and volatile like the Italians—or is it metaphysical and speculative like Plato and the Hindus? The fatal temptation in this line of thinking has always been to fasten on a single factor of nature, like climate, and proceed to discover its influence everywhere. A more credible strategy would be to regard nature as participating in an unending dialectic with human history, seeing the two, that is, as intertwined in an ongoing spiral of challenge–response–challenge, where neither nature nor humanity ever achieves absolute sovereign authority, but both continue to make and remake each other.

That is the more complex perspective suggested by modern ecology, which describes a nature that is an exquisite interacting of diverse species, a circle of interdependence and mutuality. Bring humans into the picture, and the circle of life broadens to include diverse cultures as well as biological species, all of them working to reshape one another. Nothing is ever finished in that dialectic between history and natural history. Nothing can be abstracted altogether from its context or be said to have made itself in splendid isolation.[1]

In the case of irrigation, an ecological view of history would hold that aridity has been a crucial, though not a rigidly deterministic experience for people to deal with. Whenever they attempted to overcome that condition, they gave a new shape to the environment, creating artificial rivers with dams, aqueducts, and the like. But it was not simply a one-way process of humans re-creating nature. Society, even in its so-called triumphs, inescapably came to bear the mark of the desert and of its own effort to overcome the environmental exigencies there.

Such in essence is the argument made by Karl Wittfogel, a twentieth-century scholar of Chinese civilization and architect of the controversial "hydraulic society" thesis. Where the scale of water control escalated in the ancient desert world, he maintained, where larger and larger dams and more and more elaborate canal networks were built, political power came to rest in the hands of an elite, typically a ruling class of bureaucrats. Those were the "hydraulic societies," and in their most extreme forms they became despotic regimes in which one or a few supreme individuals wielded absolute control over the common people as they did over the rivers that coursed through their territory.

Wittfogel's ecological interpretation of ancient irrigation societies has come to have a certain familiarity—though it has often been more a notoriety—among historians and anthropologists, particularly those who style themselves cultural ecologists or cultural materialists. But his theory, though it exemplifies to a remarkable degree the ecological approach to history, has older origins than the recently popular science of ecology. It had its taproot in the work of Karl Marx and his dialectical approach to history, more specifically, in those ideas of Marx, though he addressed them only fragmentarily, about the role of nature in social change and how that role might account for the peculiarities of many Asian cultures. And Marx was not the only source for Wittfogel's theorizing; it owes a great deal also to the intellectual milieu of Weimar Germany, to the sociology of Max Weber, and to the nascent Frankfurt School of radical social thought, which took as one of its main themes the study of power and domination, including the domination of the earth which derives from modern technology. What all these various influences converged to say to Wittfogel was that the most telling history is not to be found in the chronicles of kings, generals, wars, and politics; it is written in the book of nature.

Karl August Wittfogel was born in 1896 in the Hanoverian village of Woltersdorf, Germany. He grew to maturity during the most tumultuous period in modern times, the era of the two world wars, the Russian Revolution, the fascist madness, and the rise of totalitarianism. In 1920 he joined the German Communist party, subsequently becoming one of the leading Marxist scholars in the Weimar Republic. But he was also, in this chaotic swirling of ideas, a student of the writings of that other seminal thinker in Germany, Max Weber. It was Weber who first introduced him to the peculiar "hydraulic-bureaucratic official-state" in China and India, and as a student of those states, Wittfogel soon made his reputation by attempting to discover how their bureaucratic apparatus had come into being and what impact it had had on their social structures. In his first major work, *Economy and Society in China*, published in 1931, he attempted the difficult task of merging Weber's emphasis on the influence of bureaucracy on thought and power with Marx's analysis of economic class relations and politics. That significant early work was written at the Institute for Social Research

—popularly known as the Frankfurt School—which Wittfogel had joined in 1925.[2]

Just as he was launching himself on his career as an Asia scholar, however, Wittfogel's world fell apart. In 1933 Adolf Hitler took command of Germany, and immediately the young scholar found his life in danger, for he had been an outspoken critic of fascism, assailing it from the public platform in city after city. While attempting to flee the country, he was picked up by the police and thrown into a concentration camp. A vigorous outpouring of protest from English and American intellectuals persuaded the Gestapo to release him after several months, and thereupon he migrated to the United States, first to Columbia University, then to the University of Washington, where he taught Chinese history until his retirement in 1966. By that point, he had long since forsaken his early communist enthusiasms—in fact, had become rigidly anticommunist, attacking the Russians as vigorously as he once had the fascists. His was a wild, heady life, one that was always in the thick of momentous issues.

The core idea that remained constant throughout Wittfogel's long intellectual odyssey was that Asian societies had taken a different evolutionary path than those in the Occident. Much earlier, before Max Weber even, Marx had made the same observation, speaking as he did of an "Asiatic mode of production" that did not follow the European stages of development (the progression from classical slavery to feudalism to capitalism and finally to communism).[3] Marx, who in turn took the notion of a divergent Orient from James and John Stuart Mill and from several eighteenth-century thinkers before them, found it to be a troublesome aberration. How could one identify a dependable, scientific law of progress if it applied only to one small continent? Among Marx's followers, the problem of Asia became even more pressing after the long-awaited first communist revolution, for as many have noted, it occurred in the wrong place—in Russia, a country that had not yet experienced the capitalist stage, a country that was suspiciously close to those backward Asian regimes lying beyond the pale of scientific progress. Was the new Soviet order of 1918 a true harbinger of the future, or was it a betrayal of the dream, a society perfidiously using Marxist rhetorical trappings to conceal another antiprogressive Oriental state? That was the big question that came to intrigue the young Wittfogel. Finding an answer to it, strange as it may seem, led him not only to China and Asia but also to irrigation and water.

Germany in the Weimar period of the 1920s was buzzing with radical, cosmopolitan inquiry. In Berlin and Frankfurt cafés, intellectuals and activists argued over the new Soviet Union, the meaning of the late war, the colonial struggle against European imperialism, and the promise of an awakening communist East. Hundreds of Chinese students were enrolled at the universities, most of them followers of Sun Yat-sen and Chiang Kai-shek, both of whom were setting up what was seen then as a new revolutionary state in China. (Actually, it was far more bourgeois.) Wittfogel, son of a village schoolmaster though he was, threw himself with passionate concern into this international dialogue. Early on, he decided China was to become the archetypal society of his time and that it would be his mission to help westerners understand it. Just as Marx in the preceding century had chosen England as the clearest exemplar of capitalist society, so Wittfogel would explain to people what China had been and what it represented for the twentieth century.[4] It foreshadowed, he soon concluded, a scary future for humankind. Like Marx, Wittfogel did not select his country of study for its romantic, ideal qualities; rather, he found in China an unrelievedly repressive past—the China of a thousand years' stagnation and slavery—and the threat of a spreading, sinister modern influence. In the place of Marx's British capitalist, Wittfogel put the Chinese bureaucrat and his state apparatus: here was the old, and now very new, specter of domination facing the planet.

It was unclear to Wittfogel himself in the first phase of his China studies that he was headed in what might be regarded as an unpopular direction. He had found an academic and political interest perfectly consonant with the global imagination of Marxism, but ultimately these studies would lead him where most mainstream, straitlaced Marxists (not to mention typical café revolutionaries) would not want to go: to an indictment of centralized state regimes, of bureaucratic authoritarianism, and above all of those new social orders proudly bearing the label "communist."

Wittfogel remained more loyal to the Marxist cause in his dedication to promoting the scientific, materialist analysis of society. It is important, he believed, to move beneath surface details and to reveal the underlying structure of social patterns, for only changes at that basic level can produce genuine, permanent progress. That is also, of course, the theory of historical materialism as Karl Marx enunciated it. For Marx, the underlying base of any society is its "mode of production" *(Produktionsweise)*, the process by which people extract from nature their subsistence and accumulate their wealth. It is, in simplest terms, the human interaction with the earth, but there is nothing really simple about it. The mode of production involves a complex mix of ecological factors, technology, and social relations—this last including, for instance, the relations between workers and capitalists in the capitalist mode, which has dominated recent history. All social wealth comes from those elements working in concert, coming in part as the gift of nature (in the form of soil, water, coal, forests, and the like) and in part as the product of human labor.[5]

Up to this point, Marx's historical dialectic closely resembles the modern ecological perspective on culture and history. But as nature increasingly bears the impress of human energy and technique, Marx claimed, as it becomes a "second nature" of artifice, the effective terms of the dialectic change. The original conversation between a powerful, independent world of nature and a smaller, struggling world of human communities eventually gives way to one between technology and society. Hence history appears almost always in Marx—certainly European history does—as a struggle between one class of people and another, as a matter of laborers extracting a surplus from a passive physical world of "resources" lying before them like an open mine, then watching that surplus get taken away from them by those who own the tools. Nature as a real, intrinsically significant, autonomous entity gets obliterated, by workers and owners alike, in Marx's onward march of social progress.[6]

The progress of history then involved leaving nature behind as a key formative element, supplanting it with the productive apparatus and class structure contrived by humans. Marx well understood that there were psychic costs paid in that liberation, including the alienation it entailed from the rest of the natural world. Capitalism, he wrote in *Grundrisse,* has freed humans from the age-old, localized dependence on the earth and the "nature idolatry" with which it was associated.

> For the first time, nature becomes purely an object for humankind, purely a matter of utility; ceases to be recognized as a power for itself, and the theoretical discovery of its autonomous laws appears merely as a ruse so as to subjugate it under human needs, whether as an object of consumption or as a means of production.[7]

However, for Marx the alienation from nature introduced by capitalism and its technological mastery was a price worth paying, for it made possible a higher level of civilization, a fuller realization of humanity. That confidence was embedded firmly in his materialist theory of history.

Wittfogel learned much from this historical materialism of Marx, but, once again, he sidled off onto his own path, rescuing the ecological factor from Marx's neglect and placing it at the very center of his own scientific history. The natural environment and the technology used to produce wealth from it—together constituting the "means of production"—became for him more primary throughout history than Marx's social relations and forms of property ownership. In 1928 Wittfogel published his essay "Geopolitik, Geographischer, Materialismus und Marxismus," wherein he wrote: "Man and his work on one side, nature and its material on the other —this is the fundamental relation, the eternal natural condition of human life upon which every form of this life, and above all its social form, is dependent."[8] As societies try to remake nature, they remake themselves, without ever really escaping natural influences. In this spiral of history the people are by no means like helpless passengers of a boat that is being tossed this way and that in a storm; there are options open to them at every point. But always they must respond to nature, then fit themselves to their response.[9]

Having restored nature to a more pivotal role in historical materialism, Wittfogel was ready to tackle the problem of Asia and its peculiar development. What had been the mode of production in that part of the world, he asked, and what ecological forces had been involved in the emergence of that mode? In two key works he undertook to lay out some answers. The first was an essay, "The Theory of Oriental Society," which appeared in 1938 after he made a trip to China; it served as a trial run for the second and larger work, his magnum opus of twenty years later, *Oriental Despotism: A Comparative Study of Total Power* (1957). The thread connecting the two writings was running water. The Oriental mode of production, he explained, "first arises when waterworks must be undertaken on a larger scale (for purposes of protection and irrigation)."[10] During the four thousand years before Christ, in the great river valleys of Egypt, Mesopotamia, India, and China, the state took on the function of building grand hydraulic works, which in turn required centralized managerial bureaucracies to operate. Whoever controlled those means of production—in such cases it was a group of agromanagerial experts—became perforce the effective ruling class. The common techno-environmental basis in all those ancient Oriental civilizations, giving rise to similar social structures in them, was water control, mainly a program of irrigation made necessary by inadequate or unseasonal or undependable rainfall. In the case of China, there were both irrigation for its rice paddies and flood-control works to tame the Huang Ho raging down from the soft, eroding loess highlands. Together these forms of water manipulation made that country, along with its neighbors, very different from Marx's Europe.

After he emigrated from Europe and came to know his New World home better, Wittfogel realized that large-scale irrigated agriculture had been an ancient American as well as an Asian phenomenon. Consequently, by 1957 he was usually substituting the phrase "hydraulic society" for "Oriental

society" to indicate that water-controlling mode of production and its at-
tendant social order.[11] Wherever it was found, its outcome was always a
repressive use of power and the defeat of all change. Crises, whether
brought on by overexpansion or by invasion, might come and go in such
systems, but so long as irrigation continued, no real movement, no revolution, could occur in the social system. Whereas in a more fortunate Europe,
Wittfogel believed, a decentralized agriculture under feudalism and abundant rainfall had allowed the commencement of capital accumulation and
the rise of modern industrial capitalism, "the centralized structure of the
highly productive Oriental agrarian order worked in the opposite direction,
namely towards the reproduction of the existing order, towards its stagnation."[12] Big irrigation thus created a bondage of inertia.

At the time of the 1938 essay, Wittfogel was still a communist, but by
the time *Oriental Despotism* came out, he had thoroughly forsaken the faith.
The mutual tolerance pact signed by Stalin and Hitler in 1939 was the final,
decisive event. Henceforth he was an implacable foe of the Soviet Union.
When the Chinese followed Moscow's revolutionary lead in 1948, Wittfogel
began to see more clearly than ever the face of the demon haunting his
historical imagination. It was "total power," or totalitarianism: an inordi-
nately strong government that controlled the economy, the political sector,
even the thoughts of its citizens.[13] Ironically, it was not the Nazi regime
of his native Germany that he began to attack with vehemence, though he
had suffered more at its hands than at any other's. It was instead a deadly
virus spreading out of Asia, threatening to infect and destroy western
civilization, that he perceived. The ancient hydraulic societies now became
for him the precursors of the modern socialist dictatorships. Russia, he
claimed, had long been a "marginal" version of Oriental despotism, a
country infected by the conquering Mongol hordes. Now Joseph Stalin had
brought about, not a communist utopia, but an "Asian restoration."[14]
Communist China was even more obviously a case of that incurable disease
reasserting itself.

What had begun in the twenties as a search for scientific truth and
positive laws of society had by the fifties become an elaborate web of
inconsistencies, demonology, and ethnocentrism. Wittfogel's early brilliant
insight into the connection between irrigation ecology and social power lay
in shreds. The Soviet Union was totalitarian, he supposed, because it had
long ago been influenced by people who themselves had merely come into
contact with Asian hydraulic systems. This was his new theme, and with
it historical theorizing began to run wild. How could a bureaucratic power
elite migrate or diffuse across the landscape without taking its base along
—without reconstructing the mode of production that had created it? Sta-

lin's power, it was obvious to most observers, had not been established on irrigation. Aware of this embarrassment, Wittfogel abruptly chose to abandon his theory altogether. Oriental society, he began to argue, "cannot be explained in purely ecological or economic terms; and the spread of Oriental despotism to areas lacking a hydraulic agriculture underlies the limitations of such an explanation."[15] But what then was left of his theory, after such an admission, except for the flagrantly ethnocentric argument that the Chinese and Russians were, by nature, incapable of achieving the progressive levels of European capitalism and freedom? That only in western cultures could one expect to see a more humane future evolve, one committed to democratic values? The fact that Wittfogel never addressed the emergence of totalitarianism within modern Occidental society, as in the case of Germany, made his shifting logic all the more suspect.[16]

But it would be a serious mistake for Wittfogel's readers to overreact to his excesses, throwing out his genuine insights along with his logic-chopping. Though the theory of Oriental despotism may have become far-fetched and prejudicial when stretched to account for the twentieth-century failure of socialism, though no mode of production can ever explain the full essence of a society, all of Wittfogel's thinking does not deserve to be tossed onto the rubbish heap. There are profoundly important questions to raise, as he did, about the link between water and power, not in a spirit of scientism or ethnocentrism or demonism, but simply in the hope of understanding more fully the consequences of our behavior toward nature.

Even as he was wandering off into anticommunist tendentiousness, Wittfogel began to acquire a following among a new group of scholars, the cultural ecologists in anthropology. They were less interested in either his new or his old politics than in his theory of irrigation and society. In 1953 Julian Steward, an anthropologist at Columbia and later the University of Illinois, asked Wittfogel to join a symposium on irrigation assembling in Tucson, Arizona, where he would meet experts on Mesopotamia and Mesoamerica, intensely attracted to his hydraulic ideas.[17] Steward, who had himself been deeply impressed by the "Theory of Oriental Society" essay and the promise it held out for cross-cultural irrigation research, had begun to construct an ecologically based anthropology that would demonstrate how cultures evolve as they adapt to their environments. Underlying every culture, he suggested, there is a "core" (more or less equivalent to Wittfogel's "mode of production") that includes a "constellation of features which are most closely related to subsistence activities and economic activities."[18] Irrigation is one of those cultural cores, and Steward's symposium was the first of a series of studies to explore its social implications comparatively. From that meeting on, Karl Wittfogel began to lead a double life: as a defender of the "free world" against Stalin and Mao Tse-tung (Wittfogel I) and as an interdisciplinary authority on the ancient irrigation civilizations (Wittfogel II). Though once again he began to stir up his usual controversy, Wittfogel II would have a more enduring success than Wittfogel I.

Scholars still have not come to a firm consensus about the role that irrigation played in early cultural evolution, but the literature on the subject is now large and ripe for synthesis and criticism.[19] One of the most serious weaknesses in that literature, it must be said straight off, is that the modern experience with irrigation hardly appears in it. Nowhere do the ecological anthropologists—nor does Wittfogel, for that matter—seem to realize that the link between water control and social power might occur in places other than the archaic cradles of civilization nor that the past hundred years have seen more irrigation development than all of previous history.

Karl Wittfogel deserves to be remembered today, not for his Cold War dogmatism or the ultimate stagnation of his ideas, but for those bright, creative years when he raised a profound question: How, in the remaking of nature, do we remake ourselves? It is not a simple question to answer, for as we have seen here, it demands a wide knowledge of history, technology, the forces of nature, and social organization. But if we focus our attention more narrowly on rivers and their manipulation, and on the human consequences of that manipulation, as Wittfogel did, we may make the question more manageable. We may also, if we are inspired by his global imagination and ecological perspective, discover an America that we have not yet clearly seen—an America to put beside China and the other ancient hydraulic societies for comparison. It may be not only the Russians or the Asians we must worry about, as Wittfogel came to believe, but also ourselves.

THE LOCAL
SUBSISTENCE MODE

Like the taxonomy of butterflies or liverworts, irrigation societies may be lumped together and split and lumped again, until the essential question of how power evolves in them gets completely lost. The splitters are the ones who do most of the obscuring. Admittedly they are, in their devotion to finding differences, right to a point: no two water systems are exactly alike, either in natural setting or social anatomy. Some develop in narrow mountain valleys pierced by ice-cold torrents, others in broad alluvial plains drenched by monsoon storms, and still others in deserts where the streams evaporate away much of the year. Irrigation may supplement a hunter's diet with a few tubers, or it may support an agribusinessman's crop of pistachios traded all over the world. The irrigators may throw their babies into the water in sacrifice to their river gods; then again, they may worship at the altar of modern hydraulic engineering and throw away their money. The quality of uniqueness must be respected, as the splitters insist, but it should not be used to defy all generalization, for generalization is what makes critical inquiry possible. In this case, we first need to do some lumping together, locating a few unities among the varieties of irrigation societies. We can follow several criteria in that lumping: the scale of waterworks involved in each instance, the kind of managerial authority needed to operate them, and the goals pursued by the irrigators. The lumps resulting from that analysis may not suit the most inveterate splitters, but they will help focus our minds on the basic historical issues, especially the issue of how one mode of water control develops into another.

Three broad modes of water control have appeared so far in history. Each of them has had, as we will see, its own set of techniques and apparatus, its own pattern of social relationships, its own arrangement of power. There was the local subsistence mode, the agrarian state mode, and the capitalist state mode, this last found in the modern American West.

In the first and simplest type of irrigation society, based on the local subsistence mode, water control relies on temporary structures and small-scale permanent works that interfere only minimally with the natural flow of streams. The needs served by that simple technology are basic and limited: water is diverted to grow food for direct, personal consumption. Little if any of that food ever leaves the community. It is, in a sense, water flowing directly into the mouths of those who have diverted it from nature —who have dug ditches with their own hands, thrown up their own brush or rock dams, and watched the vital liquid soak into the earth around their plants. In such cases authority over water distribution and management remains completely within the local community, with those who are the users. They have within themselves, which is to say, within their vernacular traditions, all the skill and expertise required to build and maintain their water system. They are self-reliant, self-sufficient, and self-managing as individuals and as a community, though nature still sets in the main the terms on which their lives are lived.

Within this primitive agricultural economy, where production for direct use prevails, the organization of power remains loose and unconsolidated.

31

To the extent it exists at all, power follows the lines of family and kinship. There is no centralized seat of command, no stratification of people into social and economic classes, no large accumulations of private wealth, no elaborate division of labor, no state. Men may have their separate jobs, women have theirs, and those distinctions may hardly be egalitarian. But the individual, whether male or female, like the community itself retains substantial autonomy. On men and women alike the task of water management sits lightly, demanding little regimentation, involving few orders from above, and proceeding essentially by informal consensus and engrained habit rather than by imposed demands. Where everyone in the community knows roughly as much as anyone else about the process of irrigation, where the work is within everyone's sphere of competence, and where the ends of water use are elemental human nutrition, there is no compelling reason for much hierarchy or discrimination. Power is diffused, elites are inchoate.[1]

Irrigation at this most fundamental level, it has been suggested, began on dry steppes many thousands of years ago, most likely around water holes where game animals gathered to drink. There they could be easily killed by primitive hunters—too easily killed, in fact. The hunters, when they had exhausted their meat supply in those places, when they began to feel hunger, experimented with a new stratagem, scratching channels in the soil with their digging sticks and leading rainwater off to clumps of wild plants. Though many anthropologists would argue that agriculture appeared long before there was any irrigation, that farmers and not hunters invented it, the origins remain disputed and obscure.[2]

In the prehistoric Owens Valley of California, the Paiute people apparently did practice just such an irrigation without agriculture. According to Julian Steward, they did not plant, till, or cultivate the earth but cleverly watched how nature waters the grasses and bulbs, then followed suit. Eventually they learned how to throw a temporary dam of boulders, brush, and mud across a creek where it debouched onto the valley floor. Above the dam, they cut shallow ditches to divert water toward their favorite wild food species. Quite possibly this practice was a completely indigenous invention, though duplicated by gatherers living in other parts of the earth. So irrigation may have begun in some places even in advance of horticulture.[3]

Elsewhere in the American Southwest, the control of water was an idea that journeyed northward from what is now Mexico and adapted itself to local farming needs. The Pueblo societies had long been skilled irrigators when the Spanish conquistadors came in the sixteenth century and found them watering their corn, squash, and melons. The Zuni, for example, had built canals to carry the snowmelt from the mountains to their fields, and they also scattered their crops to take advantage of any springs bubbling to the surface.[4] With them, as with the nearby Hopi, decisions about water rested in the hands of the family groups or clans that made up the pueblo. But farther east along the Rio Grande, the pueblos faced a more difficult environmental challenge. The river was too powerful for any small clan, or even single pueblo, acting alone, to tame. Therefore, writes Edward Dozier, extravillage lines of coordination began to emerge, leading eventually to a more centralized system of governance. Many pueblos were united into a broad regional authority that, once perfected, could be turned to the practice of war against foreign peoples as well as to the control of water. When that happens, the local mode begins to disappear.[5]

The most extraordinary achievement in surviving the arid Southwest belongs to the Papago, the Bean People. They have dwelt for millennia in the Sonoran desert, a land that gets an average rainfall of less than ten inches, where saguaro, paloverde, and the Gila monster are among the flourishing forms of life. It was an unlikely place to take up farming, but they made a stunning success there until the white man's technology entered and destroyed their way of life.[6] Papago agriculture, supplemented by hunting and gathering, was a mobile affair, touching the desert lightly. From April to September they collected cholla buds, wild greens, acorns, and fruit from the saguaro and prickly pear. For their protein they killed bighorn sheep, mule deer, peccary, and rabbits. But it was particularly in farming that they showed the most remarkable ingenuity. Whenever and wherever the rain fell, they rushed to get a bean crop raised. The bean on which they thrived was the tepary, a fast germinator. It had to be fast given the short growing season in the desert, where erratic rainfall may cause rivers suddenly to rise only to be followed in a couple of months by soil that is bone-dry again.

The Papago and other Sonoran groups perfected a technique called "floodplain irrigation," which was confined to a few river edges and arroyo mouths. Here is how it worked: A flash flood comes roaring down the sandy riverbed on a July day. It surges into a temporary catchment basin, where it immediately soaks into the soil or forms a pond for later diversion. Cottonwoods, willows, and burrobushes, some of them artificially planted by the Indians in fencerows along the watercourse, slow the current, spreading the water over a broad, flat surface and trapping the suspended silt for fertilizer. Then, in the mud left by the flood, the Papago plant their seeds, expecting to harvest them before the earth turns bricklike again. The fields irrigated in this way are small, irregular patches—two acres here, three or four there. This technique, at which they were so skilled, was also called arroyo-mouth, or *ak-chin,* farming.[7] The traditional Papago had little margin for error or complacence, yet they can be described as a people of abundance, at least in the sense that everyone among them had enough to eat and enough leisure to spend, when work was done, on stories, games, and tranquillity.

Guiding floodwater as the Papago did required a communal effort, for no solitary individual could handle the flood torrents. In 1895 an admiring white observer, W. J. McGee, called the system "the economy of solidarity," adding that no creature, human or otherwise, could get along in the desert without it.[8] Besides cooperation, Papago agriculture demonstrated an intimate knowledge of the desert ecosystem, stream hydraulics, and agronomy. But theirs was not a science devoted to the technical conquest of nature; rather, it aimed more modestly at achieving a secure coexistence and a thrifty subsistence.

Before the Papago and the related Pima Indians appeared in the desert, their Hohokam ancestors (the "finished" or "gone" people) built far more ambitiously, and they suffered for it. Between A.D. 300 and 900, the Hohokam constructed the first large-scale irrigation works in what is now the United States. Excavations carried out from the 1930s on have gradually laid bare an advanced canal network along the Gila River near Chandler, Arizona, as well as on the site of Tempe and Phoenix, threading out from the Salt River.[9] The Hohokam dug those canals over a period of centuries, until at last they had created a spiderlike web that could tap the entire spring runoff, drawing it off upstream and taking it to their fields high above the riverbeds. The largest of their canals was 30 feet across, 7 feet deep, and 8 miles long; it was capable of bringing enough water to irrigate 8,000 acres. Rawhides and baskets hoisted on Indian shoulders were the engines that carried away the dirt dug from that and other trenches. But at last the Hohokam overreached themselves. Intensive irrigation has everywhere led to increasing concentrations of salts in the topsoil, poisoning the farmer's fields. That nemesis came to the Hohokam too, and they were forced one day to abandon their agriculture completely, leaving behind them whited fields and dust-drifted canals.[10] It was their children's children who then had to learn how to get along in the desert with a lighter touch.

Enter again the Wittfogel theory of irrigation society. The social organization required of the Hohokam was substantially different from that needed for *ak-chin* farming. The latter was a self-contained village or family operation, where individuals of more or less equal standing came together to do a common job. But with the Hohokam, as among the Rio Grande pueblos, local self-management very soon did not suffice; downstream villages had to establish control over those living upstream if they were to get any water at all. The outcome was a more efficient utilization of rivers—if efficiency means complete, total use—and a more elaborate legal framework to resolve conflicting interests. Pushed far enough along, the big-scale irrigation system, according to Wittfogel's theory, must replace local community control with a supravillage regime.

The Hohokam did not in fact have the full infrastructural base, nor perhaps did they have the intention, to go that far toward the consolidation of power. We have no firm evidence that they ever set up an elaborate bureaucracy to manage their Salt River waterworks. But were they on their way to concentrated rule when fate cut them down? Lacking supporting written evidence on precisely how the system was governed, reading only from the works themselves, archaeologists have reasoned their way to contradictory conclusions. Emil Haury and Richard Woodbury, two of the leading authorities on the Hohokam, maintain that the system could have been constructed and preserved by spontaneous, informal cooperation sustained over several hundred years. Village elders up and down the river could have worked out their peoples' differences in times of emergency without yielding local sovereignty to a central command.[11] This reasoning, however, is unconvincing, based as it is on the dubious assumption that the Hohokam were able to work with a single-mindedness and long-term harmony that other societies have not shown. A second and more credible argument comes from Bruce Masse, who has recently looked again at those Hohokam traces and concluded, "Some form of coordination or control was necessary not only within single irrigation systems but among all the systems in the Salt River Valley," especially for dealing with periods of savage, unpredictable floods or droughts. Another scholar, D. E. Doyel, has gone further to insist that one village must have come to wield economic and social power over all the others.[12] We will never know much about the actual distribution of power in Hohokam times, and what we know will always be uncertain, but that last conclusion has common sense on its side. The Hohokam, then, are an example of what can happen when a people outgrow the local mode: of the political and environmental consequences of bigness.

In other parts of the world there still survive a few examples of the local subsistence mode of irrigation, all of which seem, where details are available, to conform roughly to the lineaments of power described here. The societies trying to hold on to that mode are commonly of very ancient origin, defying the growing pressures of modern states. Unlike the Hohokam, they cause little ecological disturbance, and for that reason they are as stable as the hills from which they take their water. Some of them are found in Bali's rice-paddy country, where the farmers long ago organized themselves in *subaks*—a form of "pluralistic collectivism," as Clifford Geertz terms it.[13] Others may be Japanese irrigation cooperatives; there are over 100,000 of them in that nation, posing what some ambitious planners see as outmoded obstacles to a more scientific and profitable water management.[14] Still others are the surviving remnants in Valencia, Spain, of feudal irrigation communities where originally there was only single-canal coordination, a very limited technology, and minimal intervillage consultation.[15] Then, with at least a faint resemblance to these older varieties, there are those scattered communities in the American West made up of Hispanics, Mormons, or Montana ranchers, who continue to hang on to some part of their self-determination in the face of federal bureaucratization and external market pressures. What all those water communities have in common is that their technology, like their economy, is the handiwork of the water users themselves; it is an indigenous, not an exogenous, artifact. There is not much need for capital or for specially trained experts in their creation. Typically a river in such communities continues to run largely on its natural way, giving up only a little of its substance to human demands, answering to the need for sustainability more than for efficiency. When such communities fail, and they sometimes do, it is usually the result of bitter, persistent disputes that no one locally can resolve, or it is the result of an invasion by outside armies or progress-makers. Where such communities endure, on the other hand, the water flows and flows through history, as nature and the human community join together in a single circle.[16]

THE AGRARIAN
STATE MODE

In the preindustrial world, agriculture dominated human life, and that agriculture was a mosaic of little patches. Here a bit of wheat grew, there a grove of date trees, over there rows and rows of peas. Around those patches of crops developed a parallel mosaic of villages, often standing in sight of one another but each one largely self-contained, like an archipelago at sea. The early Chinese philosopher-poet Lao-tse speaks of hearing the cock crow every morning in the next village but never visiting the place; it was a foreign country to him.[1]

Irrigation on a limited scale did not disturb that insularity. In such cases, a river might flow through a string of villages down to the sea, sustaining and protecting their autonomy to a point. But wherever there was further development of irrigation works, that discreteness could not survive. Newer and bigger canals were built to flow, as it were, uphill to a commanding central authority. Out of such concerted efforts came a second kind of irrigation mode, the chief characteristic of which was that it interfered on a massive scale with the natural flow of the watershed, forcing water miles and miles out of its path of least resistance, running ever more complex risks of environmental degradation, requiring as a result of that danger a constant, intense vigilance. Reorganizing the fundamentals of nature in such a way demanded in turn the consolidation of the loose mosaic of villages into a broader, more powerful instrumentality. That process took place during the four millennia before Christ in some of the great desert landscapes of the world: in Arizona, as we have seen, in China, in India, and above all in the Middle East, where the Tigris, Euphrates, and Nile rivers rolled down from the mountaintops through wide, fertile, but extremely dry valleys.

This second type of irrigation society involved, in social terms, a radically disparate coupling of the humble and the grand. On the one side, there were those older villages where peasant agriculture went on much as before—local subsistence communities still trying to live as tiny worlds apart. On the other side stood a state, incipient or well advanced, with a bureaucratic organization to design and administer the water system. The state provided an adequate and dependable supply of water to the village, and in turn demanded a payment of tribute in the form of money or crops. A new redistributive economy thus appeared, wherein wealth flowed from the outlying village to the capital city and then, as expenditures for water engineering and maintenance, back outward again. Always, however, a large part of the wealth stayed in the capital city, where it paid for luxurious homes for a new ruling class or for standing armies to defend the irrigation society against its enemies, usually marauding nomads. Given enough tribute, which conversely meant given enough water supplied to the villages, the rulers could create an empire. And that is precisely what many of them did. Each time they extended their canals into new territory, they added to their domain, and, in turn, increased their tribute, until at last their domain extended well beyond any conceivable gift of water. In those desert empires, the shape of power, therefore, was like that of some primitive marine animal: a vast amorphous tissue of villages, weak and disorganized, dominated by a more highly evolved central nervous system. Wittfogel called this animal a hydraulic society. But to make matters clearer, since I will argue that hydraulic societies come in more than his one variety, we can call this second type the agrarian state.

The reality of human existence in the agrarian state was that the many did the sweaty labor while the few gave directions and took away much of the product. To get a more reliable water supply or better flood protection than their single village could provide, peasants had to pay something besides tribute; they had to perform immense, backbreaking physical labor. They found themselves not only dredging heavy loads of dirt from canal bottoms but also tugging along ornate equipages on which their new masters rode in fine style. The price paid for more intensive, ambitious irrigation, in other words, was loss of autonomy to an entrenched, extrafamily or clan authority, creating a rigid hierarchy based on the division of labor into workers and managers.

Undoubtedly there were practical economic reasons why the mass of people put up with this loss of autonomy, this heavy toil. The chief one was no doubt the need for increased food production. There may, however, have been other kinds of reasons why they were unable to protest vigorously and throw off their chains, reasons having to do with the ecology of irrigation. Both the warm climates typically found in the arid lands where irrigation was invented and the abundance of shallow waterways there created ideal conditions for the proliferation of human parasites. Often the peasant would stand all day long in a flooded rice paddy, exposed continuously to an exploding population of pathogens, and no one was, until recently, aware of the danger. The most serious of these disease organisms associated with irrigation (both in ancient times and today) was the blood fluke. It causes schistosomiasis, a chronic, nasty, debilitating ailment, which today affects as many as 100 million people. The fluke lives part of its life in the snails that thrive in irrigation ditches, the rest of its life in the human body. Adding to the health problems was the use of feces as fertilizer in countries like China. Tapeworms spread from the excrement through the water and into the peasants, until as much as 90 percent of the population was infected. One historian, William McNeill, suspects that "the despotic governments characteristic of societies dependent on irrigation agriculture" owed something to the degenerating effects of these diseases on the common people, who became too listless to resist or revolt.[2]

The rulers in this more advanced irrigation regime were, for the most part, not owners of the land itself. Land remained the possession of the peasants, acting as individuals or in common, or it was placed in the abstract hands of the state. Nor did the rulers actually claim to own the water they delivered. Instead, their power came from the technological control they exercised over the rivers; they were a managerial elite.[3] Better than the peasants, they understood when the river currents would rise and fall, how a ditch could be constructed so it would not silt up with sediment, and what the river gods wanted from humans. This group of rulers, Wittfogel points out, sponsored the first professional studies in hydraulics, astronomy, and mathematics. In fact, much of modern science and engineering has its distant foundations in water-control efforts. Religion too came within the purview of the directing elite, as priests took charge of leading the peasantry in worshipping such river gods as Isis, Osiris, Hapi of the Nile, Ninurta of Mesopotamia, and Ganga, the ancient Hindu deity who sat in Siva's wavy hair. The priestly branch of the ruling echelon reminded peasants constantly that they were to respect and obey their superiors and be thankful for their benevolent control.[4] The village may still have owned the land, but the mandarins owned authority.

In many agrarian states, irrigation helped bring to power not only a bureaucracy buttressed by priests but also a single, autocratic sovereign at the head of things. He might have been called an emperor, a king, or a pharaoh, but in any case to dominate nature was his special personal mission, his proud, egocentric boast. The fabled Assyrian ruler Queen Semiramis reputedly had inscribed on her tomb what may stand as the dominant ethos of the advanced hydraulic civilizations: "I constrained the mighty river to flow according to my will and led its water to fertilize lands that had before been barren and without inhabitants."[5] Nowhere in Papago Indian culture do we find so self-inflating an expression, so unabashedly aggressive an attitude toward the earth. It was in the larger water-control systems of the Middle East, not among the Papago, that humans first began to take the world forcefully into their own hands. They did so by setting up a representative person as a god and giving him or her absolute dominion over the desert, to redeem it and make it yield riches where before there was scarcity.

A set of high public officials, a grandiose sovereign, a program of conquest—and there you have the archetype of the ancient irrigation state. Scholars have not yet agreed which came first, the state or the heavy waterworks, and it is likely that they will never resolve the question. Do chickens make eggs, or eggs make chickens? It hardly matters when we sit down to dinner. A massive irrigation apparatus obviously could not appear in advance of the finances, planning, and technical direction of a power complex. At the same time it is clear that all of the early states emerged in arid or semiarid landscapes, all relied on irrigation.[6]

In Wittfogel's defense, it must be said that he never claimed that every state emerged initially from the single task of water control, though he did believe that irrigation must always have had a significant consolidating effect on political power.

No matter whether traditionally nonhydraulic leaders initiated or seized the incipient hydraulic "apparatus," or
whether the masters of this apparatus became the motive
force behind all important functions, there can be no doubt
that in all these cases the resulting regime was decisively
shaped by the leadership and social control required by
hydraulic agriculture.[7]

He may have been in his early years too narrowly an ecological and technological determinist, but Wittfogel was not simple-minded in thinking about
how history is made. Irrigation and the state, he indicates here, grew up
synergistically, each supporting the other. And that is where we too must
let the issue rest.

Standing before the massifying complex of water control, the ordinary
peasant must have felt himself to be very feeble, without organization or
arcane knowledge. Back in his own village, however, he lived much of the
time as his ancestors had lived, a quasi-master at least of his fate. With his
family and neighbors he continued deciding when to plant and harvest, how
to raise his children, and what to do about strictly local affairs. The overarching state was only "semimanagerial," which is to say it was far away
most of the time, lacked modern communications (canal barges and human
runners being its main methods of sending orders and gathering information), and could establish only a very limited control over peasant thinking.[8]
When the crops were all in, villagers remitted to the capital city the taxes
they owed, then withdrew to themselves once more, enjoying their beggar's
democracy for the greater part of the year.

The most important challenge to that lingering, remnant individual and
community autonomy was the corvée, a drafted army in which unpaid
laborers from the peasantry had to serve at the state's demand. In the
absence of advanced machinery, central planners relied on drafting human
muscle to do the work of constructing and keeping up the waterworks. It
was another kind of taxation, imposed in the name of the common good but
further enriching the state.[9] One of our best accounts of how the corvée
operated comes from Julien Barois, a nineteenth-century French hydrolo-
gist, who observed the system in Egypt on the eve of its abolition. Every
December the government's agents prepared an estimate of labor needed
along the Nile: the number of fellahin (peasants) needed, the number of
work days required, the irrigation repair jobs to be done. From mid-January
to the end of July, men assembled in camps, along with their wives and
children, to work under the supervision of trained engineers. Theoretically,
all able-bodied males between fifteen and fifty years old, except for the city

dwellers who owned no land and the desert Bedouins, who scorned agriculture, had to come along if called. In reality, the few rich farmers with large landholdings got exemption for themselves and their field hands by paying a sum of money. To build the Mahmūdīyah Canal for the city of Alexandria's water supply, from 1818 to 1820, about 300,000 men toiled under the broiling sun. Irrigation projects could call on similar armies. The workers' only tools were short-handled hoes and baskets made from the stems of palms. They would loosen the earth in the ditches, often working in water up to their ankles, a slippery, miry, steamy chore. Men, and sometimes children, balanced the loaded baskets on their heads and climbed as much as thirty meters up the embankment to dump them. This was, in Barois's words, "a true labor of Sisyphus, because each year this same earth slides to the bottom of the bed in high water and has to be removed with the same trouble and fatigue."[10] The standard tool of the supervising state official was the whip, laid hard on the bare backs of lagging peasants. In all of the major irrigated regions of Asia, Africa, and America, the corvée existed for thousands of years, constituting the most vivid experience the common people had of what Barois termed "despotism."

Once conscripted and taught to obey, the hydraulic army could serve the ruling class in a number of ways. Besides keeping the water flowing, it could lay down roads from the provinces to the capital city. It could improve inland water transportation. It could build ornate palaces, surrounded by lush green gardens symbolizing the rulers' command over arid nature. And it could erect pyramids, ziggurats, hilltop temples, and cold marble tombs where the dead elite could be laid out in style. Because irrigated affluence led to envy among outsiders and threats of invasion, strong fortifications had to be built. Though the peasants did not make good warriors—their diseases left them too weak to fight—they could construct the state's defenses. During the Sui dynasty, for instance, over a million workers toiled on the Great Wall of China to defend against invaders coming across the Mongolian plain. The agrarian state thus watered the drylands and raised a crop of gargantuan monuments not only to its self-esteem but also to its fear.[11]

These are the broad outlines of the ancient irrigation states, a deliberate lumping together of admittedly diverse examples to make their general principles clear. Now, however, we should do a little splitting. Hydraulic societies can be broken down, following Wittfogel again, as either compact or loose, depending on the extent to which irrigation was the norm.[12] In the compact subspecies, irrigating fields was the standard practice throughout the society, occurring on over half of all its cultivated acreage (most commonly it was concentrated in a single major river valley), or at least producing more than half the society's annual crop. The loose subspecies, in contrast, irrigated only a minor part of its arable land and depended on rainfall for providing most of its food supply. In this latter case the irrigated area, though smaller, became nonetheless a powerful economic center, exercising influence over a broad periphery of rainfall-fed villages. Classic examples of the compact agrarian state are Egypt and the Tigris-Euphrates valley civilizations, ranging from the Sumerians to the Sassanids.[13] For models of the loose type there are most notably China and India, possibly Ceylon.[14] And there are still others, some of them eluding strict classification: Vietnam, Hawaii, Fiji, the African kingdom of Benin, and the Inca empire of Peru, all of them possessing distinctive traits, all of them for the sake of brevity ignored here.[15] Seeing the essential features of the compact and loose variations on the agrarian state is the key. They can be grasped through a representative example of each.

The most famous irrigated agricultural society in world history was the compact system of Egypt, which as far back as five thousand years ago drew on the reddish-brown waters of the Nile River as it flowed northward. "Egypt," observed Herodotus and millions of schoolchildren after him, "is the gift of the Nile." Every June, with an almost clockwork regularity, the lower river began to rise, swollen by tropical rains in the African high country. By late September the whole of its floodplain had become a turbid lake. Within another month, the lake had receded back into the main channel, leaving behind an odorous residue of silt. Before humans began to plow up that floodplain to grow wheat and lentils, the borders of the upper Nile were a wild green savannah grazed by elephants and gazelles, while the delta was an intricate wetland of papyrus, reeds, and crocodiles. Away from that narrow ribbon of life stretched an awesome desert void. Sometime around 3000 B.C., during the reign of Menes, first of the Old Kingdom potentates, artificial irrigation appeared. Much later the Ptolemies (beginning with Ptolemy I in 305 B.C.) extended and intensified agriculture to a degree unmatched until the nineteenth century. They reorganized the entire water system into standardized administrative subdivisions that answered directly to the central government in Alexandria.[16] For a brief time after that, the Romans took control of the river, making Egypt the chief granary of their empire. Later still, there were the Muslims, the Turks, and the Ottoman conquerors. Out of the water, silt, and strip of green came bread and power for one autocracy after another.

In the modern era, Egypt would build dams at Aswan and other sites that would drastically alter the river's ecosystem.[17] But for most of its water history a much less intrusive manipulation called basin irrigation was the pattern. Transverse ditches created a series of entrapment basins, averaging 5,000 to 10,000 hectares apiece and imperceptibly stairstepping downstream. High water flowed into those basins via canals, flooding to a depth of three to six feet, wetting the ground thoroughly and depositing suspended mud, then draining into the next lower basin, and finally running off into the Nile and to the Mediterranean. Where gardens and fields stood too high above the river level, the Egyptians employed the swipe, or *shaduf*, a counterpoised bucket on a beam that pivoted on a pair of uprights, sweeping water up and into a trough, which led it away to the crop rows. With this ingenious tool, a single man could raise 600 gallons a day.[18]

Relying on the swipe and on the river's own steady rhythms, the Egyptian fellahin never had to face the nemesis of salt accumulation as did the Hohokam; there was enough water in the water-to-land ratio to flush the salts away. And the deposited silt was such a splendid fertilizer that the same fields produced undiminished crops for what seemed like forever. An Egyptian geographer, Gamal Hamdan, calls the basin system "clearly symbiotic," that is, it was an ecologically compatible, stable adaptation to the environment. But then he adds:

> It was an adaptation to, rather than of, nature. It was a passive adaptation; only a very partial use of the land was made while it let the bulk of the Nile water run to waste in the sea. It limited agriculture to one-third of the year and did not permit any substantial extension of the cultivated area.[19]

Following a similar logic of discontent, Egypt in the nineteenth century converted to a perennial irrigation system that required expensive storage reservoirs, more canals and headgates to regulate the passage of water, artificial fertilizers to replace sediment trapped in the reservoirs, and considerable disruption of rural life. In its favor, the new system made possible several crops a year, including cotton for exporting to the world markets. So Egypt abandoned its time-tested ways and became rich—or at least some of its citizens did. It shipped its products abroad until it no longer raised enough food to feed itself. And step by step it came to confront a mounting ecological backlash: salinity poisoning, degraded fisheries, and higher levels of schistosomiasis than ever before.[20]

Though it was by modern technical standards primitive and relatively benign in its riverine impact, the old Egyptian basin plan still required a high degree of coordinated control. A network of river watchers kept their eyes on the "nilometers" (depth scales engraved on stone pilings) that measured the water level at Memphis, Cairo, and other settlements. Up and down the Nile other officials stood ready to divert the rising current as it reached them. Laws and regulations to ensure an orderly apportionment of the flood had to be established. A program of water and agricultural planning, including food storage for drought years, helped give the capital city and its long succession of pharaohs a great influence over local people. In their book *Egyptian Irrigation,* William Willcocks and J. J. Craig concluded that "the authority of the Government in an absolutely rainless country like Egypt becomes gradually . . . autocratic," as dispersed tribunals are more and more "forced to admit its absolute supremacy." Agreeing with that conclusion, Gamal Hamdan writes: "The efficient running of the basin system depended entirely on a strong, centralized government, for every upstream basin could endanger the riparian rights of those downstream." Egypt, throughout most of its history, resembled one of its pyramids: there was a lofty pinnacle where the rulers sat and a broad base where an anonymous, voiceless peasantry toiled. Irrigation was the main factor, the means of production, creating that pyramid.[21]

One of the few dissenters from that consensus view is the American archaeologist Karl Butzer. The basin system, he claims, was naturally compartmentalized, at least in its earliest phase, and could have been operated under completely decentralized management. The rise of the pharaohs, he goes on, must have had other causes than irrigation, though he does not suggest what they might have been.[22] But even if one grants his argument, or simply puts it aside as unresolvable with the evidence available, there is plenty in Butzer's own work to show how the subsequent elaboration of irrigation could have necessitated political centralization in Egypt. When it was lacking and the water or food supply failed, the society collapsed into violent civil war, starvation, rotting corpses in the Nile, cannibalism, roving bands of marauders, and civil chaos that left the country vulnerable to outside aggressors. Governments, no matter how strong, could not always avoid such calamities, but it stands to reason that most of them tried desperately to do so and that they justified their power accumulation on the premise of preventing them.

Where virtually an entire country relied on a single grand river and the irrigation from it, as in Egypt, the flow of power to the center was simple, unambiguous, and straightforward. But in the second subspecies, the loose model of the agrarian state, the connections were more subtle, the Wittfogel theory more problematical. China is the prime test case, and a very complicated one it is, where generalizations are not easy to come by.[23] In addition to the familiar bureaucratic apparatus and teeming peasant class, there was from an early point in China's history a large group of private landowners, the gentry, who, along with city merchants, exercised considerable clout. Much of China, especially in the south, is temperate and well watered. Irrigation was not everywhere a necessity, nor were agromanagerial bureaucrats. Was China then a hydraulic society or not? Did river control there promote despotism? Was China more like Japan or Europe—a feudal world with diffuse governance? Was its evolution into empire the result of factors other than water management?

"The Chinese people," declares Joseph Needham, "have been outstanding among the nations of the world in their control and use of water."[24] Hydraulic engineering, or *shui li,* was more advanced there than in any other premodern society. Historical records going back to the eighth century B.C. mention irrigation. Like Egypt, China was never an avid builder of dams and reservoirs; its expertise lay more in flood-control works and in elegant canals, carrying both taxes to the capital city (mainly in the form of rice) and, especially in the semiarid north, water for crops. Its early triumphs include the Cheng State Canal (completed in 560 B.C.), the Chêng-kuo Canal (246 B.C.), and the Grand Canal (begun in 581 B.C.), which eventually ran the full 1,100 miles from Peking to the port of Hangchow. The rise of Imperial China, commencing with the Han dynasty of the third century B.C., owes much to some forty major water projects carried out to control "China's Sorrow," the Huang Ho, or Yellow River, which has wreaked more havoc on humankind than any other.[25] Clearly, this agrarian state did practice large-scale water manipulation and can accurately be called a hydraulic civilization. But it was not necessarily, as Wittfogel would have it, a totalitarian one.

Water became in China the profoundest symbol for understanding nature, human affairs, and the right principles for governing both. In contrast to the modern mind-controlling regimes Wittfogel knew, in China some diversity of opinion was allowed on these matters. The two most important schools of water thought were the Confucians, who dominated official circles, and the Taoists, a dissident group. In the *Tao Tê Ching,* from which the philosophy of Taoism primarily derives, water appears as the essence of nature and a model for human conduct. It is a substance that does not strive or resist, yielding easily as it does to any obstacles in its path, yet in the end it wears down the most determined opposition. A great river, it was said, runs lower than any of its tributaries, receiving into itself "all things under heaven." From this model in nature Taoists drew lessons for their rulers. They should govern with the least show of force, seeking to protect their people from violent passions and acquisitive urges; they should not become arrogant or seek to impose their will on village affairs; they should abolish the brutal corvée. The philosophy of naturalism, quietism, and humility behind such moral lessons for leaders had implications also for water engineering. *Wu wei,* the idea of moving with the flow of a stream and doing nothing contrary to nature, meant opposing structures that too rigidly confined rivers or wholly diverted them from their course. The connection between engineering and political strategies was put concisely by the Taoist engineer Chia Jang, of the Han period: "Those who are good at controlling water give it the best opportunity to flow away, those who are good at controlling the people give them plenty of chance to talk."[26]

Confucianism, in contrast, taught a more domineering stance toward water and the common people alike. Rivers must be disciplined—a favorite word of this school—by constructing strong, high dikes to pinch the water in, forcing it to move more rapidly toward the sea. Rivers too must be made to do hard work for the common good, as defined by sages and rulers. Though Confucian scholars could also talk enthusiastically about living a contemplative life on the banks of a stream, typically they advocated a more active, commanding attitude toward the natural environment. Pursuit of virtue and social welfare, respect for status, and reverence for one's elders were higher principles than following, with the Taoists, the way of nature. Operating mainly by this Confucian point of view, China's leaders transformed their country into a wealthy, powerful, hierarchically organized empire, one of history's greatest.

The Chinese landscape and society, however, were both too large and too complex ever to be brought under an unrelievedly despotic rule, whether one instructed by Confucianism or not. Wittfogel realized as much when he described China as a loose type. Undeniably there was despotism there, so that from time to time emperors compelled men to kneel and kiss their feet, mandarins may have held life-and-death sway over local populations, and peasants on irrigation projects may often have felt the lash stinging their backs and legs. But in contrast to Egypt, China's ruling class was a diverse, divided, multicentered agglomeration. The emperor had constantly to mobilize support from a wide spectrum of the population in order to stay in power; coercion alone could not work in the face of the centrifugal tendencies among the country's far-flung regions and the internal bureaucratic disputes over social goals. As S. N. Eisenstadt points out, the Chinese emperors, at times finding themselves caught between rival Confucian and Taoist forces, tried to recruit allies among both groups or to play one off against the other. And through all the cycles of dynastic rise and fall, the landed gentry maintained a position of some independence. China was,

Eisenstadt admits, a centralized state, but there was not an altogether unchecked, simple power complex running it.[27]

But if Wittfogel was wrong in seeing too much of Brave New World in Old China, in finding "total power" where there was only a powerful center, he was right to this extent: water control did enable the state partially to overcome diffusionary tendencies. By developing an irrigation economy in a critical geographical area, the state could dominate a wider territory than before, strengthening its hand against other internal forces. Intensification of agriculture in that core area produced grain tribute for the emperor and his underlings, the bureaucrats and army officers. Ch'ao-ting Chi shows how such "key economic areas" have appeared again and again in Chinese history, becoming instruments of control over surrounding, subordinate lands where rainfall farming persisted, much as setting up a string of forts can secure a claim to a frontier. Thus irrigation development repeatedly became "a powerful weapon in social and political struggles."[28] By extending this mode of production, the central government waxed stronger, though in a relative, shifting, not absolute, sense.

Taken together, the compact and the loose agrarian states created, with the aid of irrigation, one of the most distinctive relationships humans have ever worked out with nature. It was not always a sustainable relationship —in most places not nearly so ecologically stable as the local subsistence mode. It took a monstrous toll in human life and dignity, though it was less repressive than Wittfogel's tarbrush allusions to Stalinism represent. One does not have to read into that hydraulic past the totalitarian tendencies of our own time to recognize the terrible costs paid by the peasants.

Scanted by Wittfogel, and most other scholars, because it is so difficult to determine, is the more fundamental question why societies chose to pay so stiff a price to get more water. In every case there was a critical moment when they might have refused to do so, when they might have rejected large-scale irrigation and its social consequences. Once that moment had passed, however, and a decision to go ahead had been made, they found they had forged for themselves a fate they could not easily undo. It was not the desert or drylands around them which made that decision to intensify water control, though in some places a change in climate, a siege of drought, the threat of impending starvation may have left people with few alternatives. More frequently, the explanation must be that too many groups were struggling to use a limited resource, a situation that led them to require and give power to an adjudicator. In still other cases the decisive impulse undoubtedly was more a matter of ideas than hunger, of ambitions more than survival, of a thirst for power more than for water. It could also have

47

been the outcome of ideology, whether that ideology came from commonly shared beliefs and attitudes or from manipulations by a conniving few— ideology in the form of religion, philosophy, dreams, and rationalizations of conquest.[29] That ideological force, so clearly present in modern examples of irrigation development, must have been far more pervasive in ancient times than we have any way of proving. In any case, whatever the driving motive may have been, the outcome in Egypt, China, and elsewhere was that societies began the long, laborious, and dangerous task of bending the rivers of earth to human will.

THE CAPITALIST
STATE MODE

Only fragments remain today of those intricate Old World hydraulic complexes that had such decisive consequences. Today, most of the systems lie in ruins, buried in "the lone and level sands" like Shelley's statue of Ozymandias, all but vanished on the ground and visible only from the air. Water may still gurgle through a stone-embanked Chinese ditch dug over a thousand years ago, and village farmers in Madras may still wait for the annual monsoon to fill a tank hollowed out by a legendary maharajah, but fragments do not make systems. Where water control is carried out comprehensively these days, it is by means of modern technology—electric pumps that can lift an entire river over a mountain range or mammoth concrete dams that create artificial lakes over a hundred miles long. The early hydraulic societies, organized along agrarian state lines, have now all disappeared along with the apparatus they operated. In their place stand the new modern hydraulic societies, the most developed of them sprawling in the arid American West, and these societies express the reigning mind of the marketplace men, the technological wizards, and the ubiquitous state planners.

Karl Wittfogel refused to gather up his ideas about water and power and make an imaginative leap with them into that water modernity. Doing so would have required him to examine critically his new home, the United States, and he was not prepared for that inquiry. In fact, his split with the Marxists had made him an increasingly stubborn apologist for America and other western capitalist countries as promoters of freedom and progress. On several occasions he inspected the newest achievements in water engineering and always came away complacent about modern hydraulics. He insisted that the approach to social organization behind them differed from both the archaic despotisms and their recent communist descendants. In 1946, he and his wife, Esther Goldfrank, visited the Tennessee Valley Authority works, which were among the most ambitious water-control enterprises in the world. Fifteen years later the Wittfogels toured the Snowy Mountains irrigation scheme in Australia. "What I have been saying about traditional China," he wrote, "is not valid for multicentered societies." Those new "free world" projects could not be despotic because private property was now the norm, and there was no single, overpowering state in control; rather, there was in cases like the United States and Australia a balance among many countervailing forces. One found not a "ruling" but a "controlled" bureaucracy.[1] So once more Wittfogel had to scrap his original ecological argument about history. It was not, after all, the interaction of nature and technology that had made Egypt what it was, but prior social "organization." And for some reason social organization in the old desert empires had been despotic, while in the modern western countries it was open and democratic.

A few of Wittfogel's critics have completely overlooked the distinction he made between capitalist and command economies and have mistakenly accused him of branding all irrigation regimes as tyrannical. They sometimes seize on the American West as an exception to what they take to be his grim generalizations. For instance, Lon Fuller, a Harvard law professor who grew up in the Imperial Valley of California and rosily remembers that world as just and communal, has lambasted Wittfogel for casting a shadow over all irrigation. But in the course of his rambling critique of the Oriental-despotism argument, he actually ends up restating Wittfogel's own discriminations. He accepts completely the idea that water control may have led to despotism in early hydraulic societies, adding only that their problem was they "took on too difficult a social task too soon." With the invention of the marketplace, however, more benign mechanisms for sorting out conflicting interests came into being. Now we have the invisible hand of rational self-interest, Fuller believes, to resolve water disputes peacefully and achieve a fair distribution of benefits. We don't even need the courts, for individuals can now solve their own conflicts without external interference, regaining the autonomy they once enjoyed in developing river resources. All of this progress has been made possible, so Fuller implies, by the rise of capitalism. Its emergence has dispersed concentrated power, put negotiation and contract in the place of repressive authority, and assured that democracy will flourish in the desert.[2]

Unfortunately, it just isn't so. Another, closer look at modern examples of water control, as in the American West, does not support either Fuller's or Wittfogel's comforting notion of progressive liberation of humans from their tools of desert conquest. Quite to the contrary: capitalism has created over the past hundred years a new, distinctive type of hydraulic society, one that demonstrates once more how the domination of nature can lead to the domination of some people over others. Recognizing this, certain important questions must be addressed. What does this latest mode of water control have in common with its predecessors? What are its unique qualities and tendencies? How has it approached that essential substance of life, water? What path of cultural evolution has brought it to its present condition of mastery over the drylands? What inner and outer forces have driven it to achieve mastery? In what ways has that ecological domination expressed in the new water systems shaped the social order of places like the American West, creating new structures of power there, reconcentrating wealth and authority?

Interestingly, free-market liberals like Fuller and anticommunist ideologues like Wittfogel, along with some technocratically inclined radicals, have all refused to acknowledge how the fate of humans is inextricably linked to that of nature—in the present and in the past. However, like many of the most important facts in our lives, this cannot be easily proved or dismissed in the way we would handle a scientific proposition—one which says, for instance, that heating a candle will cause it to melt. Instead, we must strive to find and test a historical truth that has consistent, observable, and demonstrable expressions. When that very wise Englishman C. S. Lewis wrote, "What we call Man's power over Nature turns out to be a power exercised by some men over other men with Nature as its instrument," he had that kind of truth in mind. And when the contemporary French social theorist André Gorz declares, "The total domination of nature inevitably entails a domination of people by the techniques of domination," he too is talking about a general historical truth, not a chemical reaction.[3] A historical truth cannot be nicely calibrated or made exactly predictive without being reduced to triviality. In the case of the human implications of intensified water control, it is not possible to argue that this particular dam or that aqueduct will have precisely and in every place the same social impact. Establishing historical truths involves a looser, though still demanding, kind of analysis. It is not a strict determinism of cause-and-effect but rather an imaginative grasp of subtly interacting relationships. Only by that higher approach to historical explanation can we determine, Wittfogel and Fuller to the contrary notwithstanding, whether the fate of the hydraulic cycle in the ancient desert regimes has any modern echoes.

Another contemporary social philosopher, Lewis Mumford, has made much the same point as C. S. Lewis and André Gorz. In his *Technics and Human Development* Mumford has argued that the Age of the Pyramids has reappeared in spirit and purpose, bent as before on establishing "absolute centralized control over both nature and man."[4] He calls that restoration "Megamachine." The challenge for historians is not to whittle away his observation with positivistic knives, but to test it in specific examples, and if it seems valid, to make it as clear and coherent as possible. The best place to carry out that investigation, I believe, is in the arid American West, through a study of the history of its water-control efforts.

This third and latest mode of water control (it may not be the last, of course) is one created by the modern capitalist state. In this mode there are two roughly equivalent centers of power: a private sector of agriculturists and a public sector made up of bureaucratic planners and elected representatives. Neither group is autonomous. Both need each other, reinforce each other's values, compete for the upper hand without lasting success, and finally agree to work together to achieve a control over nature that is unprecedentedly thorough.

The agriculturists who constitute the private sector have become in recent times too rich and well organized, when compared with the archaic peasant class, to be cowed into submission by any state. Instead of serving in an involuntary corvée, they pay taxes to the state, often complaining of the high, extortionate rates, or they succeed in compelling others to pay the taxes for them to build and maintain their waterworks. In the world's labor markets they hire an anonymous human army, which they use to turn the arid spaces into green fields. In the West, those workers have come from Mexico, China, Japan, the Philippines, and India, as well as Oklahoma, Texas, and Mississippi. Those hired field hands, not their landowning employers, are the men and women who have constituted the wage-based answer to the corvée, sweating every bit as much as the Egyptian fellahin did. They also have felt the lash of an overseer or the club of a policeman, but they have had no land or village of their own to which they could escape when the season was ended. Consequently, they have been perpetual movers, with a tent or automobile in some cases serving as their only home, a city welfare office their only off-season means of support. With these wage employees, the modern domination of water becomes most vividly and unmistakably translated into hierarchy. Those who rule in that situation are not only those who hire and pay but also all those who take part in designing and controlling the hydraulic means of production. Workers serve as instruments of environmental manipulation; rivers, in turn, become means of control over workers.

The other power center emerging from this mode is the state, which furnishes as it did in archaic times the capital for big-scale engineering and the technical know-how to make it run smoothly. One of the most familiar laws of power is that he who has the capital commands. In the American West, the federal government through its Bureau of Reclamation has put up most of the capital. It therefore exerts enormous leverage over local destinies. When that same government also came to supply most of the hydraulic expertise, it gathered into its hands another means of control, one that has taken on increasing significance as the scale and complexity of water manipulation has grown. Furthermore, the state has asserted, through its various levels and agencies, the authority to settle conflicting claims, to decide which users can tap public resources, and to define what projects are worth undertaking. There is no pharaoh in that arrangement of power— no single despotic ruler who personifies human control over the environment. In the new mode, power becomes faceless and impersonal, so much so in fact that many are unaware it exists.

The most fundamental characteristic of the latest irrigation mode is its behavior toward nature and the underlying attitudes on which it is based. Water in the capitalist state has no intrinsic value, no integrity that must be respected. Water is no longer valued as a divinely appointed means for survival, for producing and reproducing human life, as it was in local subsistence communities. Nor is water an awe-inspiring, animistic ally in a quest for political empire, as it was in the agrarian states. It has now become a commodity that is bought and sold and used to make other commodities that can be bought and sold and carried to the marketplace. It is, in other words, purely and abstractly a commercial instrument. All mystery disappears from its depths, all gods depart, all contemplation of its flow ceases. It becomes so many "acre-feet" banked in an account, so many "kilowatt-hours" of generating capacity to be spent, so many bales of cotton or carloads of oranges to be traded around the globe. And in that new language of market calculation lies an assertion of ultimate power over nature—of a domination that is absolute, total, and free from all restraint.

The behavior that follows making water into a commodity is aggressively manipulative beyond any previous historical experience. Science and technology are given a place of honor in the capitalist state and put to work devising ways to extract from every river whatever cash it can produce. Where nature seemingly puts limits on human wealth, engineering presumes to bring unlimited plenty. Even in the desert, where men and women confront scarcity in its oldest form—not the deprivation of a particular industrial resource, which is always a cultural contrivance, but the lack of a basic biological necessity—every form of growth is considered possible. Undaunted by any deficiency, unwilling to concede any landscape as unprofitable, planners and schemers assure that there is water in the driest rocks, requiring only a few spoken commands to make it gush forth without end. That collective drive to make the bleakest, most sterile desert produce more and more of everything comes from aggregating individual drives to maximize personal acquisitiveness without stint or hindrance. It is an ideology shared wholeheartedly by agriculturists and water bureaucrats, providing the bond that unites their potentially rival centers of power into a formidable alliance.

The American development of that new mode of water control provides the chief substance then of the chapters that follow. To understand more thoroughly the broad theoretical issues involved, however, we might briefly do here what Wittfogel failed to do: go back to his original post—World War One milieu in Germany and to some of the social philosophers with whom he was early associated. In particular, we can find much that is relevant to understanding water and the capitalist state in the work of the Frankfurt School of critical theory. Wittfogel had been one of its first members, then drifted away; had he remained in touch with his Frankfurt colleagues, they might have opened his eyes to the contemporary relevance of his irrigation work. The common theme of those critical theorists was that domination, not the freedom promised by progress boosters, is the lot of twentieth-century humans, in the so-called democracies as well as in the unmistakably totalitarian nations. Furthermore, human domination derives from the incessant modern drive to remake nature.

The Frankfurt School, officially known as the Institute for Social Research, was established in 1923 with funds provided by a wealthy benefactor.[5] Its first director, Carl Grünberg, who served from 1923 to 1929 and was the first avowed Marxist to hold a chair in a German university, invited Wittfogel to join the institute and contribute to its orthodox Marxist studies. Then in 1929 Grünberg was replaced by the brilliant young social thinker Max Horkheimer, son of a Stuttgart manufacturer. As director, he would be anything but orthodox. With his intellectual soul mate Theodor Adorno, he soon gave the institute a new tone and direction, one that would have profound impact on twentieth-century radical thought around the world. Others who became part of the Frankfurt group included Leo Löwenthal, Erich Fromm, Friedrich Pollock, Herbert Marcuse, and much later, Jürgen Habermas, a distinct branch unto himself. There was no firm party line followed in that group, but they did share some common themes. All of them rejected, to one extent or another, what was becoming a doctrinaire kind of Marxism, one which in their view denied free inquiry, reduced cultural analysis to a sterile economic materialism, and encouraged political repression. The young Marx, the romantic idealist of the famous 1844 Manuscripts, was their kind of radical: a rebel, a humanist, a defender of the untrammeled individual spirit. Following that model, not the older Marx of *Capital* or his overly loyal disciples, they took a stand against whatever threatened critical inquiry, beginning with the bourgeois class of profit maximizers but also including the positivists, the industrial organizers, the architects of mass culture, and the bureaucracy—in sum, as Horkheimer and Adorno put it, all those responsible for creating "the world of the administered life."[6] At that point Wittfogel, despite an obvious overlapping of his concerns with theirs, walked out. He wanted a science of society, not a philosophy of values. Only much later in his life, after his main work was finished, did he renew those ties.

Perhaps the most important contribution made by Horkheimer and the others was to bring radical discussion back to the "superstructure," the realm of ideas, ideologies, and philosophies, and to treat these as decisive historical forces in their own right. They were not to be regarded merely as reflexes of a society's mode of production but as movers and shapers. Nowhere is this more true than in the modern period of the past two hundred years, when books, schooling, and mass media have enabled people to articulate their ideas and manipulate those of others on a wider scale than ever before. Ideas under those conditions may change the very basis of existence, or they may delay changes, rationalize the status quo, and protect vested interests. The study of the capitalist state irrigation mode, Horkheimer would have said, must give particular attention to the ideological matrix that has surrounded it, especially to those ideas that concern nature.

In capitalist society the prevailing way of perceiving and dealing with the natural environment is through instrumental reason. It is our equivalent for the Taoism of China, the worship of Osiris in ancient Egypt, and the animistic religion of the Papago—at once our source of faith, value, ethics, purpose, and analysis. But that comparison can mislead, for the peculiarity of instrumental thought is that it destroys traditional religion and value, denigrates all genuine philosophy, recognizes no transcending purpose, and consequently leaves a deep void in our relationship with nature. "Reason," writes Horkheimer,

> for a long period meant the activity of understanding and assimilating the eternal ideas which were to function as goals for men. Today, on the contrary, it is not only the business but the essential work of reason to find means for the goals one adopts at any given time.[7]

Instrumental reason is thinking carefully and systematically about means while ignoring the problem of ends. Business employs it regularly, for the end of business is assumed to be the obvious one of making money and only the methods for accomplishing that goal are worth bothering about. In technology too, instrumentalism tells the inventor what is needed to make a machine function more effectively, leaving the ends of innovation unexamined. There is nothing new in that way of thinking, nothing except that it has moved from the edges of human awareness, where it dwelt in premodern times, to the very center of consciousness, crowding aside all other activities, giving us increasingly a life of "rationalized irrationality."[8]

The highest form of reason, according to Horkheimer, involves more than understanding the phenomenal world and how it works and being able to manipulate it to one's advantage. Reason should deal with ultimate matters; it should define the greatest good, search out the values that inhere in things, contemplate human destiny, and sort out moral truths. By that standard, reason inevitably is the pursuit of what ought to be. But in recent centuries "ought" has been rigidly distanced from "is" and, finally, consigned to a back room. Under the influence of capitalism, science, and technology, facts alone have come to have real meaning. Values appear to be subjective preferences, which is to say they get relegated to a pile marked "private and extraneous." Like taste, they cannot be disputed, it is said, nor can they be established. An empty space therefore is left in public discussion, and instrumentalism rushes in to fill it with charts, numbers, measurements of efficiency, productivity talk, profit-making, whatever will divert attention from the awkward silence. "We must conquer the desert." Why? "So there will be homes and farms for more people." Why? "So there will be more wealth to go around." What is the wealth for? "Whatever people like, or come to decide—it's not a question we can address." Reason thus surrenders its high calling and settles for a career of calculation. "Having given up autonomy, reason has become an instrument."[9]

In an age ruled by instrumentalism, nature ceases to have any value in itself. It is no longer seen as the handiwork of God to be admired more than used, nor is it an organic being we are bound to woo and respect. A tree, a mountain, a river, and its edges are meaningless except where they can be turned to some human use by a farmer, a scientist, or a manufacturer. Nature is "degraded to mere material, mere stuff to be dominated, without any other purpose than that of this very domination." Because it is uncontrolled by any aims set by reason, technological domination is an unlimited ambition. "Man's boundless imperialism is never satisfied."[10] Here at bottom is the ideological force driving the capitalist state on and on, leading eventually to a "totalitarian attack of the human race on anything that it excludes from itself," whether it be landscapes, ecosystems, or people (Indians, Jews, and women have all at times been among the excluded) who are put outside the pale of humanity and assumed to be part of nature, not of ourselves.

The domination of nature implied in instrumentalism must not be confused with every use of specific resources, or with any and every impact humans have had on the nonhuman sphere. When a man clears a field of trees and plows it up for crops, he has not embarked on a career of technological domination, though he may have given the land a new appearance. Domination, as Horkheimer and Adorno used the term, is a repressive act that is total in intention. It springs from a hostility and an alienation that cannot tolerate the otherness of nature, that can see no worth there or respect any right to exist separate from humans, like the guard in a concentration camp who seeks to crush his prisoner's very identity. Every being on the earth influences other beings, and some exert far more influence than others. But that is not yet domination—not until the superior being tries to change others beyond all recognition and denies them any meaning outside of reference to himself. Then it becomes clear that domination is an epidemic of blindness. In his raging, uncontrolled drive for self-preservation and self-extension, the dominator loses sight of the very ends of life.[11]

Karl Marx had described capitalism as an aggressive exploiter of the earth, and the Frankfurt philosophers agreed. In the capitalist culture and its mode of production, they maintained, the domination of nature appears in its most virulent, popular form: there we find the chief expression of the destructive sickness that affects modern societies in their ecological behavior. But Horkheimer and the rest could not agree with Marx that the domination of nature is merely a side-issue to the conflict between the classes, a reflection of the bourgeois exploitation of workers. On the contrary, our relationship with nature is the central problem, the archmalady, the *Urgebrechen*, of our time. And it has roots going back before the hegemony of capitalism, and manifestations beyond its reach. For an early source, Horkheimer pointed to the Judeo-Christian tradition, particularly that often-quoted instruction by God in Genesis 1:28 to "multiply, and replenish the earth, and subdue it." (Horkheimer might have added to his indictment those other desert religions of the Near and Far East and their water-control programs.) But always, until the modern period, nature still carried some intrinsic meaning. The more immediate and decisive source of domination was the Enlightenment of eighteenth-century Europe and its "disenchantment of the world; the dissolution of myths and the substitution of knowledge for fancy."[12] The Enlightenment, though on one side devoted to the same critical reason the Frankfurt School believed in, had a darker aspect, a more influential side, which stripped value from the world, made it ephemeral and subjective, and opened wide the door to positivistic, utilitarian mindlessness. Capitalism was a key part of that ominous side—it constituted the "bourgeois Enlightenment"—but by no means was it the only part. There was also science and its imperial project to reduce nature to facts and master it, and there was industrialism, the large-scale, centralized production of goods, and its indefatigable machines, furnishing the very metaphors by which science came to understand the world. Marx, therefore, was only halfway right in focusing exclusively on capitalism and class conflict. Worse, he was, despite a romantic youth, at last too close in his own thinking to that darker Enlightenment, too close to instrumental reason, to be a wholly reliable guide.[13]

The social consequences that follow from the modern commitment to instrumental reason and the disenchantment of nature have been antidemocratic and antihuman. "The more devices we invent for dominating nature," declared Horkheimer, "the more must we serve them if we are to survive." Serving means putting ourselves in the hands of those who are especially adept at instrumental analysis: capitalists, of course, big or small and aspiring; but also a new class of experts and technocrats, whose job it is to tell us how the dominating is to be done. The contemporary engineer is the best exemplar of that power of expertise. Though not himself necessarily concerned with profit-making, he reinforces directly and indirectly the rule of instrumentalism and unending economic growth.

> The engineer is not interested in understanding things for their own sake or for the sake of insight, but in accordance with their being fitted into a scheme, no matter how alien to their own inner structure; this holds for living beings as well as for inanimate things. The engineer's mind is that of industrialism in its streamlined form. His purposeful rule would make men an agglomeration of instruments without a purpose of their own.

Democracy cannot survive where technical expertise, accumulated capital, or their combination is allowed to take command.[14]

Accepting the authority of engineers, scientists, economists, and bureaucrats along with the power of capital, the common people become a herd. They live as "docile masses governed by clocks." More and more of their needs are attended to by others, even their leisure time is organized for them. Someone decides what they should want, what will keep them amused and uncomplaining, and what they must accept as reality. Instead of maturing into autonomous, rational individuals capable of deciding ultimate issues, as one side of the Enlightenment promised they would all do in the modern age, they instead become lifelong wards of the corporation and the state. Sensing their own impotence in the midst of so much general power, they may feel anger welling up inside them; but they do not know whom or what to blame, so thoroughly have they absorbed and internalized the ruling ideas, so completely have they lost the capacity for critical thought. Genuine freedom is for the average citizen an unknown ideal. His spontaneity atrophies. The memory of alternatives dries up. The private interior is invaded by hucksters and planners. Material life alone flourishes, and for the manipulated mass man that seems to be enough: an iron cage with all the amenities will do nicely in the absence of other possibilities. "Even though the individual disappears before the apparatus which he serves, that apparatus provides for him as never before."[15]

What is to be done about this slide into "the administered life," with its frightening potential for authoritarianism and infantile regression? The remedy must begin with the root problem: the modern drive to dominate external and internal nature. No one in the Frankfurt School ever proposed that nature be liberated from every demand humans place on it or that civilizations should revert to a primitive existence. Rather, they saw reconciliation and transcendence as the rational alternative to domination. Humans must liberate reason from its instrumental straitjacket and use it to work out a new cultural perception of the earth and a new behavior. Liberated reason can reveal what a river or a valley needs for its own realization, what values it may have beyond serving as a means to profit or amusement, what moral claims it makes on humans. When set free from its bondage to money and power, reason can determine which uses of the earth are worthy and truly necessary, and which are not. It can show us how to escape the limits of nature, not by dominating with machines or dams, but by transcending through the development of human imagination and virtue. Then, these philosophers argued, that new ecology will make possible a more democratic and humanly fulfilling social order.

That history reflects nature and its fate has been the overriding theme of this chapter from its beginning. In the Frankfurt School, especially in the writings of Max Horkheimer, that argument takes on a profundity of meaning that is several levels beyond what Wittfogel, Marx, or the ecological anthropologists had in mind. More's the pity, then, that Horkheimer and the others did not apply their general analysis to the specific case of water control in the American West. They would have found it as clear and illuminating a test of the cultural implications in the rule of instrumental reason and the domination of nature as any in the world. And they had the chance to make that inquiry. For the career of the Frankfurt School became, for a brief while, directly part of the intellectual history of the West.

One month after Hitler became head of the German state, the Institute for Social Research and its staff left their native country. First they journeyed to Geneva, then in 1933 to New York City and Columbia University. Eventually, in 1941, Horkheimer and Adorno, for reasons of health, migrated to Pacific Palisades, California. They lived there as part of an expatriate colony until 1948, when Horkheimer was invited back to Frankfurt to lecture and, finally, to relocate there as rector of the university. The years spent on the edges of the desert West were only an interlude in their lives, but it was an interlude filled with opportunities to see their ideas illustrated in concrete ditches and whirring dynamos. Hydraulic society in California, Arizona, and other arid states, built on the industrial urge to dominate and repress all that is natural in nature and people, stared the two Germans émigrés in the face, but they were looking another way—at Europe, at fascism, and at the older industrial capitalist centers.

By the 1940s, the American West could boast of managing water better than any other region on the planet. Its showpiece was Hoover Dam, completed on the Colorado River in 1935, immediately ranking as one of the engineering wonders of the twentieth century. Under construction were even more ambitious projects in the Central Valley of California and at the Grand Coulee in the state of Washington. In praise of those works, J. Kip Finch, dean emeritus of Columbia University's engineering college, hailed "the increasing mastery of man over nature which has made possible our continuing progress toward a better life." "Nature," he went on, "has been harnessed to meet man's needs on a scale that not so long ago would have been regarded as completely visionary and impossible."[16] What the Frankfurt critics would have pointed out to the dean, had they not been thinking about other matters, is that such projects, like the greater project of dominating nature of which they are a part, always carry a human cost, no matter how sweet the virtuosity or how sunny the motives of the dominators.

The history of water control in the American West is a subject of much more than local interest. Out of the region's sand and sagebrush has emerged a technological complex that raises issues of world historical significance. Not to see the region in those terms is to substitute the illusion of uniqueness for the reality of continuity. It is also to fracture the integrity of both nature and history. After all, the water flowing through that dry land mingles with the common sea Oceanus, which takes into itself as well the water of China, India, Egypt, and Peru. Water is like that: it unites as well as divides, brings distant points together and gives them a common issue, transports soil from remote mountains to fertilize our homeland. It meanders across many different terrains, joining all of them into a single loop of watershed. The history of water and water control cannot, if it seeks to be true to its subject, do otherwise than follow that course. It has taken us here into famous and obscure valleys of the earth, into diverse cultures on every continent, into a labyrinth of ideas. But now it is time to leave those other rivers of history and to follow the streaming of the American West, from its wilder, freer past to its possessed and managed present.

INCIPIENCE

A Poor Man's Paradise

Oh faith rewarded! Now no idle dream,
The long-sought Canaan before him lies;
He floods the desert with the mountain stream,
And lo! it leaps transformed to paradise.

>   —*Traditional Mormon hymn (nineteenth*
>   *century)*

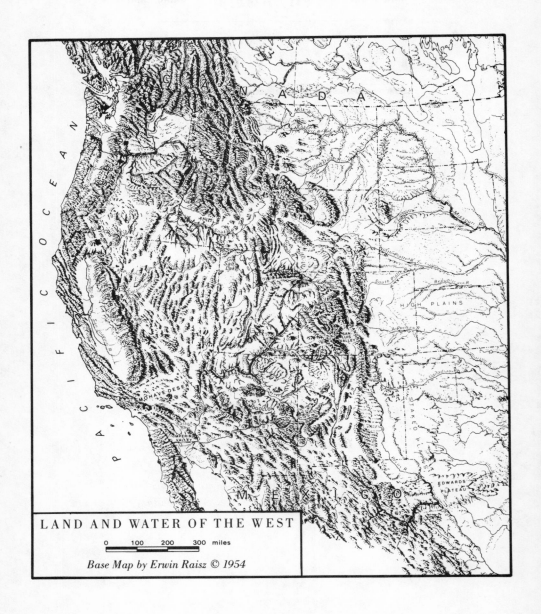

LAND AND WATER OF THE WEST

0   100   200   300   miles

Base Map by Erwin Raisz © 1954

"I'm pushing on when dawn's a-breaking, going 'cross the wide Missouri." The words of that song, the most beautiful ever written in America, tell of an experience, repeated again and again, that began with anonymous longings and ended in myth. They tell of a solitary man swimming his horse across a brown, surging river and through a sea of grass, the unbroken prairie. They tell of a woman driving a team of oxen and a covered wagon into the river, pulling up on the other bank, dripping and breathless yet eager to go on. They tell of a family on a flatboat loaded with their belongings, poling and warping their way upstream to Wyoming, Idaho, the Oregon country. Always in that endless migration there was one more river to cross. After the Missouri were the Sweetwater, the Gunnison, the Owyhee, the Dirty Devil, the Salmon, the Pecos, the Tuolumne, the Yellowstone, the Green, the Cimarron, the Escalante, the Columbia. Each was unique in character and challenge. And on the other shore, or up near the headwaters, or somewhere in the unbounded space lying beyond, there was a new life to make. There was an ancient story of exodus to reenact, a new promised land to occupy. There was a West to invent.

History compresses all those rivers, crossings, longings, and settlements into a narrative of selected details and a few generalizations. It puts brackets around periods, identifies stages, and talks of causes. None of its generalizations can be completely adequate to any situation, can encompass all the diversity in it or exhaust the human motives involved. But generalizations, nonetheless, have their use: they can describe a broad pattern of change that has enough truth in it to illuminate the present. And that is all this history of people and rivers in the American West seeks to claim. Someone else may, of course, find a contrary but plausible pattern in history. Where you choose to cross the river, whose wagon you decide to follow on the other side, may make a difference in the West you discover.

The pattern I want to describe begins as pioneers came into western valleys, made their homes there, plowed new fields, and started a process of river development. They had passed through the waters; now they turned them to their advantage. That process was one of ecological intensification —of extracting more and more economic yield from the rivers and their watersheds. It was not a steady progression, but a broken rhythm of fits and starts, of long periods of intensity, then long or short periods of consolidation or regress when development ran up against obstacles. Again and again, nature imposed limits on the settler, and often he did not have the capital, the technology, or the social organization needed to overcome them. He had reached a plateau of development and could not get off. To resume the process of intensification, the settler had to innovate and, in doing so, had to adapt himself to his innovations. Crossing that first river may have symbolized for him a break with the past, but it was the subsequent effort of getting from one plateau of river development to the next that was more decisive in the making of western society.

The process of intensification has now been going on for a century and a half in the West's river basins. It has passed through, as these chapters explain, a series of three stages, each of them lasting roughly fifty years. The first was a period of *incipience*, which began with the Mormon migration into Utah in 1847 and ran into the 1890s. It was characterized by a general dependence on local skills and means. Individuals or small communities, living rather isolated from the rest of the world, diverted rivers to the extent of their limited ability. They concentrated their energies on the smaller, more manageable streams and built primitive diversion works on them—so primitive in fact that they commonly had to be rebuilt after heavy floods. A number of private corporations also tried to harness the rivers for profit in this period, but the vast majority of them failed. The year 1902 marks the beginning of the second period, the era of *florescence*. In that year the federal government took firm charge of the western rivers, furnishing the capital and engineering expertise to lift the region to a higher plateau of development. Also in this second period, corporations and quasi-corporate entities succeeded at last in farming rivers for substantial profit, and in that success they created a sharply divided rural class structure where sagebrush and antelope had once flourished. In the third period of *empire*, extending from the 1940s into the foreseeable future, the two forces of government and private wealth achieved a powerful alliance, bringing every major western river under their unified control and perfecting a hydraulic society without peer in history.

"Roll on, roll on, you shining river." The song does not tell us much about that 150-year history of winning the water West. What it does do is remind us of that early moment when Americans stood among the sedges and cattails fringing the Big Muddy, looking westward, dreaming of what was over there and what they would do with it. Once across, they came into a land that was often more nightmare than dream—arid, hot, the air full of dust, nothing like the green world behind them. Why they went on even when disillusioned, what they did there, and how they justified it to themselves and the nation is the province, not of songs, but of history.

CONFRONTING
THE DESERT:
DEATH AND LIFE

John Woodhouse Audubon, the younger son of the famous bird painter, set out from New York City in 1849 for the California gold fields. Landing on the Texas coast, he and his party struck out across the Southwest to San Diego, following the Gila River for part of that distance, then trudging through the desert now called Imperial Valley. "Our road," he wrote, "is garnished almost every league with dead cattle, horses or oxen; and wagons, log chains, and many valuable things are left at almost every camping ground by the travelers; we ourselves have had to do the same, to relieve our worn and jaded mules, able now to carry only about a hundred pounds." Dust flowed over their shoe-tops, rose in clouds and filled their eyes, choked animals and men alike. For long stretches the only life they saw was creosote bushes, sunflowers, and a lone vulture. Ordeal, suffering, bones, death—nothing the desert inflicted could induce them to tarry awhile. It was a land to endure, a temporary price to pay for the excitement that lay ahead.[1]

The gold seekers who took the more northern route, following the Humboldt River through the Great Basin until it disappeared in the sand, leaving them all on their own to reach the Sierras, had the same negative reaction. From 1849 to 1860, about 300,000 individuals came to California by some overland route, unavoidably passing through extremely arid regions, encountering, as Patricia Nelson writes, "physical nature in its least compliant and most threatening form."[2] They followed trails marked out by fur trappers, military explorers, and Indians, but even so they had a terrible time. The desert was a hostile environment lying in wait for the slow and careless. Someday it ought to be defeated, they supposed, but now wealth was beckoning and the job of doing battle with the desert would have to wait.

Perhaps the best of their narratives, for vividness and spirit, is that of William Manly, who very nearly died in the hot sink of Death Valley. Manly had spent his childhood in cool, benign Vermont, and he had learned how to support himself from the woods and gardens around the family cabin. In Michigan and Wisconsin too, he had shown himself to be an uncommonly resourceful, self-reliant hand at frontier living. Then he made the nearly fatal mistake of setting out for the California mines. Manly joined the Sand Walking Company, which assembled at Salt Lake in October 1849 and then took off southwesterly to skirt the Sierra wall. After a few days, he began thinking back to the "bounteous stock of bread and beans on my father's table, to say nothing about all the other good things, and here was I, the oldest son, away out in the center of the Great American Desert, with an empty stomach and a dry and parched throat, and clothes fast wearing out with constant wear."[3] He tried keeping a bullet or stone in his mouth to make the saliva flow; even then he found he could not work up a swallow. He was a crack shot, but for days on end there was nothing in sight to shoot. At one point he fed on the bacon rinds thrown out by a party traveling ahead. In utter desperation he drank, with his friend and the two families they served as hunters, the black sulphurous water from wretched little holes, along with the blood of their oxen.

Months later, after they had straggled out of the desert into Los Angeles, Manly marveled that they had come through alive. It was if they had risen from a spell in their grave.

> We were out of the dreadful sands and shadows of Death
> Valley, its exhausting phantoms, its salty columns, bitter
> lakes, and wild, dreary, sunken desolation. We had crossed
> the North American Continent, from a land of plenty, over
> great barren hills and plains, to another mild and beautiful
> region, where, though still in winter months, we were
> basking in the warmth and luxuriance of early summer.
> We thought not of the gold we had come to win. We were
> dead almost, and now we lived. We were starved so that
> we had looked at each other with maniac thoughts, and
> now we placed in our mouths the very fat of the land.[4]

God had snatched them "from the jaws of death." Manly would remember, even in his seventies, every terrifying detail of that journey and their deliverance.

For a Paiute Indian, whose ancestors had survived in the desert for a thousand years, Manly's dread would have been incomprehensible. There were always chuckwallas to catch and roast, water to drink for those who knew the land. But the Americans who came into the arid West were farmers and townsmen, and none of them could read the secrets of the land like the Paiute. The only desert they had ever known was the one mentioned in the Bible, and there was nothing in that account to prepare them to love or admire the wild dry places. It was natural for them to see only what was missing in that country across the Missouri: no tall oaks or maples, no springs within a few minutes' walk, no deep, dark humus underfoot, no rustle and twitter in the underbrush, no underbrush. Such a place could only seem to them the negation of all value, the place that God forgot.

By the 1890s, however, that initial fear and hostility began to mellow into acceptance and even celebration. Americans by then had found ways of coping with western exigencies, and with that coping came familiarity, self-confidence, and eventually the seeds of delight. Life, it came to be seen, could thrive in the desert. Indeed, the West, particularly the warm Southwest, became a national sanitarium, where the victims of tuberculosis, bronchitis, or asthma could go to find relief from the dampness and polluted air of eastern America. It was as if the sick came to sit and recuperate on the bones of earlier travelers. And the healthy, once they had located a secure supply of water and food, discovered that the aridity agreed with them too, lifting their spirits and invigorating their step. In a matter of a few decades the dangers of the West had been transformed into advantages, into promises, and into copy for boosters and real-estate agents, touting the dry climate as America's best.[5]

Once that reevaluation had commenced, people came to notice that other forms of life had found the desert a good place to settle as well. The region, even in its most formidable parts, was filled with living things, and they were all success stories. The secret of their success was that they had learned how to adapt. The scientific community, particularly the ecologists, could and did contribute much to that emerging American appreciation of the desert. A small number of scientists began trekking along the same routes as the forty-niners, but moving more slowly, observing the adaptive processes that had been at work, interested in this arid nature for its own sake. In 1891, Frederick Vernon Colville led a small expedition into Death Valley and returned so intrigued by what he had found there—mesquite trees, for example, with roots going more than fifty feet down into the earth —that he began laying plans for a research station in the Southwest. Twelve years later the Carnegie Institution in Washington accepted his proposal to establish a Desert Botanical Laboratory because "it promised results concerning the fundamental processes of protoplasm as important as any in the whole realm of botany."[6] Tucson was chosen as the site for the laboratory, and William Cannon became the first resident investigator. Other early associates of the research center included Daniel Trembly MacDougal, who was Colville's companion on several collecting trips; Forrest Shreve, a graduate of Johns Hopkins who came to the laboratory in 1909 and later served as president of the Ecological Society of America; and Frederic Clements, architect of the widely influential theory of the climax stage in vegetation development.[7] Where Audubon and his party had seen only a dreary vista of dust, these later men found an astonishing variety of plants and their animal associates, all exhibiting the most remarkable attributes. There was the ocotillo, the yucca (Spanish dagger, Joshua tree), the desert lily, the rock gilia, the pinkish five-spot, the tiny sand mat, the cactuses (saguaro, barrel, organ pipe, fishhook, prickly pear), the paloverde tree with its strange green bark, the century plant with its thick succulent leaves, the aromatic sage, desert tea, heliotrope, croton, rattlesnake weed, evening primrose, saltbush, Turkish rugging, and thousands more. Searching for such botanical treasures, scientists wandered from water hole to water hole, from canyon to canyon, learning at first hand the lessons of adaptation. They learned also to appreciate what Shreve described as the "humanistic, intellectual and esthetic" values of the desert.[8]

Their preliminary studies, though often alluding to larger issues in evolutionary biology, aimed mainly at identifying the plants and plant communities of the arid region, a step that was essential in order to lay the basis for more advanced work in desert science that would come in the 1930s and after. Also among those first tasks that the pioneer scientists had to grapple with before they could pursue the problem of adaptation in detail was simply to define what a desert is and what should properly be called deserts in the West.

The word "desert" had a double set of meanings whose origins ran far back into history. It had been used at times to refer to any place without human inhabitants, at other times to denote specifically arid and usually hot landscapes. The two meanings had not always been compatible, for millions of people lived in the deserts of the Middle East and North Africa. Those were very dry but hardly uninhabitable lands. Americans had exhibited the same confusion of language, and what was more, they had not been altogether sure just how dry an area had to be in order to qualify as desert. Zebulon Pike, who crossed the prairies to the Rocky Mountains in 1808 and 1809, compared them to the "great sandy deserts of Africa" and was sure they would never be settled by Americans. Washington Irving made a similar observation in 1836: "This region, which resembles one of the ancient steppes of Asia, has not inaptly been termed The Great American Desert. It spreads forth into undulating and treeless plains and desolate sandy wastes, wearisome to the eye from their extent and monotony."[9] A number of geography textbooks followed suit, even depicting on their maps rippling dunes and camels where Kansas and Nebraska now appear. Later, as experience accumulated, the plains were more accurately reclassified as semiarid or subhumid, and the Great American Desert became for a while the Bonneville Flats of Utah. Even then there were many promoters who wanted the term banished completely from all maps of the West as a libel and as bad publicity.[10]

The scientists of the Desert Botanical Laboratory retained the word, restricted it to a condition of low rainfall (under ten inches), and drew precise maps of America's deserts. Colville and MacDougal, writing in 1903, identified two major desert areas: the Sonoran-Nevadan, extending from Sonora northward into Oregon and Idaho; and the Chihuahuan, covering parts of Mexico, Texas, and New Mexico.[11] Within those broad zones were a series of distinct plant communities, each with its own character, each with its own demands on the understanding. Almost nowhere was the American desert simply a stretch of empty sand; everywhere there was life in it. Americans had only to take the trouble to look.

Scientists, then, were a force for opening heretofore closed, averse minds to the meaning and significance of the desert. It must be added that their influence on the general population was probably small, especially in the early decades of western settlement. The botanist, the ecologist, the student of animal physiology, served to reinforce rather than to cause the shift in perception that began to be apparent in the last years of the nineteenth century. Something broader, something deeper than science was bringing that shift about, if not in every mind, at least in enough to be culturally significant. From being a loathsome and ugly environment, the desert increasingly came to be a landscape modern people would deliberately seek out. The explanation for that turnaround is simply put: for another generation of Americans deserts came to answer certain powerful needs, among them a desire for solitude, for beauty, for uncluttered existence, for the nonhuman. To seek further and even more revealing evidence of that shifting sense of priorities, we should turn to the two figures who founded what eventually became a popular American tradition of desert nature writing—Mary Austin and John Van Dyke. Both were artists, approaching the desert, not to earn a living from it, but rather to learn about it, write about it, and declare its inner truth. They gathered much from science, but the mainsprings of their reaction lay in less rational corners of modern consciousness.

Mary Austin first arrived in the West by train in 1888. She was twenty years old, traveling with her mother and older brother to take up a homestead thirty miles south of Bakersfield, California, in the shadow of the Tehachapi Mountains. Her earlier years had been spent in Carlinville, Illinois, a dull little town not far from St. Louis, and in the conventional pieties of midwestern Methodism. Despite the intense pressures for conformity, she had somehow managed to grow up independent and self-defining. To marry and settle down soon was not her main ambition. "She thought there might be a great deal to be got out of being a woman," her autobiography declares, "but she definitely meant neither to chirrup or twitter." She would spend the rest of her life in the West, identifying with buzzards and meadowlarks, not Illinois sparrows.[12]

Mary and her family filed on three 160-acre homestead claims and moved into a one-room cabin with calico curtains and bunks against the wall. Three years later she escaped from that cramped existence by marrying Stafford Wallace Austin, the son of Hawaiian sugar planters, and he turned out to be an ill-fated choice for a husband. He led her from one California town to another, from job to job, piling up debts, spinning rosy dreams, and paying little attention to her. He did, however, do two positive things for her. He made her a confirmed feminist and introduced her both to the land and people of Owens Valley, lying east of Bakersfield over the massif of Mount Whitney, and to the Mohave Desert bordering on the south. That became the setting for her book *The Land of Little Rain,* published in 1903. It is a gentle, quiet portrait of desert life—mystical, arcadian, the expression of a pagan sensibility freeing itself from Victorian and Protestant constraints.[13]

Confessing that the desert was for her a lonely place, "the loneliest that ever came out of God's hands," Mary Austin was nevertheless irresistibly drawn to it. "None other than this long brown land," she wrote, "lays such a hold on the affections." Wanting desperately to secure a private space in her life, to be free from others crowding and importuning her, she found the desert suited her exactly. She admired the way its plants tended to grow solitary, spacing themselves well apart. In the same spirit of self-reliance, she tracked coyotes prowling for their dinner, watched the cougar come silently to the water hole to drink, and walked out alone at night to marvel at the clarity of stars in the sky. Everywhere in the desert there were hills, and their aged presence suggested to her that there was "room enough and time enough" in that place to complete whatever work she wanted to do for herself. The local people she felt drawn to were likewise solitaries, or lived in small bands: a prospector hunting for a small pocket of gold ore, a sheepherder roaming with his flock, an Indian woman who supported herself by making and selling baskets. For Austin, such people were as integral to the land of little rain as coyotes and lizards. Their adobe houses, wattle huts, and patchwork gardens grew straight out of the dry brown soil —declarations of desert independence.[14]

When in the first decade of the twentieth century "modern America," in the form of the Los Angeles Water and Power Department, "laid a greedy, vulgarizing hand" on the Owens Valley, buying up land on the sly and preparing to divert the river southward to the metropolis, Austin protested and fought. The imperial city would make the valley its colony, she feared, for whoever controlled the water in that land controlled the destiny of life depending on it. Austin and the valley lost their battle in 1905, whereupon she made a painful decision. She divorced her husband and moved away, her desert pastoral, her private space, irretrievably gone.[15]

In 1898, ten years after Mary Austin's train arrived in Bakersfield, John Van Dyke showed up in Los Angeles. He was a forty-two-year-old professor of art at Rutgers University in New Jersey, the son of a judge, the author of books and pamphlets on painting and aesthetics. He was also a severe asthmatic, "just ill enough," he says, "not to care about perils and morbid enough to prefer dying in the sand, alone, to passing out in a hotel with a roommaid weeping at the foot of the bed." With a little dried food, a gallon of water, blankets, and guns, he trotted out of civilization on an Indian pony, heading for the Colorado desert. For three years he explored the southwestern country, on horseback, on foot, and by railroad car, down into Mexico among the *rancherías,* along the awesomely silent Colorado River, through the Grand Canyon, up and down the Chocolate, Boboquivari, and Sierra Madre mountains. He took a fever and was laid up for a while. He learned to squeeze the pulp of cactuses to get a drink and to build his campfire with ocotillo canes. All along he closely observed the harsh land and acquired a taste for it beyond any he had seen. In the same year Austin's book came out, he published *The Desert,* which he described as a lover's word of praise for a landscape that "has gone a-begging for a word of praise these many years."[16] Even more than Austin's, his is a study in transvaluation.

What Van Dyke discovered in the desert was how inadequate conventional nineteenth-century ideas of beauty were. There was nothing pretty there, nothing even of the picturesque that Austin had found. It was weird, grim, ugly by common standards of judgment. He claimed never to have seen the springtime flowering that can turn an Arizona hillside into a radiance of golden poppies. Flowers, he insisted, were too delicate to make an impact on that hard land. The animals he saw were lean, gaunt, fiercely aggressive, armed with fangs and poison and claws.

> They seem like a precious pack of cutthroats, these beasts
> and reptiles of the desert. Perhaps there never was a life
> so nurtured in violence, so tutored in attack and defence
> as this. The warfare is constant from the birth to the
> death.[17]

At no point does he mention meeting up in his rambles with any other human being, Indian, Mexican, or white. He was not interested in the "folk" of the Southwest—in the strings of chiles hanging from their roof beams, in the charming brown faces and black eyes of their children, in any of the staples of colorful travelogue. It was nature at its most repellent and inhuman that he came to confront and ended up loving.

Beauty is an intrinsic quality in nature, he argues in the book; it has nothing to do with human ideas of goodness or morality. It is not something men and women bestow on the world, whether by deeds or by imagination, but is independent of human beings, though it can afford sensuous pleasure. Citing the French impressionist Claude Monet, Van Dyke insists that beauty is not even a matter of form; it is pure color, shades of light, drifts of air. The desert has that quality of beauty in abundance: in dark wine-red mountains, in terra-cotta foothills, in phosphorescent moonlight, in deep blue skies, in olive and smoke-gray brush in a dry wash. A horned toad, so repulsive to us at first sight, has beauty that we are bound to respect, even if we must struggle to see it. Nature does not know favorites; it designs for the horned toad and the rattlesnake as much as for the butterfly. In this argument on behalf of the desert, Van Dyke spoke out of a distinctly modernist frame of mind, one that would sever aesthetics from all tradition and cultural bias, that would go so far as to insist on the amorality of beauty. It is not instrumental to any human ends—does not make us better people, has no uplifting mission to perform, transcends good and evil, is its own excuse for being.

Yet Van Dyke was only half an aesthete, and would not have agreed with the radical modern doctrine of pure subjectivism in taste and value. The other side of his response to the desert was archaically religious. There, more than anywhere else he had been, he felt himself in the presence of a superhuman power. The immense space, the overwhelming silence of the place, the sense of brooding mystery, were all qualities of the sublime.

Given a chance to come face to face with sublimity, what could man want with ordinary trees and lakes, or a trivial patch of grass? The desert, he noted, has often stirred in humans a strong, heroic religiosity. "The dwellers beside the desert have cherished what the inhabitants of the fertile plains have thrown away. They and their forefathers have never known civilization, and never suffered from the blight of doubt."[18] That is as much as Van Dyke would say on the matter. It was enough to suggest that he went out needing more than clean air for his lungs, that he sought, and perhaps found, a renewal of faith.

If there is a theme connecting the two halves of Van Dyke's thinking, the amorality of beauty and the sublimity in desolation, it is a weariness, a disgust with the world of humans. He speaks of the "magnificent complacency" of his fellow citizens, so sure in their own minds that the earth was made for them. Nature, he points out, "has other animals beside man to look after, other uses for her products than supporting human life."[19] Deserts are evidence of that fact. Travelers and settlers who dismiss arid places in the West with a scornful "worthless" or "useless" are trapped in their own self-centeredness, unable to take a broader, more humble view of creation. Van Dyke declines to condemn in the desert what he does not understand—and, he adds, there is a great deal humans do not understand. His stance here is a very old one, found in religions throughout history, but he gives it an almost misanthropic expression that, again, has a peculiarly modern bite to it. Go to the desert, he recommends, to get away for a while from the hordes of humanity, from their inventions, their civilization, their self-inflation, their moralizing, their assertion that nature is only a means to their continual aggrandizement.

By the time Van Dyke wrote (he finished his manuscript in 1901), irrigation had already reclaimed much of the desert, and one group of capitalists, the Colorado Irrigation Company, were preparing to turn the vast country around the Salton Sea into farmland. Van Dyke was a rank outsider, his home was on the other side of the continent, and he did not stay around to fight against their scheme. But he was outraged by the irrigation invasion and made what was at the time a novel argument for conserving the desert as wilderness. Irrigation, he warned, would make the dry, crackling air of southernmost California heavy and humid—and people required good air as much as bread and beef. "The deserts are not worthless wastes," he went on; "you cannot crop all creation with wheat and alfalfa. . . . The deserts should never be reclaimed. They are the breathing-spaces of the west and should be preserved forever." Everywhere the "practical men" had gone in America, they had cut the throat of beauty to make a dollar, chopping down northern forests, plowing up the Dakota prairies,

blackening Pennsylvania with their coal and oil, ravaging Montana's mountains for ore, leaving in their wake a chaos of weeds, derricks, shanties, and
ugly towns—"and at last they have turned to the desert!" There was little
prospect of stopping them, Van Dyke feared, but he took some comfort in
the power of nature to reassert itself in the end. "Nothing human," he was
reminded, "is of long duration."[20]

That anyone would one day write in defense of the desert would surely
have amazed William Manly and the forty-niners. But both Mary Austin and
John Van Dyke did just that a short fifty years after Manly's ordeal. They
may be said to have represented a tiny elite when they wrote, though it was
a group that would grow more and more numerous in the twentieth century,
keeping their books in print year after year until millions in the United
States and abroad had read them. A maverick woman who kicked against
the traces of marriage and motherhood. A middle-aged man troubled by
intimations of his own death, driven by antisocial feelings to oppose "progress." It would be easy to dismiss them thus as cranks. That they were
marginal to the story of desert conquest which follows is admitted. But they
were not, for that reason, unimportant. Austin and Van Dyke spoke for an
alternative side of modern America: one against domination, instrumentalism, the power of capital and technique; one in favor of freedom, wild,
untrammeled grandeur, and human humility. The West became a theater
for both versions of modernity.

THE LORD'S
BEAVERS

The Mormons, or Latter-day Saints, of Utah have sometimes claimed, in
moments of high filiopietism, that they were the first Americans to
practice irrigation on a wide scale. A more careful statement is that they
were the first Americans of northern European ancestry to do so. More
important, they were the first in the West to propagate assiduously, in deeds
as well as words, the gospel of desert conquest sanctioned by God. And they
were the first to encounter the fact that that gospel had no logical point of
closure. Its fate was that it worked and worked, until it worked its own
undoing. River valley after river valley came under Mormon command,
testifying to their religious zeal and organization. Then one day they passed
the point where it was God they were primarily serving. In the end, money

and the American marketplace had become the dominant forces driving them on. Their religion had served admirably, it turned out, as an impetus toward, and a justification for, the accumulation of capital. It had helped the Mormon people become the first commercially successful irrigators in North America. It had made them more affluent than any of their predecessors in the region had been. And then it could do no more—except impede the process of economic rationalization they had set in motion. It proved to be a good nursery for desert conquest, but a poorer guide for a lifetime career in it.

Before the Mormons founded their desert kingdom, there were the Indians and the Spanish. To understand the Mormons as irrigators, we first need to see them in relation to those peoples who came before them. The southwestern Indians, as described in the preceding chapter, had achieved a measure of water control and political concentration many centuries before white men arrived on the scene. The Spanish, whose techniques were hardly more advanced, were the first Europeans to irrigate in what is now the United States. A hundred years after Columbus's discovery they were on the Rio Grande, directing local Indians in digging a ditch near present-day San Juan, New Mexico. By 1800 they had constructed 164 *acequias,* or irrigation canals, in the upper part of that river basin. All of them were essentially communal undertakings, drawing on the peasant culture of southern Spain, on Moorish influences, and on the native pueblo experience. Other centers for their water development were the missions of California and Texas, San Diego, Los Angeles, San Antonio, and so forth, each of them an oasis in the brown land, each a means of power over the aboriginal peoples.[1]

Along the Rio Grande, where Spanish and later Mexican irrigated agriculture was most extensively practiced, each village or town had a *mayordomo,* who was responsible for constructing and maintaining the canal system and for distributing water. Church bells alerted the farmers (or in many places the peons of a large landowner) when a break in the floodgates threatened their fields. Piles of brush and large cylindrical baskets filled with stones were the materials they used to make diversion dams, which forced the river into the "mother ditch" and her smaller offspring and then into crop rows. In March of every year, men would gather to burn the weeds from the ditches, beseeching Saint Isidro, the patron of farmers, to provide a good season. Along with the Indian staples of corn, beans, pumpkins, gourds, chiles, and cotton, the Hispanic farmers planted their Old World seeds of wheat, oats, watermelons, peaches, oranges, and apricots. Their plows were simply the crotch or knee of a tree. Their fields were irregular in shape, their rows crooked, their ditches winding and complicated. By later American standards, the Spanish irrigated agriculture was ludicrously antique. "It has been pursued," one Anglo critic wrote, "merely as a means of living."[2] Confident that there was nothing profitable to be learned from either the Hispanic or Indian system of irrigation, the Yanquis dated the real history of water control in the West from their own first efforts.

The Mormons, when they came West in 1847, bypassed those older settlements, though they sent traders there and observed their irrigated fields.[3] For their refuge the Mormons chose an area that no one before them had tried to irrigate—the slope from the Wasatch Mountains to the Great Salt Lake. Despite their efforts to collect advance information, they were frightfully innocent of the first principles of water application, and they had no vernacular or folk tradition to guide them in the enterprise. Moreover, they had virtually no capital when they first arrived. What they did have was an irrepressible confidence that God had picked out a part of the desert for their homeland and would see that they thrived on it. In addition to the religious element in their determination, there was, as one of their descendants pointed out, a sense of ethnic pride.

> The Mormon pioneers . . . belonged to the civilization that Anglo-Saxon peoples had won for themselves through centuries of struggle. The gains of the civilization they must maintain. The stark desert must be subdued, but not at the price of civilized life and living. Somehow, they must hold on to the social, economic and spiritual possessions on the conquered desert as well as they had in humid regions.[4]

But merely holding on to those various possessions was not the end of it; they were also intent on making them increase forever in quantity and grace.

On 23 July 1847, a committee of Mormons broke their first ground for farming. They had just walked over eight hundred miles from Iowa to the future site of Salt Lake City. They had staked out a piece of ground near City Creek where they would plant potatoes, beans, and corn. Now they were ready to dam the creek and cut a trench from it through the hard-baked Utah ground to their new fields. Shortly thereafter, stream after stream flowing from the mountains was turned out of its bed. The means available for that work were at first primitive. Planks bolted together in the shape of the letter A formed a "go-devil," a wedgelike tool the Saints used to tear canals across the landscape. A pan filled with water served, in the absence of levels and surveying instruments, to lay out the waterways with enough decline to make the water run smoothly in them: not too fast, or the current would erode the ditch; not too slow, or the silt would settle out and clog the works. Dirt and rocks scraped together with brush made a dam. These were not much better than Indian ways, but they were only a beginning.[5]

From that first point of ad hoc innovation, Mormon irrigation diffused north, south, east, and west, creating a ganglion of colonies tied to the Mother Church in the capital city. Led by their astute patriarch Brigham Young, inspired by their murdered founder and prophet Joseph Smith, the Mormons wrote their imperial ambitions on the face of the earth for all to see. They took the bee and its hive as a symbol of their industry, but a more appropriate one would have been the beaver, for control over water became the ecological basis of their society.

One of the most remarkable aspects of Mormon irrigation was the speed of its conquest over the desert. By 1850 there were 16,333 irrigated acres in what would become the state of Utah, and on them were grown 44,000 bushels of potatoes, 4,800 tons of hay, and 107,700 bushels of wheat, along with oats, corn, and rye. Within another forty years, the irrigated acreage amounted to 263,473, and it supported more than 200,000 people. Almost every one of the 10,000 farms in the state was irrigated, and their average size was 27 acres. In forty years the potato crop had jumped over 1,000 percent, the wheat yield over 1,500 percent.[6]

The Spanish irrigation settlements, after two-and-a-half centuries of endeavor, could still not show such results. For a people who had come without even a fund of experience or capital, the Mormons had made an impressive showing. No wonder that historians, Mormon and Gentile alike, continue even now to praise them with words like "magnificent" and "heroic" and to speak fondly of their square, orderly villages with row upon row of fences and ditches lined by "Mormon trees"—tall Lombardy poplars, dark green against the barren wild.

Though they came to the arid West with empty pockets and a lack of training, the Mormons did have a system of hierarchy and group discipline, and that critical quality made possible their rapid success in water manipulation. Under their first leader, Joseph Smith, they had taken the form of a religious corporation—a theocracy (in intent if not in actuality) constructed along the lines of modern rationality. At the top of their chain of authority stood the First Presidency, the Quorum of the Twelve Apostles, and the Council of Seventy; at the bottom, the local ward bishop. In the ancient irrigation states a pattern of hierarchy had often evolved slowly, century by century, out of the intensification of irrigation. In Utah the organization was more exogenous, but it proved to work as well as any

Mesopotamian order of priests and kings in achieving river control. It provided a unified scheme of development and—within the limits of the available technology—a maximization of resource exploitation, and it freed the communities from individuals squabbling over water rights. It allowed the amassing of capital to undertake new projects and provided a cushion of security when projects failed. And, most important, it claimed to speak with the voice of God.

Before they were annexed as a territory of the United States and saddled with secular control from Washington, the Church hierarchy pursued a policy of centralism in water matters. It determined the design and location of new colonies, seeking to achieve an agrarian utopia of dispersed villages bound together by threads of waterways and ruled over by a benevolent center, reminiscent in many ways of the ancient irrigation states.[7] It parceled out land and water to its followers according to hierarchic claims, so that those at the top were given the most and adjured to hold them "in trust" for the general good. The Church asserted that all water ultimately belonged to the commonality, not to autonomous individuals. That notion, a radical one by the standards of mid-nineteenth-century America, was justified by the argument that in such an arid place, where water was scarce and survival easily put at risk, a single authority must have ultimate jurisdiction over its disposal. And what more trustworthy authority was there than the Church? Yet no matter how spiritual, centralism could also become a way to enforce the power of the hierarchy over nonconformists and dissidents.

When the federal government began to assert its preeminence over Utah, the high authorities of the Church found their hegemony threatened. As a consequence, they decentralized the water system, devolving the building of canals and dams into the hands of the local bishop or a community group. Farmers then came together, paid a tithe in the form of their own labor on the water system, and elected from among them a watermaster to supervise the work. Under an 1852 act of the territorial legislature all responsibility for water adjudication left the center (illegally, it was later declared) for the periphery—a circle of county courts. All that would seem to be a perfectly democratic manner of functioning, and in a formal sense it was. But at the same time it was a way of keeping Mormon affairs under Church influence and out of the meddling hands of the federal government, which appointed the territorial governor and Supreme Court judges. Freed from that outside, rival authority, the bishops and local courts would ensure that the Church's voice would continue to be heard. The Church might have taken a very different course, one toward a continued centralism of authority, toward a full-fledged theocracy unhindered by civil agencies,[8] had the Mormon elders had their way.

Another defensive stratagem was the Act of 1865, which allowed the organization of irrigation districts as self-governing entities. According to that law, a majority of citizens in any county or part thereof could petition their county court to let them organize and elect officers, who would decide where canals should be built and who would assess taxes, on land or on all property, to pay for them. Two-thirds of the voters in the district had to approve of any tax levy. The district could not sell bonds and incur debts. First to organize was the Deseret Irrigation and Canal Company, lying east of the Jordan River in Great Salt Lake County. By 1898 there were forty-one irrigation districts in the state.[9]

Once again the historians have been eloquent, describing the district law as the perfection of grassroots democracy, one scholar calling it "a wonderful extension of the co-operative system."[10] In reality, the act had very different aspects. It served to exclude from power and prosperity all non-Mormon farmers, who were beginning to settle in Utah, and it worked to maintain the power of the religious hierarchy. The Church controlled the definition of citizenship and voter eligibility, and, in effect, it appointed the county court judges, monopolized the best lands, and distributed them through the local bishop. When those facts had become outrageously apparent, the territorial supreme court charged, in the case of *Monroe* v. *Ivri* (1880), that the irrigation districts had become, not models of democratic participation, but "engines of oppression."[11]

There were still other ways in which the shadow theocracy asserted itself, and again, it was the control over water that was its means of doing so. Well into the twentieth century, the anthropologist Mark Leone argues, the Church dominated the most remote villages through the mechanism of religious rituals associated with irrigation and dam failures. Along the Little Colorado River in Arizona, a string of Mormon towns, with names like St. Joseph, Woodruff, and Snowflake, built dams. And whenever heavy snowmelt brought floods, those dams washed out with depressing regularity. The Rio Grande Hispanics had long had the same problem but had learned to accept it. The Mormons, however, were there to master nature, and they were not to be allowed to settle into a fatalistic acceptance. After each washout, they heard a sermon from the leadership, telling them the world was going to pieces and they must save it. In the failure of their dams God was testing them for mettle and determination; they must not fail Him. "Through a series of such sermons," Leone writes, "the hierarchy explained the event to the people, who thus explained it to themselves, and the world view of defeat was transformed into the world view of another chance to show their worthiness to be God's chosen." But it was also a "world view of permanent subordination." The common people learned that the war against nature required them to become an army of obedient soldiers who would unquestioningly march out again and again to rebuild dams, making them bigger and stronger each time in defense of the Church and its righteous cause.[12]

The Sevier River drains the Bryce Canyon uplands, traverses greasewood and rabbit-brush flats, and spends itself into the glistening alkaline basin of western Utah. In 1859, a band of Saints put up a crude earthen dam on the Sevier, watched it go in the spring freshet, put up another one, saw it fail too—then tried again. After five defeats, that group moved away, undoubtedly bearing a stigma of guilt. A few years later another group entered the scene and recommenced the war. By 1889, on the eighth try, with sixty-five tons of lava rock and log piles driven deep into the sandy bottom, they won a permanent victory. Sevier Bridge Dam, which long stood as one of the most important irrigation structures in the state, symbolized the stubborn Mormon spirit in confronting what Leonard Arrington has called the "vengeful, pitiless powers of nature."[13] In this case, no less than in several others, ultimate victory did not belong to the grassroots, to the common folk; it was the work of the hierarchy. When the local farmers along the Sevier could not manage alone, the Church did more than preach sermons about perfecting their godly doggedness; it sent out money from Salt Lake City to invest in the project—surreptitiously, as the federal government had forbidden it to provide direct capitalization for moneymaking schemes. It also, through the agency of some of its leading figures, took the lead in planning replacement structures and assembling technical skills to construct them. When the river surrendered at last and was put to work growing alfalfa, money began at last to flow out of the valley. The Church collected part of that new wealth in tithes and once again strengthened its hand over the outposts of settlement.

Had the Mormon hierarchy never migrated into the desert and become involved in river control, it would likely have had a rather different history. Its original table of organization was an abstraction. Irrigation helped make it a powerful reality. Illinois or Missouri, two of Mormonism's former homes, would not have furnished so fine a crucible for that actualization. In those states, Thomas Jefferson's ideal of independent, self-reliant farmers, freed by property ownership from hierarchy, including that of religion, was widely shared. If it had remained in Illinois, Mormonism would surely have had a great deal of trouble keeping its people from wandering off toward that ideal. In Utah, however, the Church had an excellent environment for creating an agrarian society ruled by a central power. There the hierarchy could insist, even after the federal invasion, on cohesion, dominance, and discipline.[14]

But the desert hierarchy had other problems to confront, and they were to some extent of its own making. The more the Mormons controlled nature, the more they needed science and technology. Mormonism was a peculiar mix of modern rationalism and premodern, fundamentalist devotion, a mix that was volatile and unstable. The Church required, for its own maintenance and growth, a capacity in people for unquestioning faith in angels and golden plates. However, it also depended on the expansion of hydraulic engineering, irrigation expertise, and sophisticated agricultural knowledge. At some risk, it sent its young people away to get the best training possible. John Widtsoe is a case in point. Born in Norway in 1872, he migrated with his mother to Utah, grew up in the faith, and later went off to study chemistry at Harvard. He understood that the Mormon mission "was to conquer the desert in terms of processes based on scientific study." His commitment to that conquest was, in the approving words of the Church's organ, "ardent and unlimited." As a reward for his leadership and commitment, he was made a key figure in the hierarchy—college president and member of the Quorum of the Twelve Apostles—while at the same time he helped lay the foundations for modern irrigation science.[15] In all that busyness, an elemental question seems never to have been asked by Widtsoe, namely, What was it that gave the Saints dominion over the earth, science or the Church? Others, though, might well ask that question and answer it by turning to another priesthood, that of the scientists and engineers.

An even more serious threat to the religious hierarchy came from the marketplace. Once again, the internal dynamics of Mormonism generated much of the threat, for the increase in agricultural wealth made possible by irrigation intensification was at once the Church's program and its enemy. The problem went as far back as Joseph Smith, who was, as Howard Lamar describes him, a holy man and yet also a Jacksonian man, always eager to make money.[16] His successor, Brigham Young, was equally ambivalent. He could insist over and over that the Saints must maintain their holiness by raising only what they needed for their own use, staying free of the outside world. Yet when the transcontinental railroad was opened through Utah in 1867, he was as excited as any worldly entrepreneur by the prospects of gain. Once, they had been seekers of refuge. However, after the railroad's coming, the Mormons, with Young's blessing, would be marketers. Eventually, they would put their irrigation profits into growing sugar beets instead of wheat and potatoes, they would set up a refinery to extract the sugar, and they would sell sell sell.[17]

In 1880, the state of Utah changed its laws to allow, for the first time, private individual ownership of the water resource. A key element in Mormon communalism was thus destroyed. The continuing threat of the federal government stepping into local affairs and giving power to the non-Mormon residents was one reason for the change. Vesting individual rights in water was a defense against that eventuality and the possible redistribution of water to newcomers. But we are right to see in the act another meaning: the integration of Mormonism into the mainstream of American economic culture and its free-enterprise institutions. That integration would inevitably lead to another claim to hegemony, one coming from a rising class of capitalists—agricultural and industrial—who would not interfere with the Church so long as it did not challenge their supremacy.

By 1890, capitalistic irrigation had begun to supplant the Church's program of local water development under centralized supervision. The Bear River Irrigation Company, organized in the preceding year, was constructing the most expensive canal yet attempted in Utah, a two-million-dollar excavation, much of it tunneled through solid canyon walls, to water the Bear River valley near the Idaho border, lands that originally had belonged to the Central Pacific Railroad. The money for that grand new undertaking did not come from local farmers. The farmers were to come in later, as purchasers of twenty- and thirty-acre farmsteads from the corporation. British investors had provided much of the capital, and the Church was nowhere to be seen on the project, unless it was in the form of a few leaders acting as private businessmen. The seven thousand men employed in construction looked for a paycheck from the boss, not a sermon from the bishop, to keep them going. The world-view of subordination would continue to exist in the common people's minds, but now it would be more an economic than a religious subordination.[18]

Utah is one of the most river-deprived areas in the United States. Its only large river, the Colorado-Green complex, flows deep within canyons, inaccessible to agriculture, and elsewhere its rivers are short and small, with limited bottomland. Consequently, after the Bear River scheme, Utah irrigation reached a plateau of development, and capitalists looked to other places to invest their big money and big technology. The Church, on the other hand, was not, by the 1890s, in a position to reestablish its former institutional command and lift the state to a higher plane. It had exhausted its available strategies of water control. Perhaps if there had been a Nile or Euphrates handy for it to command, and if the federal government and the marketplace had not hedged it about with laws and pressures, the religious hierarchy of Mormonism might have evolved into a distinctive, modern form of the ancient agrarian state. We will never know.

IN THE SHADOW
OF THE ROCKIES

Within the space of a few years the Mormons had broken the Hispanic-Indian monopoly on western irrigation. But then, beginning around 1870, their bold new wave was eclipsed in influence by even newer waves. About that date the center of innovation shifted to eastern Colorado, then to California. In both of those places, as in Utah, the dry air vibrated with extravagant hope. Here was a chance, perhaps the last Americans would have, to create a bright new world, with promises especially for the wretched and excluded. If a little water poured on the sterile land would make a flourishing green garden, then society too might be made over. Americans could learn to temper their aggressive individualism with more communal values: that was the great utopian promise of irrigation. Millions of little farms, all of them in the hands of ordinary people, could be created around western ditches and canals, forming an alternative to the emerging America of industrial capitalist concentration. Where the forty-niners had seen in the desert the threat of death, where scientists and writers saw intrinsic natural values, where the Mormons saw a mission from God, still others saw a grand chance for democracy to restore itself. The first place where that dream tried to achieve expression was on the plains spreading away from the Front Range of the Rocky Mountains.

In the winter of 1870 a committee arrived in Colorado looking for a site for a farming colony they wanted to establish. Among the committee members were a former Civil War general, Robert Cameron, and an agricultural writer for the New York *Tribune*, Nathan Meeker. Finally, they found something suitable: a 12,000-acre parcel on the Cache la Poudre River, four miles upstream from its junction with the South Platte. Off in the west they could see Long's Peak covered with snow; not far north was Cheyenne, Wyoming, and the Union Pacific tracks connecting with Chicago; due south was Denver, a hub for gold miners, cattlemen, and saloonkeepers. The committee liked everything but the booze on this frontier, and they hurried back to New York City to report the good news. By May, there were five hundred colonists living on the site, representing the vanguard of the Union Colony, and they were hard at work building houses in the new town of Greeley, named after the *Tribune*'s famous editor, Horace Greeley.[1]

The original plan was to settle the colonists in a compact village surrounded by farms of 40, 80, and 160 acres. In that way farmers could live together in a close-knit order and journey out from town to work their fields, much as the farmers of seventeenth-century New England and of medieval Europe had done. A community fund would be used to buy land as needed, to provide improvements, including irrigation works, a sawmill, and manufactories, and to pay for teachers and traveling lecturers. Some of the money in the fund would come from membership subscriptions ($155 was the initial cost), some from selling extra town lots to nonfarmers for stores and repair shops. Thus, private property would be the central principle of the settlement, but it would be mixed with a collectivism of finance and community planning. That combination, it was felt, would be at once practical and uplifting.

The Union Colony was the brainstorm mainly of Meeker and Greeley, two leftover idealists from the utopian-minded 1840s. They had heard about the Mormon undertaking, had traveled to Utah to see that achievement for themselves, and were inspired to revive their own fading ambitions to reform the country. As a much younger man, Greeley had been converted by the writings of the French socialist Charles Fourier and by the personal influence of Fourier's chief American disciple, Albert Brisbane. The editor had invested thousands of dollars in several communitarian settlements, including the Sylvania colony in Pennsylvania and the North American Phalanx near Redbank, New Jersey. There men and women had come together to try out on a small scale new ideas of social organization, sharing their property, living as one large "family," and dividing the work more fairly. Greeley put their point of view thus:

> Not through hatred, collision, and depressing competition;
> not through War, whether of Nation against Nation, Class
> against Class, or Capital against Labor; but through Union,
> Harmony, and the reconciling of all Interests, the giving
> scope to all noble sentiments and Aspirations, is the Reno-
> vation of the World, the Elevation of the degraded and
> suffering Masses of Mankind, to be sought and effected.[2]

It was a program, in other words, to remake America along better lines than those of capitalism by persuading people through appealing examples, not

84

by using force, expropriation, or revolution. No one need be poor or unemployed, no one need be alone and insecure, if Americans would heed the experiments.

Nathan Meeker had been a communitarian advocate too, and had joined the Trumbull Phalanx, which had been established in 1844 in his home state of Ohio. Now, almost three decades later, he still itched to see some of those ideas shining on a hill for everyone to see. He had, to be sure, come to believe that the earlier experiments had gone too far in trying to interfere with traditional family arrangements and individual accumulation of wealth, but still there was much in the ideal of association that appealed to him. Consequently, it was he who first broached the idea of making a new attempt at the old dream somewhere out on the western frontier, who presided over the first organizing meeting in New York in 1869, and who personally led the resettlement on the plains and became the Union Colony's resident leader.[3]

Arthur Bestor, one of the most perceptive historians of antebellum socialism, has argued that the utopian impulse petered out by the mid-1850s, as it became apparent that the country was too organized, too settled, to learn from small-scale, isolated experiments any longer.[4] The argument is true in a general sense, but it is important to realize that after the Civil War there were a number of communitarian revivalists at work—not always in the old places, often in the arid West. The practice of irrigation appealed to them as an ideal ecological foundation for communal living. Struggling together to command a river and apportioning the dividend among all members of the community should offer, it was thought, a far more cohesive group life than rainfall farming elsewhere. Some even referred to irrigation as a species of socialism. Meeker's Union Colony was only one example of the resurgence of earlier utopianism: there were also the Colorado Cooperative Company in Montrose County, the Anaheim Colony and San Ysidro colonies in California, and New Plymouth in Idaho.[5] Yet, if Meeker's group can be taken as illustrative, the communitarian tradition had become deeply compromised in the years after the Civil War. Not only was the old socialism overlaid by a new desire for private prosperity, but, often, there was also a new emphasis on following the principle of association for utilitarian, more than spiritual, reasons and on adopting it as an instrument to survive in the emerging corporate economy of the postwar era. Before that revised form of association could become effective, however, Meeker and Greeley had to fade away and a new generation of associationists, more pragmatic, more familiar with the local situation, had to come to the front.

Altogether, 687 memberships were subscribed to the Union Colony, mostly by rather well-to-do, not downtrodden, residents of northeastern and midwestern states. Only a portion of them ever moved to Colorado. Many of the actual settlers came in later, usually having had little exposure to Fourierism and mainly interested in getting a farm in a going community. Horace Greeley himself was content to cheer from his desk in Manhattan and offer inspiring advice from time to time. The colonists needed inspiration from some quarter, for papers other than Greeley's were not so encouraging to them. An Illinois editor, for instance, smeared the experiment as "a delusion, a snare, a cheat, a swindle" and ridiculed the site as "a barren sandy plain, part and parcel of the Great American Desert, midway between a poverty-stricken ranch and a prairie-dog village." "Wood," he added, "may be mentioned as a natural curiosity in Greeley."[6] As it turned out, getting enough wood was indeed a problem, but not nearly so serious as getting enough water. Hardest of all was keeping the faith out on the Colorado frontier, two thousand miles from the *Tribune* offices.

One of the firstcomers was J. Max Clark, a native of Wisconsin, who apparently was one of those joining the colony in some ignorance of the Meeker-Greeley dream. Few of his fellow colonists, he recalled later, expected to remain in the place for long. They wanted to make "a fortune" and get out.[7] What they got instead, if they stayed, was a long apprenticeship in farming the plains, a task their inspired leaders knew little about.

Clark remained at the Union colony for more than thirty years and died a man of modest means. During the first hard winters he and the others had to subsist on random buffalo and antelope. In the summer, cattle wandered in from the open range, trampling down their wheat, and the cattlemen laughed defiantly in their faces. Horace Greeley had laid down the rule "No fences and no rum." Both evils, he had warned, would undermine the community spirit they were to nurture. But to keep the cattle out, the colonists had to disregard Greeley's dictum and spend much of their available funds putting up a tight fence around their property. Nathan Meeker gave them advice too, and it was no more helpful. He decided the colony ought to have thousands of apple trees, evergreens, and maples to provide a homey atmosphere, so he ordered them at great expense to the common budget—and the others watched the trees die. "We had worked magic in building the town," Clark wrote, "but when we began to meddle with the supposed defects in nature's handiwork in the country, we were very soon impressed with a profound respect for the designs of the Almighty."[8]

Another failure, and one that told much about the level of communitarian spirit in the colony, was the stock and dairy association the colonists organized. They were to have a common herd and to milk it with cooperating hands. The dairy would then lead on to a bakery and a laundry, and finally to "the cooperative household." But people refused to risk their capital in the enterprise, and the herd had to be sold at a loss. So there went the noble hope of offering an alternative to capitalism. Meeker eventually grew discouraged and took his family off to the western part of the state, to the White River Reservation of the Ute Indians, where he planned to teach them how to plow and be industrious. He was killed and mutilated in 1879 by his intended pupils. The Union Colony he had brought into existence survived, but in the words of Dolores Hayden, it turned out to be "an average town with a single idealistic episode in its early history."9

As an exemplar for the radical democratization of America, the Greeley colony was a disappointment. It had, however, another contribution to make to western history, one that was more modest but more enduring, and for that it would draw on the associative principle that lay behind its founding. That contribution was a program of reform in western water law and institutions, one that would seek to identify a public interest in the alloca-tion of a scarce resource. It was the little group coming together on the banks of the Cache la Poudre that would lead Colorado and other states in the arid region, first toward a more realistic assessment of their irrigation potential, and then toward a new policy of collective, public restraint of frontier water-grabbers operating under the doctrine of prior appropriation as the basis of water rights in the West. To appreciate that Greeley achieve-ment, we must understand not only their specific situation in the Rockies but also the broader social implications in that doctrine of appropriation, the cultural consequences of the shift toward the instrumentalist view of nature that lay behind the doctrine, and the kind of problems it posed for communities.

First, their immediate predicament. One of the earliest jobs the Unionists undertook was to dig a series of ditches from the Poudre to their farms. They allotted $20,000 for the work and were chagrined to discover that the first ditch alone cost them $27,000, the complete series, $412,000. When they began digging, what they knew about the rise and fall of a Rocky Mountain stream or how much water it took to irrigate a crop could have been put in a tin cup. That first ditch was woefully small for the fields depending on it. Then they encountered another difficulty no one had foreseen. Some of the Greeley men, including General Cameron, split off and moved upstream to start a separate venture, with its own canal sucking water from the river. Came the droughty summer of 1874, and there was not even a trickle flowing past Greeley. Let down more water, they shouted to the upriver gang, or our crops and lawns will die. Nothing was done. They called for an impartial arbitrator to make a fair division, and there was no response. "From that day forward," wrote David Boyd, the colony's historian, "the people of Union Colony set their hearts upon having a law enacted to enable them to have the water of the river distributed according to the vested rights of all concerned." What that would lead them to was some form of governmental regulation to control the cutthroat competitiveness over water they were encountering.[10]

Colorado by that point had adopted the doctrine of prior appropriation of streams, and in order to understand the controversy that ensued and its outcome, it is necessary to examine briefly that doctrine and its meaning for the West. Endless words have been written on the subject, yet it remains wildly misunderstood. According to the doctrine of appropriation, the first person who came to a stream and claimed its water, or a part of it, had priority to exploit it; he acquired, in other words, a vested right to the water, made it a form of personal property. Under the doctrine, it mattered not at all how far from the river he lived or how far he diverted the water from its natural course, mattered not at all if he drained the river bone-dry. There was only one rule in that appropriation: *Qui prior est in tempore, potior est in jure*—he who is first in time is first in right.[11]

A contrasting theory of property rights in streams and rivers, derived from English common law, was the riparian principle, which held that only those people living on the banks of a river could lay claim to its flow. Ownership of riparian lands, that is, alone could give a water right. In its earliest form, however, the riparian doctrine was less a method of ascertaining individual property rights and more the expression of an attitude of noninterference with nature. Under the oldest form of the principle a river was to be regarded as no one's private property. Those who lived along its banks were granted rights to use the flow for "natural" purposes like drinking, washing, or watering their stock, but it was a usufructuary right only—a right to consume so long as the river was not diminished. The river, it was then believed, belonged to no one in particular, belonged to everybody in general, belonged to God, belonged to itself. No individual was free to enrich himself by seizing it for his personal use to the exclusion of others. Those who lived away from the banks were hardly disadvantaged by this principle. They had enough water, for every farm and village had its well. Thus there was a fundamental equality implied in the riparian doctrine, however stratified the society was that made it. It must be added that riparianism depended on there being a dependable abundance of rainfall, broadly distributed, but just as important, it rested on a popular acceptance of the idea that nature should be left free to take its course. Development of a river for "artificial" uses—damming or diverting it to satisfy desires that went beyond what was perceived as "natural" wants—would, it was feared, enrich some people at the expense of others. The original common law of riparianism, therefore, was biased against economic development. It belonged to a less aggressive, rural world that had not yet learned the modern ideas of progress and economic maximization.

The men and women who settled the American West did not belong to that older world, did not share its views about nature, and consequently rejected the traditional riparianism. Instead, they chose to set up over most of the region the doctrine of prior appropriation because it offered them a greater freedom to exploit nature. Inexplicably, historians and legal scholars, in discussing that decision of the West, have all tended to miss those reasons behind it. The standard argument has been that the arid nature of the West required a dramatic break with the English common law. Walter Prescott Webb, for example, insisted in 1931 that the doctrine of appropriation was conclusive evidence of the way a dry environment led the West to invent new ideas and institutions, thereby becoming very different from eastern America and England.[12] The riparian doctrine, he maintained, was clearly out of place in a more arid climate, for it would not have allowed the practice of irrigation and thus would have made agricultural settlement impossible. Though lawyers and judges, conservative as always, clung to foreign notions, the farmers and businessmen of the West, Webb went on, were more realistic. Eventually the truth of nature was accepted, the doctrine of appropriation was created *de novo,* economic development could go forward, and western society took a unique direction. In making that analysis, Webb relied mainly on a 1912 water-law text and on the rationalizations given by a half-century of western promoters. It is clear now that the situation was far more complicated than he or his sources realized. In truth, the West was less innovative than he thought, for the adoption of prior appropriation was part of a larger shift in thinking about nature, a shift toward instrumentalism in resource law and property rights, that was well under way back East long before anyone came West or thought of irrigation.[13]

The doctrine of appropriation had a near, immediate source for the West in its mining camps, first those up in the Sierra foothills, later those in the Colorado mountains, towns like Blackhawk, Central City, and Idaho Springs. Miners, scurrying to find and possess gold, came to those diggings and dug frenetically, without let or hindrance. Needing water for their sluice boxes, they took it without a second's thought. By the gold rushes of 1849 and 1859, they had been well schooled in the notion, radical by the standards of the old riparianism, that rivers and streams were there simply to divert into one's own pocket. The water, like the ore they were uncovering, might have belonged to the public domain, but they said among themselves, "You are in a state of nature, boys. Whatever you can use, use;

that is the right given to you by a beneficent Father. He will be pleased by your enterprise, and society will be forever in your debt." By that thinking, nature was assumed to exist for no other purpose than to be turned to private profit, and the first man on the scene was the one who could claim that profit. Older notions of property, along with any restraints on its exploitation, were no longer to be taken as sacrosanct.

But western miners were only late, rough, derivative exponents of the new instrumentalism being articulated throughout the rising world of enterprise. In its broadest terms, the doctrine of prior appropriation was the product of a new capitalist economic culture and its attitudes toward nature. Appearing first in England, that culture was organized around the institutions of the free, competitive marketplace and of private property. It promised to overcome the supposed scarcity of nature with the abundance provided by new technology. Traditional riparianism, with its antidevelopment bias, stood in its way everywhere, thwarting cotton-mill owners as much as western miners and irrigators, and it had to be replaced. Morton Horwitz, in his study *The Transformation of American Law,* shows how overturning the old common law as applied to water became in the period following the Revolutionary War the first crucial challenge for capitalists demanding the freedom to develop, to get rich, to expand the economy. Wanting to put up factories along rivers, to turn their machinery with waterwheels, and to build dams that inadvertently would flood their upstream neighbors as well as interfere with the natural flow for those downstream, they ran the risk under the common law of heavy damage suits, and they wanted relief from that prospect. In the end they got their way—got the cooperation, indeed the leadership, of the nation's judges in remaking the law to promote greater American enterprise. Through court decisions like New York State's *Palmer* v. *Mulligan* (1805), the riparian doctrine was drastically modified to allow the virtually unlimited private aggrandizement of wealth through appropriation. In that drive to replace the common law, a river became a mere instrumentality to satisfy entrepreneurial drives, a utility, a marketable commodity, to be bought and sold and made to earn money for whoever got there first. As Horwitz writes, "the idea of property underwent a fundamental transformation—from a static agarian conception entitling an owner to undisturbed enjoyment, to a dynamic, instrumental, and more abstract view of property that emphasized the newly paramount virtues of productive use and enjoyment."[14] That transformation was more or less complete by the time of the Civil War, just as the West was being opened for settlement.

By the middle of the nineteenth century, then, the doctrine of appropriation had almost wholly replaced the old riparianism throughout the Anglo-

American legal realm. True, one still had to own land on the banks of a river to use its water, but that stipulation was the merest shell of what had been the riparian tradition. The American West went one step further. It did away with the shell altogether and allowed nonriparian owners to transport water as far from a river as they liked, gaining a small measure of uniqueness while following in general the lead of eastern cultural centers.

There was a second claim to uniqueness that westerners could make. Once they had adopted the new doctrine, they tended to cling to it with a greater tenacity than did easterners. According to Horwitz, the new instrumentalism in law made all property rights, those based on appropriation included, shifting and tentative, vulnerable to invasion as economic opportunities changed. The guiding rule in property law henceforth was to be whatever would prove to be the most efficient way to use resources, whatever would produce the highest return. A latecomer who wanted to take water from a river for a new, profitable use but was confronted with a monopoly established through a prior appropriation could appeal to the instrumentalist standard, just as the first appropriator had appealed to it to break down the sanctity of old property rights. Eventually the courts, responding to a changing economy, amended the doctrine by adding the idea of "reasonable use" to any right of appropriation, which opened wide the door to challenge by the newcomer and to reapportionment. No one could appropriate more than he could reasonably use, judges learned to say, and what was reasonable was in large measure a matter of what they considered most economically productive. Thus the doctrine of appropriation appeared to serve the cause of promoting national development in its early phase, only to be discarded when and where it turned out to be an obstacle to further growth. In the West, however, the doctrine quickly became a vested right jealously guarded by agricultural interests down to the late twentieth century, a right that many economists and industrialists frequently criticized for retarding economic expansion in the region.[15]

When the Greeley irrigators shouted upstream for more flow, theoretically they had the law on their side, for they had been the first to lay claim to the Cache la Poudre. Before they arrived, the territory of Colorado, following the practices of the mining camps and the general shift toward resource instrumentalism, had repudiated the old riparian notion lock, stock, and barrel. There was no temporizing about it, no struggle to conserve and adapt the old to new circumstances. It was simply a repudiation, one so emphatic that it set a pattern that neighboring territories and states would follow, referring thereafter to the doctrine of prior appropriation as the "Colorado doctrine."[16]

In allowing any individual or group to stake a priority claim on a river and divert part or all of its current, whether for mining or irrigation, Coloradans insisted that it was essential to do so for settlement. What they meant was that row-crop agriculture could not be brought into the region without a change in water law. The place was generally too dry for rainfall farming, and though cattle ranching would have been perfectly adaptive, farming was deemed the "higher" form of use (that is, it gave a bigger return per acre). But to allow only farmers living along the banks to draw water, it was said, would give them an unfair monopoly on the resource. Therefore a principle of prior appropriation was obviously required if the land were to yield its full potential. So much was obviously true. What was not considered in that justification was the unspoken premises behind it: that the West should in fact be growing crops and building up its population, that it should be cut up into private property, that its water or any other resource should be exploited to its maximum economic potential. Take all those premises for granted, and the doctrine of appropriation made good sense. It was then rational to destroy a river completely, to send it through canals or tunnels to another watershed altogether, to wherever a man could make money from it. Indeed, it was *irrational* to do otherwise, to let the river merely flow by one's house and contemplate its motion. Question those premises, on the other hand, and what had appeared reasonable might look very different. The doctrine of appropriation was not, as Walter Prescott Webb maintained, dictated by the law of nature in an arid land, nor was it the product of timeless Reason; rather, it seemed to be natural and reasonable to a group of people who were intent on conquering, expanding, accumulating, and getting ahead.

Wherever adopted, the doctrine of prior appropriation, like its parent, the economic culture of capitalism, created difficult problems for itself. Encouraging as it did a fevered, competitive race to exploit, the doctrine led straight to a chaotic war of claim against counterclaim.

The seventeenth-century English philosopher Thomas Hobbes was one of the first to think systematically about the social consequences of the emergent culture, though he understood he was dealing with universal "human nature." Already in his own time, men were beginning to look on natural resources as private property to be sought and acquired by determined effort. One of Hobbes's leading interpreters refers to this attitude as "possessive individualism," and he makes Hobbes one of its most influential proponents.[17] Because of differences in skill and energy, Hobbes believed, some individuals must necessarily accumulate more of those resources than others, leading to jealousy and conflict, to a "war of each against all." The danger to peace and harmony in such a society of self-seekers would be avoided only by erecting a powerful authority, which Hobbes called "Leviathan." The name has come to be attached to any strong, concentrated power that controls the allocation and development of resources, but for Hobbes the Leviathan must be the state, not a private agency. Later apoloists for the new culture of capitalism were more hopeful (and naive) than he. Let everyone pursue his own interest freely, they said, let everyone use nature as he likes, and the world will become richer and richer, peace will automatically prevail.

The farmers in the Union Colony at Greeley discovered on their own the truth of Hobbes's analysis, as they watched other appropriators crowd in on them, watched the river dry up and their plants turn brown. Having begun farming and diverting water downstream, where the soil was deepest and richest, they now found themselves losing out to anyone willing to jump farther upstream and dispute their claim of priority. On and on the game of leapfrogging would go, they feared, until the man with all the water would be the man with the poorest soil. Some sort of common agreement was needed, some system of authority to enforce prior claims, some form of mutual restraint to prevent the self-destruction of Colorado agriculture. The problem was to how to get that authority without running the risk of setting up a tyrannical Leviathan.

If neighbor appealing to neighbor for the recognition of water rights had no effect, the doctrine of appropriation allowed only one recourse, the classic one in a laissez-faire society: get a lawyer and sue. From the time of the first gold strike on, Colorado courts were jammed with water suits. Those who usually came out ahead in that donnybrook were those who had enough money to carry their case to higher and higher levels—and those who practiced law. The Greeley remedy for that situation, where the modest farmer was impoverished and the most predatory was rewarded, was to take water disputes out of the courts and put them under a system of impartial administrative management. But in order for that solution to be adopted, the Greeleyites first had to overcome the hostility of the lawyers, who would lose much of their income by the change, and they had to demonstrate how little water there really was in the state. Only when scarcity was obvious to all, when it was commonly accepted as the permanent condition of Colorado agriculture, would residents compromise their possessive individualism and accept a degree of public control.

Even before their upstream squabbles began, the Greeley party had carried their case for collective action to an irrigation convention that assembled in Denver in September 1873, with delegates from a half-dozen states and territories. Representing the Greeley view were J. Max Clark and David Boyd. Prominent among the opposition were the Denver Chamber of Commerce and William N. Byers. The latter was editor of the *Rocky Mountain News* and general manager of the National Land Company, the agent for the Denver Pacific Railroad, which, through its *Star of Empire* magazine, was in the business of promoting the state and recruiting settlers. Byers, wrote Boyd, "had, or pretended to have, magnificent views of the extent of country that could be watered from the Platte and its tributaries." It was he who had induced the Union Colony to settle in the state a few years earlier, with grand promises of what a little water could do to a lot of acres. Now he brought forth authorities to argue that Colorado had the river capacity to irrigate at least 25 million acres. To this Clark rose to reply:

> I am a farmer. I till the earth with my own hands. I am
> accustomed to carry the mud of the waters of irrigation on
> my boot heels, the brown dust of the desert in my hair.
> . . . [W]e have read with fear and trembling how [Byers's
> authority], enthusiastic upon the almighty resources of our
> common country, and the agricultural resources of
> Colorado in particular, is proposing to cut a great gash in
> the earth, from South Platte canyon to Kansas City, and
> water all the land on both sides of the ridge. These things
> must "give us pause." . . . There are some things which
> are better underdone than overdone, as for instance our
> porridge and our prayers; and it seems to us this business
> of irrigation is one of them. If we have too much water, how
> easy to run it off; but if we have too little, how difficult to
> run it on.[18]

In the years following that first confrontation with the party of plenty, the Greeley colonists made their argument again and again. Theirs, they believed, was the voice of practical farmers, speaking from hard-won experience, against the visionary designs of city editors, land salesmen, and lawyers, none of whom wanted to admit that there was less wealth to be made than they hoped or that one man's appropriation must mean another man's loss.

A second convention gathered in Denver in late 1878, composed mainly of those living in the South Platte drainage area, to recommend an irrigation law for the state. It appointed a committee, chaired by David Boyd, to draw up some particulars, which were passed by the convention and, a few weeks later, were, with an exception or two, made into law. That act of 9 February 1879 divided Colorado into a number of water divisions—the South Platte basin was the first, five others came later—and into districts within those divisions, each presided over by a water commissioner appointed by the governor. The commissioner's chief duty was to establish a clear record of who had priority of appropriation on each stream and to see that in years of low runoff that claim was respected by all. Priority went to the individual who had been first to start digging his ditch. When a farmer claimed more water than he really needed (and some, with no accurate sense of flow dynamics or crop requirements, with only a primitive means of measurement, made immense claims, Amazonian claims, calling for more water than any ten streams could carry, enough water to sail a clipper ship across the plains), it was the commissioner's task to adjust and apportion. If he could. The law assumed that irrigators in a district would abide by the commissioner's rulings, but, in fact, that was not always the case. Constitutional challenges, open resistance, and petty quibbling roiled the water for many years to come. In 1881, Colorado felt compelled to go a step further toward strengthening authority by setting up a state engineer's office to supervise water claims. Even then there were failings, but, as Boyd saw it, "the law as a whole has proved a great blessing, because it put the distribution of water into the hands of one man, and so prevented the bloodshed that would have been inevitable had things remained much longer as they were."[19]

The 1879 and 1881 irrigation acts were largely the result of the Union Colony's determination to find a collective counterforce to chaotic individualism. They were the first steps toward declaring that the rivers of the West are in some sense public property and that any private appropriation can only be made under public rules and at public sufferance. It was Wyoming, not Colorado, which took that next step, in its constitution of 1890, becoming thereby a model for the rest of the region to emulate.[20] Elwood Mead, who served as a water administrator in Colorado before being named territorial, and then state, engineer of Wyoming, and who was chiefly responsible for Wyoming's constitutional clause on water, was espousing the Greeley view when he wrote:

> The needed training in cooperation and association was
> conspicuously lacking in the early irrigators. They not only
> did not know how to work harmoniously together, but they
> had inherited prejudices against submitting to the restraint
> and control needed to make associated effort a success.[21]

But a decade of training had sufficed in Colorado, as in Wyoming, to change that situation. And two decades after Meeker and his cohorts had arrived on the Cache la Poudre, the idea of public ownership and the regulation of water were becoming established policies on the Rocky Mountain frontier.

By that year of 1890, Colorado had far surpassed Utah, the early leader, as an irrigation center. There were 890, 735 acres under the ditch in the state, and each of those acres was producing $13 worth of farm products a year. Only California watered more acres, had more irrigators, and made more money at it.[22] The new Colorado laws had promoted, as in part they were designed to do, a spurt of agricultural growth. The thirsty capitalists may have been right about how wealth would increase under a more instrumental approach to rivers, but Coloradans had come to believe that it would increase even more when that approach included a system of public administration of resources.

There remained, however, a dark question hovering over the Greeley achievement. At what point did the idea of association that Meeker and his successors fought for become a vehicle of repression? In different words, how far could the concentration of social power over individuals go before it became that Hobbesian monster, Leviathan? Did the marketplace first lead to a chaos of competitiveness, then require the draconian remedy of an elaborate state apparatus exercising rigid supervision over ditches and canals in the name of harmony and economic growth? Having just been through a stage of chaos, Mead could write admiringly of a system of "absolute control of all water in one strong central authority."[23] "Absolute", however, had an ominous ring to it.

THE REDEMPTION
OF CALIFORNIA

The Reverend Thomas Starr King stood before the San Joaquin Valley Agricultural Society on 11 September 1862 to give the annual address. He was a city man, immigrant from New England, minister to Unitarians in San Francisco, and a visionary. It had been his privilege to gain a glimpse of a future California, a land of uncommon achievements yet easy ways, and now he was in demand as an official inspirer on public occasions around the state.[1] Before him stood an audience of dogged, red-faced men, the farmers of the San Joaquin Valley. At the end of another long, hot, rainless, dusty summer, perhaps they needed his prophetic vision.

This state, he told them, "which seems given over, in a general view, to the 'abomination of desolation,' is really the field of two immense 'horns of plenty.' "[2] One of them widened downward from Mount Shasta in the north of the state, following the Sacramento River, the other upward through the Kern and San Joaquin River valleys. Both horns spilled their bounty on the metropolis, the Golden Gate, the world. The thought that those horns—those rivers—of plenty might in fact have been funnels, draining the wealth from the hinterland into the pockets of urban merchants, seems not to have occurred to King. He was intent on awakening Californians to the rich agricultural possibilities around them, offering a wealth greater than gold mines and more conducive to a permanent civilization.

Up to this point mining had dominated the American interest in California, dominated to the extent of endangering other uses. By the 1860s, mining was in its hydraulic phase. Armed with dams, flumes, and canvas hoses, the miners turned streams of water onto the Sierra foothills, eroding the topsoil and gravel under intense pressure, exposing the underlying gold-bearing ore. The runoff from their assault polluted streams and covered good bottomland below with a flood of mud.[3] It was endangering the future capital of the state, King warned. Agriculture, on the other hand, would be a source of affluence that would build capital, not destroy it. The immense central valley, if it could be saved from inundation by hydraulic mining, offered a wide field for profitable labor and homes for thousands of families.

King was by no means opposed to mining, but he put the farmer's work first in dignity, morality, contribution to civilization, and religious significance: "The true farmer is an artist. He brings out into fact an idea of God." Mining only extracted from a finished product; agriculture created. The future of California required a strenuous work of creation, redeeming the land from its desolate condition, making it through farming what God had in mind for it. The vision King had of the state's future was essentially God's, who had not yet had the time or the inclination to make it real and was waiting on King and his audience to help out.

> The *earth is not yet finished*. . . . It was not made for nettles, nor for the manzanito [*sic*] and chaparral. It was made for grain, for orchards, for the vine, for the comfort and luxuries of thrifty homes. It was made for these through the educated, organized, and moral labor of man.

King excepted the mountains from this mission, for they already represented the divine idea and could not be improved. But the desertlike valley floor was obviously an unfulfilled part of nature, an ugly chaos made uglier by mining debris, requiring redemption; and it was here that the farmers could become "an implement of Providence in completing the task of Creation."[4]

In the year of that address, there were over 18,000 farmers in California doing God's work. That number would double over the next two decades and go on increasing for another fifty years, until the divine idea was at last achieved, and the state was the leading agricultural producer in the nation. A very large part of that achievement came through irrigation, for deficient rainfall was the major imperfection. There was an abundance of bright sun, fertile soil, and flat, tillable terrain. The rain, however, fell, not in the summer growing season as it was supposed to do (as it did in Indiana), but in the winter months, after the crops were all in, turning the wild oats on the hillsides a brilliant green but not watering the farmer's wheat as God wanted it to. Providence, however, had put many flowing streams within reach. Diverting them would be an act of redemption for the land.

Irrigation promised also to redeem the economic structure of California, which by the 1860s was threatening to become a feudal system where a few great landowners were served by an impoverished peasantry. Struck as he was by the urgency of saving potential farmland from the "terrible sin" of hydraulic mining, the Reverend Mr. King only briefly alluded to the "lust for immense ranches." But the situation was becoming critical for agrarian democracy. What mining did not bury would soon be agglomerated into latifundia. "All over the State," Henry George warned in 1868, "land is appreciating—fortunes are being made in a day by buying and parcelling out Spanish ranches; the Government surveyors and registrars are busy; speculators are grappling with the public domain by the hundreds of thousands of acres."[5] Most of the best farming land in the state had been deeded over by the government of Mexico, before the American conquest, to a few hundred individuals—some 13 or 14 million acres out of a total of 100 million.[6] Now a rapacious lot of Americans were falling like thieves on what was left, especially the public lands in the central valley.

"During the Civil War decade," writes Paul Gates, "an estimated eight million acres of public lands in California had passed or were in the process of passing into private ownership, a considerable part under legislation designed to make possible the establishment of farms of 160 acres." That was enough acreage to create 50,000 such farms, but in fact only 7,008 were established. Most of the land came into the hands of a group of San Francisco and Sacramento "appropriators" who lied, bribed, hired dummy entrymen, and manipulated laws to amass holdings of gargantuan size. The outcome was that, by 1871, over 2,000 individuals owned more than 500 acres apiece, and 122 of them held an average of 71,983 acres.[7] Undoubtedly in the eyes of the "appropriators" this too was part of God's design to make the desert over into a garden. But as Karl Marx observed in *Capital*, "the methods of primitive accumulation are anything but idyllic."[8]

In many cases, the land so amassed was held merely for speculation, the owner selling it for a good price later on, getting $2 to $10 or more for an acre that had cost him 60 cents or $1.25. Others, however, put their estates to use feeding cattle or sheep, which they set loose to roam across an unfenced plain. Or they turned to the more profitable enterprise of growing wheat for export to England. From the 1860s to the 1890s, wheat ruled the interior valleys. This was farming on a factory scale: using thousands of horse-drawn gang plows, monstrous steam and iron combines, and railroads that extended their lines southward from the Sacramento River over the Tehachapis into Los Angeles; raising wheat for a quick return; raising wheat across the land as far as the eye could see, year after year, exhausting the soil, but for a while making California the nation's leading producer.[9] It was a society of vast estates, world markets, bare, makeshift, sun-bleached houses, and armies of tramps on the road looking for work between harvests. There was money galore, but not to embellish the land or raise the common standard of living—it went away to Nob Hill, leaving improvishment behind. Was this really what a "finished" earth looked like? A dreary, flyspecked monotone of oligopoly?

Then it was that a trickle of water in an irrigation ditch appeared to offer renewed hope. Around the edges of the wheat domains, small farmers began to purchase whatever land they could find for sale, and to bring water to it. They had no other choice in California. In Kansas they could obtain a quarter-section homestead at no more expense than a filing fee and the work of plowing up its sod, but by the 1870s in California's major farming regions they had to pay $30, $50, even $200 an acre for plowed land.[10] At those prices a little property was all an average family could afford, and then it was likely to be located on sand or rolling foothills. In addition to high real-estate prices, they had to pay for irrigation facilities. They soon realized that this was an expensive way to farm. Put that spot of land in grapes or vegetables, however, and the family, despite its expense, could prosper, even in the midst of King Wheat. Thus was born the theory of deliverance through irrigation: irrigation as the people's choice, the benefactor of the common folk, savior of our dreams, defender of our institutions. It would take a long time to die.

The first instances of irrigated agriculture in California after the Spanish missions and whatever went on in the gold camps, date from the 1850s: the Mormon colony at San Bernardino (1852), a band of Missouri settlers on the Kern River (1856), the German immigrant colony of winegrowers at Anaheim on the Santa Ana River (1857), a few farmers in Yolo County and around Cache Creek west and northwest of the capital city (1858). By 1870, there were 915 ditches in the state, irrigating 90,344 acres, a figure that would more than triple in the next ten years.[11] An irrigated belt of orange groves began to extend from Santa Barbara down the coast to Los Angeles and San Diego, inland to Pasadena and Riverside, first growing the thickskinned, sour mission orange, then switching to the navel orange from Brazil and the Valencia from Spain.[12] North of Sacramento alfalfa became a standard irrigated crop, supporting a fine-grained landscape of dairy farms. And wherever there was water the smallholders set out grapevines, fruit and nut trees, carrots and corn. Their worth at the bank grew faster than any crop. Farmers bought land in 1871 along Los Banos Creek for $5 or less an acre, spent $12.50 more per acre for irrigation works, then found two years later that the land was worth $30 to $35.[13] More commonly, they paid out a great deal more cash for their land, trees, and ditches than that, and had to wait for three years or more to collect any receipts. But for those who could afford patience, the small irrigated farm was an opportunity that paid good rewards.

The big-money boys who had no interest in farming wheat, who had grabbed land for speculation, now were handed a golden opportunity. They could subdivide their holdings and sell out to small farmers or an irrigation colony, getting top dollar, especially if they threw in a few dams and canals. William Chapman was one of the quickest at that game. He and his associates had by 1871 acquired 277,600 acres with the intention, he claimed, of inducing otherwise reluctant settlers to come to California and make the state great.[14] Perhaps he did speed up the process of settlement—a dubious service, for which he was exceptionally well recompensed. In 1868, he sold a parcel of land on the San Joaquin plain, at twice his original cost, to three Alabama and Mississippi plantation owners looking for a new start. Their planned settlement failed, but soon there were others. In 1875, Chapman sold the first lots in what became the Central California Colony, near Fresno. The land was cut up into twenty-acre farmsteads, costing $1,000; saplings and vines had been set out in advance, water provided, and an advertising campaign launched. The first purchasers were Scandinavian immigrants, who added chickens, cows, and pigs to their tiny farms. Within three years every lot was sold, and Fresno was well on its way to becoming an island of intensive agriculture in the sea of wheat.[15]

Among the first irrigators in the Fresno colonies was Minnie Austin, who, with three other San Francisco schoolteachers, invested her savings in one of Chapman's farms. The four women put their land in a joint ownership, and in 1878 Austin moved onto the place to manage it. Her first move was to plant two acres to raisin grapes, which she picked herself, dried in the sun, boxed, and sold under her name—the first raisins from the region that one day would be world-famous for the crop. When she retired in 1886, she was harvesting 7,500 boxes a year and shipping them to the East Coast by rail. Her vineyard was surrounded by a delightful hedge of pomegranate, Osage orange, and cypress, and there were pears, apricots, peaches, and nectarines in the orchards as well. Nearby, a Danish woman was collecting $200 a year from her raisins, grown in a five-acre vineyard.[16] A writer for the *Overland Monthly* noted this tendency for women to take a more active role in Fresno agriculture:

> The work of irrigation is so light that women who bought
> their twenty or forty acre tracts in some of the colonies,
> enjoy guiding the small streams from furrow to furrow, and
> one often sees a sunbonneted figure, hoe in hand, watering
> the strawberry garden—much as, in Riverside, Pomona,
> and Pasadena, the most accomplished of women do not
> hesitate to perform out-of-door work.[17]

For independent women like Minnie Austin, enterprising women of limited means, as well as for the conventional family farmer, the irrigated homestead appeared as a door in a blank wall.

In addition to Chapman, another promoter of the irrigated colony was the Southern Pacific Railroad. Altogether that company had been given one-tenth of the state of California (11,588,000 acres) in federal land grants to encourage transportation development. Much of that land was sold to capitalists, the proceeds being put into track, bringing a direct connection with marketplace America to the entire central valley by 1876. For many wheat farmers, the railroad was "the Octopus," an enormous power squeezing life and profit out of them, "huge, terrible, flinging the echo of its thunder over all the reaches of the valley, leaving blood and destruction in its path."[18] But the railroad also sold lots to small farmers and promoted the irrigated farmstead in the valley. William Mills, who worked as chief land agent for Southern Pacific from 1883 to 1907, strongly believed that it was in the economic interest of the company to encourage diversified agriculture in the state and the growth in population it would require. He sent salesmen all over the world to promote California, and through the Southern Pacific Colonization Agency attempted to help newcomers make a go of it raising fruits and vegetables along the company's tracks.[19]

One of the Southern Pacific's enduring offspring was *Sunset Magazine*, which helped transform the California image from lair of the Octopus to desert arcadia. Among the many promotional pamphlets the magazine published and sent out to recruit settlers was one entitled simply *Fresno County California,* and it is representative of the irrigation mystique the land promoters worked to develop. The cover portrays in gentle pastels an irrigation ditch meandering peacefully between green, grassy banks. In the foreground, an orange tree hangs heavy and golden over the slow current. Across the stream Holsteins graze, and in the distance there are oak trees, red farm buildings, and snowcapped Sierra peaks. The title-page caption reads, "California Fruit for Health, California Lands for Wealth." Even now, it is an irresistible formula: a secure income for ordinary folk, effortless success, rural bliss, natural grandeur near at hand, an invigorating outdoor life, an exotic patina of palm trees, oranges, and wine applied to an old dream. John Constable with Omar Khayyám. Populism with luxury. The romance of irrigated California, contrived out of the very belly of the beast.[20]

Would it serve, whether as romance or reality, to redeem the state from the bad start it had made? Was irrigation in fact a people's weapon against bigness, against the rule of money? Was it a technique for defending pastoral ideals in a mechanizing world? Answers to those questions depended on who controlled the water, who built the ditches, and who designed them. By 1871, just as the Fresno colonists began to arrive, eager for health and wealth, evidence belying the *Sunset* portrait began to raise its ugly head.

Following the example of the entrepreneurs who had come together to create the railroad, a group of San Francisco capitalists organized on the first of September 1871 to sell real estate and to build a system of canals for irrigation, water power, and transportation to serve that land. They called themselves the San Joaquin and King's River Canal and Irrigation Company. "The farmers and settlers in the San Joaquin Valley are too poor to carry out the necessary canals and ditches by themselves," they explained in their prospectus, "and require the cooperation of capitalists."[21] In turn, the capitalists, they suggested, required aid from Congress—money derived from the sale of public lands, rights-of-way, the free use of water, access to timber and stone on the public domain. None of that proved to be forthcoming: Congress was in a railroad, not a water, mood when it came to giveaways. But the company plunged ahead, constructing in the next two years an irrigation canal that ran forty miles from the junction of the Fresno Slough and San Joaquin River and was capable of watering 16,000 acres a year. They talked airily of an even bigger ditch, 180 miles long, 100 feet wide, costing as much as $30,000 a mile to dig. They would drown the Octopus and free the valley from its tentacles.

A key figure behind the canal was Henry Miller, who supervised its construction and eventually came to own a controlling interest in it. Miller was a German immigrant, born to the name Kreiser in 1827, who had made his fortune in the gold rush selling beef to miners. His picture at age eighty shows a grizzled man with a thrusting beak of a nose, his eyes fixed on a distant point—undoubtedly a For Sale sign, for Miller was an ardent land buyer, accumulating with his partner Charles Lux a total of 328,000 acres in California alone. He owned portions of the San Joaquin River banks over a 120-mile distance. Cattle was what he knew and loved, cattle to feed and butcher, but he was not slow to see what might be done with the river too. Through discussions with an engineer who had worked on irrigation projects in Egypt and India, he hatched some grand designs to irrigate his pastures and ship his steers to San Francisco Bay slaughterhouses by barge.[22]

Miller also owned property farther south along the Kern River, and there he had a worthy rival for water dominance: James Ben Ali Haggin, the "Grand Khan of the Kern." Haggin was from Kentucky, a lawyer turned entrepreneur, a mogul of Nob Hill associated with Lloyd Tevis in utility companies, mining interests, and railroads. From his friends at Southern Pacific, he picked up a large part of Kern County real estate, then added whatever he could pry loose from other sources. From 1873 to 1890, when he and Tevis established the Kern County Land Company, he acquired 413,000 acres, an estancia that would remain more or less intact for a century thereafter.[23]

In addition to purchasing railroad grant land, Haggin pieced out his domain by manipulating the Desert Land Act, passed by Congress in 1877 to encourage irrigation. The act directed the commissioner of the Land Office to turn over 640 acres of public land to any individual putting down an initial 25 cents an acre and promising to bring water to them in three years. Upon proof of irrigation and the payment of an extra $1 per acre, title passed to the individual. It was in conception an absurd law and in execution a corruptible one. When the average size of a Mormon irrigated farm was less than thirty acres, when the same amount of land would ensure a comfortable living to a Fresno colonist, the 640 acres given by the act was clearly excessive—enough to create twenty or thirty farms. Just as clearly it had other purposes: to allow cattlemen, using their own and their hired hands' claims, to come into possession of a grand spread,[24] or to turn over the public domain to ambitious, deserving men like James Haggin. Within weeks of the act's passage, Haggin had lined up "dummies," who would enter claims at the Visalia Land Office, put down money furnished by him, give him a mortgage on their claims which they had no intention of paying off, then go back to their city jobs at Wells Fargo or Southern Pacific. In defending this fraud, Haggin maintained:

> My object has not been . . . to monopolize large bodies of land, but I desire to make valuable and available that which I have, by extending irrigating ditches over my land, and when these lands are subject to irrigation, to divide them up and sell them out in small tracts with the water rights necessary for irrigation.[25]

But in the absence of a vigorous campaign to recruit settlers, Haggin's professions could not be taken seriously. What he really had in mind was to create what one admirer called "the greatest farm in the world."[26]

If Haggin's explanations did not hold water, his canals did. And that was enough finally to hush his critics, who had to admit that only big capital like his, concentrated on a single water system, could develop the Kern efficiently. As the Visalia *Delta* paper said, "All that is desired is that these barren plains should be made to blossom as the rose. And all that is necessary to make them bloom is to give them away in chunks."[27] Taking over the Calloway Canal near Bakersfield, one of the earliest and largest irrigation structures built in the state, Haggin proceeded to add to it an elaborate subsidiary network, drawing off water that once would have flowed into Buena Vista Lake.

One river, the Kern, small and erratic, with no outlet to the sea. Two claimants, with large, insatiable appetites. In 1881 they met in court in the case *Lux* v. *Haggin* (Lux was Miller's partner and stand-in) to settle which man would rule the desert, and until the state supreme court resolved their dispute five years later, the California law of water rights hung in the balance. Miller claimed the river was his under the common law of riparian rights, which the state had implicitly adopted in its constitution of 1850. He owned land along the Kern's banks, making the stream his property (if one stretched the riparian doctrine of usufruct and natural use beyond all recognition). Haggin, on the other hand, claimed the river through purchase of rights of prior appropriation, which, in California as in Colorado, had emerged out of the mining frenzy. The courts, he argued, had established those rights, beginning with the case of *Irwin* v. *Phillips* (1855), and so had the state legislature, in the Civil Code of 1872.[28] Thus the battle was joined, not between an archaic, foreign riparian idea and a modern, indigenous appropriationist idea, as the historians sometimes describe it, but between two versions of capitalist grab.

As the battle of the Kern River barons commenced, California agriculturalists began organizing themselves into rival water camps—for Miller or for Haggin. The word "rival" comes from the Latin *rivalis,* "one using the same brook as another," usually referring to parties standing on opposite banks trying to monopolize the flow. In California of the 1880s the rivalry was not of one bank against the other. Instead, it pitted the riparian landowners, who as a rule were cattlemen, against those living at a remove but needing water if they were to grow grapes and oranges. The riparianists took Miller, of course, as their champion and were sure that he would vindicate their rights. The opposing appropriationists had the clear majority, for most people wanting access to water did not, and could not, live along a river's banks. Whether they had come early or late, whether they possessed twenty or twenty thousand acres, they claimed the rivers ought to be available to them too. James Haggin, they believed, was fighting their case in court.

The dispute quickly took on false ideological tones: a struggle of democracy versus elitism. At stake, the appropriationists argued, was whether a small, privileged group of men could achieve a monopoly on a resource, thereby denying economic opportunity to the masses. In 1883, a state irrigation convention assembled in Riverside to make that argument loudly and forcefully to state legislators. The next year, the convention reassembled in Fresno and put their case thus:

> Which is better? That a few men, the limited few who own the [river] bank, should have exclusive use of the stream to water their stock, all irrigation be stopped, all the progress of the past be blotted out, and ruin and destruction be brought to the prosperous and happy homes of which now irrigation is the cause, the life and the only hope; or that the stream be used so as to irrigate the greatest amount of land which it is capable of irrigating so as to stimulate production to its widest limits, so as to build up homes of plenty and happy firesides, and rich and prosperous communities and peoples, even if the stock men do have to sink a few wells to water their stock? Which is best; the desert, with a few herds and their scattering attendants, or green fields, orchards, the vine, the olive, the orange, the ripening grain and the happiness and prosperity which attends [*sic*] safe and certain husbandry? . . . The consequences

of depriving all, or all but riparian owners, from irrigating
are simply frightful to contemplate.[29]

The legislators, they demanded, should establish once and for all the
doctrine of appropriation and free the state from the dead hand of the past
—from a riparianism that was like a medieval suit of armor, imprisoning
the youthful energies of California and preventing its natural growth. Making appropriation the sole basis of water law in the state would promote
"natural justice," they asserted, and assure the triumph of democracy.

The convention's statement obscured the real issues confronting democratic land use in California. In the first place, irrigation was practiced to
some extent by both sides in the dispute, though the riparianists typically
relied on stock raising for their main source of income and used the water
only for raising native grass or a little alfalfa in the bottomlands. Second,
no one in the convention proposed to take Haggin's lands away from him,
though they had been acquired by dubious means, and distribute them in
twenty-acre irrigated homesteads to the world's poor. The appropriationists,
though more numerous, could hardly be said to represent agrarian democracy when their number included some of the biggest land monopolizers
around, when it included investors like Haggin who lived far off in San
Francisco and bought up appropriation claims as readily as railroad or
mining stock. Third, the doctrine of appropriation could create an elite as
small as, or smaller than, the riparian principle did. Under appropriation,
a single individual could acquire rights to an entire river and, conceivably,
take its water a hundred or more miles away, leaving streamside dwellers
with a dry bed. Water taken out and used immediately along the banks
might find its way back into the stream, or most of it would, but appropriated water was commonly lost water for all who lived downstream.

The notion that appropriation was a more democratic approach to water
rights rested on a single assumption, unexamined and unsubstantiated in the
convention: that democracy was promoted by intensive reclamation of the
desert. The more land that was irrigated, the more wealth it produced,
the nearer the state would come to realizing democratic ideals. It is obvious,
the convention's statement implies, that following the legal principle of
appropriation must mean more irrigation development than is possible under
riparianism. *Ipso facto*, democracy must flourish. That assumption will be
considered in greater detail later on. Suffice it here to say that, according to
such thinking, a James Haggin must appear a greater benefactor than a
Henry Miller, for there was more money to be made in irrigated corn, wheat,
and fruit than in cattle fed on irrigated pasture. Haggin would bring the
earth to its highest yield. He would make the most dramatic change in the

arid landscape. To recall the words of the Reverend Thomas Starr King, he would play more nobly the role of "an implement of Providence in completing the task of Creation."

The riparian doctrine had been updated radically so as to accommodate the unlimited private acquisitiveness of Henry Miller. Still, it was unacceptable to many Californians because it was identified with what they regarded as an inferior ecological niche, stock raising. That niche was too narrow for all the people who wanted to crowd in. It could not support a large human population, nor did it make intensive use of resources. And, as always in discussions of the merits of crop agriculture versus ranching, there was the hint that the latter instilled less desirable behavior traits: a rambling, unsettled style of life; an indifference to domesticity; an individuality that belonged to the past; a primitive mentality that now must surrender to progress.[30]

Given sentiments like those expressed by the irrigation conventions of 1883 and 1884 and by most of the newspapers in the central and southern parts of the state, it came as a shock and an outrage that Henry Miller won his case. In 1886 the California supreme court, in a split decision, upheld the riparian doctrine and gave Miller priority over the Kern. Immediately, there were charges that he had bought the justices. There were Jeremiahs who predicted that the state would be left behind in the western rush for development. And there was a move initiated to get the constitution changed, a move that would take forty years to accomplish. For his part, Henry Miller proved to be a magnanimous winner. Having established that he was indeed lord of the waters, he turned around and offered a partnership to Haggin. The two barons agreed to build an upstream reservoir on the Kern to provide enough water for both, with Miller to get one-third of the downstream current thereafter, Haggin two-thirds.[31] After all, they were big men, and big men act big, even over a little water.

It would be too simple to say that the 1886 decision in *Lux* v. *Haggin* fastened on the state a riparian system of water rights. Nowhere was the law more complicated, more filled with compromise, than here. In contrast to Colorado, where prior appropriation under state ownership and regulation was the rule, California threw together a ramshackle system that came to be known as the "California doctrine." The state adopted the riparian principle but accepted appropriation rights derived from the federal government, which in its Mining Act of 1866 had conceded such rights on the public domain. Where an individual had bought state land or a Mexican grant, the water rights were declared to be riparian; where he had claimed water from the public domain before 1866, he had a right of prior appropriation that could be exercised or sold as personal property. All grants after 1866, state or federal, came under the riparian rule, which in California meant that the appropriator could divert only as much water as riparian owners allowed. Whenever they decided to use the river, the appropriator had to relinquish, no matter how long he had irrigated, no matter how established his orchards and gardens, no matter whether his farm died.[32] In Colorado and the seven states that followed its lead (Wyoming, Montana, Idaho, Nevada, Utah, Arizona, and New Mexico), the right to appropriate was a right to "beneficial use" of water only—a right, that is, to take as much water as was needed for a legitimate purpose, a purpose that was in the public interest, that would earn money and add to the state's prosperity. But in California, until 1928, the riparian owner was restricted only in relation to other riparian owners (by the idea of "correlative" or "coequal" rights, which made all those owners equals). Against an appropriator, on the other hand, he could make extravagant demands on the river and use its water with stubborn inefficiency and waste.[33] He could not, however, insist that the stream flow undisturbed by his porch, affording an amenity to enjoy, nor could he protect it as the handiwork of God. Both would have been indeed unreasonable and wasteful. The western law of waters, as with natural resources generally, insisted in every state that instrumental values must always prevail.[34]

Although it was a messy fusion of riparian and appropriationist thinking, the California doctrine was emphatically clear in one particular: it put the irrigator without stream frontage at a disadvantage—potentially a fatal disadvantage for his fortunes. For that reason, irrigators felt compelled to find a way to undo the court's ruling, and the best immediate chance for that, they decided, was to pass a law authorizing the formation of irrigation districts around the state. A Modesto lawyer, C. C. Wright, was elected to the legislature on a promise to do just that, and one year after his election, he delivered. The Irrigation District Act became law in late February 1887. Put briefly, the law permitted agricultural communities to organize as official governing units to construct and operate collectively the irrigation works they needed. It went further than the similar Utah district act of 1865. When fifty freeholders (or a majority in an area) petitioned the state to form such a district, an election was held. Two-thirds of the voters living in the designated area had to approve of the idea. The act did not measure voting power by the acreage owned, for it was feared that a few large landowners might thereby sabotage the community will. Once approved, the district elected officers, and they were given broad authority. They could take by the power of eminent domain any land they needed for an irrigation canal; they could make contracts to build works and tax property in the district or sell bonds to pay for them; and most important perhaps, they could condemn all individual water rights, including riparian, and purchase them in the name of the district. The Wright Act was, according to Thomas Malone, "California's major nineteenth century contribution to irrigation law."[35] It also snatched victory from the strong, blunt fingers of Henry Miller.

In the formation and financing of an irrigation district, a big rancher like Miller had but a single vote. His lands could be taxed, his water rights condemned, and his river control broken by a rabble of little farmers. It was one thing to cooperate with a Haggin, quite another to be tied down by the Lilliputians and have to go along with their schemes. Soon Miller was back in court, fighting for his dominion, along with other large landowners in the state. All the way to the United States Supreme Court they went—and they lost. In the case of *Bradley* v. *Fallbrook Irrigation District* (1897), brought by a nonresident landowner against a new district, the highest court ruled that the Wright Act was constitutional. It was permissible, the opinion read, to take private property for public uses, and irrigation development was such a public use, one that no individual should be allowed to thwart.[36] Unlike the confrontation between Haggin and Miller, this battle had been unmistakably fought between the Minnie Austins around Fresno and San Bernardino and the power elite of Nob Hill. If California were to be redeemed from concentrated wealth, if irrigation were to be the means of that redemption, giving to the ordinary men and women of the state control over rural life, then, so the hope went, it would be the effect of the Wright Act.[37]

Shortly after the act was passed, the United States census revealed that California now led the nation in irrigated acreage. There were 1,004,233 acres being watered in the state, and the average size of an irrigated farm was 73 acres, more than twice the size of those in Utah. Each of those California acres produced a market value of $19 per year, the highest return in the country. But it also had to be said that California had far more potential for hydraulic engineering than its people had yet realized. According to one of the state's leading civil engineers, C. E. Grunsky, "Irrigation is not general throughout the State."[38] In contrast to Utah, where almost every farm was irrigated, California had only one in four farm units under the ditch. Elwood Mead, who came to the state to conduct a general survey of irrigation progress, blamed the slow progress on prejudicial attitudes that still favored the cattlemen and wheat kings.

> Men pride themselves [here] on great undertakings and on
> doing whatever they undertake on a large scale. . . . The

owner of a range herd was more than a money-maker, he
was practically monarch of all he surveyed. The cowboy on
horseback was an aristocrat; the irrigator on foot, working
through the hot summer days in the mud of irrigated fields,
was a groveling wretch. In cowboy land the irrigation ditch
has always been regarded with disfavor because it is the
badge and symbol of a despised occupation. The same
feeling, but in a less degree, has prevailed in the wheat-
growing districts of California, and for much the same
reason.[39]

Given the widespread criticism of Henry Miller and the riparian landowners, it is difficult to credit Mead's explanation completely. Haggin had
demonstrated that irrigation too could be a large undertaking, perfectly in
tune with the most passionate enthusiasm for grandeur. The stagnation in
irrigation development that was apparent by the 1890s had another cause
than prejudice: there were simply not enough Haggins around able or
willing to furnish the capital needed.

Almost everything that could be done to rivers with limited funds, with
local capital, had been done by the last decade of the century. What was
required next, if the state was to escape from its plateau of water development, was to find the money to buy more advanced engineering. The Wright
Act sought only to overcome the obstacle presented by riparian priority; it
did not put more money in the pockets of the small farmers living far off
from rivers. Its authorization of bond sales helped, but not much, for bonds
had to be repaid, with interest. Some districts quickly discovered that they
had sold more bonds than they could repay, and yet not enough to complete
the works they wanted.[40] What use was it, they began to wonder, to hold
elections and obtain water rights if the district had no money? State Engineer William Hammond Hall, itching as much as any district officer to
extend the mastery over nature, stated the problem and then suggested a
solution: "The great majority of the streams of California," he wrote, "are
of such a character that the work of the farmers can avail nothing. There
must be strong associations and large capital."[41] From the vantage of the
1890s, corporate power looked like the only way to get off the plateau, but
that would mean falling back into the hands of the moguls.

After several decades of colonization, court decisions, crop experimenta-
tion, and ideological sparring, California found itself mired in a dilemma.
The redemption of the desert could not go forward without help from
concentrated capital. The redemption of society, however, depended on
liberation from that same capital. It was God's wish that nature's desolation

be turned into a garden. It was also His wish that that garden be ruled by men and women of modest means. Unfortunately, He had not said how both could be done.

THE IDEOLOGY OF
DEMOCRATIC
CONQUEST

Surely it is a poor land, and an impoverishing one, that must have water brought to it. The early farmers who came into the West must have said that to themselves many thousand times, for their common sense told them that a grave deficiency in nature, especially of a necessity like water, must work against them. Only the desperate farmer, shut out of opportunity in more favored places, would consider the desert for a dwelling, like untouchables pitching their tent on a dunghill. But there were other Americans who came ready to believe in miracles, who began to insist it was precisely that deficiency which made the West so promising. By the 1880s they were propagating the view that out of aridity would come a level of prosperity beyond anything Americans had seen before, making the West the home of the future. More striking yet was their confidence that conquering the desert through irrigation would produce a more perfect democracy. To make that assumption, they had not only to overcome an initial pessimism but also to ignore considerable contrary evidence from elsewhere, including warnings from their own countrymen about the antidemocratic tendencies of irrigation societies.

One of the first warnings was sounded by a military man, Lieutenant William H. Emory, a topographical engineer who traveled to California with General Kearney in 1846. Emory was thirty-five years old at the time, a Marylander, as unacquainted with arid lands and irrigation as he was with the moon. On his way across the Southwest from the Arkansas to the lower Colorado River, he repeatedly came upon Mexican and Indian agriculture. It was strange to find only narrow strips of crops growing along the shallow streams, but it was even more disturbing to his American principles to see the concentrations of personal power such agriculture created. Irrigation, he observed, "involves a degree of subordination, and absolute obedience to a chief, repugnant to the habits of our people."[1] The chief in charge of

111

water control had to be implicitly obeyed, and those who failed to do so were severely punished. Without such command, water would be wasted, the embankments would be breached, and the welfare of the community put in jeopardy. Emory's was a cursory judgment, made only in a brief passing, but it was one that could have been corroborated by many Old and New World examples.

Almost thirty years later came another and more elaborate warning, this time from the American ambassador to Italy, George Perkins Marsh. He was particularly interested in conservation and land-use practices—indeed, was something of a world authority on the matter, with considerable study to his credit throughout the Mediterranean basin as well as his native New England. His fellow citizens, he noted, had had little chance thus far to observe the effects of irrigation on either the earth or society; it was still a novelty to them. Not so among the southern Europeans, for they had water systems dating back hundreds of years, as well as massive new works like the Cavour Canal, one of the most expensive ever built, in the Piedmont region of Italy.

"The tendency of irrigation as a regular agricultural method," Marsh concluded from that history, "is to promote the accumulation of large tracts of land in the hands of single proprietors, and consequently to dispossess the smaller land holders." Italy had a long record of water litigation, especially in the Po valley, which had left control over its rivers and best lands in the hands of a few grandees, and they farmed their estates "on a scale hardly surpassed in England, or even on the boundless meadows and pastures of our own West." A large tenant class did most of that work. Over them stood a single supervising head, who was needed to control the distribution of water. This discouraged individual initiative, as did the fact that the water network, once constructed, must "remain as immutable as the arteries and veins of the human system," and agricultural progress and improvement must cease. The only exceptions to that pattern of entrenched power and conservatism were in the high mountain valleys, where there were many small but copious streams, primitive technology, and limited arable land. In those places, the poorer farmers had been left to run their own affairs, without regimentation.[2]

There were other problems associated with irrigation besides the emergence of a power elite. Marsh noted that it saturated the soil, as the level of groundwater rose near the surface, and provided a favorable environment for disease.

> All irrigation, except where the configuration of the surface
> and the character of the soil are such as to promote the

rapid draining of the water, or where special precautions are taken against its influence, is prejudicial to health. In most localities the increased dampness of the atmosphere is injurious to the respiratory system, and in others the exhalations from the watered soil and moistened manures tend powerfully to favor the development of malarious influences, and to aggravate, if not to occasion, febrile diseases.[3]

Moreover, the soil became harder and more compact. Soil nutrients got flushed away. Corn, wheat, and vegetables lost much of their taste and nutritional value under constant irrigation. And there was always the danger of a dam bursting, water rushing out of reservoirs, flooding and drowning.

As serious as those disadvantages were, Marsh could not bring himself to recommend against irrigation for America. A little caution was in order, he wanted to emphasize, along with vigorous state supervision of all water development. The government of every American state where irrigation was practiced should declare the rivers to be public property and make itself the exclusive owner of all the principal reservoirs and canals, rather than let them fall into the hands of wealthy individuals or corporations. The state should also establish low water rates for small farmers to protect them against being squeezed out. Marsh's remedies had little to do with the ecological problems he had cited, nor did they reveal any concern that the state, given so much leverage over wealth and privilege, might itself become a despotic force—apparently he was unfamiliar with such ancient irrigation states around the Mediterranean as Egypt. His warning was given in a more optimistic mood: "We are in a position to protect ourselves and our posterity by, if I may use so hard a word, *prophylactic* measures—to supply the remedy before the disease manifests itself; whereas in the Old World irrigation had become a widely-spread and deeply-rooted agricultural method before its mischiefs were appreciated, or even suspected, and a preventive policy came too late."[4]

Both Emory and Marsh saw in irrigation a potential threat to American liberal and democratic ideals. Such a threat, let it be noted, would come out of the West, from the frontier. In attempting to introduce agriculture into that region there was a danger that the individual would become subordinated to a rigid social structure, that hierarchy would replace equality, and that only the wealthy would succeed. So long as the West was considered an inferior and unpromising land, it would be left to the dispossessed, to the have-nots. But once Americans set about transforming it into a more appealing place, then it might become a dangerous influence. In its winning it might be lost. The last refuge of the poor man might become his prison.

Had warnings like these been heeded, irrigation would have been introduced more cautiously by Americans. They were not. On the contrary, by the end of the nineteenth century irrigation had become a veritable crusade, urged on moral, patriotic, religious, economic, and scientific grounds. Above all, it came to be regarded, through a process of legitimation, as the flowering of American democratic values and institutions. That process tells us much about what was meant by democracy in the United States and how it was manipulated as a social ideology.

Legitimation involves the transforming of what might be regarded with skepticism or hostility into something acceptable, even honorific. Max Weber defines it as a process of establishing that something is right and proper, or that it is rational to do, when there is no custom or tradition behind it.[5] A bastard child becomes a rightful heir. An unsigned painting becomes the acknowledged work of a master artist. The bourgeoisie take their place in the highest echelons of power, viewed no longer as ignoble upstarts but as leaders and benefactors. A revolutionary government gains support by arguing that it is the genuine voice of the people. In all such cases of legitimation there is at once an appeal to reason—or it may be an effort to redefine what is reasonable—and an appeal to tradition, demonstrating that the new is in fact organically linked to the old and established. When the claimant is a class, government, culture, or mode of production, legitimation usually involves the creation of an ideology, a set of ideas that will justify the claim. To create that authenticating ideology requires the recruiting of a group of persuasive ideologues, whose skill with words and reasoning can overcome opposing ideas, make the outlandish familiar, and motivate people to act in desired ways.[6] Irrigation, as a new technological and social system introduced into American agriculture, went through such a legitimation process, as its ideologues attempted to establish that it was the genuine article—at once the perfection of reason and the fulfillment of tradition.

One of the commonest defenses offered for irrigation was that it was the epitome of scientific agriculture, that therefore it advanced the cause of progress toward a more rational society. By "rational" and "scientific," irrigation ideologues commonly meant control over the forces of nature. Therefore, the more perfect the agriculture, the less it left any part of production to chance. Water in the West, despite its scarcity, was more dependable, if it were captured by irrigation works, than rainfall in the East. Practice in manipulating rivers would make farmers there more intel-

ligent than their humid-land counterparts. The Johns Hopkins economist
Charles Brough pointed out that irrigation "puts a premium on brains."[7]
Trained in the use of their intelligence, western farmers could be expected
to be in the forefront of adopting new agricultural techniques of every sort
—chemical fertilizers, pest-control strategies, marketing approaches, ge-
netic experiments. They would bring farming out of the dark ages of
folkways and into the new industrial era. An Ohioan, James Reeve, author
of *Ten Acres Enough,* exemplified this celebration of western agricultural
rationality: "The superstition and traditions of peon and peasant are giving
way before modern progress, and the true husbandman is coming at last
to his own."[8]

A related argument on behalf of irrigation was that it would promote
more businesslike farming. Bankers would be willing to lend more money
at lower rates to the man with a dependable source of water. Consequently,
western agriculture could solve one of the farmer's chief problems, access
to adequate credit. Investors would be attracted to an agriculture that was
more industrial and scientific, where the profits were as reliable and substantial as in a factory. Reeve cited the example of a northern New Mexico
company that had spent $350,000 in buying 70,000 acres and furnishing
them with storage reservoirs. They later sold that land for as much as $30
an acre. Nowhere else in America were capitalists so enthusiastic about
agriculture as in the West. And the farmers who bought and watered that
land were on their way to becoming capitalists too, for "there is no other
legitimate opening for commercial enterprise that will at all compare with
this in extent and in promise of large returns."[9]

Other ideologues hailed the new farming based on irrigation as an agency
of American imperialism. By the last quarter of the nineteenth century,
driving toward empire was an established national preoccupation, though
Americans liked to contrast their methods with those of the European
imperialists. We conquer empty wilderness, it was said; they subjugate
other people. But that "peaceful" (peaceful if one disregarded the warfare
against native Indian peoples) conquest of nature had run up against a
barrier in the desert, and it could go no further without the aid of irrigation.
To stop before that obstacle, to reject irrigation, would mean a failure to
achieve national greatness. According to Reeve, "One who has complete
faith in the destiny of our country can only believe that that destiny will
be best accomplished by developing to the utmost every material resource
as rapidly and fully as it can be done." There was a heavy burden of
responsibility in this imperial mission. The irrigator must carry on the
heroic movement begun by preceding generations, and he must help restore
manliness and dedication to a society that was beginning to enjoy life on

115

too easy a set of terms. If the ideologues discovered that such exhortations to civic duty were not enough, they could refer to the charge God made to Adam when He placed him in the Garden of Eden—an irrigated garden, it was often noted—to multiply and exercise dominion. "Upon us," wrote the Pacific Northwest irrigation expert Frank Nimmo, Jr., "rests the obligation of the Divine mandate—'Subdue the earth.' "[10]

One of the most expansive of the irrigation imperialists was Morris Estee, a California lawyer and Republican party figure. In his 1874 address to the State Agricultural Society in Sacramento, he portrayed irrigation as the best possible schooling for "the empire of success." Out of the discipline of desert conquest would come a spirit of national greatness, of unflagging enterprise. Some years later, he chaired the State Board of Trade's Committee on Arid Lands, which reported on irrigation prospects. "The public lands," his report observed, "are almost exhausted." Territorial acquisition overseas offered one possibility of replenishing American *Lebensraum*, but the morally superior course was to reclaim a like amount of space from the arid lands. "We see what an empire would thus be brought into practical use," Estee's board enthused, for there would be room for hundreds of millions in that reclaimed land, while abroad there were vast indigenous populations in the way.[11] The American empire lay waiting in the western desert, and with the irrigated produce from it Americans could go overseas as agricultural merchants, opening up markets throughout the world, opening up the hungry, insatiable markets of China and India, winning through trade what the Europeans must win through bloody arms.

These claims for irrigation offered, like a Wagnerian opera, plenty of bombast and show. Science led to rational, businesslike agriculture; these both led to empire; religion and nationalism made a swelling chorus; and at the end of the performance were money and world power. But an empire based on water needed legitimacy among the ordinary folk too, the people who were not yet ready for the grand opera of Progress. For them, irrigation was urged as a means of satisfying their interest in achieving a quiet, simple competence. They did not have to demand, it was advised, that the privileged share their well-watered farmlands in eastern America. They had no cause to resent a policy of wide-open immigration of the world's poor to America or feel pressed to the wall by them. They could find homes and farms enough in the desert, and it would not be on a dunghill either.

"If no more unoccupied lands are made fit for use," Estee and the Board of Trade feared, "landholding will soon be the privilege of the rich, and tenantry the only hope of the poor." "The best safety that capital can have," they added, is "universal ownership of the soil."[12] The relationship of capitalism to the agrarian dream is nowhere put more clearly than that.

Urban men of wealth like Estee were often among the most sentimental and enthusiastic defenders of small farmers. It was blissful beyond telling, they liked to repeat, to live as as an independent farmer on a little patch of earth and tend a few beans, with no rancor toward capital, enjoying many more satisfactions than a lawyer or a steel-mill owner. Their dream of America was of a peaceful nation populated mainly by contented farmers, with here and there, inconspicuous and unbothered, a few big capitalists like themselves.

The beauty of irrigation, in the minds of the ideologues, was that it seemed to be a natural antidote—Marsh and the Italians notwithstanding —to capitalist monopoly and the social tensions that it would generate. William Hammond Hall, the state engineer of California and one of the country's leading irrigation experts, directly refuted Marsh's argument that irrigation promoted concentrated power with evidence from the West Coast. Where Fresno County had been held in 20,000-acre tracts, it was now being divided into 20-acre lots; hence, he insisted, "irrigation is a blessing to the country, [for] it enables large owners to cut up their lands and sell out to the many." The Seattle *Sunday Times* pointed to corroborating evidence in the state of Washington: In Vineland County, near the mouth of the Snake River, irrigated farms averaged only four acres—and these, the paper insisted, were farms "from which people get a living." Similar examples could have been collected from every part of the West, except where irrigation was only a supplement to cattle ranching, suggesting to the hopeful that a new order of rural life was in the making.[13]

The problem with such examples was that they led too quickly to generalizations. In their eagerness to bestow legitimacy, Hall and others ignored contrary cases like Haggin's Kern County Land Company, where there was enough will and capital to irrigate on a grand scale. That James Haggin's plans were larger and more centralized than those of the neighboring large landowner who subdivided was more important to the course of irrigation than any intrinsic qualities in this new agriculture. The apologists also failed to notice that the typical great estate that was cut up had easily accessible water on it, or small farmers could never have undertaken irrigation there.[14] Estates with no small, manageable rivulets, where the water lay deep underground in aquifers, where it flowed past in a great torrent, or where there was no water at all, were not subdivided, and they were in the majority. There were, in other words, some ecological reasons why irrigation in some places produced a small-scale agriculture but would not do so everywhere.

The main reason why irrigation seemed to be an irresistible force for democratic ownership had to do with economies of scale. Hall again, in his state engineer's report of 1880, argued that water application required considerable skill and close supervision. No single individual could efficiently irrigate 160 or 640 acres: it was too much land. The wheat farmer or rancher could personally handle hundreds of acres, or he could live far off, hire men to plant and harvest or ride herd, and devote his life to other matters. Indeed, he did not have to be a farmer or rancher in the ordinary sense at all. But the irrigator could never be a big-scale suitcase or sidewalk farmer, showing up only once or twice a year. He must be a permanent resident on his land. And he could not farm by hired labor—virtually every observer was adamant about that. Here is Hall:

> Hired labor, and consequently all labor on large land holdings in California, can never attain to great skill in irrigation, because it is that of a transient population unused to the soil, the slopes, the appliances, and works of the fields in which it is called upon to manage the water.[15]

And here is the conclusion of Senator William Stewart of Nevada:

> Irrigated land can not be monopolized, because it requires so much personal attention and supervision that hired laborers will not produce the best results. It is the mode of farming suited to families and they can make one acre of irrigated land produce more for a term of years than five acres of the best land in the Mississippi Valley where rainfall is relied on for moisture.[16]

Arguments like these, founded on the idea of an economy of scale, were as numerous as they were unreliable. Within a few more decades, irrigating farmers proved to be willing to hire as many laborers as they could get, and to use that labor to expand their domains beyond all precedent in row-crop agriculture. Then the ideologues would make precisely the opposite argument: that economies of scale require getting bigger, not smaller. What is the right scale in farming is, after all, decided not by the economist's numbers but by the farmer's appetite.

Easily the most prominent ideologue for irrigation in the late nineteenth century, and one who had an unbounded faith in its democratic potential, was William Smythe. He was an unprepossessing man with sad, drooping eyes, thin, lank hair parted in the middle, a beard and mustache above a starched collar: the type, one would have thought, to minister to a small brick church in an obscure village, not take on the role of national high priest of irrigation. He was from Massachusetts, the scion of a Pilgrim line that most recently had produced wealthy shoe manufacturers. Paradoxically, he was also an admirer of Horace Greeley and the utopian principles of Fourierist association. In 1888, at age twenty-seven, he went West to work as editor of a Kearney, Nebraska newspaper. Within two years he found himself living through a tragedy of drought and farm failures. It was then that he discovered the wonder of irrigation, and until his death in 1922, it became for him "the Cause", a means to save the West from economic ruin and, still more important, to create a new and better world.[17]

In 1891, a reporter from the Nebraska *State Journal* caught Smythe in the first flare of excitement over his Cause:

> Tell the people of Nebraska [he said, surely with a sweep of his hand] that we are going to make homes for millions of men; that in these homes irrigation shall guarantee industrial independence and the small farm unit a reasonable degree of human equality. Tell them that the foundation of our industrial philosophy will be the systematic production of what each family consumes. Tell them that electricity will be the partner of irrigation and that the densely populated agricultural districts of the new Nebraska will have all the advantages of town life and few of its evils, all the charm of country life without its present loneliness. Nebraska's best days are before her. The historian will record them as the irrigation era.[18]

That excitement continued unabated through the decade and beyond, as Smythe organized experimental colonies, spoke at irrigation congresses all over the West, and commenced publishing a new journal, *The Irrigation Age*. Then in 1899, on a remote ranch in Lassen County, California, he finished his book *The Conquest of Arid America*, which was published the following year. It offered a wealth of information on the progress of irrigation in western states. More important, it was an exercise in legitimation, often muddled, confused, and unsystematic in strict philosophical terms, but fired with zeal; and often there is nothing more effective in legitimation than to enlist the zeal of a true believer.

The word "conquest" in the title of Smythe's book, meaning of course the technological domination of nature, is a key one in his social thought. It was for him a cornerstone in the foundations of democracy, an indispensable means for achieving that more humane order of life. Because irrigation

119

of the desert landscape represented such domination in its most advanced agricultural form, he was ready to believe that it must be peculiarly efficacious as a liberalizing force. "The essence of the industrial life which springs from irrigation," he declared, "is its democracy."[19] Though that assumption was familiar enough by the time he came to write, was even a cliché, Smythe made it more compelling than anyone before him had done, or anyone after him would do. His success in promoting it among the public showed he was far more in tune with the main currents of the day than either William Emory or George Perkins Marsh, for in sounding their warnings they had gotten nowhere—there were too many other, contradictory cultural values in their way. Along with the majority of his countrymen in a position to count, Smythe simply could not imagine any conflict between desert conquest and democratic institutions.

In making the leap of faith from domination to democracy, Americans had been well tutored by more than two centuries of liberal social philosophers. From the time of James Harrington and John Locke, the founding fathers of classical liberalism had preached to the common folk over and over the sermon of democracy triumphant over nature. If you want a more egalitarian life, they had explained, you must begin by working for it. You must march into the wilderness and wrest your wealth from unappropriated nature, whether from the soil, the forest, the mine, or the sea. Then, so long as the elite few are not allowed to monopolize that wealth, taking what they have not earned, there will be enough of everything to go around and democracy will begin to flourish. Emancipation from inequality, in other words, was made to depend substantially on that movement of labor (especially agrarian labor) into unsettled space, into a raw, open country. From its seventeenth-century beginnings, liberalism was a philosophy of environmental activism, of progress, of economic expansion, of acquisitiveness— though there were disagreements among the philosophers as to how far private acquisitiveness should be tolerated—and of material abundance. It was the ideology of an aspiring middle class who resented the power, property, and conservatism of the established gentry and who wanted the freedom to take directly from the land, or later from mills and markets, their means to independence.

By Smythe's time, however, that ideology of democratic conquest had begun to encounter a few problems that were making people anxious. For one thing, the ideology had required for its credibility an environment of natural abundance easily accessible to individual enterprise. By the opening of the twentieth century, such places were becoming scarcer. The world of unexploited nature that had invited Locke and Thomas Jefferson was becoming well-settled ground, and opportunity seemed to be disappearing.

Smythe refused to accept that darkening prospect. Citing the statistics of the American achievement to date, the farms made out of wilderness, the railroads linking them to cities, the factories furnishing them with plows and fencing, statistics drawn in part from Andrew Carnegie's "inspiring" book *Triumphant Democracy*, Smythe had neither any doubts about what had already been achieved to date in the country nor any intention of letting the process come to a dreary end.

> Can there be any reasonable doubt [he asked] that if the
> policy of material conquest over new areas can find another
> field on which to operate, and that if it be entered upon
> with the old vigor and faith, it will confer another century
> of prosperity upon the nation so fortunately endowed?

His own inventory of prospective frontiers, added to that of Carnegie, was wholly reassuring. "The resources of the earth," he proclaimed authoritatively, "are yet very far from a state of thorough development. There is room for incalculable expansion. . . . The sum to be added to the world's wealth and comfort by the conquest of the waste places is literally beyond the dreams of avarice, even in a day when avarice has large conceptions." There were still spectacular possibilities left for extending the empire of democracy westward, and that empire would be clean and virtuous, would ennoble Americans and the rest of humanity as well.[20]

In a later book, *Constructive Democracy* (1905), Smythe discussed another threat to the traditional hopes of liberal democracy: the drift toward monopoly, the rule of concentrated wealth. In the urban, industrial East "plutocracy" was now firmly in the saddle, riding the economy, the political system, and the working class. Smythe's response to that development was not to call for breaking the power structure down into smaller pieces, as the Populist radicals he knew in Nebraska wanted to do, or to seize the wealth through sudden revolution and redistribute it to the majority. Quite the contrary: he would remove all obstacles from the path of consolidation, letting the corporations ride freely as far as they could go. "The result would be the solidarity of the industry," he wrote, "with a virtual monopoly at home and advantages abroad which cannot possibly be matched by the warring competitors of other countries. In a word, we would achieve the highest economic efficiency."[21] Centralization of capital and power was, in his opinion, a blessing. It would lead to greater social harmony and unity, whereas the old small-scale competitiveness had produced only diversity, discord, and inefficiency. A better future lay with bigness—of that he was emphatically sure. But all the same, how guarantee justice and opportunity in that future great society? The chief drawback apparent to him in the progress toward larger and larger agglomerations of capital, higher and higher levels of social organization, was that millions of people would become "surplus." What to do with them, the technologically unemployed, whether factory workers or bankers, the men and women who no longer would be needed to make the machinery run smoothly?

Here again is where irrigation and the West came into the picture. Irrigated lands were not only a frontier for further expansion but were also an outlet for the human surplus of the industrial East. Redundant Americans could simply head West and find an irrigated farm, returning to the soil as earlier generations had done, and win their stake in life.

> No other part of the Republic can possibly compete with [the West] as an outlet for surplus population. No other region offers such fertile soil for the growth of institutions suited to the social and economic needs of a new time. It is here that the Nation is to find the means of relief from many of the perils that encompass it. Long neglected, ridiculed, even despised, its day has come, at last.[22]

The America surging forward in the East then would be a single, integrated corporate structure, an industrial state that one day, Smythe hoped, would learn to use its immense, concentrated force to redistribute more of its wealth to all its people. Meanwhile, in the West, an alternative irrigated empire would emerge, offering unbounded opportunity to those Americans who wanted the independence, the work, and the challenge that the industrial system could no longer furnish.

The West, however, was not to be taken as a throwback to an older agrarian world losing out elsewhere, a temporary reprieve against modernity, but rather as a new kind of frontier that would reinforce the nation's inexorable move toward corporatism. Smythe pointedly celebrated irrigation as an agricultural counterpart to industrial organization, a stance that has not been sufficiently appreciated by historians. For instance, Lawrence Lee, the foremost authority on Smythe's life, has argued that he saw in the arid region "a sanctuary for the traditional American society nourished in agrarian simplicity and protected from the forces that were undermining the old order in the East."[23] True, there are throughout Smythe's writings many traces of nostalgia, many longing glances back to an earlier, less structured time when struggling entrepreneurs had a more open field for their talents, when farmers and townspeople lived more on a level, when the local village or milltown was the locus of community life—all of which was gone, swallowed up by Big Capital. Smythe speaks repeatedly of the "independence" possible on a self-sufficient, forty-acre irrigated farm. But those instances of looking backward are overbalanced by his enthusiasm for the social changes in progress. The word that he uses most frequently in *Conquest* to characterize the irrigated West is not "agrarian" but "industrial." By industrial he means a plan of rationalized, complex economic organization similar to the one appearing in the East. Irrigation would indeed bring Americans back to the countryside, but they would come to carry out the modernization of farming and the industrialization of the West —Smythe is clear and positive on that point. They would erect on the base of scientific water control what he calls an industrial "superstructure," an economy utilizing power generated by massive hydroelectric dams, power to run factories as well as farms, an economy of international marketing, technical expertise, and high consumption.

Smythe's preferred model for the irrigated West was not, therefore, the New England village of his ancestors, with its vernacular technology and loose, casual social structure. Rather, it was the bustling little nation of Holland, which had pushed back the North Sea with sophisticated hydraulic engineering. "The Dutch combined and organized their efforts in order to keep the water off their lands," he wrote, "just as the Westerners combine and organize to bring the water on." In both places there was a need for "associative enterprise" to conquer nature. "Associative" was a vague word, to be sure, ranging across a wide scale, suggesting capitalism as easily as socialism, and it could involve various degrees of individual coercion. Smythe gave some indication of what he had in mind when he quoted extensively from a book describing Dutch social organization: "The people are a vast civic army," his source noted, "subdivided into brigades, regiments, and companies, all accustomed to discipline, learning the first great lesson of life—obedience." They are "not selfish and individual," but have learned to take orders, follow directions, and accept leaders.[24] The Dutch, in other words, pursued the domination of nature through the subordination of the person to the group and through erecting a firm hierarchy of authority. That behavior seems to have been what Smythe wanted for the arid West. Whether he was right or not about the Dutch is not material here; what does matter is the social qualities he singled out for emulation.

In the democracy created by irrigation, the surplus men and women of the East would travel West, pooling their capital and efforts in order to master the region's aridity. Smythe wanted to see the federal government step in to give them a hand in the construction of their dams and canals (and soon he would have his way with the passage of the National Reclamation Act in 1902). Though he did not expect or want big capitalists to be included in this movement into the desert, he did expect that the small farmers would operate pretty much as the capitalists did—that is, by the ethos of conquest and accumulation. They might, he indicated, even begin to hire laborers, as capitalists do, to help them make money in their fields (Indians and Mexicans were recommended for that role, but Smythe would send the Oriental "serfs" back home). The irrigating farmers would not live on an absolutely equal basis—at least not in the foreseeable future—for every proprietor must be free to increase his wealth as he chose. Progress still demanded individual initiative and reward. It was the Mormons in Utah, Smythe believed, who had worked out an ideal, model arrangement, one worth putting alongside that of the Dutch: their system, he said, was "nothing but a joint-stock company," in which everybody had a share in the benefits but not an equal ownership.[25] There, in a phrase, was Smythe's ideal America, a world where everybody would be a member of the corporation, a stockholder in the company. That was what his democracy would mean up and down the irrigation ditch.

In sum, what attracted Smythe to an agriculture based on irrigation were in large part the qualities found in any modern business corporation. Both brought together scattered individuals who on their own were ineffective in developing and deploying advanced technology. Both the corporation and the irrigation community grew out of, but superseded and rejected, John Locke's individualistic, agrarian liberalism. Both professed to be the vanguard of a new type of democracy, though it would be democracy with a more regimented face, following strong lines of command and tolerating economic inequality (though Smythe was less comfortable with that inequality than the typical capitalist). Both aimed to win markets for their products in a widening world sphere—to enjoy "advantages abroad which cannot possibly be matched by the warring competitors of other countries." The Cause of Irrigation, then, was at once an antidote for and a mirror of America Incorporated.

Legitimacy is a slippery thing. Today you have it, tomorrow it may slide out of your hands. In a liberal society, where ideas, along with corn and clocks and bib overalls, enter a more or less open marketplace, every form of power depends on securing legitimacy. The price of that power is eternal vigilance against all critics, all cynics, and the means of retaining it is a troop of industrious, watchful, persuasive ideologues who can smooth away doubts, find appealing arguments, and skillfully manipulate the culture's values and ideologies. Irrigation had such a troop, and it was led by men like William Smythe. Thanks in no small part to their efforts, reclamation of the West was readily accepted by Americans, gaining a legitimacy because it was easily linked to an existing, widely held ideology of democratic conquest, and also because it gave that ideology a convincing rationality, the argument that conquest in the modern world must be collective if it is to succeed. So long as Americans continued to hold to the ideology, the control of water would seem to them a perfectly benign, progressive relation with the earth. But if one day they awoke to discover that their mastery over natural forces had not in fact produced a more democratic society, then that legitimacy might be abruptly withdrawn. The hydraulic society they had built might then find itself in a crisis of credibility.

At the end of this first period of irrigation intensification in the West, the period of incipience, some significant contrasts between the American and the ancient hydraulic civilizations had become manifest. In the latter, the initial decision to irrigate and the subsequent moves to intensify the system seem to have been the outcome of slowly evolving relations between people and rivers. Most likely, the pressures of a burgeoning population on available food supplies were the decisive forces, driving those civilizations to undertake the command of water. In the case of the American West, however, such ecological pressures were far less obvious and decisive. The white man came rather suddenly into Utah, Colorado, California, and other arid states and hastily set about turning them into paradise. There were a mix of reasons for his entry, but none of them had anything to do with a genuine national shortage of basic nutrition. For some people the motivation was religious security, for others an interest in social experiment, for still others a sense of curiosity or a quest for adventure or an urge to accumulate. Almost always they came because their society told them to do so. It said that there was not enough room or opportunity or future for them in settled America. That message need not have been taken as true, but it was so taken and the desert gave way.

FOUR

FLORESCENCE

The State and the Desert

The conquest of nature, which began with progressive control of the soil and its products, and passed to the minerals, is now extending to the waters on, above and beneath the surface. The conquest will not be complete until these waters are brought under complete control.

—W. J. McGee, *"Water as a Resource" (1909)*

In this age of radio the chasm of the western night sky fills endlessly with invisible voices. Each one has its own timbre, each one wants to be heard, each claims an identity, an individuality. Yet at some nebulous point they touch and merge, their sounds become one, a single rhythm, a blended throbbing in the air, a blur of whispers, shouts, pleadings, and threats. Let your attention drift from their uniqueness, and it's easy to hear them as a common voice. There can be no hard shell around them. They constantly mix their vibrations, until even the most carefully designed separateness is lost in the great babble.

Society is like that sky full of sounds, where the unique and the common weave in and out of the ether. Much of social thought has to do with deciding how much attention to give the individual sound and how much to give the general blur, or with whether there is any virtue in listening at all. In America, we proclaim that the people's voices must be heard. Our air is a continual buzzing, louder and more cacophonous as years go by, and it is anybody's guess what the voices have to say in concert. How tempting, if you are a politician, to heed only the voices that have the sound of money in them. Yet it is also an old American belief that the individual can speak more clearly here than anywhere else in the world—and not just one with a warning to make or an ego to express. Any individual in this society is allowed, so the official theory goes, to have an important, self-contained voice. Indeed, some say we pay so much attention to those private sounds that we ignore larger collective cries of anguish and protest. That we are too much a nation of discrete transmitters. That we turn a deaf ear to the common good.

The state is supposed to be the agency that listens to all those voices of Americans, to their demands, their complaints, their enthusiasms, and responds to them. That has always been so since the state, which is to say the national government, was first established, though for a long time it listened with only a sporadic and narrow attention. However, in the twentieth century especially, it has increasingly had the responsibility of being not only an ear but also a voice in itself, speaking of protection, assistance, and mercy for less fortunate Americans: the state as the people's voice of conscience. Arguably, it has seldom spoken very well—maybe because too many have never approved of the mission and have done their best to sabotage it.

This chapter is not, for the most part, about the state as either the ear or the voice of conscience in American society. There is another, and separable, role that the state has been given. It begins with the first clamorings for "internal improvements," with importunings for canals, turnpikes, and railroads to open a continent for exploitation. The state in this capacity has been an agency for conquest. Americans, in particular those with the largest influence, have not been slow to call on it for help whenever they have run into difficulties overcoming nature and turning it into wealth. "Here I am, over here, come give a hand, I'm engaged in a great work, the nation will profit, this is the state's job too." The voices that have been loudest in American history have been those calling for the aid of the state in the pursuit of domination.

I suspect it is more in the character of any state to respond to demands for the conquest of nature than to serve as a moral conscience. The state is an agency of power, and power has a way of feeding itself first rather than the powerless. It is a recent hope among welfare statists that that old pattern can be reversed. Build up the power of the state, they have believed, and the strength to do good is increased. A plausible idea, except that it overlooks two facts: the ability to do damage is also multiplied, and, more serious yet, strength has an old, notorious tendency to become an end in itself.

In the American West, the individual voice is, according to popular myth, clear and self-reliant. It has a rough masculine sound, audible above the din, hard-edged, isolate, claiming a large space for itself. The reality is somewhat different. Lone, autonomous individuals could not conquer the desert. The ecological situation demanded group effort. What was not specified was how far westerners should be willing to go in that conquest —and how much individuality they should be ready to surrender.

By the 1890s, the West had gone as far as it could on its own hook. It had tried partnerships, theocracy, foreign and local capital—and still most of the rivers ran on freely to the sea. The Columbia, the Missouri, the Rio Grande, and the Colorado all eluded their grasp. So they raised their voices in one loud, sustained chant that could be heard all the way to Washington, D.C.: "We need the state!" And the federal government responded by passing the National Reclamation Act in 1902. It has been the most important single piece of legislation in the history of the West, overshadowing even the Homestead Act in the consequences it has had for the region's life. The West, more than any other American region, was built by state power, state expertise, state technology, and state bureaucracy. That is another way of saying that it has been, and is, the most thoroughly modern of American regions, and therefore that its experience, particularly in the matter of water, has been most instructive for deciphering the confused messages of that modernity.

``A COMMONWEALTH WITHIN ITSELF''

The census of 1890, thanks to Frederick Jackson Turner, is well known, but not so the one that came ten years later. The first told Americans that the frontier, defined as a broad band of sparsely settled land, a zone of from two to six people per square mile, was gone. The second told them quite the contrary, that the frontier was not all settled, indeed that it had, for the first time in the nation's history, gained on civilization. A decade of drought, beginning in 1888, had thrown the line of western settlement back eastward. "Man," lamented Edwin Erle Sparks, professor of history at the University of Chicago, "has retired before hostile nature." The depopulation was most dramatic across the entire state of Colorado, along the major rivers of New Mexico, on the high plains of Kansas, and out on the Llano Estacado of Texas. It was apparent too in scattered parts of northern Wyoming, western Montana, western Idaho, the interior valleys of Washington and Oregon, and the basin country of northeastern California and Nevada. Sparks wrote: "Lines of posts with occasional strands of wire, dry irrigation ditches, and abandoned dugouts or sod houses show where over-confident man has retreated from the unequal contest."[1]

There was another kind of drought that plagued the West through the 1890s: a lack of enough private capital to build the irrigation systems desired. In the previous decade there had seemed to be plenty of money from investors, including many in Glasgow and London, to put into district bonds and into speculative land and water projects. However, in 1893 an international depression began, and investors suddenly turned off the flood of dollars, with no warning, leaving many hopeful settlers stranded and dry. Turner ignored that money drought when he wrote "The Significance of the Frontier in American History"; otherwise he might have had a different

131

story to tell. But westerners could not ignore it. They were forced to admit that in order to sustain their population advance in the face of an adverse climate, they needed irrigation—and on a big scale, bigger than anything they had so far tried. More and bigger irrigation required more and bigger money, however, and those who had that money were now unwilling to risk it. That was the real significance, and predicament, of the western frontier in the nineties.

Nothing more should have been needed after those two droughts to bring a tone of sobriety to the region's boomers, who had been heralding the arrival in the West of all the poor, the enterprising, and the wealth seekers of the world. But not so: they were more determined in their expansiveness than ever. Somehow, they were sure, the money for irrigation would be found. In 1893, the second International Irrigation Congress convened in Los Angeles (the first had met two years earlier in Salt Lake City), and there, in the midst of red, white, and blue bunting and massed choirs singing odes to water, delegates let their imaginations run loose. William Smythe, the instigator of the congress idea, pushed through resolutions declaring that irrigation would make possible homes for millions more in the desert, that land grants should be limited to forty acres per family, and that it was time for the federal government to assume some responsibility in the matter. Prizes followed for the biggest tomato raised by irrigation, for the juiciest grapes, for the heaviest wheat. "O glorious land! O glorious land!" sang the choir, "where fruits purple, crimson, and golden roll forth from plenty's horn." Ignore the empty ditches and the abandoned dugouts, for there is still an empire here to make if Washington will deliver water to us.

The only discordant note in that upbeat affair came from John Wesley Powell, a short, stocky, whiskery man with an arm missing, now in his last months of employment at the United States Geological Survey. There is not enough water in the arid region, he told the astounded delegates to do all that you want to do. There is not even enough to water one-third of the land already in private ownership, and even if we had the money to build more dams and canals, even if the droughts were over, irrigation would forever be a limited remedy, capable of reclaiming at most a mere 12 percent of the region. "I tell you gentlemen you are piling up a heritage of conflict and litigation over water rights for there is not sufficient water to supply the land."[2] In the storm of outrage that followed those blunt words, Powell was silenced. It was the last anyone would hear from him publicly on the West and its settlement. Within another nine years he would be dead.

Although he was not at all a popular figure in 1893, John Wesley Powell has fared much better among later generations. He is now, in most places, a bona fide American hero, even among the boomers. It is hard to fix precisely why he has come out so much better than his critics in the eyes of posterity. Maybe it is because he was a complicated man, for it is easier to find in the complicated man or woman something to admire—heroes need more than one face to sustain their fame. In Powell's case, there was the hero who, in 1869, led the first exploring expedition down the Colorado River, from Green River, Wyoming, to Grand Wash Cliffs near the Utah-Nevada border. That Powell was a wild-river enthusiast, letting go of civilization to ride the surging spring currents over rapids and through deep canyons downstream to the unpredictable. In stark contrast to that face, there was another and very different Powell: the technocrat, the man of science who wanted to plan the world, to control its future. That Powell was eager to take on the work of "redeeming" the West by capturing its rivers that were "running to waste." Then there was the Powell who was a competent, dedicated bureaucrat, head of the Survey from 1881 to 1894, author before that of the famous 1878 *Report on the Lands of the Arid Region of the United States*, a model of ecological realism in an unsympathetic age of unbounded expectations. And there was still another Powell, one who remembered the rural Midwest of his youth and wanted to see an arid-lands America built on a similar foundation of decentralized, democratic institutions, where ordinary people would be in charge of working out their own relations with water, free of outside interference. That last Powell has gotten the least attention, and it is a Powell we especially need to recall today.[3]

A complicated man, filled with such inconsistent impulses, Powell is a difficult man to read in the sum. In contrast, he was always perspicacious in specifics. In 1874, he first put on paper what he saw as the essential western *problématique*:

> About two-fifths of the entire area of the United States has a climate so arid that agriculture cannot be pursued without irrigation. When all the waters running in the streams found running in this region are conducted on the lands there will be but a very small portion of the country redeemed, varying in different territories perhaps from 1 to 3 percent. [At the Los Angeles congress he said 12 percent —in both cases being a realist, but also a waffler.] Already the greater number of smaller streams, such as can be controlled by individuals who wish to obtain a livelihood by agriculture, are used for this purpose; the largest streams, which will irrigate somewhat greater areas, can

133

only be managed by co-operative organizations, great capitalists, or by the General or State governments. It is of the
most immediate and pressing importance that a general
survey should be made for the purpose of determining the
several areas which can thus be redeemed by irrigation.[4]

Over the next twenty years he matured a plan both for that survey and for
the irrigation settlements it would suggest.

The central assumption of his plan—and it seems to have been Powell's
controlling idea through his entire Washington career—was that the wild
rivers of the West had to be mastered. "All the waters of all the arid lands
will eventually be taken from their natural channels," he wrote in his *Arid
Region*, (presumably including in that "all" the Colorado River, which had
given him some thrilling times), for now that the age of exploration was
over, the goal must be "the greatest possible development" of industry,
agriculture, mining, and manufacturing, in the region. The West was to be,
in Powell's mind ought to be, a technological civilization, militantly modern, bent on the complete domination of nature. Every streambed should
be drained dry, so that not a drop of water would escape. The Colorado was
wasting its energy by cutting canyons through sandstone and shale; in the
coming age, it would be put to better work generating electricity for a brave
new world. Its waters would all be taken for crops, providing food for the
miners and factory workers of the future West—indeed, for the world, for
this was to be the premier agricultural region of the country. With the death
of the rivers, the drying out of those arteries of the natural earth, a new
order would rise, the regime of the eternal, indefatigable machine, spewing
out a steady flow of material abundance.[5]

That much in Powell was perfectly in tune with the visions of the power
elite of his time, in both the West and the East. It was his vision of how
this technological civilization built on water control was to be governed that
differed. Was it to be run by capitalists or by the people? Powell's answer,
given as emphatically as anyone in government service has ever given it,
was that the people should be in charge. And the West presented a grand
opportunity, he believed, to plot that technological democracy, whereas the
older industrial centers were already firmly under capitalism's control. To
be sure, there were in the 1870s and 1880s many men of large private
wealth eagerly buying up the West as well as Pittsburgh and Chicago. The
hour was late, he warned, but if Americans moved quickly, they could save
the region, or most of it, from the fate of private monopoly as experienced
in the East.

Powell was not unaware that irrigation had a suspicious record in history, associated as it had been in its advanced stages with antidemocratic forces. "In the practice of agriculture by irrigation in high antiquity," he admitted, "men were organized as communal bodies or as slaves to carry on such operations by united labor. Thus the means of obtaining subsistence were of such a character as to give excuse and cogent argument for the establishment of despotism." But, he was confident, "such a system cannot obtain in the United States" because here "the love of liberty is universal."[6] Americans, defying all precedents, would hang on to their freedom as they advanced their civilization. In fact, their freedom would grow with civilization. Technology would rescue them from the sweat and subordination found in the ancient desert world, leaving nature as the only slave around, and on the basis of that new slavery a classless democracy of free citizens would arise.

The opportunity to survey and plan a technological democracy, to see it emerge out of shortgrass plains where the buffalo had roamed, out of clumps of cottonwood and willow and mesquite, out of high alpine meadows where the water ran clear and cold, was Powell's consuming passion. He was at last given his chance when Congress authorized, in a joint resolution in March 1888, an irrigation survey under his direction. He was given $100,000 the first year and $250,000 the next to identify all lands in the public domain that would be suitable for reservoirs, ditches, canals, or irrigated agriculture. Such lands were to be off-limits to entry or settlement, so that speculators could not rush in and grab them up, until the survey was complete and disposal could begin by some unspecified procedure, or until the President intervened to make specific lands available. By 9 December, Powell had a corps of young engineering-school graduates learning the art of stream gauging under Frederick Newell's direction at an encampment on the Rio Grande. That was the hydrographic branch of the survey. Another group traveled by horse and rail, looking for reservoir sites while compiling a series of topographic maps of every western river basin, beginning with those in Colorado, Nevada, Montana, and New Mexico. First the grand map of the West, Powell decided, with statistics on precisely how much water was running through the land. Then could come the grander scheme, the mapping of a new society.[7]

Opposition to the irrigation survey had come at first from easterners who feared it would be the opening wedge for a program of government-financed dams and reservoirs: "socialism" creeping into the land of self-made men. The chief congressional proponent of the survey, Senator William Stewart of Nevada, had assured them in the solemnest tones that he had no such alien program in mind. And he did not, for Stewart was unquestionably devoted to serving the money interests. Over much of his career he was notoriously a footman for the San Francisco moguls, especially Collis Huntington of the Southern Pacific Railroad Company, and had also worked for James Haggin and the Bank of California. He had still other capitalist friends, other personal interests, in mining, in cattle, in timber. The admirer who edited his reminiscences had this to say of him: "In the mad scramble for wealth in the treasure vaults of El Dorado, young Stewart was in the fore, and obtained his share. [I]n him the money-making instinct is highly developed."[8] What this public servant had in mind was simply to let the government do the work of finding the best irrigation prospects and then open them up for private capital to exploit. What he saw happen instead was that little, maimed John Wesley Powell had settled in for at least a six- or seven-year term of mapmaking, during which no private interests would have any access to those water sites. At that point Big Bill Stewart feared that the idea of a survey, originally his idea as much as Powell's, had gotten out of hand. He wanted a West that would be wide open to men of large ideas and heavy pockets, a West that would be developed fast, where fortunes could be made tomorrow. Naturally, he assumed that was what his constituents wanted too, certainly the constituents whose voices he heard. He therefore found himself moving abruptly to oppose Powell, and with him went a number of powerful senators and representatives from the western states.[9]

Stewart had himself set up as chairman of a special Senate committee on irrigation, and in August and September of 1889, he led the committee —or more accurately represented it, since most of the members put in only a perfunctory appearance in their home state—on a fact-finding tour. They began in St. Paul, swung across the plains and Rockies to the Pacific Northwest, tacked southwesterly, and ended up in Ogallala, Nebraska, completing a circuit of 14,000 miles. During their travels, they heard from almost four hundred individuals (including William Carr, Haggin's man on the Kern; plenty of businessmen; and a few actual farmers, even on one occasion a member of the radical Farmers' Alliance), enjoying all the while the hospitality of the railroads and innumerable chambers of commerce. Mainly it was Stewart's roadshow, with Senator John Reagan of Texas, Powell's chief supporter on the committee, there much of the time to represent the minority Democrats. Also in the Stewart entourage was Powell, doggedly trudging along, saying nothing, listening to Big Bill day after day. The upshot of the tour was a proposal from the committee majority to take the irrigation survey out of Powell's hands and give it to some new office in the Department of Agriculture. They would also repeal the Desert Land Act, guarantee free access to water holes on the public domain for the cattlemen, and reserve rights-of-way for irrigation developers, thereby giving "full play," as they promised, "to the enterprise of the pioneers of the west."[10]

Hearings began on the Stewart proposal in January 1890, and it was clear from the outset that Powell was not going to get to make either of his maps. The most serious charge against his direction of the survey was that he had wrongfully diverted irrigation funds to make topographic maps—and it was a patently trumped-up accusation. A more discrediting issue was whether those maps were really needed for water development, and on that question some of Powell's own lieutenants deserted him. Senators from the northern plains demanded to know why he had not spent more money to prove that there were wonderful artesian-well possibilities in their states. However, the burning anger in that hearing, so hot it was hard to express, was over delay —over locking up resources for a few years while the experts tried to rationalize the process of settlement. Making an aggravating situation worse, the General Land Office, backed up by the Attorney General's and the President's opinions, declared that no public lands in the West of any sort would be available for sale until Powell was finished. In effect, they said Congress had, in its authorization of the survey, repealed every land law—the Homestead Act, the Desert Land Act, and the rest. That decision was not Powell's work, but it was one he did nothing to discourage and, in fact, welcomed. So the real motive behind the hearing was to get rid of an uppity bureaucrat thwarting and starving the land-hungry westerners. "The ambition of Major Powell to manage the whole subject of irrigation" was what stuck in Stewart's fleshy throat, and when he could not swallow something, he got nasty. Outside the committee room, he launched a campaign of vilification and innuendo, trying to get Powell removed from office ("I have made some inquiry and find that his habits with women are scandalous"). He did not succeed immediately, for the survey remained in Powell's hands. But he did manage to cut the director's funds drastically and thereby demoralize him to the point where finally, in 1894, he resigned.[11]

In the course of the 1890 hearings, Powell at last revealed to the senators the new society he would like to see take shape in the river valleys of the West. Two articles in *Century* magazine, appearing simultaneously with the hearings, presented to the public the substance of his testimony, serving as a kind of defense against his critics and implicitly asking for popular support. The explanation he prepared for the senators was sober, dignified, and rooted in practicality. Its only color was in the maps Powell brought with him to illustrate his ideas. The magazine articles, on the other hand, were flamboyant and theatrical, straight from the painterly school of Albert

Bierstadt: "The lofty peaks of the arid land are silvered with eternal rime . . . and the deep canyons thrill with the music of laughing waters"—a laughter, Powell forgot to add, that he would silence. Taken together and with all their limitations, these statements constituted the single most comprehensive blueprint ever put forward for the region.

Powell's maps showed that the boundaries of the arid region ran on the east along the hundredth meridian and on the west from Monterey Bay inland, up the east side of the Sacramento Valley, and north along the Cascade Mountains to the Columbia. It was an area of 1,340,000 square miles, and, according to the 1890 census, already 3.6 million acres of it (0.4 percent) were being irrigated. Powell's scheme was to divide the region into two or three hundred "hydrographic basins," or watershed units, and to organize settlement within those basins rather than by the prevailing township and county system. Nature in its drainage network had indicated the patterns of rational settlement, and the topographic maps expressed that logic. "I early recognized," Powell said in the hearings, "that ultimately these natural features would present conditions which would control the engineering problems of irrigation and which would ultimately control the institutional or legal problems."[12] It was, in a sense, a strategy of ecological adaptation he was proposing. The watershed gives shape to the technology that conquers it, and the efficient functioning of that technology requires a society organized along watershed lines, so that the jurisdiction of laws and courts and community planning are coextensive with the resource base. An eminently scientific, modern approach, one Americans had never tried before—had never felt the need to try. In the West, Powell was saying, the scarcity of water imposes on us, if we are to make the most of the place, a new rationality. The old approach to settlement—buying land from an abstract gridiron of lots, a 640-acre square here, a 40-acre block there, and letting the narrow economics of an entrepreneur rather than the broad economics of resource maximization control development—must be replaced.

Powell illustrated his "natural districts" scheme with the oldest and one of the longest of American rivers, the Rio Grande, the Great River. Up near its headwaters, in the broad, arable San Luis Valley of Colorado, he would establish what he called a first-class district. It would be a single social, political, and economic unit, with the right to use all the water collected within its boundaries. Downstream, say in the vicinity of Santa Fe, El Paso, and Laredo, there would be several second-class or river-trunk districts. Each of them would build dams on their side-streams and at points on the main river to store all the local water runoff. Third-class districts would be organized elsewhere on minor streams with no issue to the sea. Eventually all the flow of the Rio Grande would be stored in reservoirs, and then there would be enough water for all. Rights to the use of that water would be assigned according to the district of origin. Headwater districts should have first claim, for they contributed most to the river current. Water rights would thus be unalterably fused with land ownership, ending the threat of separable monopoly control over the right to that critical commodity. All reservoir and canal sites should forever remain in the district's collective possession.[13]

The scheme undoubtedly owed much to the irrigation-district legislation of Utah and California, but in its sweep and implication it was, as Wallace Stegner argues, a "revolutionary" idea.[14] And there was more to come. Powell would limit every future settler to 80 acres of irrigable land within one of the districts. No other lands there should be open to private purchase or appropriation, and the cattle barons—now the tension, the incredulity, in the hearing room must have been palpable—must cease making free use of the public domain. Furthermore, the timber companies must not be allowed to buy up the mountain forests. All nonirrigable lands, except for mineral and coal areas and townsites, should be kept as federal property in perpetuity. Their use and protection should be left to the districts, not to the United States Army, as some proposed, or to any other corps of outsiders. Westerners themselves should be "organized into bodies corporate and politic and constitute commonwealths for the regulation of irrigation, the division of waters, the protection of forests, and the protection of the pasturage lands, and for the utilization of all of these values."[15] In short, neither the capitalists nor the far-off bureaucrats should be permitted to control the destiny of the West.

There were 100 million acres to be redeemed, Powell wrote in *Century*, affording enough land for 1.25 million farm families. In their hands should lie the decisive power over most of the region's resources. First, though, they had to command the rivers, and it would take a billion dollars to do that. No less a figure than Brigadier General Nelson Miles, the most famous Indian fighter in America and soon to be commander-in-chief of the United States Army, proposed in May 1890 that the government furnish that capital. "The enormous amount of money required to place the desert lands in a productive state would have to be furnished by the government," Miles insisted, "as it would be impossible for the States and territories to complete such a system as is in contemplation; and the funds expended should, by a well-matured and comprehensive plan, revert to the treasury of the general government from the sale of its lands thus improved."[16] A single water law, he added, ought to extend over the entire arid region and its irrigation system, rather than the hodgepodge of conflicting state laws.

Miles was a centralizer. So were some of the leading irrigation experts in the western states, men like Elwood Mead in Wyoming, who believed that the control of water should be put in each state engineer's office. Powell, however, wanted to go down a different road. "Hands off!" he urged. "Furnish the people with institutions of justice, and let them do the work for themselves."[17] They could construct their own headgates and weirs, using labor in the place of capital, if necessary. They could contract with private corporations for the jobs they were not able to do. They could mortgage their lands, put their water rights up as security, borrow what they needed from the banks. In that way only could they maintain the love of liberty that would distinguish them from those despotic irrigation societies of ancient times. The sole responsibility of the government should be to furnish the districts with the best scientific information it could, as Powell was attempting to do with his survey and maps.

"The accumulation of facts for the people."[18] Scientists in Washington in league with grassroots America: that was Powell's aim and that was to be the foundation of democracy in his coming technological society. In this advancing civilization knowledge was, and always would be, the major means to power. Already there were difficult technical questions to answer. How much water is available to spread around? Where is the best location for a dam? Which design should be used in its construction? What should be the gradient of a canal? Those who knew the answers would determine who got the profit from dominating nature. The capitalists had access to the best expertise money could buy, forcing the people to become informed in their own self-defense. "Facts for the people" was the bedrock issue in the 1890 hearings over the Powell irrigation survey. It may have been that Stewart and the committee majority did not ever see that issue. It may even have been that most westerners, most Americans, did not see it, or seeing it, did not share Powell's concern. He was nonetheless undaunted. "The conclusions which I have reached are not hasty," he said, "for I have given to the subject the best thought and energy of my life." We have spent enough time on "generalities," Stewart retorted. "What we want now is to hear from any person present who has practical ideas as to what can and ought to be done to facilitate irrigation."[19] Quick results, not a laborious process of conveying information. Dams built, land available to exploit now, not a lot of maps and data with farmers poring over them, scratching their heads, trying to figure out what they meant and how to proceed.

Stewart and a few historians since him notwithstanding, Powell's watershed settlement plan could have been as practical as people in the West wanted to make it. That is all practicality ever is, a matter of definition and acceptance, of willingness to work for one scheme rather than another. Powell's was rejected as being too impractical. It is hard to say in the last analysis by whom it was rejected: clearly by Stewart and the Congress, undoubtedly by the Haggins and Millers, possibly by run-of-the-mill westerners and would-be westerners, who failed to rise up and support it vociferously, if they ever heard of it. But regardless of its fate, it had some good features, enough to make it memorable in later years, when the control of the West came to rest, as Powell had feared it would, in fewer and fewer hands. However, the plan also had some serious problems that Powell himself never addressed and some internal contradictions that could not be resolved given his assumptions, his paradoxes of character. They are problems that must be dealt with in any effort to erect a democratic society on a modern technological base.

The natural district would be, Powell wrote, "a commonwealth within itself."[20] The phrase suggests the democratic qualities of autonomy and self-determination, of decentralization of authority and power. Yet almost immediately he was forced to concede the need to resort to external decision-making. In the first place, there was the problem of adjudicating water claims up and down a river, across state lines, even between nations. The Rio Grande had all those complications. In the southern part of New Mexico, where irrigation had long been well established, farmers insisted they had priority of use over newcomers upstream. Owing to diversions in the San Luis Valley and the severe drought, there was no water at all in Rio Grande south of Albuquerque in the summer of 1889, when the Stewart entourage came through. "The sand was blowing across the channel of the river," Powell reminded the senators, "and instead of the space being covered by waves of water it was, when I saw it last, filled with sand dunes."[21] South of the border in the Juarez neighborhood of Mexico, farmers cursed the gringos and demanded reparations from the United States government. There was, in other words, a complicated web of existing water claims that would make the district idea, with its proposed new hierarchy of precedence, very difficult to introduce into a watershed. And even if there were a less encumbered place to try it out, it would soon break down if all the inhabitants along the river tried constantly to maximize their own or their district's wealth—and they would if they were typical Americans of their time. Wherever economic maximizers and resource scarcity coincided, some kind of external presence, some form of Leviathan, would become inevitable. In a case like the Rio Grande, seething with rivalries and bitter disputation, Powell's remedy of proliferating reservoirs might suffice, but only for a short time. Sooner or later, the federal government would be called in to decide where and how the river would be divided.[22]

Another kind of intrusion on the autonomous commonwealth threatened to come from the expertise Powell believed was indispensable in the future. There could be no triumph over nature, no industrial empire in the West, without trained intelligence to direct it. Whose head then would the irrigation district actually use, its own or that of some expert? In an old agrarian culture of modest ambitions and strong vernacular traditions, the problem would never appear, but it most certainly would in Powell's technological society. Amazingly, a million and a quarter families, all of them new to the region and unfamiliar with irrigated agriculture, were to create the most advanced productive system ever, and thereby be given a big say over all urban and industrial growth in the region. They would have to create water-control works that were massive and efficient, yet manageable and safe.

A tragic event just one year before the hearing underlined the risks in what Powell was asking. The Johnstown Dam in western Pennsylvania suddenly gave way in the spring of 1889, and its floodwaters rushed down the Conemaugh River valley, drowning two thousand people. Powell himself wrote an article on the disaster, making recommendations on how such things might be prevented in the future but insisting that it would be irrational and unprogressive to turn against the idea of building dams because of mishaps like this one. Johnstown was the result of inadequate science; the lesson was more expertise. "Modern industries are handling the forces of nature on a stupendous scale," he wrote, mixing warning with pride. "The coal-fields of the world are now on fire to work for man; chemical forces, as giant explosives, are used as his servants; the lightnings are harnessed and floods are tamed. Woe to the people who trust these powers to the hands of fools! Then wealth is destroyed, homes are overwhelmed, and loved ones killed."[23] The new power was not one to leave carelessly in the hands of ordinary people; there would have to be experts in positions of oversight and management. Could these experts in turn be trusted with that power? If Powell would not trust the federal government to oversee the western environment, who would watch the watchers? Powell would not trust capitalists to produce a fair, just society. He would not trust "fools" to construct and operate the new-age technology. Who then was left? Could the simple farmers of the West be expected to do better than the fools at Johnstown? Obviously, they would require a great deal of help, and a great deal of direction, from an elite cadre of technocrats. And trusting those technocrats as he trusted himself, Powell could not see the potential for profoundly antidemocratic tendencies in that situation.

Powell's dream of a "commonwealth within itself" was spoiled by the existing settlements, culture, and history of the West, over which he had no control, and by his own paradoxical commitment to the absolute domination of nature. Neither problem was irremediable, though it would have taken a more fundamental revolution—something more drastic than what Wallace Stegner meant by "revolution"—in American thinking, and in Powell's too, to find a solution. As it was, there was no revolution of any sort. The director left his survey, got hooted down at Los Angeles, and passed off the stage. A short time thereafter, the state took over the reclamation of the arid lands, just as General Miles had proposed. Henceforth, it and big money would continue to rule, the technocrats would get a piece of the action, and the people would go along for the ride.

PASSAGES TO INDIA

In the latter part of the nineteenth century they could be found all over the West, sitting together in the dining parlors of hot, dusty hotels, camping in tents on some lonely benchland or playa, peering through their theodolites, marking down angles and measurements. They were the brigade of hydraulic engineers, and they had more to do with making the modern West than all the fur trappers and cowboys and sheepherders there ever were. Many came from the East and had been educated at the Massachusetts Institute of Technology or Yale's Sheffield Scientific School; others had attended the University of California at Berkeley. Most worked for private land and water companies, a large minority for the United States Geological Survey or a state engineer's office. By the standards of the region they were exceptionally well educated, farsighted, and cosmopolitan men. They understood that they were engaged in a mission of conquest that was going on in all the arid parts of the world—in India, Egypt, the Sahara, Australia. A great and noble work it was, which ought to be well done if it was to be done at all. And everywhere around them they could find outrageous examples of incompetence and irrationality, work as good as it had to be and not a whit better.

Mary Hallock, the daughter of Hudson River Quakers, married one of those engineers, Arthur DeWint Foote of Connecticut, and followed him West. Her reminiscences and other writings tell us much about a professional's life in the new land, about the frustrations of being an engineer in a capitalist economy, and about the sacrificing, sharing, and sometimes

143

questioning life of a spouse. They first went to the mining camps of California, Colorado, and Mexico, before Arthur got involved in an irrigation development on the Boise River of Idaho. Undaunted by his lack of training in water control, he organized a corporation to dig the New York Canal, which would reclaim 300,000 acres. "One old, tough business pirate" from Staten Island, as Arthur described him, was the chief backer, along with a family of iron and steel merchants in Baltimore. Although new at the game of business as well as water, Arthur showed for a while a talent for raising funds and advertising his product. The cover of his company prospectus depicted Egyptian fellahin in loincloths, staggering along under water pots, surmounted by this inscription from the Psalms: "I have removed his shoulder from the burden; his hands were delivered from the pots." Clarence King, the Footes' friend and John Wesley Powell's predecessor at the Geological Survey, declared when he saw it that "the quotation ought to build the canal." Unfortunately for Arthur, it did not. His canal work, begun in 1883, came to a halt seven years later when his capitalists failed him. He thereupon went to work for Powell and the irrigation survey, before going back to mining and California. "We did not leave our bones on that battlefield of the Boise canyon," Mary wrote later, "but we left pretty much everything else we had. My husband left the crown of his years and the greatest of his hopes, the dream that satisfied the blood of farmers and home-makers in him, and the brain of the constructor he was born to use."[1]

The most interesting figure in the New York Canal group was Mary herself, both in her fine talent for describing sympathetically the life and motives of the hydraulic engineers and in her ambivalence toward their mission. "Darkest Idaho!" she exclaimed when she first arrived, "thousands of acres of desert empty of history."[2] But soon she was drawing pictures of that frontier and writing a novel based on her life there, *The Chosen Valley*, which was published in 1892. Its theme is the conflict between engineering, as dream and technique, and business, which makes use of the engineer but usually puts profit above his integrity. Though she is on the side of the Arthur Footes of the world, Mary can see the virtues of both parties in the conflict: the technologist's dream is incomplete without the capitalist's skill at organizing labor to make it real, while the capitalist, without the engineer's imagination to raise him up, is a petty, grasping sort. But finally Mary wonders whether the conquest in which both are engaged can ever be worth its cost, whether it can ever deliver on its promise.

The chief figure of the novel is Dunsmuir, a fiercely idealistic Scotsman, trained in his profession on the Lower Ganges Canal of India. He has come to the American West certainly not to make money but to create, to do a

godlike work, to help in the process of colonization, to . . . it is at last
impossible to say why he is there, why he has put discouraging year after
year into cutting a canal through canyon rock. "The man himself is his own
best reason for what he does," he lamely explains at one point. His sometime partner, sometime rival, is Price Norrisson, an entrepreneur pure and
simple who has gotten into irrigation for no more exalted reason than
because it is to be "the next big boom." Their children form a chorus
around the two antagonists: young Norrisson, an engineer who identifies
with Dunsmuir; Dunsmuir's daughter, Dolly, who shares her father's hopes;
and her brother, Alan, who, hating "this arid-land business," rebels against
his father and leaves the country. In the end Dunsmuir is forced to accept
work from Nourrisson, who has squeezed him out of his own project;
against his own judgment, he constructs a dam without a strong bedrock
foundation. The valley people christen the dam in a "Marriage of the Ditch"
ceremony, heavy with the symbols of sexuality and fertility. The river then
begins to rise against the dam, which collapses under the pressure, and
Dunsmuir drowns in what is really a suicide. Now Norrisson goes into
action: "This is Dunsmuir's dam!" he shouts, and it *will* be rebuilt, just
the way the Scotsman would have done it. Five years later it stands complete, "as solid as the hills." The water flows to the crops, the valley
prospers, and Dunsmuir's name will hang forever on a plaque.

Doubt kept creeping around the edges of Mary Hallock Foote's admira-
tion of the work of reclaiming the wasteland. She could enthusiastically
celebrate the work, as in her splendid drawing "The Irrigation Ditch," in
which a mother with babe in arms smiles down on water purling through
a meadow edged with poplars.[3] But she could also write feelingly of the
pre-irrigation landscape, of wind across the sagebrush hills, of wild roaming
animals and a cowboy's lament. One side of her speaks through Alan
Dunsmuir when he asks, "Isn't there land enough, with water belonging
to it, without spending millions to twist the rivers out of their courses?
. . . I should let it stay so. My father can build other things besides ditches."
And in the last words of the novel Mary speaks of the "cruel expansion of
our country's material progress." Every noble scheme is compromised by
greed, envy, and deaths like that of Dunsmuir. "Victory, if it come," she
concludes on a sober, melancholy note, "shall border hard upon defeat."[4]

Mary Hallock Foote's irrigation novel and other writings are a good introduction to the brigade of engineers on the water frontier, the self-effacing,
industrious servants of society whom she called the "sons of Martha." They
were prideful Americans, whether by birth or adoption, intensely loyal to
their country and often to the West, but at the same time they belonged

to an international fraternity of experts. Arthur Foote carried with him into the Idaho wilds a treasured library of irrigation books, reports, and pamphlets. They defined for him, as they did for other engineers, the world leaders and principles of that fraternity. In his library there were, for example, Colonel Richard Baird Smith's two volumes on the canals of Piedmont and Lombardy and Sir Colin Scott-Moncrieff's writings on India. The Foote circle would have been familiar with names from abroad like Jean Charpentier de Cossigny, Nadault de Buffon, William Willcocks, and Robert Burton Buckley, and with names from America like Richard Hinton, Herbert Wilson, Carl Grunsky, James Dix Schuyler, and Franklin King— all authorities on hydraulic engineering or irrigated agriculture. They would likely have known Edward Wegmann's *The Design and Construction of Dams,* and it would have told them about the Bear Valley Dam in the San Bernardino Mountains of California, or the Sweetwater and LaGrange dams in the same state, or the Poona Dam in India, the grand old Alicante in Spain, the Furens in southeastern France, and the Aswan site on the Nile.[5] The books in their library told of far-off, exotic places and stupendous achievements, of esprit and adventure. Above all, they held up a professional ideal of exacting standards. The problem for an engineer like Foote was how to measure up to that ideal in Idaho, where there were many pressures to compromise, and where often there was not enough money or time to do the job as it ought to be done.

An Australian commission came to the West in 1885 to study American irrigation technique and observed the damaging effects of those pressures. Alfred Deakin, the commission's leader and later a prominent political figure in his country, was appalled at the lack of finish in that technique. Most canals were dug with a few teams of horses pulling a Fresno scraper, a primitive cast-iron scoop; the ditches were unlined and the seepage from them was enormous. In the Mussel Slough area of the San Joaquin Valley, Deakin found five ditches where one would have done the job. "Extreme simplicity and economy" was the rule, as was "running a certain risk whenever it can be shown to be profitable." In contrast to Australia, he observed, the government stayed completely out of the irrigation business, with the result that engineers were seldom hired and the works were thrown up for the short run. "When built by a capitalist, whose only object is to get rid of his land, poor works are often constructed, he being indifferent as to their permanence, so long as they last until he has sold out."[6]

The most serious deficiency, from the perspective of the perfection of technique, was the lack of comprehensive planning in the United States. Piecemeal development, carried out by competing interests, meant the underutilization of river resources, and underutilization was, in the words of one expert, "a sin."[7] Scientists and engineers were early on among the most ardent critics of irrigation haphazardness and inefficiency. And they commonly were enthusiastic centralizers, for to bring water development under one head, be it a single large private corporation or the government, was in their view to promote the rationalization of the West. And that rule of reason, it hardly needs saying, was the rule of instrumentalism: reason in the service of productivity, economic maximization, and domination, reason not about ultimate ends but about means.

In 1874, Congress appropriated its first monies for an irrigation investigation, and the report that emerged from the study is a clear instance of those centralizing inclinations of expertise. Three commissioners were selected to reconnoiter the irrigation potential of the Sacramento and San Joaquin basins, or what the commissioners termed "the Great Valley of California." The three included Lieutenant Barton Alexander and Major George Mendell of the Army Corps of Engineers and George Davidson, a professor at the University of California and a scientist with the United States Coast and Geodetic Survey. It was Davidson who wrote the report and went on to establish a reputation in irrigation matters. He was a Scot by birth, brought to the United States by his parents; later he graduated from the University of Pennsylvania, served for many years as president of the California Academy of Science, and became one of the leading mapmakers of the West Coast, with his name affixed to sites from San Francisco to Alaska. With the two Corpsmen, he proposed a sweeping plan for the valley—so ambitious, in fact, that it would take a hundred years to develop the central power required to put it into operation.[8]

The essential feature of their plan was to take water from the northern end of the valley, where there was two-thirds of the rainfall but only one-third of the arable land, to the southern and drier end. Every stream falling out of the Sierra Nevada would be dammed, several times over in some cases, and broad, lined canals would carry the water southward. Twelve million acres stood ready to drink the water, and California, in the short space of two decades, could with this plan become "the granary of the world." But it would take "some authority" to plan and execute a "proper system to bring that artifice to fruition. If left to themselves," the commission pointed out, "the farmers in any country of large extent can never devise or execute such a system." Operating on their own, they would produce a "disastrous" effect. Clearly, the commission argued, it was "the duty of the Government to teach the value of irrigation, and lay out a comprehensive system, and enforce proper laws on the subject."[9]

A few months after the report appeared, in January 1875, George Davidson left the country on a federal mission to inspect irrigation works in

China, India, Egypt, and Italy. He was the first of a number of American travelers to go abroad to meet the world leaders in the hydraulic fraternity, study water laws and customs, and bring back ideas to try out. What he saw, especially in India, fairly took his breath away: audacious engineering, monumental designs, works grander than the pyramids, a grace and sophistication of technique that made American efforts seem shabby and amateurish. Abroad they built with stone, built to last. They manipulated immense armies of laborers. They flooded whole principalities and harvested bounteous crops to feed the world's densest populations. All of that was made possible, Davidson said on his return, by the power of centralized government. Only the state could afford such investments, wait patiently for the returns, and assemble a permanent body of expertise to manage the technology. Regretfully, he had to admit, Americans were not yet ready for that degree of centralization. He was, however, more convinced than ever that "the whole system of irrigation should be designed and projected by the government, or by each State, and constructed and maintained at the expense of the land benefitted, under the protection and direction of the State."[10]

Another American who journeyed overseas to learn at first hand what his foreign counterparts were doing with water was Herbert M. Wilson, one of John Wesley Powell's bright young men in the irrigation survey. He went with a considerable field experience behind him in the West, for he had traipsed around Montana for Powell, drawing topographic maps and shaking his head at the general backwardness of the people's methods. The Yellowstone, the Gallatin, the Missouri, and the other rivers there, he had reported, could, if properly exploited, water 18 million acres and support a population of more than 3 million.[11] Then he was off to India, arriving in Bombay on 13 January 1890 (just as Powell was facing the Stewart committee) to see how things really ought to be done. There he discovered that the British colonial government had been constructing irrigation works for thirty years. Particularly in the northern provinces, where fabled rivers poured out of the Himalayan foothills, they had much to show him. For the twelfth annual report of the Geological Survey, Wilson prepared a two-hundred-page report on the India model, summoning American engineers by a trumpet blast of data to meet the world competition.

Although most of the Indian peasantry still lifted water from hand-dug wells by bullocks and pulleys or relied on the ancient Persian wheel, circling with its buckets in a shallow pool, to irrigate their fields in the dry season, the British were making vast changes quickly. Already they had spent $360 million on hydraulic engineering, more than ten times the American amount, and were watering 25 million acres, easily ranking them first in the world. The Great Ganges Canal, begun in 1847, alone had cost $15 million. With its branching distributaries, it ran for four thousand miles and provided water for a million acres. There were also the Swat and Sirhind canals in the Indus basin, the Kaveri scheme in southernmost India, and east of Bombay, in a landscape resembling Arizona, the gargantuan Bhatgur Reservoir, backed up behind a dam almost a mile long. All these had been built in part by women robed in saris, carrying rocks on their heads up steep slopes. "India," wrote Wilson, "stands preeminent for her gigantic engineering undertakings." In America, on the other hand, he had to admit, "there can scarcely be said to have been constructed a single irrigation work designed on sound engineering principles" before 1882.[12]

There were further differences between the two countries. In India, all land and water belonged to the government, all works were the government's doing and the government's property. When the construction was done, public engineers remained on site to keep the apparatus repaired, police the use of water, and maintain the system at a peak of efficiency. In contrast, the unsupervised farmers in the American West were a careless lot, capable of letting gophers burrow into the canal banks and open leaks. That slovenly management extended to their farming practices as well. "The engineer," complained Wilson in a speech to his colleagues, "is not called upon to decide whether the soil is suitable or whether paying crops can be raised or what is the financial prospect."[13]

Then there was a wide disparity between the two nations in the "duty of water," a quaint phrase that speaks volumes about the perception of nature. "Duty" refers to the amount of water needed to mature crops; it is the standard measure of irrigation efficiency. Technically, it is defined as the number of acres that a second-foot of water (one cubic foot per second) flowing continuously through the growing season can irrigate. The rule of thumb in America varied widely. Some experts estimated the American standard at 60 acres per second-foot, some at 80 acres, some at 100, depending partly on location. In northern India, the standard was 250 to 300 acres. Only in a few areas in southern California did the Americans match that efficiency. The difference was due in no small part to better distributaries and more careful management in Punjab and Uttar Pradesh. But Wilson could optimistically write that "as the influence of capitalists and educated engineers is brought to bear on the cultivators, and as the experience of the latter is increased, the duty of water is constantly rising" among the Americans.[14]

A final set of differences lay in the purpose controlling irrigation development in the two societies. For the British in India, a major goal was to feed a teeming population and prevent social unrest, which in 1857 had boiled over into the Sepoy Rebellion of the natives against the Crown. Another ambition was to raise more agricultural exports, thereby earning more money and using the colony as colonies are meant to be used, for the enhancement of the empire. That ambition had at once an old and a very new aspect. As William Willcocks wrote, the British were engaged in "the resurrection of this ancient land."[15] For thousands of years, power in the Orient had been achieved and maintained through control of water. These latest conquerors were following a long-established pattern. At the same time they wanted to put hydraulic India, Egypt, and other possessions on a modern commercial footing, to make them profitable in the world market-place. In the American West, on the other hand, the purpose of irrigation was to induce settlement in an empty land, to fabricate an empire *de novo* out of yeoman farmers, miners, and manufacturers. But whether set up on old or brand-new foundations, whether involving the subjugation of one's own land only or of a foreign land and people together, empire in the late nineteenth century meant world economic dominance. The arid lands were to be the instruments of that dominance, and irrigation the methodology.

British and American hydraulic engineers, men like Willcocks, Wilson, and Scott-Moncrieff, were willing tools in the late-nineteenth-century international struggle for power and wealth. Being tools of respective empires meant that however fraternal they were in a professional sense, they were also rivals. In Montana and Idaho, near Cairo and Delhi, they strove for their nations' triumph in the battle, ready to work for whichever entity gave the most promise of achieving national success. Since the ultimate justification for the rivalry was the maximizing of markets and money, both the American and the British engineers were inescapably, if sometimes indirectly, in the employ of capitalism and capitalists. But as the India experience demonstrated, it was the state that could command the largest resources in the rivalry for empire. Somehow, many American engineers came to realize by the 1890s that they must induce the federal government to take a more active role in desert mastery for the sake of their own personal interest, for the sake of instrumental reason, and for the sake of victory.

The American engineers who went to India and other Old World irrigation regimes were classic studies in innocence abroad. They carefully copied down the figures they were given on the height of dams, on the number of acres watered, and on the costs of materials. But they commonly failed to notice less flattering details. They paid no attention to the despotic social organization associated with the control of water. They ignored the disastrous impact of new British and French hydraulic technology on traditional native cultures. And they were oblivious to the ecological problems which that technology created, just as they were at home. Standing on some finely crafted stone bridge flanked by massive carved lions, the common ornaments of British Empire design, looking down on smoothly flowing canal waters, the Americans were simply awed. They had four weeks, five weeks, two months, to see it all and make their report—no time, even if the motive had been there, to measure the costs of that triumph. Or if in rare cases they saw them, they found arguments to rationalize them away. Had they been prepared to absorb the full scene, however, there was a good deal of contemporary evidence spelling out how heavy those costs really were.

The peripatetic Alfred Deakin of Australia was a more acute observer than any of the Americans. After his trips to the American West and to Italy and Egypt, he went to India in 1890 and 1891 to study irrigation. What he witnessed both impressed and disturbed him. "We found a despotism," he wrote, "and we preserve it, striving not to alter, or weaken it, but to make it sympathetic and just." The irrigation system was under the absolute command of a bureaucratic army, answerable only to the viceroy. "In northern India the engineer is a ruler of men," Deakin noted, and the peasants came to him with requests and complaints, as they once had come to their local rajah. But decisions about hydraulic works, their location and expense, were not open to popular influence. "The Indian ryot [or peasant] . . . is never consulted in any way or at any stage in the construction," Deakin went on. "Government initiates designs and executes the work, offering him the water if he likes to take it, and relying only upon his self-interest to induce him to become a purchaser." There was not the slightest trace of self-government permitted in British India. White and native alike had no vote, living as "mere ciphers," exercising "only such illicit influence as is permitted to women in England and Australia." Everywhere he journeyed, it struck Deakin that "the Government is anti-democratic in every respect."

> The aim of the State is to do for the Hindu what he will not or cannot do for himself, and its *régime* is therefore in every sense of the term paternal. . . . The country has been won by the sword; its Government is imposed upon the people by force, and is administered by foreigners, upon a policy independent of their interests, far more enlightened than theirs, but nevertheless to them strange, uncomprehended, and unacceptable.

151

However benevolent its intentions, Deakin realized, the water regime was all the same a tyranny. And the hydraulic engineers, in their role as dominators of the rivers, became for the average farmer the immediate agent of that tyranny.[16]

Deakin had come face to face with the darker side of the imperial thrust. He found it amazing that the British, who at home were often disciples of Herbert Spencer's libertarianism, were quite capable abroad of asserting the unbounded power of the state. Like the Americans, he admired intensely the technological expertise which that state power made possible, and he wanted some similar monuments for his own country. The solution to the dilemma, it appeared to him, lay in separating the technology from the politics. Though irrigated India, he concluded, has little to teach us in the way of laws, administration, or the relation of citizens to bureaucracy, it has much to teach about the mastery of water.[17] A nice distinction, but could it be maintained? Or was the tyranny inextricably part of the advanced hydraulic technology? Once more, the old confidence that one can rule nature without being ruled oneself lulled even a perceptive observer into complacency, and Deakin went away without answering those questions.

How benevolent the irrigation imperialists really were is a complicated question, but its answer must take into account the damage done to traditional ways of living. Those ways had their own rationality, though it was often incompatible with the market and technological rationality the British imposed. In the case of India the foreign experts sought to transform a peasant agriculture into a modern, commercial one by means of the water innovations. What they achieved was something less than that—and more. The traditional pattern in most Indian villages was to water crops by individual wells, but only when they were in danger of dying. It was a simple, cheap strategy. The new British canals, as the historian Elizabeth Whitcombe shows, destroyed that strategy and tried to put in its place a perennial, systematic irrigation. Peasants subsequently came to depend on the government works completely. They became prisoners of the high-cost agriculture those works represented and, tragically, let both their wells and their old life cave in. The modern water system was far more expensive than the old—too expensive as it turned out for raising anything but export crops: cotton, sugarcane, wheat, and opium. India, it is true, made more money with the new system, becoming in many commodities a major world exporter, but that success did not improve the lot of the poorer classes. The peasants themselves and their livestock actually had less to eat than before.

Whitcombe writes, "Only that minority of the rural population already in a position of prosperity and sufficient power to maintain some independence of action had access to the benefits of innovation."[18]

With the grand new canals and reservoirs also came unexpectedly severe environmental damage, mainly through the excess of water now brought to the land, threatening health and livelihood. In some areas, where drainage was poor, water perpetually stood in puddles and shallow lakes. Fields became swamps, crops died from rising water tables, malaria-carrying mosquitoes swarmed, endoparasites like liver and lung flukes thrived and infected the villages. And then there was the salt, the curse of *reh*, a mineral efflorescence brought out of the soil by capillary action, coating the surface like snow and destroying arability. A government chemist reported in 1891 that four to five thousand square miles had been damaged by salinization in the North-West Provinces alone.[19]

The salt nemesis was one the Americans might have observed at home but did not, or observing, they dismissed it. Eugene Hilgard, the University of California soil authority, had been studying and writing about the problem in his own state from the early 1880s on. He called it "the rise of the alkali." Near Bakersfield, he reported, one could pick up salt by the handfuls. Intensive desert irrigation had put it there. Hilgard, an enlistee himself in the cause of environmental conquest, had a few remedies to offer. Where there was good drainage, his recommended treatment was to pour more water onto the land, flushing the salt away and into the sea. But where drainage was poor, where the soil was waterlogged, he recommended installing tile drains under the surface—a very expensive undertaking, adding to the burdens of the small farmer who got caught in the irrigation trap.[20] (Even where affordable or practicable, these remedies only solved the salt problem on one's own land; the runoff would poison rivers and lakes elsewhere, killing aquatic life.) However inadequate or unaffordable his recommendations were, Hilgard's work on salinity and alkalinity was world-famous and more heeded abroad than at home. While America's hydraulic engineers went overseas to be inspired, other countries, plagued by their own pace-setting progress in creating the modern hydraulic society, sent agents to talk to Hilgard. In 1884, for instance, an English engineer came over from the British colonial government in New Delhi to compare notes with Hilgard and gather insights into curbing the salt backlash. Unfortunately for him and for the farmers of India and America, the problem was inherent in massive, sustained irrigation. No amount of expertise in soil management and environmental protection could overcome problems generated by an unrestrained drive to build larger and larger water projects. Nor could the course of empire be stayed by such petty details.

"We are establishing the oldest form of agriculture known to man in as utter disregard of the experience of other lands as it is in defiance of the best intelligence of our own."[21] That warning came from Elwood Mead, state engineer of Wyoming and member of the American Society of Irrigation Engineers, before the society's 1896 annual meeting. In another three decades, he would become the foremost professional name in irrigation in the United States, and one of the most widely traveled and knowledgeable authorities on the matter in the entire arid world. No more than the average member of his engineering fraternity did he ever criticize the darker side of imperialism, bureaucratic centralism, ecological destruction, or the adverse impact of advanced irrigation on the structure of rural wealth, tradition, and power. But along with many engineers, he was capable of a fine outrage when he witnessed other forms of irrationality, other lapses from scientific intelligence.

The most glaring irrationality the irrigation engineers faced was in nature itself. No competent earth designer, it was often suggested, would have left over a million square miles of the American land without sufficient rainfall to raise a crop. Aridity was *ipso facto* a defect, an illness requiring a physician to heal it. A rational nature, a healthy nature, would be a nature of uniform productivity, where there was no waste, no excess, no deficiency, nothing but a steady yield of the useful forever and ever. In that world, rivers too would be transformed into models of reason. No skilled engineer would devise a river that meandered this way and that on its way to the ocean; intelligence always runs in straight lines. Nor would a trained expert be guilty of allowing so much variability as was found in western rivers. For most of the year they typically amounted to a mere trickle; then with a sudden thunderstorm or an early thaw they raged and rampaged, tearing out everything put in their way, wreaking havoc over a vast floodplain. All those natural imperfections would have to be set right. Science demanded a nature without flaws.

The word used by engineers to refer to that work of rationalizing the rivers of the West, and nature in general, was "conservation." Dating from its first appearance in the Middle Ages in reference to the River Thames in England, conservation, or "conservacie," had long had the meaning of "protection." A writer in 1720 explained that "conservacie doth extend to the preservation of the stream, and the banks of the rivers, as also the fish and fry within the same."[22] For the American hydraulic engineers of the late nineteenth and early twentieth centuries, however, conservation had nothing to do with protecting rivers from harm, with preserving their integrity, or with saving them for posterity's enjoyment. Conservation meant, to a great extent, the pursuit of technological dominance. It meant putting rivers, and eventually their entire watersheds, to work in the most efficient way possible for the purpose of maximizing production and wealth. The first stage in that intensification of use was to dam and store the natural flow, until not a single drop escaped control.

Frederick Newell, an engineer and graduate of MIT, a friend and disciple of John Wesley Powell, and from 1890 on head of hydrological studies in the U. S. Geological Survey, was a prominent leader in the engineers' movement for conservation. "The stability and permanence of the commonwealth," he wrote, "are assured by the conservation of water resources which otherwise would go to waste." It was for him a program in which business and engineering had a common stake, for conservation, he insisted, "really implies good business management." Later, he added that the model for that water conservation could be found, not in the hastily contrived, fastbuck irrigation schemes of many western capitalists, but in the emerging corporate structure, ruled by "captains of industry" who, in their great combinations, demonstrated that success "is attained . . . by the economies which are possible in operations on a large scale." For him, conservation was a movement to apply the corporate principle of centralized management to the natural environment.[23]

In addition to the irrationalities of nature, there were man-made irrationalities spoiling the engineer's design, calling for his attention all over the American West. A private party owned the rights to this bit of water but lacked the land to use it on; another party had good land for irrigating but had no water. Each state had set up its own laws and then amended, revised, and contradicted them, creating a legal bramblebush. The technology of water control was large and intricate; the social structures were diffused and chaotic. Was this craziness never to end? Was what was potentially the greatest hydraulic empire in history never to be realized? Why should the New World continue to be inferior to the Old? Would the promise of science and technique be enjoyed only by the miserable ryots and fellahin of archaic places, while the Americans watched their opportunities flow unseized past their door?

"We have in the Colorado [River] an American Nile awaiting regulation," wrote the California engineer Joseph Lippincott, "and it should be treated in as intelligent and vigorous a manner as the British government has treated its great Egyptian prototype."[24] In other words, there should be and there must be an American Nile. And an American Ganges. And a rival to the Indus and the Euphrates. Reason said it could be done, that

155

empire was within the Americans' grasp. But it would require moving beyond the divided imagination of a John Wesley Powell and beyond the narrow self-interest of a Senator William Stewart. Neither man understood how indispensable the national government was to the task ahead. Thanks to examples like British India and Egypt, a growing number of American engineers had come to take an enlarged view. They stood ready to serve with personal modesty and patriotic devotion, if their own state was at last prepared to ask for their services.

A LONG, STRONG
ROPE

T hrough the 1890s the West milled around, frustrated and uncertain, on a plateau of water development. It was a small but expanding plateau, some 3.5 million acres in extent when the decade began, over 7 million when it ended. Not a bad achievement in itself, perhaps, though most of the increase came in the first few years of the decade before the droughts set in earnest. But the achievement stood in the shadow of a looming prospect, a vast upland of potential, ranging in size from Powell's 100 million acres to twice, three, four times that amount. Who could say how large that upland was until people were actually there? It was difficult to take much satisfaction in what had been won when so immense a promise lay just out of reach. Westerners itched to climb, but they could not find a toehold in the wall before them. Despite Powell's encouragement, they had little faith in their ability to make their way unaided up that wall. What they needed was a rope let down from above. Eventually they would stop milling and seize the long, strong rope of federalization, but first they would try a tangled assortment tentatively thrown down by the western state and territorial governments.

Federal aid to this point had been worse than useless. Simply handing a settler, or purported settler, a square mile of desert with the requirement that he bring water to it, as the Desert Land Act did, was a snare and a delusion. It was mainly cattlemen who took advantage of that laissez-faire policy, along with speculators who accumulated vast tracts under the act and held them for future sale. In 1891 Congress cut the acreage in half, eliminated a residency requirement, and allowed farmers to group into associations to go after water. The result was only a marginal increase in

156

irrigation. The reclamation party, in reaction against that record of failure, became altogether fed up with the federal policy of laissez-faire, and with admonitions to pull oneself up by one's bootstraps. They wanted bolder action and more vigorous aid. At the first National Irrigation Congress, they called on the federal government to cede to the states (that is, the individual states as opposed to the nation-state) all the arid lands in the public domain, allowing those states to undertake large, well-planned irrigation projects on them. James J. Hill, president of the Great Northern Railroad, said it should be done; so did William Mills of Southern Pacific; so did engineers, lawyers, real-estate agents, and journalists like William Smythe. The farmers said little, for they were too busy farming to attend congresses—and perhaps too preoccupied with their existing farms to worry much about reaching that upland. But the principal westerner developers were agreed, and they began to demand state ownership of their region and state planning of its redemption.[1]

Congress, whether out of wisdom or jealousy is hard to say, refused to bow to their demand. It would not give away the West, or even a substantial portion of it, to westerners. But three years after that demand, in 1894, Congress did agree to an experiment called the Carey Act, named after Joseph Carey from Wyoming. The federal government, according to the act, would give each desert state one million acres to irrigate and sell to farmers, provided the federal treasury received the sale money. The state would draw up plans, find a construction company to do the developing, and guarantee them a profit. Settlers on the projects could acquire up to a maximum of 160 acres at a nominal cost—50 cents an acre, plus the price of the waterworks negotiated by the state. In Idaho, the Carey projects charged $10 to $25 an acre for the water facilities, and a farmer could acquire a quarter-section irrigated farm there for as little as $240 to $480, with ten years to pay it off. Now, it was said, big projects could go forward. Construction companies need not fear losing their investment, thanks to state backing, and the farmer could not ask for more generous terms. The Carey Act, however, was a dismal and discouraging failure. Eight years after it had become law, only four of the ten eligible states had applied for federal lands, and altogether they had selected a total of only 669,476 acres. Apparently the states were not willing to do the job, particularly when they had to take all the financial risks by underwriting water investments and got nothing in return, or at least nothing but a bigger tax base. The act, nonetheless, remained on the books, and by 1958 the western states had managed to patent among them slightly over a million acres under it, two-thirds of them in the single state of Idaho.[2]

Still, across the plateau impatient voices rumbled, "Give more rope to

157

the states." One of the loudest of those voices belonged to Senator Francis Warren of Wyoming, a cattleman but also, breaking all the stereotypes, a proponent of irrigation. As governor, he had hired Elwood Mead to oversee water development, and the two performed as a duet on state initiative for a long time thereafter. Warren thought in simple, direct terms: let Wyoming have that portion of the public domain within its borders, let it dispose of those lands to private parties (he was suspected of being himself in the market to add to his cattle spread), let the proceeds be used to aid capitalists in irrigation projects, let all hands join to pass the money round and round.[3] Try as he would, he could not make many in Washington see the logic in that proposal. It was Mead who was more apt to get their ear, for he had some cogent arguments on behalf of "home rule."

The federal government owned almost all the land in the West, Mead pointed out, and therein lay the cause of stagnation. In the nine core arid states, 84 percent of the land belonged to the national government; the proportion ranged from a low of 64 percent in California to a high of 96 percent in Nevada. The only states that had much irrigation in place were California and Colorado, both on the low end of the scale. The other states did not have the financial resources to push their own development. How could Nevada be expected to pay for reclamation when its tax base was so tiny? And federal monopoly of the land, Mead went on, interfered with comprehensive state water planning. Take, for example, the case of Wyoming: it had instituted the region's most progressive water laws, but practically speaking, they applied to only 6 percent of its area. The water anarchist could go onto the public domain, divert water from it to his lands, and thumb his nose at the state engineer. Wyoming, to be sure, like Colorado, had declared that all water belonged to the state, not the federal government, but it was another matter to enforce that decree, for jurisdiction was still disputed. The way out of the impasse, Mead hinted, was to put everything in one basket, ceding the federal lands, uniting control over water and soil in the same capable state office. The federal grazing lands, he added (though it was not what Francis Warren wanted to hear), would then be leased out by the states, largely to irrigation farmers to supplement their 160-acre farmsteads, and the lease fees would be invested in more irrigation.[4]

Mead's remedy made some sense—but not enough. States outside the desert core, like South Dakota and Oregon, wanted more irrigation too, and they were left out of his proposal. Many states were less advanced than Wyoming in centralized planning. Why bother with that burden, they wondered, if someone else would do the work? States whose rivers came from outside their borders were less likely to agree than those with their own headwater sources. State cession, the former feared, would not ensure that interstate streams were apportioned fairly or that waters in storage reservoirs located in distant mountains would be made accessible to all. Nevada was one of those downstream states, for its most promising irrigation prospect, the Truckee River, came out of Lake Tahoe and California. Mead could expect few supporters there. He spoke for a Wyoming that wanted to follow its own inclinations. Nevadans, in contrast, wanted someone to make sure that whatever rope got thrown to them would not be cut off by California.[5]

Year by year, the crowd on the plateau argued over the best way up, tested one possibility after another, until at last federalization seemed to be the only recourse. Even then, as William Lilley and Lewis Gould have observed, they came to that decision with the greatest reluctance. Federal aid was a rope they distrusted when they reached for it, and one they would go on distrusting every inch they climbed.[6] At first they told themselves they would require only half a rope; they would ask the federal government to build only a few storage reservoirs for them. Francis Warren, who would brook no interference with state rights and state control but who would happily accept federal assistance, inserted an amendment in the River and Harbor Act of 1896 that authorized a survey of reservoir sites in Wyoming and Colorado. Hiram Chittenden, a West Point graduate with the Army Corps of Engineers, was assigned the work. His report appeared in 1897, naming a few good sites but, more significantly, recommending that reservoirs be built on them and elsewhere by the national government. "If it is properly a Government function to preserve the forests in order to conserve the flow of the streams," he argued, "surely it can not be less a Government function to execute works which will conserve that flow even more positively and directly."[7] Not a man to let a good idea lie idle in a report, Chittenden proceeded to lobby hard from his Army Engineers post, writing letters to Mead and other influentials and speaking from the platform of the National Irrigation Congress. Let the government hire experts to design the finest dams ever built, he urged, dams capable of lasting forever, and let the states continue to rule over the canal end of irrigation. It was a great American compromise, one that almost all westerners could live with, and they gave it their enthusiastic support. It turned out, however, to be something of a stalking horse for a more ambitious federal program that soon followed.

The impatience to find a way up the blank wall continued to mount, forcing many to alter their early thinking and bringing to the fore new leaders who were willing to risk losing regional self-determination for the sake of more water. Elwood Mead was boisterously applauded by his fellow engineers and by politicians alike when he complained of the slow progress

159

in developing the West. Many of us are giving the best years of our lives to the mission, he said, and "would like to see some more tangible results." At the current rate of agricultural expansion, it would take two hundred years to turn the region into "productive assets," and by then he would not be around to glory "because," he threw in, "the good die young."[8] A lawyer from Sonoma, California, George Maxwell, grew tired of the delay too, and in a Kansas hotel room in June 1899, he formed the National Irrigation Association to rally support for a complete federal takeover. The president of the Santa Fe Railroad signed up with the Maxwell campaign immediately and brought with him other pragmatic corporate leaders who had become disillusioned with the state cession idea and were now ready to put their money to lobbying Congress for an irrigation program. Maxwell was going too far for the old guard around Francis Warren, who denounced him as an upstart, a mercenary, and an agitator, one who would "foist upon the West rigid and exclusive National control of its waters."[9] But by 1900, a substantial number of westerners, including Mead, were ready to be foisted upon. One indication that year of the region's changed mood was that two of the national political parties—the Republicans and the Silver Republicans—courted western support by including in their platforms a plank advocating a national irrigation program.[10]

Then on 26 January 1901, the congressman from Nevada, Francis Newlands, introduced a bill in the House of Representatives that would place money from the sale of western public lands into an "arid land reclamation fund," which would be used for constructing irrigation projects. The lands in those projects would be sold to individuals in parcels not to exceed 80 acres, at a price to be determined by the water-development costs and to be reimbursable in ten annual installments. Repayment would create a revolving fund, with no other claims on it than more and more reclamation. Newlands expected the public domain to be the site of most of those projects, but the bill also allowed the federal government to develop water for lands already in private hands, at the sole discretion of the Secretary of the Interior, provided no one received water for more than 80 acres.[11] Federalization was now a full-fledged proposal, with a clear method of financing and a wide scope of application. If accepted, it would set up a development program completely independent of congressional appropriations, managed in every particular by an executive department and its bureaucracy. It was, let no one misunderstand, a proposal that came out of the West, devised by a western politician and promoted by a well-oiled and well-funded western lobby that had been organized by a native son of the golden West. On 17 June 1902 it became the law of the land.

In its final form, the National Reclamation, or Newlands, Act differed from the first bill in only one significant particular: the size of the farms created could now be as large as 160 acres. That change came at the insistence of the railroads, who feared that 80 acres would sound dreadfully small to prospective settlers, though in fact an irrigated holding of that size was, in most western states, a handsome bit of capital. To control that generosity, Section 4 of the act allowed the Secretary of the Interior to establish a much smaller farm size, as little as 40 acres if he chose, the intention being to give him the flexibility to decide how much land "may be reasonably required for the support of a family." The acreage limit was clearly a family, not an individual, standard, and it applied in all cases, whether the land to be watered had been in private ownership for a hundred years or whether it was newly segregated out of the public domain was immaterial.

> No right to the use of water for land in private ownership shall be sold for a tract exceeding one hundred and sixty acres to any one landowner [i.e., a single family], and no such sale shall be made to any landowner unless he be an actual bona fide resident on such land, or occupant thereof residing in the neighborhood of said land, and no such right shall permanently attach until all payments thereof are made.[12]

Other clauses specified that federal reclamation would not interfere in any way with established state water laws and private rights acquired under them, that the reclamation fund should be spent largely in proportion to the land sales made in the states, and that "no Mongolian labor" could be hired to work on construction crews. Only white American family men need apply.

The act passed easily. In the Senate, there was hardly any debate, and the individual vote went unrecorded. In the House, where there was some outspoken opposition (all of it from midwestern and mid-Atlantic states) the tally was 146 in favor, 55 against.[13] Historians have been explaining ever since why it passed and what it reflected of American culture of the time. Their explanations generally follow one of two lines. First and more simply, it has been said that the act was the achievement of consummate political leadership, either that of Francis Newlands or of Theodore Roosevelt. Second and more abstractly, it has been argued that the act rolled through on a wave of something called "Progressivism" or "Conservation." Neither theory is fully convincing. They are either too narrow and dependent on personalities or too grandiose and abstract. They both fail to pay enough attention to what was actually said in Congress on behalf of the act—to the specific reasons urged for its adoption, which, in the absence of proof of congressional artfulness, we are obliged to take at face value as open expressions of intent. But before analyzing those reasons, the prevailing historical explanations, despite their weaknesses, deserve at least a brief hearing.

Undoubtedly, Francis Newlands, who had armed himself with the best available professional advice, was a persuasive advocate of his bill, especially when working behind the scenes among his sometimes dubious western colleagues. After mid-September 1901, he had a powerful ally in the person of Theodore Roosevelt, who was elevated to the presidency on the death of William McKinley. Newlands was a Democrat, Roosevelt a Republican. Together they carried the day, then fought over who ought to get the credit. Their impassioned articulateness, their adroitness at political opportunism, at seizing a growing popular cause and riding it to victory, were impressive, and without them the 1902 act might have moved more slowly to enactment. Still, even granting the role of their personal motives and political skills, Roosevelt and Newlands were not the major reason for federalization. They were two minor, late-appearing, marginal voices on the water plateau. And that they snarled at each other even after their triumph should give pause to those who maintain that somehow they were simply disinterested allies in a common public cause.[14]

Did the federalizing of irrigation then occur because of the rise of two intertwined movements called Conservation and Progressivism? Both Newlands and Roosevelt, not to mention a number of other reclamation figures, have been identified with those movements. Ergo, Reclamation, it is often assumed, must equal Progressivism. The problem with that explanation is that historians cannot really decide what those movements refer to. An early supposition was that Progressive conservation was a drive in the first two decades of the twentieth century to democratize the national life and defend natural resources, including water, against the threat of private monopoly.[15] Roosevelt and Newlands, so it has been said, were guided by that democratic vision. Then a rival interpretation appeared, mainly in the work of Samuel Hays, which convincingly demonstrated that the Progressive conservationists were not in fact very democratic, apart from a few rhetorical flourishes now and then, that, on the contrary, they wanted to impose on American society a rule of centralized expertise, of scientific efficiency and use, and that federalizing western irrigation was where they wanted to begin that program. It remains a provocative interpretation, and some of its themes have been reflected in these pages. But finally it has the fatal flaw of identifying Progressive conservation with that amorphous process

162

social scientists have called "modernization."[16] By modernization is meant, obviously, the process of becoming modern. Unfortunately, what one means by modern is whatever one wants it to mean. Two abstractions overlaying one another seldom afford much illumination. When one of them is the murky abstraction "Progressivism" and the other is the still more cloudy and insubstantial "modernization," darkness descends over the entire subject and men and women had better fetch a small candle to find their way about. Until someone succeeds in giving Progressive conservation a clearer reference and narrower borders than all of modernity (and this is not the place to essay that formidable chore), we are better advised, if we want to get on with understanding this pivotal moment in American water history, to set the entire explanation aside and simply examine the arguments made pro and con in the matter of the 1902 act.[17]

The debate over federalization opened in the House of Representatives on 21 January and extended fitfully until 13 June, with arguments added by the Senate in the same period. A majority report from the House Committee on Irrigation of the Arid Lands, chaired by Frank Mondell of Wyoming, with a minority statement from George Ray of New York, summed up the opposing sides. The burning question in that debate, and it was at times a hot one, was not the preservation of democracy or the conservation of natural wealth or the threat of monopoly to either. If those matters entered Congress's mind at all, it was tangentially, around the edges, adding a spark here or there. What they really were wrangling over was the wisdom of the traditional American policy of economic expansion and its future direction in the new twentieth century. Did the country need more farmland in production? Was the westward movement now outmoded? What impact did expansion have on older settled regions? Was it wiser to expand overseas or at home? Answer those questions one way, and federalized irrigation was an idea whose time had come; answer them another way, and the West would stay on its plateau.

On the first day of House debate, the gentleman from Pennsylvania, Joseph Sibley, rose to denounce the bill as a poisoned chalice pressed to the lips of the farming classes. Eastern farmers, he pointed out, were facing "a man with the hoe" life. Their land values had fallen 50 percent in a generation, they suffered from overproduction of crops, they were working sixteen hours a day to make ends meet, across states like New Hampshire their farmhouses and barns stood empty, the brush growing up to the eaves. Now Newlands proposed to add arid-lands irrigation to the eastern farmers' woes. "So long as we have a large exportable surplus of agricultural products," he asked, "let the farmer meet, as others must, private, but not governmental competition."[18]

A few weeks later an Ohio congressman inserted in the record an editorial from *Country Gentleman,* which picked up the argument against expansion. The American government, the editor complained, gave protection to domestic industrialists from foreign competition, but when it came to the farmer, no help was available. Quite the contrary: the government had long held that door wide open for immigrants to come and set up here in farming, and now it was preparing to depress the agricultural sector further with reclamation. It was time for Americans to husband their existing farm settlements and proceed with care in adding new ones.

> A century ago, no doubt, the country needed development; but, great heavens, what is the haste to develop it further just now? Are we not numerous enough, strong enough, as a people? Could any nation on earth dream of invading our territory? What in the world are we gaining, what can we possibly gain, by this frantic, breathless haste to develop, to fill up our whole country with people, any and every kind of people, foreigners very largely, the off-scourings of the earth in no small part?

Westerners, the editor wrote, wore two faces on immigration. They clamored for more farmers from Europe to come into the country and take up an irrigated farm, but they were equally zealous to get the Chinese excluded from the West Coast, where they were regarded as "unfair" competitors. The easterner was satisfied, or at least this one was, that the United States had enough inhabitants of every sort, and he would save the West to be developed in due time for the natural increase in population that would occur.[19]

A bigger America was no longer a better America. To that fundamental argument the bill's opponents added other, closely related objections, all of them mixing legal, fiscal, and moral conservatism with expressions of regional self-interest. Federal reclamation would end up costing a great deal of money, more money than the land sales could provide, and the West would only too soon be back asking for regular appropriations (not so! not so! shouted the other side). The Constitution, strictly construed, did not give the federal government the license to do such work. It was squeezed under the Constitution's famously expandable "general welfare" clause, but in this case the land-sales receipts, which belonged to all Americans, would go to help enrich a few individuals. There were no public benefits in view, only private ones, including the welfare of the railroad corporations. The bill, like every other western land law, would end in corruption and fraud. It was, moreover, a waste and a bad investment. If the states could not make irrigation pay, if private capital could not, then how could the federal government succeed? Hepburn of Iowa thundered that this was, "the most insolent and impudent attempt at larceny that I have seen embodied in a legislative proposition . . . to give an empire to order that their private property may be made valuable." On that note of outrage the opposition may be said to have rested its case.[20]

They were not, however, going to carry the day. With the heroic example of an expansionary past behind them and with a new century beckoning them on, the majority in Congress were not ready just yet to stop filling up the West. They boomed out their defense of the bill with all the candor of the securely powerful.

Senator William Stewart of Nevada: "Here is a vast store of wealth, almost incomprehensible if irrigation can be carried on," and it will "increase the grandeur and power of this Republic."

Senator Augustus Bacon of Georgia: "The wealth which would be added to the nation is beyond calculation. Better that we spend our hundreds of millions of dollars in the creation of this new world within our borders than squander it beyond the seas."

Senator Jacob Gallinger of New Hampshire: "We are engaged in New England largely in manufactures, and we are seeking new markets for our manufactured goods." A reclaimed West "will open a new market" for those goods.

Congressman Elmer Burkett of Nebraska: "The people of this country are pushing out for markets. . . . We want markets. Markets! Markets! has been the watchword of the Republican party ever since it raised its head in the cradle of liberty for the protection and betterment of mankind."

Congressman John Bell of Colorado: "My friends speak of the overproduction of agriculture. That is nonsense. America must supply the shortage of the earth."

Congressman Thomas Glenn of Idaho: "It is right for the Government to create and improve everything that will facilitate the creation of wealth."[21]

And so forth and so on. Judging by the frequency of arguments, one must conclude that the Newlands bill passed, whether it was constitutional or not, whether there was a national need for it or not, because it promised to augment American wealth and muscle. A story of empire was being written across the land, and Congress refused to stop before the last chapter was finished. There was an irresistible logic to that story; it simply had to be completed. When the last chapter was written, when the West had been reclaimed and was supporting a hundred million, two hundred million people, then there would be a sequel to write: "The Orient," a continuing saga of American trade and markets, of the Republic's endless realization. In the light of that compelling adventure, the plight of eastern farmers was a trivial matter. From its beginning, the westering impulse had unsettled old ways, disturbed traditional communities, forced the backward to pay a price, and encountered resistance from mossbacks. But always it had gone forward. The opponents of the bill, gibed Congressman Reeder of Kansas, "had they lived one hundred years ago . . . might have been regretting that Columbus had discovered America."[22]

The federalization of water development was the work of men who more than likely thought of themselves as staunch conservatives. In at least one sense they were conservative: their support for enlarged federal power in this case was designed in large part to enhance the established social order in the West and in the country as a whole. The typical eastern farmer had never been part of that order, so if it came to that, he was expendable. The federal reclamation of the West would open markets to men of wealth and property. It would give the nation (which is to say those same men) a stronger hand abroad. True, it would entail spreading the federal largesse more widely, breaking the North and East's monopoly on the pork-barrel budget, but the South and the West quickly came together on that goal, recalling their earlier foiled embrace over the free coinage of silver and vowing this time to make the partnership last until the Yankees gave them their rightful share of the "internal improvements" money. But in joining forces on the water issue they were not making some wild old Populist attack on Wall Street. Reclamation, unlike free silver, was a regional program in Wall Street's best interest too. Moreover, with an intensely nationalistic president in the White House and an international prospect opening to Americans, the old regional squabbles were beginning to wear thin. Men of wealth and property in every part of the country had compelling reasons to make common cause in national development. Only in backwater rural areas were people unprepared and unwilling to take that broader, forward-moving view. As Senator Henry Hansbrough, who led the fight in his branch for the bill, read off the list of newspaper supporters—the *Times, Tribune, World,* and *Sun* in New York; the *Transcript* and *Globe* in Boston; the *Inquirer, Ledger,* and *Press* in Philadelphia—it was clear that the West could count on powerful conservative support in eastern urban centers.[23]

Federal irrigation was seen then to promote the accumulation of profit and power, two conservative ends served by innovative means. It was also supposed to offer the men of property and wealth a means of maintaining social peace—a safety valve for the discontented, unemployed, unruly class in the cities. Virtually every argument for the bill as a democratizing force had that manipulative idea in mind. Senator Thomas Patterson of Colorado called the Newlands scheme "a great pacificator," for it would open an outlet in times of economic unrest. When there is "danger of great social disturbances in the great cities, instead of meeting for the purpose of concocting trouble," the down-and-outers, he predicted, would load their families into a wagon and go West to seek an irrigated farm. The bill, therefore, would be "better than a standing army." Congressman Wesley Jones of Yakima, Washington, insisted that the bill's purpose was "to furnish homes for the homeless and farms for the farmless." Where people work for others, he warned, the result is "anarchy and anarchists, disorder, and revolution." If that was a plea for democratizing America, it had at the same time a distinctly authoritarian ring to it.[24]

That the 1902 bill represented a triumph for the little people of America has become a widespread myth among historians. Francis Newlands and Theodore Roosevelt, so the myth goes, stood up for farmers and insisted that the West be theirs. However, in the congressional debate, that poor man's theme occurs only rarely, and when it does, it appears as an argument from expediency more than from sympathy or moral principle. Here is Newlands:

> Lord Macaulay said we never would experience the test of our institutions until our public domain was exhausted and an increased population engaged in a contest for ownership of land. That will be the test of the future, and the very purpose of this bill is to guard against land monopoly and to hold this land in small tracts for the people of the entire country, to give to each man only the amount of land that will be necessary for the support of a family. . . . Convey this land to private corporations and doubtless this work would be done, but we would have fastened upon this country all the evils of land monopoly which produced the great French revolution [,] which caused the revolt against church monopoly in South America, and which in recent times has caused the outbreak of the Filipinos against Spanish authority.[25]

In this passage, the most elaborate antimonopoly statement in the debate, Newlands, himself a very wealthy man, married to one of the Comstock mining heirs, was not arguing for democracy on its own merits. A wide diffusion of land ownership, he was saying, was a wise strategy for averting serious, violent threats to the structure of power. That is not to say he was without feeling for less fortunate members of society. Certainly he was as broad in his sympathies as many of his opponents, and he was in a firm position to take them to task when they supported, as some of them did, the United States' "war of subjugation against a foreign people desirous of independence" (the Philippines) while refusing to release money for the West's war against the desert. But Newlands, for all his antimonopoly language, did not address in his bill, nor in any other he authored in his legislative career, the most serious form of monopoly in America: industrial, corporate monopoly. His reclamation bill was an evasion of that problem of concentration which, more than any other force, threatened the common people's control over their lives. The bill was an evasion and a distraction, for it suggested that something effective was being done out on the remote fringes of the arid lands to solve those problems and that nothing more was needed. In offering it, Newlands was listening to Macaulay's upper-class fears of mass revolt, to the similar anxieties of the American men of wealth and property, and to the ambitions of western go-getters. There is no evidence, however, that he was listening to the poor, excluded masses of the nation. Had he been, he might not have assumed as easily as he did that agricultural expansion was a cure for monopoly or concentrated wealth.

"Home building," wrote Dorothy Lampen, an economist, in her 1930 study of federal reclamation, "was perhaps the most popular argument of reclamationists."[26] Among the public at large that may well have been true, though it was not the main line of appeal in the congressional speechmaking. There, if home building had a place in the argument, it was in the form of the markets and rail freight promised by a more populous West and the economic development there that new homes and farms would make possible. As a selling device, the prospect of millions of homesteads—"homes for homeless people," as Lampen put it—was undoubtedly persuasive. It had long been a useful device among politicians, capitalists, industrialists, and their legitimizers for easing the tensions in the society they were creating. There would always be an agrarian America somewhere farther west, they told themselves and the public, always someplace to find a piece of property to own, to get a start on the way to success, to make a complex, highly structured nation seem simple again. The beauty of national reclamation was that it could at once hold out that promise and promote industrial might and world empire.

Poor men and women in the city were unlikely in 1902 to want to traipse off to Nevada or New Mexico and learn how to farm the desert. Nobody thought to ask them for their opinion of the bill, but if someone had, they would surely have replied, "Help us instead keep our factory jobs, find a way to stop these depressions, give us better housing." Farmers were likewise conspicuously voiceless on the nationalizing scheme. They had never been a major part of the irrigation congresses, they did not bankroll George Maxwell's lobby, they were outsiders in Washington politics. Where their voice was echoed at all in the Newlands bill debate, it was in opposition to opening more farmland to immigrants. Perhaps the ordinary farmers of the West, in contrast to those of the East and South, ardently applauded Newlands and his bill; in the absence of evidence we cannot say for sure. It does not matter much, for as the debate made clear, they were not the main intended beneficiaries of federalization. The irrigation centralizers, whatever region they represented, were overwhelmingly an elite group promoting an elite program. Their overriding aim was to enlarge, for their own ends, the country's wealth and influence. To secure peace and stability at home. To earn profits at home and abroad. And to pursue power, always power.

FAILURE

Success breeds generosity and convenient lapses of memory. Francis Newlands, who had begun his political career by denouncing John Wesley Powell as an obstructionist, was now regarded as a Powell protégé. Others among the federalizers began to honor Powell's memory in fine words, though they had quietly rejected his idea of leaving rivers in the hands of irrigation commonwealths. They celebrated his "vision" and "humanity" without acknowledging how radically different their scheme of federal control was from his decentralist thinking. He was, so they told it, their great bearded prophet crying in the wilderness; they were the more practical men who came along later to adjust his methods and realize his vision.

Ironically, their own scheme of centralized reclamation quickly proved to be even more hopelessly unrealistic, expensive, unworkable, and naive than his. Within eight years it was in such straits that a loan from Congress had to be secured. During the first two-and-a-half decades following its signing into law, the program lurched along under four successive directors and went through one congressional revision after another. By 1930, it was so manifest a failure that, had there not been powerful groups and strong cultural imperatives supporting it, federal reclamation would have died an ignominious death. The practical men who created and promoted it—politicians, lawyers, engineers, railroad executives, and the like—placed the blame for failure on this element or that, on anything but their own shortsightedness. A few washed their hands of the whole affair. Others, the most practical men of all by the standards of bureaucratic survival, worked to keep the program alive until a new justification for its existence was found under the New Deal.

Although there were many problems that plagued federalized irrigation, the central reason for the failure was a yawning gap between economic and technological ambitions on the one hand and social vision and understanding on the other. That had been Powell's weakness too, but at least he had a fairly clear idea of the society he wanted to see emerge in the West. The federalizers did not. Nor did they have any evidence in hand on how many Americans were in fact ready to take up residence on the new irrigation projects, or how well prepared those people were for the venture. More serious yet, when they pushed their program through in 1902, they had only the vaguest notion of what kind of communities would be likely to emerge from it. They were as unconcerned as the British in India about the social impact of advanced hydraulic engineering. Hence, the subsequent history of the Newlands Act confronted Americans with at least three consequences that they were for a long time unprepared to grasp or to handle: those who could reap the benefits were a much smaller number than anyone had supposed; they had to be organized into tight hierarchical and corporate entities which violated traditional rural culture; and the bureaucracy administering the program had to become adept at social as well as environmental engineering. There was, in other words, an unforeseen price to pay for the national conquest of the arid lands. If any of the practical men did suspect it, they did not mind the price. They, after all, were not the ones who would have to do the paying.

Three weeks after the act passed, the Secretary of the Interior set up within the Geological Survey a new division called the Reclamation Service. Frederick Newell moved over from hydrographical investigation to take charge. In 1907, the division became an independent agency, and in 1923 it was renamed the Bureau of Reclamation and put under a commissioner, who presided over a subordinate staff of engineers, project managers, and laboratory technicians.[1] From an initial staff of two-hundred-odd persons it grew to number thousands and become the largest bureaucracy ever assembled in irrigation history, though not the most powerful. In its first few embryonic years, when thanks to Congressman Newlands's efforts it was free to use the money from western land sales as it saw fit, the Service was a power unto itself. Later, when it began to live off yearly appropriations instead, that budgetary freedom was more circumscribed, though the Service maintained, and in some ways augmented, its clout through increasing control of expertise. As the Service enlarged its reach, other, nonfederal employment opportunities for irrigation experts diminished, eventually giving the federal reclamation bureaucracy a position of technical hegemony in western water development.

For the fiscal year ending on 30 June 1902, income from western public-land sales amounted to $4,585,521, a paltry sum for watering an empire.[2] That year and for several years thereafter, the Service was obliged to spend half the money on the states with the largest sales of public lands, including Oregon, Washington, North Dakota, and Oklahoma, although irrigation was needed most in exceptionally arid states like Nevada and Arizona. The first project selected was along the Truckee and Carson rivers in Congressman Newlands's backyard. Others authorized in the first three years included Salt River and Yuma in Arizona; North Platte in Nebraska-Wyoming; Shoshone in Wyoming, where Buffalo Bill Cody had turned farm-and-water salesman; Milk River, Huntley, and the Lower Yellowstone projects in Montana; Belle Fourche, north of Deadwood, South Dakota; Payette-Boise River in Idaho, the aborted project of Arthur Foote; the Yakima and Okanagan valleys in Washington; Klamath and Umatilla in Oregon; the valley of the Strawberry in central Utah; Uncompahgre (the incomparable valley with the unpronounceable name, President Taft called it) in Colorado; and the Rio Grande in southern New Mexico. Too many projects for the available money, certainly too many to do well, and in several cases projects that had been the despair of private developers. The cheap, easy, high-return sites had long since been skimmed off. Now, the frequent question was whether the Service could make orange groves and alfalfa fields out of lemons.

The original intent behind the 1902 act had been that the federal government would mainly concentrate its reclamation efforts on the public domain. After a site had been selected, homesteaders would file on their free claims and reside on them for the standard five years required to get title, while enjoying the water gurgling in ditches through their fields. It did not work that way at all. The appearance of Service engineers and a construction crew in an area touched off, particularly in the early years, a frenzied rush of speculators. They grabbed up the free homesteads, intending not to settle there but to sell them a few years later, whenever the water arrived, at a stiff price to latecomers. Those who had to pay the inflated price were heavily in debt from the beginning. Even more unexpected was how much reclamation was done on the private, not the public, domain. By 1910 there were thirty projects in the works, and some of them had not a single acre of public land. Altogether, they included 1,063,111 acres of federal domain, 136,815 acres belonging to the states, and 1,402,702 acres of private property.[3] By and large, federalization worked to enrich speculators and enhance the holdings of established owners, not to furnish inexpensive new homes for homeless folk from the overcrowded cities.

A striking instance of the tendency to develop existing private property was the largest and most spectacular of the early Service undertakings, the Salt River project surrounding the town of Phoenix, Arizona. From the time Jack Swilling of the Texas Rangers began irrigating from the river in 1867, the valley had laid out fourteen canals, some of them following the traces of the ancient Hohokam system. Then the nineties drought threw the farmers into violent feuding and court battles. In a fearful meeting at the Grand Opera House, they resolved to appeal for outside help, and John Wesley Powell's nephew, Arthur Powell Davis, a Geological Survey engineer, agreed to locate some prospects for capturing more water and preventing bloodshed. Then George Maxwell, fresh from his triumph as a Washington lobbyist, came out in 1902 and convinced the warring parties to invite the Reclamation Service to reorganize and develop the valley. There was not a single acre of public domain there, but the Service, eager for success, assumed command.[4]

Some sixty miles east of Phoenix, the federal engineers found a wild, rugged gorge where they could construct a gigantic storage dam. Work began in 1905, using local rock to raise a masonry wall curving upstream against the river's current. Surmounted by stone turrets with gothic windows, the dam, named in honor of Theodore Roosevelt, had the dark, grave elegance of a medieval fortress. But the workers who erected it were unmistakably southwestern Americans: a crew of Apaches, not twenty years removed from Geronimo's warrior bands, with a scattering of local Hispanics and of Anglo hoboes recruited from farms and freight cars. When finished in 1911, Roosevelt Dam was the highest in the world, standing 280 feet above bedrock. A 16-foot-wide road for automobile traffic crossed it, and enough water lapped up behind it to cover 1.4 million acres of land a foot deep. Three hundred thousand cubic yards of rock went into its arched wall, 3 million feet of lumber were chopped out of the surrounding forests for construction use. To generate the enormous quantity of electricity required to move the stone into place, the engineers forced the river to turn a turbine, and when the dam was complete, they had energy to sell and help pay off the $10.5 million cost of the project. Though a novice organization, the Service astounded the world with its ingenuity, resourcefulness, mastery over nature, and grace of design. Roosevelt Dam soothed the hostilities of the valley, and as an added bonus, Phoenix began to hum —a desert metropolis in the making. When the construction was over, the Apaches, Mexicans, and hoboes went elsewhere looking for jobs. And the Salt River valley farmlands, now with an ample, assured supply of water and worth far more on the market than before, remained in the same old hands.[5]

Remember that by the terms of the National Reclamation Act, no farm family was to be allowed water for more than 160 acres, whether the land had been privately or publicly owned before project status. That provision was, from the beginning, never to be rigorously enforced by the Service in the Salt River valley. Indeed, as late as 1946, almost half a century after its authorization, the project still had an entrenched group of noncomplying owners—134 of them by government accounting, farming 30,720 acres, or 12.5 percent of all irrigated land in the project area. Even those numbers were deceptively low. The Bureau of Reclamation was calculating by its own self-defined standard, for it had decided in a 1916 departmental ruling to reinterpret the act's language to allow 160 acres *each* for a husband and a wife—320 acres for a married couple. That generous ruling could benefit only a small, privileged minority of farmers. Small-scale agriculture was the common pattern in the valley, in 1946 as it had been a half-century earlier. Using the Department of Interior's definition of the word, there were 19,136 "ownerships" (out of 19,782) that were under 80 acres. That pattern owed nothing to federalization and survived in spite of it.[6]

The laxity in acreage-limitation enforcement, which might have made more land available for the landless, contrasted starkly with official public pronouncements. In 1905, agency head Newell told delegates at the National Irrigation Congress in Portland, Oregon, that the federal program was set up to make homes, not simply irrigate the wasteland. To make available more home sites, large landowners seeking water would have to sell off their excess property, or they would be left out. "Not one dollar will be invested," he warned, "until the Government has a guarantee that these large farms will ultimately be put into the hands of small owners, who will live upon and cultivate them." Bitter complaints were hurled at him from some in the audience. An Oregon old-timer protested the "enforced sale of your private rights, your private property"; a Californian retorted that he and his neighbors would never consent to have their lands liquidated by federal order, even if it meant no federal project for them. The trim and dapper Newell refused to give way to their anger. If you don't want to comply, he told them in tough, forthright words, the Service will go else-where to people who want to cooperate. The money is limited, and there are many worthy projects to spend it on.[7]

That was the government's voice, cool and professional, firm and exact, on the public platform. But along the Salt River and elsewhere the Service's actions belied its words. So sporadic was acreage-limitation enforcement generally that a 1916 review board concluded it "closely verges on fraud."[8] What kind of rural society, then, did the federal bureaucrats and engineers really want to see emerge in the West? Was it one in which concentrated ownership was broken up, as Newell had promised, and the land consis-tently put into the hands of small farmers? Or was it one in which advanced water development would be allowed to enhance the wealth and power of an existing elite? Salt River strongly suggested that the Reclamation Ser-vice would devote its very best efforts to building magnificent dams, more often than not in areas of established private landownership, and that those technical triumphs would not be matched by equally bold, strenuous, heroic efforts at distributing the benefits to America's have-nots.

In the Service's defense, it must be said that the eager hordes of landless Americans climbing into their wagons and heading West to irrigation pro-jects never materialized. And if far fewer prospective settlers were showing up on the free public lands than anyone had predicted, who was there then to pay $100 an acre and up to buy the excess acres on a Salt River valley farm? The absence of substantial demand, even for free land, was a problem that became increasingly serious. But the vision of long lines of families escaping from urban America or the slums of Europe along the old Oregon or Santa Fe Trail continued, in the face of changed circumstances, to appeal to diehards. Commander Frederick Booth Tucker of the Salvation Army insisted that "there are millions of [poor Americans] prepared to move at a few hours' notice from all quarters of this and other lands. . . . The talk about their unwillingness to leave the cities or go back to the land is pure, undiluted moonshine."[9] What was needed, he and men like William Smythe argued, was a program of financial assistance to get the slum dwellers relocated. Nothing of that sort was ever done, and the dreary experience of the handful who did resettle on a reclamation farm should have persuaded the Tuckers and Smythes of the impracticality, and the inhumanity, of their solution for poverty.

The families that came out to an undeveloped irrigation project on the harsh alkaline flats of Nevada or the cold, windswept northern plains of Montana had as hard a life as any farmers have faced in twentieth-century America. In many ways, their lot was also harder, if simply by contrast with what was then available to them elsewhere, than that of men and women on an earlier frontier. Pioneers in the East and Midwest had had acorns for their pigs, free wood for their cabins, wild game to supplement their diet, adequate rain to raise a quick crop of corn and wheat. They brought with them the folk skills to manage their environment successfully without outside help. In contrast, reclamation pioneers went through an ordeal of severe deprivation and sometimes galling dependence. Edward Gillette, state treasurer of Wyoming, pointed out: "Conditions are such on most of our reclamation projects that only a foreigner with a large family, used to the plainest living and disregarding the education of his children, can be successful." Even an enthusiastic supporter of the program like Thomas Means, who was resident manager of the Truckee-Carson project, had to admit there was a large gap between visions and realities, though he blamed the visions on settlers themselves rather than on the western promoters who had done much to oversell irrigation.

> The man in the gloomy back office in Chicago, who reads of the sunshine and freedom of the West, where a man can wear overalls and a flannel shirt and yet be respected, often overlooks the fact that he will have to wield the business end of a pitchfork in the hot sun, instead of a pen beneath the cheerful buzz of an electric fan. He thinks of the cool shade of a grape arbor and has an idea that, by sitting on the back porch, he can pull a string which will lift a gate and irrigate the back lot. When he gets into the real practice of irrigation, and his ditch breaks down and drowns half his crop and the other half dries up before the ditch is fixed, and his whole year's work is gone; or when, in the middle of a hot afternoon, the blinding sweat is pouring over his face as he pitches a few more tons of hay on the wagon, he thinks of that Chicago office with the electric fan as one of the most attractive places, and it is no wonder he becomes a bit discouraged.

In contrast to the established large farmer along the Salt River, for whom federal water was a windfall, those settlers who came to live on the raw public-domain projects typically went through hell.[10]

The extreme rigors of work and weather were bad enough, but then the settler also had to put up with the cost overruns, the confusion, the insistent demands, and the insensitivities of the reclamation bureaucracy. Making the desert blossom was a slower and far more expensive process than anyone in Washington, including representatives from arid states, had imagined. Ten years was the specified repayment period for federal projects. Not one project ever met those terms. The reasons were complicated and numerous, but all of them came down to the simple fact that irrigated agriculture, as the government tried to carry it out, was not an economical proposition. Consider again those hydraulic marvels the Reclamation Service fashioned: Roosevelt Dam on the Salt River, the even higher Arrowrock Dam on the Boise, massive Elephant Butte Dam spanning the Rio Grande, the tunnel drilled through Colorado granite and shale to divert the Gunnison River into the Uncompahgre Valley.[11] Men sweated and died to build them; others then had to sweat and worry to pay for them. Under the federal irrigation program, the cost of the engineering jumped from $9 per acre watered (pre-1900) to $30 (1900–1910), then to $50 (by 1915) and $125 (by 1925). Settlers entered the Payette-Boise project on the understanding that their cost would be $25 an acre. When the Service finished construction, it announced that the cost had gone up to $80. Arrowrock Dam, which had not been part of the first estimate, was the main cause of the inflation. Settlers, to be sure, wanted it and needed it, but they had no idea how much it would cost them, and having no means when it was done to pay for it, feeling put upon and misled, they filed suit against the Service to reduce their burdens. Adding to the embarrassment was the delay in development on many projects. Even when demand for land had been high, bringing a project to full utilization took at least twenty years. The new federal schemes, plagued by low demand, would after fifty years, an agricultural economist predicted, still not be watering more than 80 percent of their lands. Worse yet, in the allotted repayment period they could expect to raise crops, and an income, on only 50 percent of project land. The poorest farmers, those without capital to tide them over, were the first to lose heart and sell out to someone better fixed for waiting.[12]

So, in a highly charged, acrimonious atmosphere, there began a series of adjustments and legislative amendments to the 1902 act. In 1910, Congress loaned the Reclamation Fund $20 million to speed up construction and get water to the settlers. The next year it passed the Warren Act, which allowed the Service, where it had a surplus of water and a shortage of users, to sell project water to outside farmers to supplement their supplies. Not good enough, said the beleaguered projects; we must have easier terms of repayment. Director Newell's response to that demand was swift and unyielding. He accused them of trying to renege on a solemn agreement signed with the Service. The settlers countered that Newell and his engineers had been wasteful and unbusinesslike in fulfilling their part of the contract. A critic from the Carlsbad, New Mexico project angrily declared,

"There is no limit to the liability of the settler for the work of absolutely irresponsible engineers." His neighbors, he reported, had a saying, "To settlers under a Government project all is lost but a sense of humor." Actually, he had little humor left, denouncing Newell as he did in the most vehement terms, pointing out how much the Service had spent and how little land had been reclaimed, and ending with a hard right to the jaw:

> This is the most autocratic and irresponsible department
> of our Government, wielding absolute authority over the
> entire personal fortunes of thousands of free citizens of
> these United States, and doing it by means of their money,
> with personal accountability to no one.[13]

This critic must have been profoundly gratified when Newell was dismissed in 1914 and his job given to his second-in-command, Arthur Powell Davis.

Before his firing, Frederick Haynes Newell had been one of the most prominent engineers of his day and one of the first of the new breed of engineer-administrators in government. He represented, as Edwin Layton, Jr. has written, a group of professionals who "had little faith in democracy as a social remedy . . . they expected society to be saved by a technical elite."[14] In Newell's mind, and in that of his defenders, the issue behind the project turmoil was whether selfish, incompetent settlers should be allowed to spoil, through repudiation of their debts, a noble work begun by noble experts in the name of national welfare. Among the defenders of the experts was the southwestern publicist George Wharton James, who discerned in the Reclamation engineers "a great heart of pulsating brother-hood under the cold or grim exterior." Democracy, he cautioned, would be ill-served if disgruntled settlers persuaded Congress to begin intervening in the irrigation program, for disinterested planning would then give way before special-interest pleading, professional decision-making would be replaced by pork-barrel politics. But in the eyes of his critics, Newell was intent, not on the public good, but on his own self-aggrandizement. The magazine *Irrigation Age,* claiming to speak for ordinary farmers, was gra-tified by his departure, for he had created, the editor charged, a "powerful bureaucracy" after his own image, "cold-blooded, self-satisfied, with little or no sympathy for the settlers." If that were so, it was not clear how his individual departure would change matters much, nor how the problem could be avoided so long as westerners insisted on having the bureaucrat-engineers do a job for them.[15]

Shortly before Newell was retired to private life, Congress passed a settler relief bill known as the Extension Act of 1914. It gave the legislators, not the engineers, the authority to appropriate money from the Reclamation Fund. It doubled the repayment period to twenty years and set up an easier, graduated schedule of payments. It reaffirmed the policy of requiring owners of more than 160 acres to sell their excess before they could enjoy federal water—before even construction could begin—along with the policy of requiring residence on or near the land to be watered. And it gave the Secretary of the Interior the right to determine the selling price of that excess land to prevent windfall profits. Now we have enough, the settlers said, to make our plight bearable.

Momentarily the tumult ceased—that is, until the agricultural depression of the 1920s tipped the projects once more into insolvency. In the aftermath of World War One, commodity prices plunged downward, knocking the pins from under farmers across the nation. Federal-reclamation farmers suffered more than most, for they had the highest fixed costs. From 1919 to 1922, the annual crop value on project farms fell from $153 million to $84 million. By that latter date, four in ten project farmers were delinquent on their water-construction payments. As of 1923, only 11 percent of the $143 million spent on federal irrigation had been repaid.[16] This time the failure of federalization to be a financial success could not be blamed simply on Newell and his lack of sympathy. The drive to reach that promised land of western empire was faltering badly and had to be reconsidered in the light of twenty years' experience. Was there truly a national need to conquer the desert? Why, even before the agricultural depression, had there been so many economic difficulties? What kind of rural society was appearing in the federalized West? Could new leadership achieve better results? Or was it time to abandon the effort?

The reassessment lasted through the entire decade of the twenties. It revealed, among other things, that two decades of expensive water engineering had produced only a small dribble of new crops and homes. No more than 1.2 million acres were being irrigated on federal projects in 1923, out of a total of nearly 20 million acres irrigated in the West. By far and away the greatest growth in irrigation was due to private investment, which had rebounded as a source of capital. Taken together the federal projects counted 34,276 farms and 131,194 people, but two-thirds of those farms predated the government's program. No one had ever inquired into precisely how many of the bona fide new farmers had truly been unemployed and homeless people, desperate for a new start and raging against the established order, nor whether they had been successfully transformed into pacified, law-abiding, prosperous property owners.

The question of national need had another dimension than alleviating poverty. Was western food and fiber really indispensable? The crops raised on the projects largely duplicated, contrary to all protestations to the contrary, those raised in other, nonirrigated regions. Three out of four acres were planted to alfalfa, wheat, cotton, and pasture grasses. That was true of western irrigation generally and explains why, except for the minority with oranges or lettuce, farmers in the region were poor by national standards. They were trying to sell products that could be produced more cheaply elsewhere. According to a Department of Agriculture study carried out in the prosperous year of 1917, the average yearly income among the Corn Belt farms of Illinois was $870, and in Chester County, Pennsylvania, it was $789; but on irrigated farms in the Salt Lake Valley of Utah it was only $417. And the average federal farmer, with far more costly water than in the Utah valley, was worse off yet, living not much better than a southern sharecropper. This, then, was the reality of empire: a family fighting to hold on to a forty-acre place in the sun, grubbing out sagebrush and cactus to raise a redundant crop like wheat, stuffing rags into the cracks to stop the winter wind moaning through a bare-board shack, all for so little income, so uncertain a future.[17]

Uncontrolled speculation made the picture even darker, for it was turning the public lands into a social wasteland. Despite the residency requirement in the law, project after project was heavily populated by tenant farmers while landowners lived far off. At Belle Fourche in South Dakota, after a decade and a half of development, only 27 percent of the 965 farms had owner-residents (the majority had no occupants at all). On another project only 31 percent of the land had owner-residents. A common pattern was for one owner to rent a half-dozen of his neighbors' farms and plant them to wheat, while they kept their jobs in some city. Or a speculator, while waiting for the land's market value to rise, would rent it temporarily to some ne'er-do-well wandering through, seeking a little bread money. Frederick Newell, looking on in disgruntled retirement, argued that "real farmers" were not often being helped by federal reclamation. Actors, artists, teachers, undertakers, and railroad workers had all claimed an irrigated homestead. Now they were saying to the Bureau of Reclamation, "For Heaven's sake, give us less advice, less talk, but get us more and better tenants."[18]

Born out of vague but intense ambitions to see the West become a strong new arm for the nation, federalization had unraveled steadily into social disaster and disgrace. To determine what should be done to restore the program's credibility, President Calvin Coolidge appointed a "fact finders'" group, the elite Committee of Special Advisors. It included the former governor of Arizona, a former Secretary of the Interior, a Denver water lawyer, the president of the American Farm Bureau, the Mormon irrigation scientist and college president John Widtsoe, and the ubiquitous Elwood Mead. Men of that stripe were not about to call for repudiation of the 1902 program. "These projects," their report concluded, "have helped in the conquest, for human good, of the more difficult places of our country and thereby have shown the great value of the arid and semiarid region, as a part of the domain, which in the providence of God has been given to our country." A tediously long list of sixty-six recommendations followed those stirring words, but their common theme was that "construction of irrigation works would of itself" not create "irrigated agriculture." Environmental engineering was merely the first step. Then must come a process of fitting rural people to the apparatus: selecting settlers on the basis of capital, skill, and teachability; showing them how to farm in the new, intensive, regimented way; reorganizing them into a competent local managerial agency; furnishing them aid and direction at every point. Men and women simply had to be made capable of living up to the engineering. Otherwise, dams like Roosevelt, Arrowrock, and Pathfinder would never deliver their full promise.[19]

For reclamation farmers, the economic incentive to participate in this process of rural redesign was increased substantially when Congress, heeding the Special Advisors' urging, extended the repayment period to forty years. No interest was to be charged over that entire period. It was, in effect, a subsidy, one of the most generous ever given by the federal government, four times larger than the one in the original Newlands Act. Over in the Department of Agriculture, eyebrows arched and tongues began to clack. Ray Teele, one of that department's chief economists, rued the effect the subsidy would have on his campaign to discourage farm production in the country. Encouraging irrigation, he thought, was exactly what the nation did not need to do any longer. The subsidy, he went on, was given to one privileged acre in 765 nationally. Though many irrigators may have needed some help to survive, others were profiteering on government largesse. For example, on the Rio Grande project, farmers had not been required to make their first payment until fourteen years after the water arrived. Their total cost was set at $90 an acre, but with the long free period and the no-interest feature, Teele calculated they were collecting a subsidy worth $465 per acre. For farmers with 20 or 40 acres in less lucrative Montana, that amount might have been justified, but for farmers in warmer climates like New Mexico, and for farmers hanging on to more than their allotted 160 acres, the subsidy was less easy to justify. The USDA examined the Salt River project and discovered it had been enjoying a subsidy of $276 an acre. A man with over a thousand acres there, and there were a few such, was growing rich at the expense of middling and poor farmers across the country whose taxes were being used to pay interest on western irrigation construction. Those examples were calculated for the twenty-year payment plan. Now, with the period doubled, the subsidy in all cases had become substantial, and in some cases had become princely. Newell, now convinced that the program he had once administered had outlived its usefulness, decried the "enthusiasm" and "sentimentality" behind western irrigation, for it was concealing the fact that money was unjustly and unnecessarily being "deftly taken from the pockets" of American taxpayers.[20]

Another inducement offered was more local control. The enforcement of the excess-land requirement, having been a general failure in the Bureau of Reclamation's hands, was, according to the 1926 legislation, to be turned over to the projects themselves. In fact, the Bureau was henceforth to devolve several of its responsibilities onto local organizations, especially the collecting of payments, which had become a nightmare in public relations. But first, before local control could become acceptable to the government, there had to be the right kind of local organizations in place. From its beginning, federalization had had the effect of consolidating loose clusters of rural people under single, overarching authorities. In the Salt River valley again, farmers had been forced into forming a broad water-users' association to get federal investment. Courtland Smith and Harland Padfield describe the process of local reorganization that went on there as the fitting of social institutions to the demands of water-resource development, creating what they call a "waterspace," which is a unified technological and social unit. Under federal pressure, the "space" reached its mature form along the Salt by the late 1920s and has remained constant ever since.[21] Put another way, the impact of federal influence accelerated a process of local incorporation. A large agency like the Bureau was understandably not eager to work with a scattering of individualistic farmers. Its natural inclination was to refashion the community for instrumental effectiveness, encouraging the formation of a local bureaucracy. It would be headed by a few local men to carry on negotiations with the experts, and its jurisdiction would cover as large an area as possible. The Bureau's label for this agency was "a public corporation". In some places it was called an irrigation district, in others a water-users' association.[22]

It has not always been clear what the ideal of local autonomy and local control has meant to its twentieth-century American advocates. Do they want to see power distributed in small-scale, diffuse groups, infused by a communitarian spirit, or do they want power collected into modern corporations, public or private, infused by a spirit of profit and enterprise? In the reevaluation of federal irrigation which went on in the 1920s, that ambiguity ran through much of the reform talk. It is time to end "federal paternalism," the Special Advisors declared. Western farmers ought to take command of their own projects, work out their own payment schemes, distribute the water as they like. Yet other recommendations ran precisely in the opposite direction, toward creating a more structured set of institutions that would mesh neatly with national agencies. Farmers need more supervision, it was said. They must be transformed into modern organization men, able to manage the advanced hydraulic technology on which they depend, able to compete in the world marketplace. The ambivalence may have been more apparent than real. It soon became clear that local control was to be allowed only so long as it was the right kind. And that right kind of local control was, in its origin and outlook, not really local at all.

The man who most fully articulated the new emphasis on social engineering and "businesslike" local control was Elwood Mead. In 1924, President Calvin Coolidge named him commissioner of the Bureau of Reclamation, a position he would occupy until his death in 1936 at the age of seventy-eight. Behind his round, cherubic visage there worked the mind of a consummate survivor, just the sort of mind the Bureau needed if it was to transform failure into success, a loss of purpose into a renewal of mission. Mead was an engineer by training and an irrigation administrator with more than thirty years of experience. He had stood apart from the rush to federalization, supporting it to a point, but anxious to maintain state control. Jealous of Newell's reign over the new federal agency, he became a critic from his position as head of the rival Department of Agriculture's Office of Irrigation Investigations. Then, seeing little future for himself in the Washington reclamation establishment, he left for California and Australia. Yet here he was again in Washington in 1924, popping up to assume command at last, leading the Bureau through its crisis and into a new age of ambitiousness. Under his direction, the agency would undertake and finish its single most heroic engineering feat, the building of Hoover Dam on the Colorado River. It would then go on to tackle the remaking of the major river systems of the West in their entirety under a program of comprehensive, multipurpose planning, underwritten by hydroelectricity revenues. Ideologically, Mead would slide glibly from Coolidge's reactionary administration over to Franklin Delano Roosevelt's New Deal. He would acquire a not altogether deserved reputation among historians as a man of humanitarian values and progressive vision.[23] A chameleon changing his coloration to fit the changing times, an opportunist cultivating those with jobs to offer, and withal a matchless mirror of official reclamation thinking, reflecting all its ambiguities and contradictions, Elwood Mead had a greater influence than any other individual on the course of western hydraulic society.

Mead grew up on a farm in southern Indiana and hated the work it involved. As soon as he could, he left it behind. His first ambition was to become a professor teaching agriculture. Later, he set his sights at becoming a bureaucrat administering agricultural policy. America, he believed throughout his life, needed the blessings of rural life, needed as many people as possible down on the farm, working hard and developing a high moral character. A large, thriving rural order would prevent the division of the nation into warring classes and would ensure the future of a democracy where citizens were neither capitalists nor laborers but amalgams of both. However, the old agrarian ideal, if it were to be capable of saving democracy, had to be updated. Irrigation became for Mead the basis of that newfangled agrarianism. It would make possible the reconstruction of the distasteful, unattractive farm life he had personally rejected, transforming it into something competitive, scientific, and profitable. The mind of the farmer must be "organized to meet the business mind of the city." Irrigation was capable of that effect, and thereby of the regeneration of American society. So it became Mead's mission to make irrigation a social success and then stamp its mold on rural life everywhere.[24]

Mead's dream for the American West, as it was revealed in bits and pieces throughout his life, was essentially of a society composed of petty-bourgeois farmers. White farmers, it should be added, for Meade regarded Asians and Mexicans with undisguised distaste. Unfortunately, he discovered, farmers often did not share that bourgeois dream. Many were recalcitrant and had to be reeducated. His biographer tells the story of how Mead, as Wyoming state engineer, imperiously lectured farmers on filling out the forms he sent them neatly and carefully in ink, not pencil. Though a trivial matter, this demonstrates Mead's character perfectly. All his life he showed a "passion for orderliness": he loved efficiency, hated waste, insisted on rules.[25] Directing the flow of water in the desert satisfied him immensely. The farmers, however, would never behave quite so well as the water did, would never run in the ditches he had dug for them. Not seeing that he had their best interests at heart, they repeatedly broke the rules, refused to become organized, were unthrifty, and made foolish demands. Irrigation, Mead had hoped, would be a training ground for a new breed of farmers, but the debacle of the federal program in its first two decades demonstrated how much work with rural folk remained to be done.

Before assuming the commissionership, Mead had two administrative experiences that solidified his thinking about irrigation settlement and the formation of a new social order. From 1907 to 1915, he was director of the Victoria State Rivers and Water Commission in Australia, which was engaged in colonizing the outback. Intensely desirous of getting immigrants from Europe to develop its agriculture, the Victoria government was willing to go to great lengths to make farming easy and appealing. Mead sold the legislators on the idea of buying large estates and subdividing them into small irrigated farms, with the land to be cleared, graded, watered, and fenced at government expense and with low-interest, long-term loans and cash advances to be extended to the settlers. "Scientific colonization," he called it. Then Mead traveled to England, Scotland, Denmark, Italy, and other western nations to find settlers. While in those countries, he discovered that their governments had under way their own resettlement programs, enticing their farmers to stay at home. In Denmark, for instance, the government helped tenants buy the land they worked from their landlords, a policy to stop the drift of penniless rural folk into the city or to places like Australia. Mead was impressed by the more active role of government in Australia and Europe. Their collective approach and willingness to undertake community planning bespoke a sympathetic understanding of the needs and problems of poor farmers. America, he came home saying, was twenty-five years behind other advanced societies in expanding the responsibility of government to promote social welfare.[26]

What Denmark was doing, however, was very different from what Mead had tried to do in Australia and what he wanted to do in the United States. The Danes were redistributing land to people who had farmed it for generations but had never received the full product of their labor. But Australia and the United States were not really engaged in agrarian reform; they were primarily empire builders. The former activity aimed at enhancing the status and livelihood of the individual farmer, the latter, for the most part, at increasing the wealth and power of the country. That distinction explains why Mead's notion of reform did not send him back to his native Indiana to redistribute land there to poor white and black farmers. Rather, it was to be achieved indirectly through reclamation of the desert. Mead was a reformer, but he was also an expansionist. If forced to choose, he would put national economic development ahead of democratic self-determination. Just before leaving Australia, he told the Royal Commission on Closer Settlement that "the individual cannot be considered in a matter of national development. The individual must give way in the interest of the state."[27] That statement reveals as well as anything he ever said the nature of Mead's "reforms." In no sense was he seeking to free oppressed people from their oppressors. He was a reformer of the type who seeks to impose on nature and society his vision of what the world ought to be like. There was much benevolence in the man, and a strongly felt, if arms-length, agrarianism; but those qualities were mixed with, and subordinated to, a capacity for asserting authority when those he was aiding failed to do as they were told.

The second experience came on his return from Australia, when he was put in charge, from 1915 to 1924, of California's new Commission on Colonization and Rural Credits. Here he wanted to apply the Australian directed-settlement idea by buying fertile farmland and organizing irrigation colonies on it. With a small state appropriation, he purchased two sites, one at Durham in 1918 and another at Delhi in 1919, to launch his new America. Mead had in mind turning Durham into a showcase of small-scale dairy farming, while Delhi would be an exemplar of fruit raising. Both would be high-profit operations, capable of getting the most return from irrigation and demonstrating the social planning needed in irrigated farming. In its enabling act of 1917, the California legislature intended that the settlements would provide "employment and rural homes" for veterans who had fought in World War One. In actuality, veterans never amounted to more than half of the settlers. Indeed, the Settlement Board, out of desperation to get the lands peopled, ended up taking whomever they could get, including an African big-game hunter, a dressmaker, and a banker. As he had done in Australia, Mead undertook to subdivide the land into farms (28 acres was the average size at Delhi, 52 acres at Durham, with minuscule allotments for farm laborers) and ready it for production. He lent up to $3,000 to help settlers get started. With his resident superintendents and visiting professors from the University of California, he designed a total environment for them—houses, community halls, roads, fences, fields, crop types, water systems, drains, and a cooperative dairy on the Danish model. Government should become "a more effective business partner," Mead explained in justification of these measures; otherwise, the United States would pay for its "lack of expert direction in public affairs."[28]

For the first few years, the settlers worked hard and cooperated with Mead. Prepared budgets told them what kind of house they should want and whether or not they could afford a new car. "Left to decide matters for themselves," he wrote, "it is certain that some of the settlers would have made grave mistakes." But then it became steadily apparent that the experts had made a few mistakes too. The Delhi land they had bought at premium prices was mainly sand, unfit for orchards, land that nearby experienced farmers had shunned. In some places, there were windblown dunes on it. Water there rapidly soaked away, and soil nematodes flourished and killed the young trees. Like the federal reclamation projects, Delhi and Durham were plagued by poor agricultural planning, long delays in getting a crop harvested, and resultant high costs, which the settlers had to absorb.

When they asked Mead for relief, he refused it, calling them "anarchists" and threatening them with ouster if they did not behave. Then he left town on an expert mission to advise Zionist settlements in Palestine. The people in Delhi, angered by Mead's intransigence and neglect, broke into the community hall, cut a painting of him from its frame, and hung it in effigy above the road. "The celebrated Doctor [Mead] preaches," they complained, "but fails to practice [humanitarianism] here." One sixty-five-year-old man explained his anger thus: "My money is all gone and I have suffered a very substantial loss by attempting, in good faith, to prove the land to be adapted to the crops that I was assured it was adapted to, but was not, in truth and in fact, adapted to produce such crops." On his return, weary of the struggle to realize his dream, Mead resigned. The state appointed a temporary successor, eventually forgave most of the settlers' debts, and bowed out of the projects. Mead, undeterred by his failure, moved on to bigger and better things at the Bureau of Reclamation.[29]

As commissioner in Washington, Mead's agenda for reforming the Bureau's program followed the recommendations of the Special Advisors' report, most of which he wrote. He supported the more generous repayment schedule and subsidies. For a short while, he was chary with new projects, at least until the old ones were in better shape. He established selection panels in the West who interviewed prospective settlers and allowed into public-lands projects only those candidates with enough capital, experience, and moral fiber to be good risks. He installed supervisors in the field to watch how families spent their money and to show them how to farm in the proper way. The Durham superintendent and Mead's close friend, George Kreutzer, went along with him to Washington, where he became director of reclamation economics. With Mead, he believed in a program of "aided and directed settlement," where there would always be an adviser "with his hand on the settler's shoulder at all times. We have found," Kreutzer added, "where we have that kind of assistance it produces results."[30] The Bureau's hand on the shoulder would push irrigating farmers along the path to better business practices, more reliance on technical authorities, and more association with neighbors for marketplace clout. In other words, Mead and his associate introduced the idea of social engineering. Though it had failed in Delhi and Durham, it was supposed to save the federal program from dying a dismal death.

Once the advanced domination of western rivers made possible by federalization began, the inevitable next step was toward social engineering. A modern hydraulic society could not be constructed with the ragtags and "bobends" of an older rural order. A new kind of agricultural community was demanded, either one evolving quickly on its own or one designed and promoted by the experts. People and their agricultural institutions had to be reshaped to make the technology work efficiently: that was the lesson of the first two decades of national reclamation.

Unfortunately, social engineering was a bigger job than anyone in the 1920s, including Elwood Mead, quite knew how to handle. Mead was the best-prepared man of his time to undertake it, but throughout his tenure as commissioner, he could hardly claim a resounding success. In his favor, it must be said that he made a better pass at it than any of his predecessors had done or wanted to attempt, and the projects began to move ever so slowly toward prosperity, progressive business thinking, and cooperative association—toward his ideal of "organized industry." But that promise of florescence soon wilted. Shortly after Mead assumed command, the Great Depression commenced and knocked his reclamation reforms into a cocked hat. With the crash of the stock market in 1929, federal money dried up drastically and the Bureau of Reclamation, its hydraulic as well as its social engineering, became a popular target, especially in the East, for pruning if not elimination. Mead then had to abandon his planned-settlements idea and concentrate simply on bureaucratic survival, redefining the Bureau's mission as an agency of public works contributing to economic recovery.

As late as the 1930s, in short, federal reclamation had not really succeeded. It had merely survived. Its leaders and defenders had managed to ward off persistent attacks by those who found no economic need for it, and little economic rationality in it. In the course of seeking to shore the program up, the federalizers had discovered several inescapable truths. They had come to see that the average farmer, especially the poor struggling, marginal farmer, was the worst person to recruit for the new western society—unless, that is, he or she could be made over in Dr. Mead's school. The federalizers had come to understand that technology and society are not two separate spheres, but are interdependent and mutually transformative. They had to acknowledge that climbing up the federal rope would leave its mark on western society. Those reaching that upland of maximum irrigation expansion would be a different people from those who had occupied the lower plateau.

See all this the federalizers did, more or less clearly. Worry about it they did not. They were in the end not much abashed by the degree of social change, selectivity, and reeducation that was involved. If Roosevelt Dam was good, and no one really doubted that it was, then the social institutions and communities required to build and operate it must also be good. That underlying faith held firm despite all the settlers' trials and tragedies, all the Bureau's economic woes, all the questioning on how much water control was really needed in a nation with chronic overproduction and rural shrinkage. For federal reclamation, like the commercial and individual assaults on western rivers before it, answered to a deeper urge. It was compelled by an unrelenting American cultural imperative, one that could not be shaken by any amount of failure. John Widtsoe, who served with Mead on the Special Advisors Committee, put that imperative thus:

> The destiny of man is to possess the whole earth; and the destiny of the earth is to be subject to man. There can be no full conquest of the earth, and no real satisfaction to humanity, if large portions of the earth remain beyond his highest control. Only as all parts of the earth are developed according to the best existing knowledge, and brought under human control, can man be said to possess the earth. The United States of America . . . might accommodate its present population within its humid region, but it would not then be the great nation that it now is. By the vision of its statesmen and by its marvelous power of accomplishment it has made use of the country west of the hundredth meridian which lies under a low rainfall. The nation is now one country: not two strips of country, with a desert between. We possess our country. . . . And all the world will be helped by the conquest. It is an imperial problem which as it is solved will satisfy a world-wide need.[31]

Total power, total possession was the program. Nature in the West could not be allowed to defy it, nor could human cussedness.

FLORESCENCE

The Grapes of Wealth

*What America is to Europe, what Western America
is to Eastern, that California is to the other Western
States.*

—*James Bryce,* The American Commonwealth
(1888)

In a rainy country water falls abundantly on the just and the unjust, the poor and the rich, the little fellow and the big one, without discrimination or prejudice. No more than the air can it skew the structure of society, for it cannot be usefully hoarded in one place by a designing few. It eludes the clutches of would-be monopolizers, spills over cupped hands onto the fields of the lowliest sharecropper or peasant. There water does not work against democracy, egalitarianism, and freedom. That it is readily accessible to all does not, of course, guarantee that a people will be free, but it can help.

The political tradition of America, rooted in the rain-rich eastern states and in Europe, has tended to take water for granted in its thinking about the relation of resources to freedom and independence in the social order. Land, on the other hand, has been another matter. Experience taught early on that it could be easily bought and fenced off, could be transformed into private property and made a foundation of class and privilege. Tutored by the Old World's landed aristocracies, the Americans understood that potential well, and they collected land as fast as they could, determined to secure thereby a guarantee of status, independence, and power. So long as there was more land than there were accumulators, it seemed as though everyone in America could become an aristocrat. Then when the land began to run out, when there were fewer places left to go, Americans witnessed some of the consequences of resource scarcity for democracy.

Those lessons in land and power impressed men like Thomas Paine and Thomas Jefferson, and after them a succession of agrarian reformers: the Free-Soilers of the antebellum period, followed by men like Henry George and Horace Greeley, along with a sprinkling of Populists and New Dealers, tenant-farmer organizations and labor unions, all of them shaken together into a party of democratic protest by the emergence of New World land baronies. But though concerned about the social implications of concentrated landownership, they were far less prepared to see the antidemocratic potential in mastering aridity, in the intensive control and development of water where that vital resource was in limited supply. Their agrarianism, in fact, led them to an uncritical enthusiasm over the prospect of total water management. It could deliver more land into impoverished hands, and that was all they were ready to see and understand.

In a dry country, unlike a wet one, rain can be grasped and held. The hands that do the grasping are also powerful shaping hands, capable of doling out life and death, wealth and status. They may not personally own the resource they handle. Typically in arid places water is regarded as too precious and irreplaceable a part of nature to be left long in purely private hands. At some point in its development it usually comes under a public agency, which gains power through the exercise of technical expertise, that is, through the reservoirs, dams, siphons, and canals it lays out and maintains. Such an agency, emerging as a technical elite, grows more and more influential with each elaboration of water control, making itself ever more indispensable and authoritative. Its rule can be challenged, of course, but always it has a formidable defense in its command of special knowledge and in the people's awe of and dependence on that knowledge.

Designing a hydraulic system in a water-poor landscape thus makes the water experts a power to be reckoned with, just as erecting a fence does for the land accumulator. These strategies, however, are rather different routes to power. The fence requires for its maintenance little in the way of special knowledge, but much in the way of private money or fraud or muscle. It surrounds a piece of stable property that can be easily demarcated and held in perpetuity, protected by No Trespassing signs: those signs depend for their effectiveness on the strength of the institution of private property in the popular mind. Water, on the other hand, is a more mobile resource that must be collected and delivered to be of any real force.

Try though they did, westerners never quite succeeded in fencing in water as they did land, a failure that left them with a more complicated rural situation than the East's, more complicated than they realized for a long while. Westerners were caught between *two* structures of power, one symbolized by federal dams and ditches, the other by private fences and signs —two structures heading inevitably toward a confrontation. Would the men owning the fences win out in that rivalry, forcing the water technocrats to discriminate in their favor? Or would the wielders of expertise come to dominate the social order of the region, letting the water dribble out only to those people and classes it liked?

California was the major setting for that confrontation—California, and with time, Arizona. There, to a greater degree than in other parts of the

West, the men of the fence succeeded in making themselves a ruling class. They were the nation's vanguard of a rising agribusiness elite, "factory farmers" employing hundreds of thousands of laborers, marketing fruit, vegetables, and cotton to far-flung consumers, exercising immense influence over local and state politics. Only one essential element, and it was the most essential of all, eluded their control: they constantly had to have water, and plenty of it, to stay on top. And to get that water, they eventually came to need the men of the dam and ditch. By the 1930s, California had worked up the nation's biggest thirst. Thirsty men are desperate men, often willing to bargain away much of what they own to get a drink. Those who can fetch water for them are a threat as much as a savior. That fact was felt strongly by the private landowners of agricultural California, who had come to control the land in the southernmost valley of the state, Imperial, and farther north in the Great Central Valley. Their very success in transforming wastelands into marketable commodities left them increasingly vulnerable and dependent.

The principal threat to their undisputed dominion came from the rival elite of water-bearers, mainly the federal Bureau of Reclamation. Failing to make much progress elsewhere in recruiting inexperienced folk to live on its projects, facing cutbacks and even elimination by a depression-era Congress, the Bureau moved from the marginal outskirts to the highly profitable core of western agriculture, the California valleys. Indeed, it came running there, carrying water on both shoulders, eager to be of service. Then it slowed down and began to size up the situation, hinting as it did so that here was a new, unfamiliar power of bureaucracy and expertise waiting to be asserted. It was a power the men of the fence came to fear and fight against.

The rural ruling class also had to deal with a small, noisy pack of agrarian critics, notably writers like John Steinbeck and Carey McWilliams, who resented the private fences of agricultural capitalism and wanted them to come down. Not until very late in the day did they see how truly vulnerable was this western agribusiness, or wherein its vulnerability lay. Nor did the agrarian reformers see any danger to their democratic cause from the Bureau's army of experts. On the contrary, they looked on them with even less suspicion than the ruling class did. Though denounced as dangerous radicals, the agrarians were not radical enough to move beyond conventional thinking and to comprehend the western predicament for what it was: a struggle between two forms of wealth, symbolized by the land as accumulated capital and the water as accumulated expertise.

A PLACE NAMED
IMPERIAL

In the first few decades of the twentieth century, the command over rivers in the West could hardly be said to have commenced. Nowhere was that more apparent than along the Colorado. As late as sixty years after John Wesley Powell's explorations the great red dynamo still ran unchecked to the sea, a symbol of the wildness remaining in the region, of its freedom and adventure. *Río colorado*: the words continued year after year to speak of independence, danger, and mystery, of the earth's blood spilling into the sea. Even scientists resorted to animistic language to describe the river, referring often to its "viciousness," its "whims," and its capacity for "vengeance." Bringing such a superhuman force under control would be a very different and more demanding achievement than putting down Indians or plowing the prairies. It would take vast sums of capital instead of cavalry bullets, technological prowess instead of homesteader muscle, and complex social organization instead of family determination. The mastery of the awesome Colorado would be another form of winning the West, and in that winning an old West would be irretrievably lost.

The peculiar mystique of the Colorado River derived from its stupendous geological achievements, unmatched for scale anywhere in the nation. In part it came from the river's imposing length—a current running 1,440 miles from the Rocky Mountain divide to the Gulf of California, draining portions of seven states and a small section of Mexico, some 244,000 square miles in all. The amount of water the river carried over that course was not especially impressive—only 14 million acre-feet a year, a mere trickle compared to the Mississippi or Columbia. What made the Colorado seem so formidable was the gargantuan work it had done over its route and the energy, the violence, with which it continued to do that work. Eons ago it had had thrust in front of it a massive plateau of sandstone and shale, rising almost as fast as the river could cut it away. In its last thirteen million years of existence the Colorado had washed away more than a quadrillion tons of rock, sand, and gravel from that plateau, leaving behind the most spectacular canyons on earth. Deeper and deeper through the resistance it had wound its way, cutting meanders as much as a mile down, for hundreds upon hundreds of miles. All rivers are indefatigable workers, but this one had a fanatic's determination in its industry. It would accept no compromises, make no detours, in the pursuit of its end but would push on night and day until the plateau was gone, until there was no more work to be done and it had died of its own labors.[1]

Debouching from its multihued canyons, the Colorado carried in its lower reaches one of the heaviest silt loads of all the world's rivers. The suspended sediment floating past the site of Yuma, Arizona, amounted to 160 million tons a year, more than all the railroad cars ever made could carry. For months at a time the river would run low, a slack, sluggish ooze gulfward; but with the spring thawing of the mountain snowpack or with a torrential summer storm, the sediment-carrying river would become a chaotic avalanche. Entire boulders would tumble along in the churning current. Then the river, overloaded with rock, dirt, and water, would slop over its banks onto the surrounding floodplain and lay down some of its burden. The deeper the river sawed into that plateau upstream, the higher its bed rose above the lowlands downstream. Eventually the lower Colorado ran along a self-made ridge, well above the desert floor. In its struggle for equilibrium, tearing down here to build up there, the river was setting the terms for its conquest. All of it would have to be mastered, or none of it could be.

When it encountered the still, absorbent ocean, the river at last had to stop moving. At that point, as though losing its fanatical determination in a confrontation with a force it could not budge, it broke down into a delta of dozens of interlacing waterways, now following this channel, now that one. Gradually the Colorado's delta broadened into a fanlike plug, cutting off one end of the sea. The water in that cutoff end, now forming an inland saltwater lake, eventually evaporated, leaving behind an empty bowl, the Salton Sink. Now and then the river would become decisive again, suddenly cutting through its rim and plunging down into that bowl, filling it anew with silt and water.[2] But always the plunge over the edge was a temporary aberration; silt would soon close the cut, the river would return to its old, shifting, uncertain channels, and the lake would dry up once more in the intense, blistering heat of the Southwest. All that kept the river high on its ridge and delta, heading toward the sea instead of veering off into the sink, were soft earthen banks fringed with arrowweed, mesquite, screw bean, willow, hemp, and wild cane. In most seasons that vegetation was enough to restrain the western dynamo.

Even before Powell's canyon trips there were American entrepreneurs who thought this immense, complex Colorado phenomenon could be made to flow handily into their pockets as cash. A New Orleans physician, Oliver Wozencraft, on his way to the Sierra gold fields, was the first to see the possibilities. He came close to persuading Congress to hand over to him, free of charge, the entire dry sink, a half-million acres of the Colorado

Desert, and to let him irrigate it with the river.[3] In 1891, John Beatty took the dream over, forming the Colorado Irrigation Company and hiring Charles Rockwood as his engineer to make it work. Reorganized a few years later as the Colorado Development Company, under Rockwood's direction, the scheme continued toward realization. Rockwood took on a couple of associates to help him with the project. One of them was a sharp, avaricious operator from the Kern County Land Company, Anthony Heber, and the other was an entrepreneurial genius, George Chaffey, who had made an international reputation for himself in irrigation in the Los Angeles basin and on the Murray River of Australia. It was Chaffey who showed them how to get the water to run their way. He made a cut in the riverbank at Pilot Knob across from Yuma and led the current through it and into Mexico, where an old river channel, the Alamo, could be utilized to bring the water in a loop back across the border and into the sink. It was also Chaffey who, following a local banker's golden flash of inspiration, renamed the desolate, furnacelike sink the "Imperial Valley."[4] In May 1901, these three bold men diverted their first water into what they hoped would become one of the richest agricultural empires yet seen in the West. Time would prove them right, though ironically none of them anticipated how little money they would personally make out of their achievement. Nor did any of them have a remotely adequate idea of the social force, the organization and capital, needed to tame the canyon-gnawing Colorado.

In January 1901, even before the water arrived, the first settlers appeared, all of them immigrants from the Salt River valley in Arizona. Within three years there were 7,000 people in the renamed sink, many of them living on Desert Land Act tracts, and they were scrambling madly to get more of the land into their hands.[5] Eager developers were throwing together the new boom towns of Calexico, Brawley, El Centro, and Holtville, and laying railroad tracks to them to ship the irrigated produce to market. Imperial Valley was a brilliant, overnight success, or so it seemed. Then the implications in what had been so boldly attempted began to come plain. An empire was not to be so easily won from the desert and the river.

Each new acre of land brought under cultivation meant that more water was needed from the river, and, in turn, more Colorado water meant more silt to deal with. It was the responsibility of Rockwood and the company to remove that heavy sediment before it clogged the channels and ditches, stopping the flow and endangering the farmers' crops. By late summer 1904, the company was losing the game. Its main canal was fast plugging up over a four-mile stretch from the river's intake point. Chief Engineer Rockwood, in a desperate gamble to gain the upper hand, decided to make a new notch in the bank downstream from the old clogged one, across the border in Mexican territory. Before he could get approval from the government in Mexico City on the design of a controlling gate, the Colorado went on a rampage. During the first half of 1905, flood followed flood, until the last one found its way into Rockwood's unguarded cut. Quickly the entire river changed its course, forsaking its delta path to the gulf, racing over the rim and down the side of the bowl into the sink below. By mid-June 90,000 cubic feet of water were pouring every second into the new agricultural settlement. Imperial Valley was once again on its way to becoming a lake, not a farm, threatening to drown the ambitions of the entrepreneurs and those who had trusted them in their miscalculations.[6]

Putting the Colorado back on its on its high road to the sea and keeping it up there, letting down into the sink only the water the farmers needed, it was now apparent, was a big job, one requiring bigger men than Rockwood and his company. Unable to stop the flooding on their own, they appealed for aid to E. H. Harriman, the New York-based railroad king and one of the wealthiest capitalists in America. Harriman had acquired the old Octopus, the Southern Pacific Railroad (adding it to his interest in the Union Pacific and almost every major line around the country), and thus he had a clear stake in the valley's future. His price for helping save Imperial, however, was steep: he would make the river behave only if he could oversee the management of the Colorado Development Company. Once his terms had been accepted, and Rockwood and Heber had no real choice but to accept them, Harriman began to mobilize his vast corporate machinery. Straightaway he sent in one of his crack engineers, H. T. Cory, an erstwhile college professor, to supervise the battle. Over the next year and a half, as the entire nation looked on, Cory fought the Colorado with a desperate tenacity. Though bankrolled with $3 million of Harriman's capital and commanding the combined labor of six local Indian tribes, he lost to the river again and again. Finally, in February 1907, his army succeeded in filling the hole in the soft bank with enough rock, brought in by an endless chain of traincars from distant quarries, to stop the flooding. Imperial was saved at last, though meanwhile the river had washed four times more earth down into the sink than had been excavated for the Panama Canal, had wiped out thousands of acres of farmland, and had sent enough water surging through to create the Salton Sea, a new desert lake fifty miles long and fifteen wide.[7]

The rescue of Imperial Valley was as dramatic a story as any in the history of the West, and it brought writers and film-makers running excitedly. In 1911, the best-selling writer Harold Bell Wright published a maudlin account of the salvation, *The Winning of Barbara Worth*. It was followed three years later by Ednah Aiken's *The River*, and in 1926 by the silent-film classic, *The Winning of Barbara Worth*, directed by Henry King and starring Ronald Colman, Vilma Banky, and, in his first screen role, Gary Cooper. The common theme of these popular entertainments was how heroic private enterprise had triumphed over treacherous nature. In Wright's view, which was representative of the lot, the saga of Imperial Valley demonstrated that the entrepreneurial Americans were the master race come at last to command the desert.

> The forgotten land held its wealth until Time should make the giants that could take it. . . . The kingdoms of earth, air and water yielded up their wealth as men grew strong to take it; the elements bowed their necks to his yoke, to fetch and carry for him as he grew wise to order; the wilderness fled, the mountains laid bare their hearts, the waste places paid tribute as he grew brave to command.

"They were the advance force of a mighty army," Wright declared, "ordered by Good Business—the master passion of the race."[8]

As others before them had done in celebrating the westward movement, these popular mythmakers professed to admire the nature that had been conquered. The Colorado, they acknowledged, was a giant that ought to be respected, even in its defeat. Its grandeur and strength, they went on to suggest, would be preserved in the character of the people who subdued it, the men and women of Imperial who would become what the river had once been—an indefatigable force remaking the Southwest, destroying to build again. As victors representing Good Business, they would create money where the river had made a delta. They would be a new kind of river, an unstoppable flow of high-minded acquisitiveness that would carry the world before it.

But would business, as the new ruler of the West, remain for long under the direct control of the people residing in Imperial Valley? Already their emergency appeal to Harriman and Cory argued strongly that local strength was not up to the immense challenge of environmental management. Yet the overwhelming sentiment in the valley was against letting the Colorado River become Rio Harriman. Big capital, the valley felt, was as much to be feared as big nature. Harold Wright reflected that local concern when he grimly described "the methods of capital" as "impersonal, inhuman—the methods of a force governed by laws as fixed as the laws of nature, neither cruel nor kind; inconsiderate of man's misery or happiness, his life or death; using man for its own ends—profit, as men use water and soil and sun and air."[9] It was a tricky question the valley faced: how to capture the river and use it safely without in turn being captured and used by outside corporate powers. The solution hinted at by novelist Wright, and it was one he never systematically or practically explored, was somehow to keep the primary locus of finance close to home, where private capital, so Wright thought, would be more apt to serve the people rather than its own ends, where it could be under the close influence of popular pressure. Given the grand imperial dreams of the valley, however, that hope would prove to be quaint and unrealistic.

Early one June morning J. Smeaton Chase, a Congregational minister, trotted out of Palm Springs, California, on his pony Kaweah. The First World War was echoing in his ears from the other side of the earth, far away from the Colorado Desert where he rode solitary and quiet. Behind him, across the mountains, lay San Diego, Los Angeles, and Hollywood, sprawling new cities filling rapidly with people eager for release, for a better life, for throwing off their midwestern privation. Chase had deliberately turned his back on that world too to seek out the alternative of desert hardship. By living with the hot, arid wilderness through its most dreaded season, he hoped to learn something "of its lonely heart, its subtle, uncomprehended spirit, its repellent yet enthralling beauty, its agelessness, changelessness, and weariness, its implacability, solemnity, and terror."[10] In his rambles that summer east and south of Palm Springs, he came again and again to confront the old terror, a powerful thirst foreshadowing death, which a succession of forty-niners and gold prospectors before him had faced. In scattered Mexican adobes, where strings of chiles hung from the rafters and tiny candles burned in corner shrines, he ate *frijoles* and *tasajo*. He studied, as John Van Dyke had also done not twenty years earlier, the sparse gray vegetation, the flame and violet of sunsets, and the rough upthrust rocks. What he could not do, however, was truly escape what had become, by the second decade of the twentieth century, the pervasive hand of civilization. In the night, camping with his pony in the hills, Chase could see the headlights of automobiles speeding across the new Imperial Valley, carrying farmers, merchants, and tourists from Yuma to the coast. The desert still held some mystery for him, some secret promise, but it was less of a refuge than he had anticipated.

For long stretches in his travels there would be a vast emptiness all around him. Then the rider would come up hard against a fence, a field of alfalfa, a herd of milk cows grazing, telephone poles lined up to the horizon. Ramshackle houses scattered over the new rural landscape, each surrounded by a detritus of cans, bottles, and baling wire. In the summer, Chase discovered, Imperial Valley was a man's world; farm and town wives packed up and headed for the oceanside, escaping the searing temperatures, leaving the men behind to tend their crops in the heavy heat and dust. In the evenings, the lonely farmers slept out in the open under brush ramadas, next to burlap sacking sprayed with water to cool the breeze. Their hard life was made somewhat easier by a profusion of saloons across the international border. Someday, many of them hoped, they too could flee the inferno, when they had reached the point where they could hire a few Indians or Mexicans to do the work for them or when they could sell out at a big profit to an eager newcomer. "It is a miracle," Chase admitted, "the transforming, within a dozen years, of a tract of strict desert into a farming region of the highest fertility."[11] On the other hand, this empire was so far not an aesthetic or a social success. Compared with the unredeemed desert grandeur he had come to explore, Chase found the reclaimed land an uninspiring prospect. The aggressive agriculture that had entered showed an ugly, wretched visage, an unstable, empty character; and he went away from it in haste.

Others were a good deal less inclined than Chase to cavil, were in fact wildly excited by the miracle of desert eradication going on. Looking back to its natural period, they saw nothing of value or interest in the place; looking ahead, they saw only a perfectly benign oasis, one that would set the pace in productivity and affluence for all of American farming. "Imperial! Imperial! Imperial!": the name went round and round, catching on, firing imaginations, creating unbounded hopes among water engineers, real-estate salesmen, farm investors, railroad boosters, and the breathless fraternity of local journalists. "Lands of Imperial Valley," noted the University of California irrigation professor Frank Adams, "have developed more rapidly than any other large area in western America."[12]

By 1925 the population of the valley was 50,000, half of whom were living in incorporated towns. Property values amounted to $140 million. Every month of the year, the crops streamed out on Southern Pacific tracks to urban consumers in the East: cotton, cantaloupes, lettuce, milk fat, watermelons, peas, asparagus, tomatoes, milo maize, wheat, alfalfa hay, sheep, poultry, and eggs. Exotic forests of date palms grew up in the Coachella neighborhood, their trunks squatting in water ditches, hinting of a Babylonian luxuriance. In 1927 the valley counted 4,769 farms. Some of those farms were as large as 3,000 acres, and the overwhelming majority of them were operated by tenants, not their owners, who were at last finding their way out of the sweat and toil. Altogether there were almost 400,000 acres under cultivation, plus another 156,000 acres served by the Imperial irrigation system across the Mexican border. In a year's time 3 million acre-feet of water came from the Colorado River through the valley's canals.

It was still heavily laden with sediment, but now the sediment was under better control. Sixty dredges, operated unceasingly by over a thousand men, prevented it from choking the system, though the cost of that maintenance was high—a half-million dollars annually. The low-lying valley was plagued too by drainage problems and salt accumulation, but with high crop profits, with rigorous supervision, those foes, it was confidently believed, could be kept at bay.[13] And presiding over this apparent success story, furnishing the water that made it possible, holding the desert and the river in its indefatigable grip, was a new force on the scene, a homegrown agency of power, the Imperial Irrigation District.

The District came into being in 1911, a quasi-governmental agency by the terms of California law, with the ability to assess all property in its prescribed area to raise funds for its operations. It was the largest such water district in the West. Its first bond issue of $3 million enabled it in 1916 to purchase from Harriman the complete water-distribution network, freeing the valley at last from the embrace of the Octopus and its New York owner. In 1927, the District had an income of $2.4 million, part of which came from town properties within its jurisdiction, part from farmland assessments.[14] A board of directors, elected by local people, determined how that income should be spent. Here, one might have said, was a model of American democracy, the realization of Harold Bell Wright's hopes for local control. On the surface, so it appeared. In reality, however, democracy in Imperial water management was more nominal than effective, for the agency soon found ways to limit participation in its decisions. As it gathered the water into its hands, it simultaneously wedded its own bureaucratic and technical mission to the financial interests of a propertied elite.

In its first decade or two the IID became the chief battleground for deciding who was to control the valley's future. Although the agency was set up as a means whereby ordinary farmers could own and manage their own water system, few farmers won seats on its board of directors. Instead, four of the first five directors were from business (banking, real estate, merchandising), and they were intent on using their position as water dispensers to keep the right people running valley affairs. Opposed to them for a while were an insurgent mass of small farmers and would-be farmers. ("Unemployed poor people," one director called them; a "great horde of unwashed from Texas," said another.) Their leader was a crude, dirty, loud-mouthed farmer named Mark Rose, who identified his own eagerness to get rich with the aspirations of that riffraff. Though they finally succeeded in electing Rose to a directorship—in fact, elected him repeatedly from 1920 to 1944, making him a force to be continually reckoned with—the insurgents were never really able to wrest command from an emergent business-agribusiness alliance. Though they rocked that alliance with challenge after challenge in the early years, it nonetheless succeeded in consolidating its position and gaining the upper hand.[15]

The transformation of the Imperial Irrigation District into a local power complex, immune to many residents' needs, was in large measure the achievement of a succession of hired managerial experts. Perfecting an irrigation system covering over 500,000 acres, they realized and convinced others, was not a job for struggling, hard-pressed farmers or their spokesmen. Nor was it, for that matter, a job for part-time directors, with other business responsibilities to look after. Consequently, the IID early on hired a general manager, Munson Dowd, an engineering graduate of the California Institute of Technology, to carry on day-to-day operations. Dowd was the man who created in the valley a modern, efficient hydraulic apparatus, though he did so by bringing the agency's finances under more centralized direction and by insulating much of the decision-making from the turmoil of political struggles. With the coming of the depression in the 1930s, as the agency, despite all of Dowd's efforts, slid into desperate insolvency, another voice for the rule of expertise appeared on the scene, a formally uneducated but shrewd, talented administrator, E. T. Hewes. Determined to make Imperial safe and stable for a long time to come, Hewes, like Dowd, believed that the valley's future must lie with large-scale industrial farming. Therefore, the key to the agency's success with its water plans lay in putting foremost the needs of the big agribusiness irrigators, not the small, marginal ones. One of Hewes's first moves in carrying out that strategy was to convince the head of the Bank of America, A. P. Giannini, that the valley was a secure investment for the bank's money. Other outside investors followed Giannini's lead and purchased IID bonds, allowing the agency to get back on its feet and return to the task of extending its technological mastery. By the late thirties the pattern was clear: big capital and big water planning would henceforth go smoothly hand in hand. Water in this place would be managed more as a private than a public interest.[16]

The evolution of the Imperial Irrigation District is a case study in a familiar twentieth-century phenomenon: the collusion between scientifically oriented managers and holders of large private wealth. The first group speaks the language of efficiency, instrumental reason, and environmental domination; the second assents vigorously to that language and proceeds to hire the managers, confident they will end by serving its interest above all others. The common institutional framework for that alliance has been the modern business corporation. Although Imperial was a raw desert farm community, far removed geographically from the main scene of American corporate elaboration, it had leaders with up-to-date vision. Under the leadership of men like Dowd and Hewes, the IID quickly learned the virtues of the modern technician-capitalist alliance, modeling itself into a kind of private corporate entity, one producing water instead of automobiles or refrigerators.

Imperial's flowering into a private rather than a genuinely public agency, manipulating the Colorado River in the service of agribusiness needs, followed the advice of some of the leading irrigation experts of the day. Those experts looked suspiciously on democratic ideals, small-scale farming, and community participation in water planning because these endangered the maximization of technological and economic efficiency. A case in point is George Chaffey. His experience in "socialistic" Australia, with obstreperous settlers at Mildura and Renmark, convinced him that authority must be safely removed from popular pressures. As his biographer writes, Chaffey "saw clearly that a democracy of water users, or even a board made up of either elected or appointed representatives of the several mutual water companies, could not be entrusted with the great irrigation works, which simply must afford uninterrupted service year in and year out."[17] He made that point emphatically from the beginning of his involvement in planning the Imperial system.

Chaffey might be dismissed as an obviously self-interested private entrepreneur who was worried about what interfering people would do to his designs and profits. More disinterested, and more official, was the similar advice coming from the head of the Reclamation Service in Washington, Frederick Newell. He had been known on occasion to speak boldly for "Progressive," antimonopoly principles, yet warring in his own mind with those principles were contradictory ideas that put technical success above democratic involvement. In 1912, Newell spoke at a succession of Reclamation conferences, making at each of them a pitch for more businesslike management of irrigation projects. In Chicago, he held the railroad oligopoly up as an example of good management. Western irrigators, he argued, should ape the consolidating efforts of the railroad kings (he might have had E. H. Harriman in mind) and merge their little, decentralized waterways into a few "great systems." Then in Salt Lake City, Newell had this to say as a justification for a new order in water management:

> The present is a time of transition in many parts of the Arid
> West from the old easy-going way of handling irrigation
> canals to more effective and systematic modern methods.
> In cases where the farmers have gradually built the works
> by their own labor and where each man is well acquainted
> with his neighbor and with the operation in general, there

is possible an easy-going way of distributing water between neighbors, each of whom has learned through years of experience something of his duties and responsibilities. This is not possible in the case of the larger systems built by corporate investment or by the Government, where hundreds of farmers representing the various types of experience, nationality and religion are brought together from all parts of the country.

The absence of a grassroots communal tradition in the new West, he was saying, could be remedied only by putting decision-making into the hands of a trained water manager. The schemes had outgrown a neighborhood scale. Now "there must be a strong central organization," Newell went on, "headed by a manager who is removed from the danger of being influenced by individual water users, and who has enough assistants, responsible directly to him, to enable him to carry out effectively the general plans and policies." A few weeks later in Berkeley, California, Newell recommended that irrigation farmers put their affairs under the direction of "a business manager whose experience and ability are comparable to those of the general manager of a railroad or of any large industrial institution." Without that expertise, and without its forceful expression, farmers, he feared, would go on in their old, self-devised, inefficient ways of putting water on their crops. The danger in that situation was that the land would not deliver its greatest possible return. "The most efficient manager of an irrigation system," Newell insisted again, so there was no mistaking his inspiration, "is usually one who has had experience in large corporations and who has had training in handling large affairs."[18]

Newell, it must be said, did not at all mean that the *benefits* from more professional, corporate-style water management should be concentrated in only a few hands. But in promoting the ideal of a technical authority standing over farmers, removed from their direct supervision, in pushing for greater efficiency and economies of scale, he was playing directly into the hands of agribusiness interests. This became clear when his advice began showing up in campaigns to promote corporate farming on the West Coast. For example, two farm and water experts, M. L. Requa and H. T. Cory (the engineer who saved Imperial Valley from flooding), quoted Newell extensively in making the case, from their San Francisco bank offices, for turning water over to immense private farms organized along factory lines. "The same ability that has successfully guided the great corporations," they urged, must be brought into California irrigated agriculture. Here was a field of untapped opportunity, of enormous economic potential, if developed by the right hands. In the single year of 1916, exports of fruits, vegetables, wine, and grain from California amounted to almost $500 million—and that was achieved under an antiquated pattern of little patchwork farms and jerry-built ditches, under scattered, amateur control. Reorganized into "syndicate farms," each covering thousands of acres and employing scientific methods, the state's agriculture could be far more productive, capable of supporting a much larger population. "An irrigated farm," Requa and Cory pointed out," is distinctly *not* a poor man's operation." The costs were too high, the people too incompetent to make the most of it. A more rational approach, in their opinion, was to turn the land and water over to "a central czar-like corporation, strong financially" and capable of steering "a far more profitable course than a lot of unorganized, or even wonderfully well organized, farmers."[19]

Imperial Valley was in an unusually good position to put such advice from Chaffey, Newell, Requa, and Cory into practice. From the beginning it had been a creature of business enterprise, promoted and then salvaged by corporate money. It had no old-fashioned agrarian past to complicate its institutions. It had attracted a number of large investors who were not about to lose control to the lower ranks. And it had a single concentrated source of water in the strong, defiant Colorado, requiring, it seemed obvious, a concentration of social power capable of river mastery. Imperial was therefore a community destined by all those elements involved in its making to be on the leading edge of the new agriculture and to become the shining exemplar of, the unexcelled formula for, the rural society which that agriculture would bring into being.

During the first four decades of its history, Imperial's emerging shape of power was a dimly understood subject, one that neither critics like the desert-seeking Smeaton Chase nor celebrants like the novelist Harold Bell Wright were in a position to forecast accurately. Had they been so prepared, they would have found in the valley a lesson in consequences. An agricultural empire, they would have realized, was not to be contrived out of the most desolate country in the American West without some new, potent instrumentalities. By the 1930s, the main outlines of those instrumentalities had become much more discernible, though they were not yet fully matured. And a good deal later they were unmistakable. In 1972 a student of political science, Ernest Leonard, after an extended stay in the valley, concluded that a mutually reinforcing confederacy of technicians of water control and agribusinesses was now incontestably in command of the area's resources.

> The community of the Imperial Valley is a "company
> town" in every respect except ownership. It is dominated
> by a single industry which in turn is dominated by a
> cohesive elite. . . . The Imperial Irrigation District's organi-
> zational success is based upon its recognition of the spe-
> cialized and powerful interests in the valley and its alliance
> with that element including absentee owners. . . . The
> agency has developed a conservative, paternalistic and
> self-protective managerial system.[20]

Those who were left out of that alliance were the poor and landless, in
particular a huge army of farm workers, most of them with Hispanic
surnames, toiling on the ditches and in the fields. Leonard discovered that
the IID, though still nominally a public body open to the electoral process,
had succeeded in insulating its policies from democratic participation by
that army of laborers and other dissident groups. It had done so by wrap-
ping itself in the supposedly neutral language of scientific management, so
that all its decisions were made to appear so utterly rational, so perfectly
wise, that ordinary citizens did not challenge them, did not feel confident
enough in their own knowledge to question or oppose them. The result was
rule by technocracy, and not surprisingly the chief beneficiaries of that rule
were men of property and standing. Water had indeed made this desert
bloom, and the crop was oligarchy.

Could that local "cohesive elite," drawn closer together year by year in the
tasks of water management and irrigated farming, destined to rule over
Imperial Valley's future without fear of usurpation, also command the
mighty Colorado River? It could not. Internally, it might aspire to unques-
tioned dominance. Externally, however, it was a puny force by contrast with
the river, having at best a capacity for defense against silt buildup and for
end-distribution of the resource but lacking the conclusive means to make
the Colorado do its will. Quite simply, the river did not recognize the IID
as its rightful master, and without that recognition, the agency could not
be truly secure in its dominance. To secure its structure of power at home,
therefore, the valley oligarchy, through its servant agency, had somehow
to appeal for help to powers beyond its borders, some of them dwelling well
upstream, some of them across state lines, some of them far off in Washington. That was a risky business for the local elite, because to win more
security from the river they had to accept the possibility of interference by
those outside powers, had to accept as the price of their survival a significant loss in their dominion.

There were three principal threats to the nascent elite. First, there was the river itself. Even after Cory closed the breach in its banks, it continued to rise and fall in violent floods, any one of which could destroy the valley. In dry cycles the farmers might lose all their crops; they had no way to assure a minimum supply. During the 1920s, only 20 percent of the current made its way into their canals, the rest going off into the sea. There were undeveloped desert lands which could have used that "wasted" water, but they lay too high above the gravity-fed channels, and the costs of pumping water uphill to them was prohibitive. The Colorado was, for fully three decades after Chaffey's cut in its side, still an untamed, undocile beast, refusing to wear the Imperial harness.

A second threat came from rival human interests who might take the water for their own enrichment, to the detriment of the valley moguls. Although there were a few small claimants beginning to appear on the river's headwaters and on the opposite bank in Arizona, the most serious immediate rivals, because they lay outside the jurisdiction of American law, were those in Mexico. Among them was the Colorado River Land Company, holding a principality across the border from Imperial and having as its chief stockholder Harry Chandler, owner of the Los Angeles *Times.* It leased some of its 840,000 acres to Chinese, Japanese, and Mexican farmers, who constituted in the eyes of the Imperial settlers a dangerous, "alien" challenge to their success. Then there were, incongruously enough, bands of anti-Yankee land reformers and revolutionaries roaming the same Baja California countryside, threatening to expropriate the Imperial water passing through their lands.[21]

The third threat was the United States Reclamation Service, which longed to have the entire Colorado River handed over to it for comprehensive development. From the first, the valley believed, they had had to fight off a conspiracy on the part of the federal government to discredit their private efforts and grab the water. In 1901, Department of Agriculture soil experts, in an infamous report, had dismissed the valley as being too alkaline to raise crops profitably. Then the Service had sought to get the river declared navigable, thereby establishing its priority over local water appropriators, though boats were as rare a sight on the Colorado as good whiskey under Prohibition. One of the local eminences, banker L. M. Holt of Holtville, wrote in a fit of indignation:

> The Reclamation Service had an inordinate ambition to
> wipe off the slate all irrigation enterprises so far as the
> Colorado River and the Colorado Desert was concerned, to

the end that they might have a free hand to construct the
largest irrigation system in the United States.[22]

Holt went so far as to blame the 1905–1907 disaster on the federal conni-
vers, arguing as he did that Rockwood had made the ill-fated cut south of
the border to remove his scheme from American government interference.
If that was so, and the evidence suggests it was indeed part of Rockwood's
strategy, then he had ironically delivered the valley into the even more
menacing grasp of Mexico. Either way they went, Imperial could not win
the game they had started. Too many other, larger, outside forces wanted
the river for their own ends and would not let a few local claims stand in
their way.

Put those various threats together and the rational course was clear:
Imperial had better give up a little freedom of action to get protection and
further its development. In January 1919, the valley submitted to a partnership with the long-resisted Reclamation Service. Federal engineers, it was
agreed, would build for Imperial an "All-American Canal," lying wholly on
their side of the border, and through it they would bring water for sixty
miles across rippling, Sahara-like sand dunes to both the valley's settled
and its unsettled lands. The cost would be a whopping $30 million, but its
repayment would be spread out over many years, with no interest charged
to residents, as provided in the 1902 National Reclamation Act and its
amendments. At the same time, Imperial agreed to join in a "unified
Colorado River project," which would put storage dams upstream to even
out the monthly flow and prevent flooding. Under those two programs the
IID was in effect declaring itself to be a ward of the central government,
acknowledging that, in a final sense, its own power flowed down to it from
higher agencies.

Only with the greatest reluctance did valley leaders accept that second
program of upstream storage dams. At first they hoped that the Reclamation
Service would enter their territory to dig their aqueduct for them, would
subsidize its repayment, then would fade away, leaving them alone with
their river. The chief counsel for the Imperial Irrigation District, Phil
Swing, went to Congress to lobby for just that limited involvement and
nothing more. It would not wash. Congressman Carl Hayden of Arizona was
not about to let the Imperial Valley go its own way, refusing to help bear
the costs of mastering the entire river. The recently formed League of the
Southwest, made up of governors, city officials, and businessmen dedicated
to making the region "the greatest empire on the face of the earth," would
not let the valley take an independent course. And then there was Arthur

208

Powell Davis, the head of the Reclamation Service and the nephew of John Wesley Powell. Davis had made the conquest of the Colorado his main ambition, his burning obsession. "I . . . considered problems in all of the Western states," but none of them, he admitted, "excited my interest and imagination and ambition so much as the development of the Colorado River basin." What he wanted were dams in those deep upriver canyons and on the lower reaches, dams that Imperial affluence could help pay for. Against those concerted pressures Phil Swing and the valley moguls caved in, accepting the fact that they must go along with centralized planning or go home with nothing.[23]

The story of the forging of the Colorado River Compact has been told with considerable skill and detail by historian Norris Hundley. The main actors included, in addition to Davis, the IID factotum Phil Swing, who was elected to Congress in 1920; Hiram Johnson, the senator from California; Delph Carpenter, an astute water lawyer from Denver representing upper-basin interests; a scattering of other state delegates; and, presiding over the negotiations, Secretary of Commerce Herbert Hoover. Meeting in Santa Fe in 1922, the delegates accepted Carpenter's scheme to divide the river into two basins, upper and lower, the division point being at Lees Ferry, with each basin to have 7.5 million acre-feet of water to use per year. That amount, Hundley notes, was based on a too optimistic calculation of Colorado flow. The river would not, in most years, deliver that much water, would not be able to fill all the demands put on it.[24] But for the first time in the West neighboring states had sat down to make a treaty over a scarce supply of water instead of seizing it first and squabbling in the courts ever after.

All did, that is, except Arizona, which refused to ratify the compact until 1944. Arizonans regarded the lower river as their rightful possession because it cut across their lands and received their tributaries, though the vast portion of its current came from Rocky Mountain snowfields. They worried that a bigger, more advanced neighbor like California, a state which contributed virtually no runoff to the river, would get the larger mouthful to drink. Sympathizing with Arizona's complaint was the writer Mary Austin, who saw in the compact a replay of the earlier Owens Valley–Los Angeles controversy, where the smaller, weaker party lost out to the more powerful one while the federal government looked on and abetted. Now along the Colorado the government was once more throwing all its aid to the invading party, giving to the Californians residing in Los Angeles and Imperial Valley 4.4 million acre-feet a year of the lower basin's apportionment—the lion's share. It is a case, Austin wrote, of "the rape of the natural resources of one State *against that State's consent,* for the advantage of another State."[25]

A sparsely settled state's grumblings would soon be drowned out in the acclaim evoked by the bold, extravagant technological feat that followed the signing and ratification of the compact. With enough cooperation secured up and down stream to proceed, the reclamation engineers got to work in the early 1930s on bringing the river to heel at last. In Black Canyon, thirty miles southeast of Las Vegas, Nevada, they began pouring concrete for the largest dam ever attempted. Four giant diversion tunnels were drilled through the dense andesite canyon walls so the river could be turned out of its bed during the construction phase. Then, as thousands of workers swarmed over the site, working in devastating heat, a spectacular arch dam, shaped like a giant shell wedged upright in the canyon, began to mount from bedrock. Layer on layer of concrete rose bulging against the current, 3.4 million cubic yards in all, flanked by glittering steel pipes and penstocks, by stately intake towers and whirring turbines in a massive hydroelectric power plant. A smooth, sloping wall 726 feet high, a quarter-mile long at its crest, forming a plug big enough to back up water for over a hundred miles, big enough to store the entire flow of the Colorado for two full years, big enough and deep enough that it would not fill with silt for a few centuries. The dam was completed in 1935.[26]

Ecstatic Americans called it one of the greatest man-made wonders of the world. It was that, all right, the first of the modern world's high dams. Given his obsession with the river, the dam should have been named after Arthur Powell Davis. Instead, it came to be called Hoover, in honor of the role he played in the compact negotiations. More than any other single structure, Hoover Dam and its power plant turned the desert Southwest into boom country, affording as it did a sudden new abundance of electricity and domestic water supplies for cities and stabilized water for irrigated agriculture. But Hoover Dam was at the same time a shining alabaster monument to emergent social powers. Chiseled as it were across its imposing face were the names of those powers. In boldest letters was the name of the United States Bureau of Reclamation and the centralized authority behind it. In somewhat smaller letters were the names of Los Angeles and the coastal Metropolitan Water District, representing the rising new metropolitan forces of California. Prominent too was the new Colorado River Commission, made up of southwestern state representatives. There were also the names of the Six Companies, the consortium of private contractors and financiers which did the actual construction. They included Henry J. Kaiser,

Morrison-Knudsen, W. A. ("Dad") Bechtel, Utah Construction, Mac-Donald-Kahn, J. F. Shea, and Pacific Bridge, actually seven of them in number, many of them destined for world eminence, all of them leaders in creating the new corporate empire of the West. If he did not have his own name up there in the public consciousness, Arthur Powell Davis could at least take comfort in that the Colorado was on its way to becoming what he had wanted it to become, a managed ditch running meekly from its headwaters to its mouth under the strict supervision of the federal engineers. As Hundley observes, the conquest of the Colorado marks "the emergence of the government in Washington as the most powerful authority" in western water management.[27]

Among those not served by the new river regime, and not included in its roster of power, were the various Indian peoples living within the Colorado basin. Though some of them had been depending on the water for far longer than the Imperial farmers and had worked hard to save them from the river's floods, they were left out of the new hydraulic society. No one asked them to participate in the Colorado compact negotiations, and the Bureau of Indian Affairs, supposedly their guardian angel, failed to look out for their interests there. What's more, much of their reservation land, in that watershed as elsewhere in the West, was taken from them and sold to whites, who developed irrigation farms on it. The public justification behind that policy of termination was that the reservations had become desolate ghettos, entrapping native peoples in endless poverty, that they would be released from them and "assimilated" into the mainstream of American life. Termination, however, was a suspiciously convenient way to redistribute Indian land and water to whites. On the Yuma reservation, for instance, the native owners were allotted a mere 5 acres apiece on which to raise their food with irrigation, while 6,500 acres left over from the distribution were sold to whites in 40- to 100-acre parcels. That breaking up of the reservation not only made land accessible to outsiders but effectively limited the water demands of the Indians, freeing the river for others to grab.[28]

And what of the white man's contrived paradise, Imperial Valley, the place that had given itself so big a name? Where did it stand in the new roster of power? Nowhere near so high as Rockwood, Chaffey, and its other investors and promoters had hoped. It had not after all proved to be the main seat of an arid-land empire, but was more of a province, an appendage to the river and its controlling agencies. It was now caught inextricably in a complicated web of bureaucratic structures, countervailing demands, and distant decision-makers. By no means had it become a helpless fly in that web, nor had it been impoverished by the entanglement. It was, nonetheless, unmistakably less the master of its fate than it had been before its ambitions and insecurities drove it into the arms of a once-dreaded antagonist. One evidence of its diminishing influence was that the valley, which had bent so far against its wishes as to accept centralized Colorado River development, found itself the last to be served. Its pet scheme, the All-American Canal, did not get started until well after the Hoover Dam was completed and did not carry its first water until 1940.

There was a comforting postscript for some of the white entrepreneurs. Imperial Valley did manage, with federal help, to salvage an important measure of local (which is to say, local elite) control. Within days of going out of office, the Hoover administration blatantly abrogated the national reclamation law to safeguard the estates of the Imperial agribusinessmen. According to the Boulder Canyon Project Act of 1928, the canal was to be paid for by residents in the valley, "as provided in the reclamation law." That meant, and could only mean, that no water was to be provided for tracts exceeding 160 acres in size, farmed by owners living in the neighborhood. Hoover's Secretary of the Interior, Ray Lyman Wilbur, declared in a letter dated 24 February 1933 that Imperial Valley did not have to comply with that provision, since it had been using Colorado water prior to government construction and there was therefore no *sale* of new water but merely the *delivery* of old water in which the valley had a vested right. That the Reclamation Bureau was charging a price for its water delivery here as elsewhere, using precisely the same no-interest repayment formula it applied in all other reclamation projects, was passed over as irrelevant. It was hardly a coincidence that the Wilbur letter was prepared by an executive assistant who, after leaving office, served as the IID's lawyer in Washington. Succeeding Interior administrators, whatever they may have thought of the opinion's validity, found it much easier to acquiesce in it and get on with the more pressing task of river control than to challenge and disrupt the valley establishment.[29]

The upshot of this bureaucratic rule-making was that, at least for the next thirty years, Imperial's oligarchy was not to be disturbed within its borders. Having surrendered the Colorado to Washington, they were then granted a carefully circumscribed freedom from interference in the accumulation of local power and wealth. The river was bound now to behave itself, to work steadily the year round, the humbled servant of its human masters. Imperial's capitalists and technicians could thrive so long as they remained discreetly on the edges, taking advice, paying the bills, and speaking the language of cooperation.

212

"I NEVER KNOWED THEY WAS ANYTHING LIKE HER"

In the nineteenth century, there had been several centers of hydraulic innovation in the West, all stumbling their way forward by trial and error, all making some special claim for historical precedence, all bidding for regional supremacy. The Mormons had their unique combination of small-scale rural communities and centralized church authority. The Coloradans promoted the legal doctrine of prior appropriation of water rights while at the same time, along with Wyoming, they counterposed the Greeley-inspired idea of coordinated public planning. Out in California the irrigation district emerged as a novel institution, along with a peculiarly convoluted system of water laws, a large-scale mentality in agriculture, and a dependency, first through ocean transport, then through refrigerated railroad cars, on distant markets. For a while, each center existed more or less separate from the others. Each went its own way, without much hindrance from outside powers, without much attention to what the others were doing. The important story of the twentieth-century agricultural West, however, has been the steady elaboration of a cross-regional hierarchy, one not completed even now, one perhaps never to be finally perfected, but a hierarchy all the same.

The core (or what the Chinese scholar Ch'ao-ting Chi called the "key economic area") of that western hierarchy was to be California.[1] From 1920 on it would increasingly command the region's water resources, not all of them, but enough to establish its supremacy. Already it far surpassed its competing centers in wealth and influence. Agricultural investment capital was beginning to flow from it to the other, neighboring states, while water and profit, as Arizonans bitterly realized, were beginning to flow out from them as a kind of tribute. Colorado and Utah, along with the Yakima valley in Washington, the Milk River settlements in Montana, the Pecos and San Juan communities in New Mexico, and dozens of others, were beginning to look to California for inspiration, for leadership, even while competing with it for position. Someday soon they would constitute a fringe for the Golden State's core, a ring of economic subordination, overmatched and overshad-

213

owed, treated at times like colonies rather than equal partners in empire. And that fringe would not stop with the backwaters of the West but would extend far eastward into humid farm areas, which also would be forced to acknowledge California's primacy. One day it would even extend into foreign countries, where the core would take its products to sell and its methods to try out. Artificial water, mixed with human enterprise and labor, would eventually make California the premier agricultural center of the entire earth, a modern kingdom by the sea.

In 1909, California trailed behind Colorado in irrigated acreage. Then in a spurt of development over the next decade the West Coast state moved to take the lead, never to relinquish it. The census of 1920 showed 4,219,040 acres under the ditch in California, or one-fifth of the nation's total, with Colorado, Idaho, Montana, Utah, Wyoming, and Oregon following after. Capital invested in California farm water systems amounted to almost $200 million (a figure that would more than double in the next decade), compared to only $32 million in Utah, $30 million in Washington, and $35 million in Texas. Out of California's fields came an overflowing cornucopia of diversity—foods and fibers introduced from almost every part of the earth, representing almost every imaginable set of growing conditions. Almost 9 million orange trees grew in the state in 1920, ranking as the leading money earner. Half a million acres of alfalfa hay under irrigation. Seventy-three million grapevines of bearing age, and twice that many by 1930. After those the leading irrigation crops included, in a descending order of value, rice, peaches, lemons, plums and prunes, potatoes, beans, walnuts, cotton, sugar beets, barley, apricots, spring and winter wheat, other small-grains cut for hay, kaffir, milo, cantaloupes and melons, apples, tomatoes, flower and vegetable seeds. California farmers harvested more than two hundred commercial crops in all, many of them grown nowhere else in the United States, most of them incapable of surviving without an artificially augmented supply of moisture.[2]

Why this state should surge into western agricultural dominance is not a question to be answered in a phrase or two. Environment, of course, had much to do with it: the hand of nature had marked California, its residents had told one another over a long while, for greatness. They had plenty of water in the Sierras, a benign winter climate, an immensity of space broken up into a rich mosaic of ecological zones, an urban concentration unusual in the West, providing hundreds of thousands, then millions, of city mouths hungry for fresh food, and they had several splendid seaports giving access to the rest of the world. California farmers, moreover, were organized to take advantage of those environmental assets, and that may in fact have been the indispensable element in their success. Simply, they knew how to come together in concerted action. Irrigation, Elwood Mead observed of California, was "a nursery of cooperation."[3] Whether that spirit of cooperation was acquired in an irrigation district or in a mutual water company organized as a joint-stock corporation was immaterial. The main thing was that California agriculturists learned, and learned faster and better than their competitors in other states, the ways of group action.

As a nursery of cooperation the irrigation district was slow in proving its worth. Only after 1897, when the large landowners succeeded in regaining the upper hand over financial matters, removing thereby an old bone of contention, did the districts begin to thrive. Later on the state set itself up as an outside overseer of district organization and finance in order to win the confidence of San Francisco and eastern bond buyers, and to that same end it pushed the districts toward more professional local water management. Then farmers began to discover too that the district was, in the words of a modern lawyer, "an extraordinarily potent engine for the creation of wealth."[4] By 1921 there were seventy-four such engines in California, covering a third of all its watered acres. Through the power of property taxation, they could force recalcitrant farmers in their midst to improve their lands, grow more lucrative crops, and in general join the march, in the words of a slogan draped across the Modesto railroad depot, toward "Water, Wealth, Contentment, Health." Commonly it was a local bank president or merchant who took the lead in forming a district, and alongside him, pushing hard too, were men like S. T. Harding, an engineer and for a while a Department of Agriculture employee. For men like these, the attraction of the district lay in its promise of greater returns through economic union. Harding went about the state preaching that

> one of the greatest needs of the locality is a greater spirit
> of co-operation in other things . . . as well as in irrigation
> matters and the development of leaders who have the land
> owners' confidence and who can carry through any organi-
> zation that be to the best interests of all concerned.[5]

Those "other things," he was aware, would begin to follow in the wake of improved water organization. After irrigation would come success in the cooperative marketing of farm products, then success in the coordination of labor recruitment and control.

In the mid-1890s, the irrigated fruit farmers of California, plagued by recurring crop gluts and by a handful of dealers who had them over a barrel, began to ask themselves whether they should try to pool their energies to do their own marketing, thus putting into their own pockets the middleman's profit. To that end, they began organizing themselves into producer cooperatives. The first to be formed was the Orange Growers' Protective Union, established in 1895 (later renamed the California Fruit Growers' Exchange, then the Sunkist Growers, Incorporated). Within fifteen years, the cooperative was selling $20 million worth of citrus fruit a year, gathered from six thousand farms. By the twenties, the state's cooperatives were so skilled in their work that California farmers barely felt the nationwide agricultural depression of the decade. For one thing, they had learned the trick of name-brand identification and advertising, so Americans everywhere had begun to hear of and buy their Sun-Maid raisins, Sunsweet prunes, Diamond Brand walnuts, and Blue Ribbon peaches. To meet the demand they generated, the co-ops set up immense, industrialized packing sheds where workers shaved the fuzz from an endless line of those peaches, where they shelled almonds by the carful, or where they washed and boxed a plentitude of broccoli for grocery display. From the packing sheds went beans to Cuba, eggs to London, and rice—it was a great boast—to Japan. Truly, exulted an agricultural editor and a college dean, "the world is California's market." With enough cooperation, they predicted, "we shall utilize all but the thud in the packing box and bucket."[6]

By the present century agricultural cooperation had unquestionably become a popular notion in the state, but its meaning, its virtue, was nonetheless carefully hedged about. Despite their willingness to join forces in acquiring water and selling crops, farmers were not at all ready to give up their private dreams of accumulating great wealth. In that regard they remained steadfast individualists. A Stanford economist, Ira Cross, complained that cooperation was a very superficial ideal in California. Growers could understand the advantages to be gained from promoting a cooperative in which they had a self-interest, in which they held stock, but they refused to concern themselves with other collectivities or with a generalized notion of community welfare. The reason for their narrowness was that, in Cross's words, the cooperatives "seem to have been organized with but one object in mind, and that is to make money for their stockholders. They are mere profit-making associations." It was hard, he concluded, to find any real difference between rural cooperation as perfected there and "that which characterizes the stockholders of the ordinary business corporation."[7]

Karl Marx, in contrasting the ancient with the modern world, had made a similar distinction between the species of cooperation. Past societies like the Egyptian, in the task of erecting the pyramids and bringing water to the desert, had, he wrote in *Capital,* practiced a "simple cooperation," colossal in its results, exploitative in its governance, but uncomplicated in its practice. In that long-ago time, workers had toiled like bees in their communal hive. They took for granted a common ownership of the means of production, at least within their villages. They were still tied by a psychological umbilical cord to their tribe or community. In the modern economy, however, cooperation had come to be something very different— it was "capitalistic cooperation." Individual property ownership replaced communalism, and while workers were freed from the enforced labor of the corvées, they were also permanently cut off from their native communities and made to wander in search of work and wages. According to Marx, "cooperation ever constitutes the fundamental form of the capitalist mode of production."[8] But it was now strictly the cooperation among a group of capitalists in the pursuit of private gain. It did not reach across class lines.

So it was in irrigated California from the late nineteenth century forward. Brought together by the task of water control into the most cohesive economic class yet seen in American agriculture, one united in its commercial goals and in that only, the state's farmers undertook to recruit the last element needed to make their supremacy complete: a large body of laborers. What would emerge was a work force tireless and cheap, hired in a tightly rationalized, controlled market. It would be disorganized without employer rule, but once so organized, it could be sent to and fro, here and there, up and down the state, wherever there was a demand for work. It would be controlled with all the ease of making water run in a ditch. Without those people, the water and the land on which it was used could not be brought under a true domination. Without the managed water, on the other hand, there would be less need and much less inclination to recruit and manage those people.

During the Great Depression of the 1930s, Americans first became widely aware that there was a negative side to western, and in particular California, agriculture. Or at least they came to see some of the darker *human,* not the ecological, consequences of that agriculture. What they discovered was that, contrary to traditional rural ideals, a pronounced system of class relations, and of the raw exploitation of one class by another, existed out there. Somehow Americans had always assumed—and westerners were not different from other citizens in this respect—that the region could be won from nature by the unorganized, self-employed labor of middle-class individuals and their families, struggling with their own properties. In fact, the flowering of the West was, and had to be if the dreams of absolute environmental conquest were to become reality, the work of a dominated underclass of hired men and women. The failure to see that was due to a long-persisting epidemic of wishful thinking. It was also due to a tendency among white Americans to ignore the social consequences of desert mastery when people of color were used as the chief instruments of that domination.[9]

A few prescient observers escaped the wishful thinking, but not the racism. Jefferson Davis, for example, who had been a Mississippi cotton planter before serving as a United States senator, then as president of the Confederacy, understood that the West presented a profound challenge to established northern ways of arranging rural work. In arguing against the Compromise of 1850, which admitted California to the Union as a non-slaveowning state, Davis insisted that slavery was better suited than free labor "to an agriculture which depends upon irrigation."

> Till the canals are cut, ditches and dams made, no person can reclaim the soil from Nature; an individual pioneer cannot settle upon it with his family, and support them by the product of his own exertion, as in the old possessions of the United States, where rain and dew unite with a prolific soil to reward freely and readily the toil of man. It is only by associated labor that such a country can be reduced to cultivation.[10]

His method of securing the necessary labor was to make the West an extension of the South: to take black slaves into the deserts—he believed them to be better adapted than whites to toiling in the hot sun—and make them do the work. To its great credit the West rejected that brutal solution, but then found itself without a supply of labor. Some substitute had to be found.

Jefferson Davis had assumed that cheap, abundant labor would be needed mainly for the initial construction of water systems, but in fact it was the ongoing, daily tasks of irrigation farming that created the more important labor demand, one that persisted and grew with each extension of control. As settlers exhausted the easy possibilities of river diversion, as their hydraulic apparatus became elaborately engineered, the water sluicing to their fields became, not surprisingly, more and more costly. Expensive water brought an end to any expectation that families might subsist by their own labor on their own lands. In that situation, a high-return cash crop was the only rational form of land use, not a diversified smattering of grains, livestock, fruits, and vegetables on every little farm, supplying every little family from its own backyard. One must feed the market, not oneself, to make irrigation pay. Consequently, California farmers began early on to specialize in those crops they could raise with substantial profit. Here they put forty acres into tomatoes, over there twenty acres into oranges, and beyond that a hundred into cotton. A single acre of staked tomatoes took over a thousand man-hours to plant, cultivate, and harvest. And when such labor-intensive crops were ready to be harvested, many hands had to be found to do the job—and do it quickly, before the fruit began to rot. The inevitable outcome of irrigation intensification, in other words, was a loud, anxious cry for harvest hands who would come running, get the crop in efficiently, and then leave before they became a useless burden on the grower's income. Given the institutions of private property and the market-place, nothing in that chain of consequences, once it was set in motion, could have been avoided. The only imponderable in the equation was where the supply of temporary farm laborers could be found.

In the days of the Spanish and Mexican missions and haciendas, Indians had been the main pool of workers in orchards and fields, but the ravages of disease and overwork had left few of them available for the American irrigators to hire. Roaming across the countryside were thousands of white farm workers, the so-called bindle stiffs or fruit tramps, and for a period they furnished the largest number of field hands. But there were never enough of them that could be lured out of the cities to put in a few weeks of transient labor, so out of desperation farmers turned toward distant Asia. Four years after Davis's speech in the Senate on introducing slavery into the West, the *California Farmer* hit upon that remedy: "The Chinese! . . . [T]hat population, educated, schooled and drilled in the cultivation of these products are to be to California what the African has been to the South. This is the decree of the Almighty, and man cannot stop it."[11] By 1880 one-third of all laborers in California agriculture were Chinese, and the percentage used in intensive cropping was much higher than that. Besides working for extremely low wages, the Chinese brought the advan-tage of agricultural experience. Their own society had been irrigating for thousands of years, using massed corvées of rural folk. They knew the techniques well, knew how much water to apply and when, knew how to slog along day after day in mud and heat. No one has yet made a study of the contributions those immigrants made to the hydraulic West, but it must have been decisive in the incipient period, when California was taking its first uncertain steps in that direction. Theirs was, in any case, a short-lived employment. Howls of resentment mixed with violent deeds by white labor-ers who feared the Chinese low-wage competition led to the Chinese Exclu-sion Act of 1882, which forbade any further immigration. The act was renewed ten years later and continued, through subsequent legislation, up until 1943, when at last it was repealed in a spirit of wartime cooperation. Gradually, under the threat of white hostility, the remaining coolies re-treated from the fields and into the cities.[12]

When irrigation began to pick up momentum once more after the doldrums of the 1890s, farmers had begun to cast about for a new labor source. If not China, then maybe Japan would do. In 1900 the Japanese had come to number 10,000 in California, and they were performing much of the labor on irrigated farms, especially on those raising sugar beets in the Salinas Valley and citrus fruits around Los Angeles. Within another six years that immigrant population had increased by 400 percent, enough to trigger demands once more for Asian exclusion. The so-called Gentleman's Agreement of 1906 stopped the influx of Japanese workers. Meanwhile, employers were discovering that the new group was far less inclined than the Chinese to toil docilely for them. The Japanese came with a hunger for property and a determination to take their place among the landowning elite. They worked closely with one another in a tribalistic spirit unfamiliar to most Americans, threatening to strike where conditions were unacceptable, helping one another to save money from their wages, and eventually, renting and even buying their own farms. On marginal lands that other farmers had ignored, like the low, marshy Sacramento delta, they settled into business for themselves, draining and diking where necessary, fertilizing with their own excrement where required, turning those lands into vegetable wealth. By 1910, there were 1,816 Issei, or first-generation Japanese immigrants, operating farms in the state. Now it was the white farmers' turn to feel the pressure of Asian competition, and they responded by forcing the passage of the Alien Land Act of 1913, which prohibited foreigners (the Japanese had not bothered with or been encouraged to take out citizenship papers) from owning land, restricting them to leases only. If the purpose of the act was to force the Japanese back into wage-labor status, it failed. They were through with that life, and employers again had to locate a fresh supply of people to squat and stoop and pick their crops.[13]

The connections between the American and Asian hydraulic civilizations ramified with the introduction of a third nationality group, the "rag heads" from India. Simultaneously with the Japanese, more than 10,000 Hindustanis entered California as farm workers, and their lean brown bodies and white turbans moving down the rows were reminiscent of scenes along the Ganges and Indus. One of their number, Dhan Gopal Mukerji, an educated young man from Calcutta, described thus his school vacations when he signed on with a crew of his countrymen to work in California fields:

> It was a ghastly performance. We got up at half past three, and before the first faint daylight was visible we were ready for work. We were paid by the piece, and if we filled up a whole box of asparagus we received ten cents. They gave us miles and miles of asparagus rows. As soon as I had

knelt down with my knife and cut out one head and put
it in the box, there would be another one sprouting before
me. Then I would have to stoop again, and it was continuous picking and stooping that made it a terrible form of
exercise. It is walk and bend, bend and walk, from half
past four or thereabouts, until seven in the evening.[14]

Mukerji was astonished to find that the men with whom he toiled took to
the fields with irrepressible enthusiasm. What he did not add, what any
employer knew only too well, was that they also refused to stay on as farm
hands whenever the chance for landownership came their way.

Still another group of Asians introduced into California irrigation were
the Filipinos. They arrived on the scene in the early 1920s, most of them
young, single males herded about by labor contractors. There were 30,500
of them in the state by 1930. Employers regarded them with suspicion, for
they had a fighter's reputation, were quick to respond to abuse as well as
to organize and strike.[15] In addition, a few European and Middle Eastern
immigrants came to work for a while—Italians and Armenians mainly—
but they too moved rapidly up to the higher status of farm operator and
themselves began looking for cheap hires. And then, after those experiments in distant immigration had been tried and usually had failed, there
came the Mexicans. It was they who worked alongside the remnant white
American laborers, filling out the planting, watering, and harvesting crews,
then working alone when the Anglos finally went away. It was they who
proved to be the most reliable, accessible foreign recruits of all. Over the
course of the twentieth century, they became the persistent presence, the
dominated class, the despised race, the men and women who made the water
empire a success.

For centuries, the Mexican peons had been tied down in involuntary
servitude to the great estates of their homeland. Not until 1911, with the
overthrow of Porfirio Díaz, did their prospects begin to brighten. However,
in the period following the revolution, as Mexico went through a continuing
turmoil of assassinations, of American invasions, and of civil war waged by
Pancho Villa and Emiliano Zapata, the peons gained far less than they had
expected. They began to look across the border to the American irrigated
farmlands, where they could earn a wage, no matter how small, and return
home richer than before. With World War I, which brought a nationwide
labor shortage to the United States, a door to the north opened for them,
and it would not close until the Depression. Initially, they trekked into
Imperial Valley. By the late twenties, one-third of the laboring population
there was of Mexican origin. From Imperial, they diffused northward in

California, until by 1930 the Mexican population of the state stood at 368,000. Those were the legal immigrants. It was anyone's guess how many illegal border crossers there were in the state or how many "wetbacks" there were elsewhere in the Southwest, how many peons had waded the Rio Grande in the night or walked over mountains and deserts to find jobs in Yankeeland. What the American farmers did know, and know well, was that the Mexicans, whether legally or illegally present at their gates, were undemanding and ready to take whatever was offered. If any of them caused trouble, they could be easily deported—dumped back across the border from where they came.[16]

The agricultural story in neighboring Arizona was that of California on a smaller scale, with water, cotton, some truck cropping, and Mexican labor affording the chief features. After a struggling start, Arizona found its future in 1912 when 572 acres were planted to cotton. The next year the Salt River Valley Egyptian Cotton Growers Association formed to recruit pickers for the crop. Local white workers refused to handle the Pima variety grown in the state. They disliked intensely its small boll, which was harder for them to handle than the big-boll upland varieties cultivated in the South. It was also a very tall plant by harvest time, and down in the irrigated rows, where the cooling breezes were shut out, a picker could collapse from the heat and high humidity. Making matters worse, the pay was low—one to two cents per pound. For an average adult male, this amounted to a dollar and a half or, at most, three dollars for a ten-hour day. When whites could not be recruited, the state's Indians had been tried and found to be an unreliable source of substitute labor. The Navaho from up north stayed away from the fields under advice from the Bureau of Indian Affairs. The Papago could be induced to do the work when drought ruined their own reservation crops, and they did it well. With the arrival of good rains, however, they quickly departed for home. Consequently, by 1920 the growers felt compelled to send recruiters and trains into Mexico, bringing out thousands of families to undertake temporary work that no one else would do.[17]

There were some who worried publicly, who ranted and made ominous noises, about the social consequences of the turn toward large-scale irrigated farming. The state's labor leaders complained bitterly about the importation drive both because it put the Mexicans in a new state of peonage from which they could not easily escape and because in the off-seasons they wandered about the state looking for work, competing against Americans and driving wages down. A banker argued that cotton was a "roulette-and-faro crop" that made the state's economy more unstable than before. And a Phoenix newspaper editor protested in 1920 that "by adding an inferior race to our population, every form of vice and crime is promoted that a few rich men may grow richer." He went on to complain that "our courts are congested with the trial of criminal cases, arising from depredations committed by these underpaid, half-civilized people who creep under the fence all along the international line. This extra cost comes off the entire community and not from those who enjoy the special privilege." All of the protests, the well-founded ones and the vicious, the plausible and the absurd, were to no avail. Arizona farmers, using water furnished them by the public subsidy of federal irrigation projects, were fast creating a major cotton-producing center, one that would compete successfully against the Old South, and the Mexicans were to remain the chosen human instruments of their success.[18]

The Depression brought a momentary halt to that international labor arrangement in California and Arizona alike, as it did in Texas grapefruit orchards and Colorado beet fields. Protests from urban taxpayers, forced to give relief to Mexican nationals hanging about their towns unable to get work, became at last too loud to ignore. Luckily, a new labor force for the hydraulic society was already in the making farther east, a native-born force, and it was beginning to drift westward. For a while, it would be relied on to take the Mexicans' place. It was made up of destitute whites, loosely known as "Okies," most of them former sharecroppers and tenant farmers who had been thrown off the land and were even more desperate than the Mexicans to scrape together a living. Those poor whites understood cotton —it was as much a part of their lives as corn pone and grits—and by the 1930s there were hundreds of thousands of acres of cotton drawing them west as pickers. These same workers could learn the techniques of harvesting grapes and oranges too. They loaded their meager possessions into wheezy old cars and came looking for jobs in the irrigated fields: men in faded blue jeans and shirts, heavy work shoes without socks, and grimy hats; barefoot women in flour-sack dresses, with hard lines around their mouths; and children with sores and smiles on their faces, in hand-me-down clothes, all expecting to work. From 1935 through 1938, officials at the plant quarantine stations on California's borders counted 285,000 migrants entering the state to seek manual employment. Some observers called them "dust-bowlers," but the causes for their uprooting were in most cases farm mechanization, a depressed economy, and soil exhaustion in the cotton belt, not the dust storms and droughts of the plains.[19] One in five farm workers coming into Arizona hailed from the single state of Oklahoma; one in ten in California was from there. With their fellows from Arkansas, Texas, and the Mississippi Delta, they would manage to do what the Mexicans had not been able to accomplish: bring attention to the structure of power and poverty associated with a maturing irrigation system.[20]

The itinerants who came into Arizona inherited the squalor of the Mexican labor camps. In one of those camps, for example, over two hundred shacks had been thrown up for harvest crews. There were no floors in them, no glass windows, no furniture, no stoves, no screens, no electric lights. The sour smell of too many bodies packed in too small a space blew out of open doorways. On other farms a few shabby tents were scattered along the narrow space between the roads and water ditches. The San Carlos reclamation project south of Phoenix had some of the worst living conditions of all. Built by the Bureau of Indian Affairs on native peoples' land, which was sold to whites, the project had turned out to have few bona fide resident farmers. Walter Packard, sent out in 1936 by the federal government to find land for resettling poor white migrants on the San Carlos project, discovered there hordes of hired laborers huddled in work camps, not self-reliant family farmers tilling their own fields. In one area, he found that only a single widowed proprietor was still living on her holding; the other eight owners were all nonresidents, among them a certified accountant whose home was in San Francisco. All of those farms had been rented out to tenant operators, some of them working more than 800 acres with migrant workers. Housing for the employees was made of cardboard and flattened tin cans. As many as eight families of laborers were crowded into each hovel, subdivided into apartments by chicken wire. According to Packard, "the area was a rural slum of the worst type."[21]

California subjected its farm workers to an equally wretched style of life, in their housing, in their health care, in their nutrition, in their income and job security. Conditions were especially bad in Imperial Valley, the inspiration of Hollywood movie-makers and the home of the IID, that prime beneficiary of federal largesse and engineering skill. One survey described the valley as offering agricultural workers "the absolute low for the entire state." A California State Relief Administration report described this Imperial scene:

> Many families were found camping out by the side of irrigation ditches, with little or no shelter. One such family consisted of the father, mother, amd eight children. The father hoped there would be some work in the valley later in the year. The mother had tuberculosis and pellagra and it was because of her health that the family came to California. One of the children had active tuberculosis. The family had no home but a 1921 Ford. The mother was trying to chop some wood for the fire. . . . A meat and vegetable

stew was being cooked in a large, rusty tin over a grate supported by four other cans. A cupboard and a table had been constructed of boxes. There were no toilet facilities, Nature's needs being attended to behind bushes. Some water was brought from the ice plant in El Centro for drinking purposes, but for cooking and washing, water from the irrigation ditches was used. The family had been sleeping on the ground. The blankets were kept during the daytime in the car. There was no possible shelter. . . . The mother told the worker on the survey that she had been known as the best housekeeper in her home town.

A year earlier the same agency had estimated that the average family in California required at least $780 annually for a "minimum subsistence" income and $972 for a "health and decency" budget. But the average migrant family in agriculture could expect yearly wages of only $289. The sizable shortfall had to be made up by limited federal assistance or by state relief programs, though to qualify for such aid migrants had to be able to prove a year's residency in California. The landowners employing these families, once they had their crops in, took little notice of their housing or income needs.[22]

Even had they been more inclined to exercise their cooperative skills in solving the degraded farm-labor working conditions, California and Arizona growers would, it must be admitted, have had a task too big for their own resources. There were simply too many refugees from social problems elsewhere who were pouring into their states seeking jobs. By 1939, two or three migrants lined up for every available picker's position. When they could not find work, some of them stubbornly refused to accept any form of government aid. A proud, individualistic lot, they were often culturally unequipped to understand the organized agricultural world into which they had come and tended to look back homeward in nostalgia rather than try to meet the requirements of that world.[23] Just as the federal reclamation engineers had trouble on their projects remaking old-fashioned farmers into modern, successful irrigators, so the West Coast growers were bewildered by the adjustment problems of the "Okies," by the task of transforming them from sharecroppers into a regimented flow of harvesters, moving on cue from crop to crop. It was far easier to bring water to the fields and drain it away than it was to handle the human problems generated by intensive irrigation and its rhythms—or for that matter, the human problems flooding in from the Depression, from historic southern and foreign poverty. That the growers did not want that responsibility and did not much care about finding solutions only escalated an already difficult situation into a tragedy.

What the growers were much better prepared to do was draw together into a cohesive class and seek to defend themselves from the human flood of poor eastern whites. Sure that the new immigrants would prove to be the most intractable laborers of all, the most prone to violence when they did not like their conditions, certain that trouble was brewing on the horizon, employers organized into hiring councils, into protective agencies, and, especially, into anti-union brigades. The most effective of those groups was the Associated Farmers of California, which was formed in 1934 with financing from railroads, utilities, and banks interested in the stable profitability of the state's agriculture. Three years later, the group expanded into a larger group called the United Farmers of the West Coast, moving outward from the core to enlist members in Arizona, Oregon, and Washington. Having subdued nature, they were not about to let a rabble of Okies disrupt their success. Within five years of its founding, the group had a state membership of 40,000 in California alone, plus the full cooperation of the police in most locales (not to mention a private arsenal of guns, tear gas, and pick handles) with which to keep down "radicalism" in the fields. Potentially pitted against them were the 250,000 farm laborers roaming the state, plus an indeterminate number of "reds" and "Communists" who had begun to discover in the made-over desert a cause that demanded their own organizing zeal. The farmers' ditches had become, as it were, a set of moats encircling a besieged fortress in which they lived.[24]

Even before the defense was organized and armed, a rash of agricultural strikes had begun. In 1928, Mexican field hands in Imperial Valley joined together as La Unión de Trabajadores del Valle Imperial and walked out of the cantaloupe patches. Unwilling to seek support from the Filipino workers in the fields, alone and vulnerable in their militancy, the Mexicans had to abandon that strike. But only two years later they were back on the picket lines, this time with Filipino support, surrounding the lettuce crop near Brawley, refusing to let it be harvested until their wage demands were met. This time too they had the help of the Communist party and its Trade Union Unity League. That show of solidarity was enough to stir the Imperial oligarchy into a frenzy of vigilante action and repressiveness, and they had the Communist organizers imprisoned. Meanwhile, other strikes broke out farther north, and some of them involved the new white migrants: there was Santa Clara valley, 1931; Vacaville, 1932 and 1933; the Pixley cotton strike and others in that extraordinary year, 1933; then back to broiling Imperial in 1934. In Pixley, caravans of armed growers opened fire on strikers and their families, killing and wounding men, women, and children, while the highway patrol watched from hiding. In Arvin, the sheriff's deputies lobbed tear-gas into worker picket lines and arrested strikers for "rioting." Year after year of strikes, eruption after eruption of violence, blow after blow rained on workers' heads—until finally the workers' militancy had subsided, had spent itself in futile protest, until the growers had won.[25] Against the coordinated determination of the ruling irrigation order, the tatterdemalion army of stoopers and pickers proved to be completely ineffective. They lacked enough cohesion, interethnic harmony, effective leadership, financial resources, and outside friends to successfully take on and fundamentally change the agricultural power complex that had developed in California. Henceforth, they would have to move quietly along the canals, as the water did—or go away. Much to the relief of the growers, the Okies generally chose the latter course, forsaking the fields for armaments factories and shipyards when World War Two came. Once more, the Mexicans, and Americans of Mexican ancestry, filed back into the vineyards and orchards to do the sweat work.

Fail though they did to force a sharing of power in the hydraulic society, the farm laborers did manage at last to make a vivid impression on the American consciousness. Their breakthrough to recognition came in 1939, when two California writers, John Steinbeck and Carey McWilliams, published books on the laborers' world. Steinbeck's novel *The Grapes of Wrath* was released by Viking Press in mid-April, and it was at the top of the best-seller list by May. It remained near there for the rest of that year and the next and took the Pulitzer Prize in fiction. McWilliams's study of migratory labor, *Factories in the Field,* appeared shortly thereafter, and it supported Steinbeck's fiction with a lawyer's factual details and argumentation. The discovery of appalling poverty in the midst of so rich a farm abundance had impelled both men to write, and they found a nationwide audience among Americans sensitized by a decade of economic depression, ready to feel the misfortunes of an underclass living in far-off, unfamiliar desert places. In many parts of California, however, the two writers were seen as an outrageous pair of libelers, using lies and distortion to discredit a remarkable achievement. The Associated Farmers, for example, described McWilliams as "Agriculture's No. 1 Pest."[26] The farmers feared that a new kind of power was entering their valleys, based not on the control of water or land or labor but on the strength of words—the power of a critical mind to indict, persuade, and help overthrow their agricultural structure.

Neither Steinbeck nor McWilliams, however, was as much a threat as he might have been because neither ever quite understood the hydraulic society for what it was. Looking at what admittedly was a complicated socio-ecological system, they seized on only a part of it. They focused on concentrated land ownership, not on the water regime that made agricultural capitalism so potent and well organized. That failure to see and describe the whole picture hobbled their criticism, tied it up in knots they could not undo, and led to partial, unconvincing remedies. It left, too, a legacy of misanalysis among western American historians and social thinkers, who have continued, as those two writers did, to celebrate the conquest of arid nature in the region while naively hoping for some ideal form of postcapitalistic society to appear there. In the case of Steinbeck and McWilliams, the confused analysis undoubtedly derived from their cultural background. Both were native sons of the West. The first had grown up around ranches, irrigated farms, and small towns of the Salinas Valley of California, while the second came from the Yampa River basin of Colorado, where his father traded real estate and raised cattle.[27] In those rural milieus, the virtue of transforming dry land into a lush productivity had for so long been been promoted as an article of faith that only a complete, crabbed misfit would have been free to question it—and neither man was that. As a result, the fact that the West's agriculture was evolving into a regime of exploitation and violence could not be connected by either man to the manipulation of water. Some other, narrower explanation had to be sought.

Of the two, Steinbeck was more ready to see a connection between the social and the ecological realms. In his novel the main characters, the Joad family of Oklahoma who migrate to California seeking work, are people who have derived their enormous strength and virtue through a long, harmonious relationship with the earth. They exemplify a natural goodness uncorrupted by the modern ideology of economic maximization. In their original setting they are a close-knit family, three generations dwelling together in one household, their identity emerging organically from their farm life. Though the farm is rented, it is theirs and they belong to it, neither dominating it nor being dominated. On that piece of land they are able, to a point, to control their own destiny, though that control is limited by the lack of ownership. As Robert Benton has written, Steinbeck's ideal human community is a modest one existing as part of a vast, complex ecosystem, the human and nonhuman linked together in a single unity.[28] The tragedy of the Joads in Oklahoma is that their unity is shattered by an intruding capitalist economy and its technology. Tractors sent in by some distant corporation to extract more profit from the land force them to pack off to the West Coast, and abandon a life-style that provides an autonomy and a large part of their self-definition. The difficulty for Steinbeck lay in seeing how that same process of destruction might be operating in California; not merely through private land accumulation—he saw that well enough—but also through the elaboration of irrigation.

The Joads carry west with them, as others before them have done, an extravagant, *Sunset*-magazine dream of relocating in an easy oasis life. In California, so they hope, they will escape forever all toil, all hunger, and enjoy a complete release from deprivation. "They's grapes out there," Grandpa says, "just a-hangin' over inta the road. Know what I'm a-gonna do? I'm gonna pick me a wash tub full a grapes, an' I'm gonna set in 'em, an' scrooge aroun', an' let the juice run down my pants."[29] It is an extravagant dream because the high cost of achieving it is never weighed by the Joads, who in their determination to escape and their eagerness to achieve something better, tend to discount their own past. As it turns out, Grandpa himself is not to experience that juicy immersion, dying as he does before the family is out of Oklahoma; he belongs, Steinbeck is aware, to a culture of hard work, humble expectations, and self-restraint. However, Steinbeck leads us to hope that the younger Joads—Ma, Pa, Tom, and the rest—have the possibility of entering and participating in that promised land. They can substitute a man-made California garden for their Oklahoma farm and live better than ever. All that is required is to pass through the desert; then that paradise will be theirs. And as they emerge from their deadly nighttime passage through the Mohave, as in the morning they surmount the Tehachapi Mountains from which they can see the long-anticipated irrigated landscape, they stop in awestruck wonder, admiring the green fields stretching away below them, the rows and rows of orchards, the money represented in those well-to-do farms. Pa speaks for them all when he says, "I want ta look at her. . . . I never knowed they was anything like her."[30] Embodied in that rush of excitement is a colossal innocence about the valley and the forces that had made it. Unfortunately, it was Steinbeck's innocence as much as the Joads's. He had forgotten that his characters had been formed in the environment of another, freer, more natural world and that they could belong here only if they radically changed, became less independent and far different people. If they wanted to be part of the valley, the only conceivable place for the Joads would be under somebody else's thumb.

Nowhere in *The Grapes of Wrath* does Steinbeck draw attention to the elaborate hydraulic apparatus that has been required to create the California garden. In fact, the process of irrigation does not even appear in the text. Grapes, carrots, cotton, and the like are the products, it would seem, of spontaneous nature, not the contrivances of advanced water engineering and the social organization it has required. The Joads, unfamiliar with the new landscape, are understandably angered when they discover there is no place for the likes of them in this paradise. Nature has never been ungenerous to them before, and they cannot comprehend why this new "nature" is different.

Another migrant, who has had his hopes dashed, gives them his version of what has gone wrong: "She's a nice country. But she was stole a long time ago."[31] Steinbeck agrees too quickly with that simplified analysis. The problem in California, he indicates at many points, is that a few greedy landowners have monopolized the garden and want to keep the Joads out. If that were the only problem, then the sufficient solution would be to challenge their ownership, and, in fact, that is precisely what Steinbeck does recommend, along with setting up some clean, government-funded labor camps, pushing worker unionization, and redistributing the economic rewards of the valley. Those were all humane, useful ideas, all planks in the New Deal platform of social reform, but the reader senses that Steinbeck's heart is not really in them. To put deep confidence in such distributional changes, he would have to alter drastically his original argument. He would have to insist after all that the land should be remade by advanced technology and that the corporatized social order carrying out that redemption can everywhere, in Oklahoma as well as in California, be a good home for people like the Joads. And he does not quite believe any of that. He is more pessimistic about the promise of the technological dominance of nature. The inconsistency between Steinbeck's efforts at solution and his analysis of the underlying causes is damaging to the book, rendering it in the end unconvincing and half-hearted. A moving indictment in its early chapters, it becomes in the second half a straining, reformist tract. The main source of his difficulty is that Steinbeck is not prepared to admit in California what he can perceive so clearly in Oklahoma: that it is finally the apparatus and ideology of unrestrained environmental conquest which lies at the root of the Joads' affliction.

Steinbeck's portrayal of the Joad family tragedy was complicated to the point of despair by his ambivalence about the past and present. He looked back with a sense of loss to a decentralized rural society that had developed in the more humid East, yet he also affirmed (or tried to) the new, modern hydraulic order of the West, with its technology-based luxuriance of production. Carey McWilliams, in contrast, was not nearly so complicated in his loyalties. His *Factories in the Field* was a much simpler book, offering in the end an unambiguous formula for people like the Joads: collective ownership of the farms, a social revolution against capitalism. That remedy was taken from the standard leftist textbooks of the 1930s. By applying it to West Coast agriculture, McWilliams broke down the mental barriers separating the region from the rest of the nation. He joined the plight of its farm workers to that of textile employees in New Jersey, coal miners in Kentucky, and assembly-line automatons in Detroit. He came to believe that in each of those places there was a similar small handful of industrial capitalists who owned the means of production, while a repressed proletariat slaved away for them at minimal wages, or worse, got laid off in slack times, stood in breadlines, beat the streets for a job. For a boy from a Rocky Mountain backwater, McWilliams learned that urban Marxist analysis very quickly and grasped its relevance for the rural West. And unhesitantly he joined the battle. With other intellectuals across the country, he allied himself with that struggling proletariat, including workers of all races— with whomever he felt had been dealt a losing hand in American life.

Unfortunately, there were two elementary problems plaguing that conventional leftist stance and spoiling its appeal for Americans, then and later on. First, it was too trusting in the forces of modernity to be thoroughly credible. Already in Europe groups like the Frankfurt philosophers were demonstrating that the repressive impact of industrial society required something more than collective ownership of the means of production. Second, the standard leftist analysis—and it was certainly so in the case of McWilliams—failed to make room for nature, either as a historical actor or as a moral issue. In that respect, leftists were no different from capitalists, both standing for the conquest of the natural world, and their visions of the future tended to converge toward the same technological utopianism. Their differences might not seem profound enough to make a fight for a socialist revolution in the West worth the trouble.

McWilliams's book is at once a historical study of the class struggle between farm workers and owners and a report on the violent events of the day. He tells the bloody, ghastly story of the Wheatland riot of 1913, when the Industrial Workers of the World were driven from California fields; of the birth of the communistic Cannery and Agricultural Workers' Industrial Union; of the militant strikes from 1929 to 1935. Out of those events emerges a pattern of what he calls "farm fascism," an organized, centralized, authoritarian effort by groups like the Associated Farmers (many of whom, he reveals, openly admired Hitler and the storm troopers of Germany) to keep the Okies and Mexicans under control.[32] Fascism, he argues, is the last stage in capitalist agricultural development, a final desperate effort of the oppressive few to hold on to their position. It is hopeless for them, however, for they have created the very agent of their own defeat: a system of agriculture that is "large-scale, intensive, diversified, mechanized" but which, through their greed, has been rendered chaotic, inefficient, and irrational. The contradiction between the system and its present fascist owners is too great; a socialist future of collectivized agriculture has increasingly become inevitable, a future when all classes will be abolished, when reason will be unshackled, when efficiency will be triumphant, when peace will come at last to California.

Irrigation has a more prominent place in McWilliams's account than in Steinbeck's, but nowhere is it systematically examined or taken into account. His Marxist-like logic tells McWilliams that private property, not the domination of nature, is the source of all abusive power, and in agriculture, he assumes, private property must mean private, concentrated landowner-ship. To be sure, he acknowledges at one point the inadequacy of that theory when he points out that rural California is a "forced plant—the product of irrigation."[33] Later he goes on to show how the the development of an artificial water supply leads to new crop patterns, new labor require-ments, new concentrations of capital, and new employer solidarity: that it is mainly irrigation, in other words, which makes the "factories in the field" work. Far more than concentrated landownership, irrigation has promoted the industrialization of farming in the state. Yet despite the shock implied in the title of his book, McWilliams has nothing to say against industrialism per se nor is he at all opposed to large-scale irrigation.

> California agriculture is a magnificent achievement: in its
> scope, efficiency, organization and amazing abundance.
> The great farm valleys of California, rescued from sage-
> brush and desert, are easily among the richest agricultural
> regions of the world. The anachronistic system of owner-
> ship by which they are at present controlled must be
> changed before the valleys can come into their own.[34]

Put the new-fangled hydraulic society under socialism, he suggests. Make nature obey the dictates of the collective ownership, and the West will be set right. Power will then belong to all the people, which is to say it will cease to be a social problem.

For many American readers of 1939, the prospect of establishing collec-tive irrigated farms in the West must have summoned up the recent experi-ence in the Soviet Union. Under orders from Joseph Stalin, millions of liberated serfs there were herded onto the lands of the dispossessed kulaks, lands now owned by the state, and set to toiling for the common good. Those who refused to conform, who revolted against the state and its commissars, were reviled, beaten, or shot down.[35] Carey McWilliams was not by any means a Stalinist, nor did he intend to advocate any authoritarian strategy; undoubtedly he had in mind some more humane method of bringing collec-tivism to rural California. Unfortunately, he did not tell anyone what that method was, or how it could be made to work, or what the blueprint would be. Would he call in a gang of bureaucrats who would take over from capitalists the day-to-day management of California agriculture? Would the technicians of water control retire from the scene and put simple folks like the Joads in charge? How would McWilliams enforce the industrial or hydraulic work patterns among hitherto individualistic workers? Those were some of the questions that had to be addressed if people were to know how to act, were to see what was possible and efficacious. However, other than by a few, passing catchphrases, *Factories in the Field* did not address these questions. Had they been more carefully addressed, Americans might at least have had a clearer sense of the options available to them, if in fact there were any. As it was, the option already in force was the only one they were really equipped to understand, and the vague suggestion of a socialist future could only summon up a nightmare of repression at least as bad as the one already going on in California.

By the end of the thirties, the unresolved conundrum was whether there was any conceivable social instrumentality that could be trusted to carry out the modern reclamation of the arid lands. No one was yet willing to consider abandoning the general project, but no one could show how it could be continued without risking severe human costs. The situation seemed clear but unfortunate: someone would have to be put to doing the sweat work, while someone else would get most of the profit and power. In fact, it was an inescapable predicament, inherent in the very nature of the project of technological domination. Unable to understand and solve it at the time, Americans decided to ignore it—or at least to postpone its consideration to another day.

WHO RULES THE GREAT VALLEY?

The revolutionary winds that have blown through history have flattened the strongest fences, uprooted the richest crops, and overturned the most carefully defended societies. For California growers in the mid-1930s, such a wind seemed to be rising in their labor camps and in the shantytowns of desperate migrants: a hot, fierce wind that threatened to wither their vines hanging heavy with ripe bunches of grapes. They were expecting such a wind, and expecting it, they were prepared to defeat it. What they did not anticipate was that a wind from an altogether different quarter might blow up, one bearing the smell of rain, and that it might have its own potential for making radical changes in the prevailing power structure and

233

farm operations of the state. That wind, when it came, blew from the federal water bureaucracy. It was a strong wind—far more so, it turned out, than the one coming from the direction of the camps. To be sure, at first it seemed more benign, but then wet winds can be destructive too, can knock down fences and blow away a ruling class. The problem for the growers was to determine whether that federal wind was to be another revolutionary threat to their estates or whether it could be relied on as an ally against revolution.

From the vantage of the farm laborers, the growers' position seemed impregnable, defended as it was by a heavy phalanx of police and guns and politicians. But had they been thinking ecologically, the laborers and their supporters might have seen how really vulnerable that position was. The growers needed water, and more and more of it, to maintain their cohesion, to expand their wealth, to stay in business. Imperial Valley's vulnerability has been discussed. An equally perilous condition existed in the Great Central Valley, especially in its naturally dry southern parts, from Fresno to Bakersfield. By the early twenties, the water there began to run out. District after district had borrowed funds and built advanced water systems, until the surface supply had been completely appropriated. For example, by 1930 the Kings River, a secondary stream out of the Sierra, was irrigating over one million acres, more than any other river in the world except the Nile and the Indus.[1] The consequences of that overconsumption ramified all the way to the sea. Low or no flow coming downstream made enemies and rivals, destroyed grower unity, and overloaded the courts. It also produced profound environmental changes in the major estuary of the state, San Francisco Bay, and let the ocean invade from San Pablo and the Carquinez Strait up the Sacramento–San Joaquin delta, leaving farms and towns there with salty instead of fresh water.

The electric water pump appeared in the nick of time to postpone that water crisis in the making. Under the dry surface, moving slowly through the deep, permeable alluvial soils of the valley, was a seep of underground water of immense proportions, a natural reservoir stored in the pores of sand and gravel deposits lying at depths of hundreds, even thousands, of feet. A pump was the only means to tap that pool, to suck it out. Racing to get their share of the new bonanza of water, farmers began punching down wells right and left, in the foothills, on the sandy plains, in areas where no irrigation before had been possible, opening up new lands for investment. Tulare County, directly north of Bakersfield, had 739 pumps going in 1910; by 1919, there were 3,758 of them, a major reason why that county had become the fourth largest producer of farm wealth in the United States. From 1918 into the early 1920s, a series of droughts intensified the pumping. Then came the familiar, dreary denouement to entrepreneurial expansion: rapid resource depletion, increasingly expensive technology to beat the competition, a diminishing number of survivors. From 1921, when the state first began systematically to measure the number of wells and their capacity, to 1939, the average groundwater level in the upper San Joaquin area fell 39 feet. And old neighborhoods, old communities, began to fall with it.[2]

The social effects of the underground water depletion appear in a couple of examples, both suggesting a new concentration of wealth in the wake of scarcity. Jimmie Palmer, manager of a 600-acre orange grove in Tulare County, was one of the few who had access to the means to stay in the race, but even for him survival was not easy. His water bill in 1930 amounted to $32,000. Three of his wells went dry in the middle of the growing season, forcing him to drill a new one, going down 507 feet and costing a thousand dollars.[3] Undoubtedly his less affluent neighbors were not so fortunate. In Kern County, an even bigger man appeared and began buying out failing farmers: Joseph DiGiorgio, an Italian immigrant who had for a while, as a young man on the East Coast, successfully contested United Fruit's international market dominance. DiGiorgio came West in 1915 with a large bankroll earned in the banana trade and began putting together what would eventually be a "ranch" of 10,000 acres in the vicinity of Arvin, almost all of it in grapes—row upon row, staked and wired, of White Malagas, Red Emperors, Alicantes, Tokays, Thompson Seedless—raised for raisins and for wine. As his neighbors' wells went dry, he bought them out and sank new shafts, outfitted with enormous gasoline pumps costing $10,000 apiece. Equipped thus to reach the water that no one else could, DiGiorgio went on to create around him a private fiefdom. He shipped 10 million boxes of fruit a year to his winery, to stores everywhere, and hired a permanent resident labor force, freeing himself from the complete dependency of other, smaller growers on the migrant tides. DiGiorgio also gave the lie to the creaky myth that irrigation would always be a force to break up huge landed estates into family farms. On the contrary, he showed that at a certain point in its intensification, irrigation had precisely the opposite effect, replacing a loose rural egality with a hard knot of command.[4]

Even a DiGiorgio, however, could not go on pumping indefinitely, going down deeper and deeper, spewing out water from the bowels of the earth. Some other solution had to be found for depletion than a better pump. One possibility was to declare all underground water to be public property and then designate the state as a rationing agency, much as New Mexico did in its pioneering legislation of 1931. The American Farm Bureau Federation, at a 1935 meeting in Los Angeles, called for just that solution, but it was never implemented; too interfering, was the California growers' reaction.[5] Their rejection of controlled pumping left only one other hope, if disaster in the San Joaquin and Kern river country was to be avoided. New water would have to be located and brought in from some outside source.

The star candidate for that augmented supply was the Sacramento River in the north. There, it had been common knowledge for a long time (at least since the Alexander Commission report of 1874), could be found two-thirds of the water in the Great Valley but only one-third of the arable land. Obviously, the imbalance was a monumental error, a defect in the design of nature, and it had to be corrected. Californians forthwith set about with awesome determination to put things right. It was the sort of adjustment, writes historian John Caughey, "that God would have made had he known the facts in the case."[6] God surely would have if He had been an agricultural capitalist bent on unlimited expansion.

Or, if He were a visionary sort like Colonel Robert Bradford Marshall, a geographer in the employ of the United States Geological Survey and the Reclamation Service. After arriving in California in 1891, Marshall had, for reasons known only to him, given long private hours to working out the essentials for remaking the valley. He had dreamed, in his words, "that dream of EMPIRE BUILDING that every man of vision at one time or another has dreamed when he views California's millions of acres parched and burning in the summer and her millions of acre feet of water pouring into the Pacific in the winter." In 1919, in a pamphlet entitled *Irrigation of Twelve Million Acres in the Valley of California,* he had sketched a blueprint of water engineering that would make the state, he promised, "the world's greatest garden." It involved the construction of a dam near the headwaters of the Sacramento and, from there, a set of canals running southward, first downhill to the lowlands around the capital, then uphill (using pumps) to the Tehachapis and over them into the Los Angeles basin. The price would be a mere $1 billion, or twice the cost of the Panama Canal. "This is a day of large undertakings," Marshall declared, adding that "small ideas have no place in California."[7]

For a while it must have seemed that large ideas had no place there either, as year after year Marshall lobbied unsuccessfully to get his dream accepted by the people. Fortunately he managed to plant its main features in the minds of some authorities who counted more than he: a group of technicians and bureaucrats in Sacramento government offices, zealous centralized planners who wanted to put their expertise to work making the valleys and rivers of the state over into what one historian has described as "a more rational economic order."[8] Marshall's scheme exactly suited their ordering ambitions. In 1920, they began a series of water-resource studies for all of California. Ten years later, those studies yielded the State Water Plan, the most comprehensive scheme of its kind anywhere in the West but still not quite up to the standard of dreaming set by Marshall. The plan, for instance, omitted the Cecil B. DeMille stunt of lifting a river over the Tehachapis, and it carried an initial price tag of only $160 million. California voters liked its more modest scale and, though in the midst of a depression, voted in 1933 to sell bonds and begin construction. All did, that is, except the private utility conglomerate, Pacific Gas and Electric, and the disgruntled folks of Los Angeles. The former resented the competition from public power to be generated and sold by the state and the latter, who had had to pay by themselves to drain water out of the Owens Valley and the Colorado, were not happy about using their credit to get a water supply to the Great Valley farmers.[9]

Measured by strict cost accounting in the private sector, the plan to send the Sacramento south would have been regarded as a losing proposition. No private grower, not even the most flamboyant risk-taker, would have dared undertake it if he had to foot the whole bill. It was feasible only if a government agency did the borrowing, and then only if it could borrow the funds at a mere 3 percent rate of interest or less, only if it could have fifty years to pay them off, and only if it could spread the costs to taxpayers. Had the scheme been left solely in the hands of the state of California, more than likely it would have been shelved, for the state was not in a position to get such favorable financial terms nor, as it turned out, was it really in a mood to undertake so large a debt on its own. Californians fully expected that the federal government would take the project off their hands. Then it would not only be Los Angeles clerks or Imperial growers who would be paying for the Great Valley's overexpansion and depletion of resources but also clerks in Chicago, lumberjacks in Maine, and poor sharecroppers in the South.

The year California approved its state water plan, 1933, found the federal Bureau of Reclamation in sad shape, starving for funds and under attack. It was then at the dead end of thirty years of failure. To be sure, there was Hoover Dam rising majestically on the Colorado, a river now under the Bureau's sole management, but otherwise the agency was in emergency distress. Three decades of its projects in the West had produced a disappointingly small number of new family farms, and most of those were barely surviving. The Bureau's yearly budget, based on repayment by settlers into its revolving fund, had dribbled down to $8 million. More serious yet, eastern congressmen were demanding to know why, in a time of national economic crisis, staggering poverty, and crop surpluses, the Bureau existed at all, why it should still be promoting western settlement, why it kept asking for loans from the federal treasury.[10] All of the objections raised in 1902 against federalized reclamation and pooh-poohed by westerners now had been thoroughly vindicated. The Bureau, however, was not about to close down shop, admit that its mission was over, that its reason for being was no longer compelling. It was not about to die quietly by its own hand. Bureaucracies, like natural organisms, have an intense desire to survive and reproduce themselves, to extend their range and influence even where they are beset by hostile forces. In 1933 the Bureau, under Elwood Mead's directorship, began casting about hungrily for new food on which to feed. It promoted a new private lobbying organization, the National Reclamation Association, bearing the ebullient banner "Without Irrigation Western Progress Stops."[11] The Bureau also set about redefining its niche in the scheme of things, seeking first to exploit the depression environment of the thirties and, beyond that, to nose into the emerging agribusiness vineyards of the West Coast.

What the Bureau wanted, and what it had to have, was precisely what in 1902 it had promised never to request: a regular appropriation from the federal treasury. Among themselves, many western leaders supported such an appropriation on the old, scarcely concealed ground that it was the West's manifest destiny and right. The senator from Idaho, James Pope, promised that an expanded reclamation program "could not fail to pave the way for an expected and almost inevitable population movement to the West." Of all the arguments for the Bureau and its budget, this was the most insensitive and inept, blithely assumming as it did that eastern states would be delighted to subsidize their own decline. Luckily there were shrewder men around to make the case that reclamation was not a gift but a sound "business policy," an investment that would enrich many easterners too. As late as 1939 that rationalization was still being trotted out: since its beginnings, it was said that year, federal reclamation had produced over $2 billion worth of crops; it had cost a mere $170 per acre watered; federal projects contributed less than 1 percent to the national surplus in wheat, corn, and cotton; over 50,000 new farm homes had been created, along with schools and churches; and those project farmers were spending their income on manufactured goods from the East. Never mind for the moment that they would have done the same had they been kept on eastern farms. The point was that reclamation meant economic expansion, "a greater America," and no one could kick against that.[12]

Stirred by such drumbeats, Congress consented at last to open the public purse. In 1936, the Bureau was given $16 million in general funds (it took in only $1.3 million from repayments that year), an amount that doubled by 1939, doubled again in 1940, and, following World War II, shot even higher and stayed there: $118 million in 1949, $314 million in 1950, $124 million in 1960, $154 million in 1968. And those sums did not begin to indicate the enriched diet on which the agency now was feeding, for also in the thirties it discovered that the generation and sale of hydroelectric power from its western dams was the very elixir of bureaucratic life.[13]

The old imperative of domination had not begun to be satisfied. There were rivers in the West not yet utilized, bleak dry valleys not yet redeemed. A sense of historic inevitability was pushing Americans on in the thirties as it had been doing for a long time to possess the continent, to settle its most trying places, and then to say, "We mastered even this, we made it pay." The Bureau understood perfectly that traditional American cultural imperative, knew how to absorb and utilize it to serve its own institutional ends. But for those Americans no longer stirred by the dream of domination, and there were more of them in the age of the Great Depression than ever before, the Bureau had another, more appealing pitch to make. It could become an agency of salvage as well as conquest, and salvage was an undisputed thirties program. All over the country were communities, urban and rural, in desperate straits, needing salvage: poor, threatened communities that had been ground down by the industrial apparatus and tossed aside, or that had inherited a legacy of land abuse and were trapped in it through no fault of their own. Among those communities, the Bureau decided, was the Great Valley of California. It too needed salvage, and the Bureau stood ready to the task.

In 1930, a joint federal-state commission recommended that the national government put money into the California State Water Plan. A study done for the Bureau of Reclamation by three state residents, Frank Adams, David Morgan, and Walter Packard, stated the reasons for that recommendation. "If an additional supply of water is not brought in," they warned, "there will be an agricultural retrogression and an impairment of values that will adversely affect not only the entire southern San Joaquin Valley, but will be felt in more distant centers to which the trade and commerce of southern San Joaquin Valley contribute." Lured by the hope of abundant groundwater, many had wildly invested in land and now were heavily in debt, with those prospects of aquifer irrigation falling rapidly, with foreclosure by the banks a looming threat. Thousands of existing farms might soon have to be abandoned. A sorry scene, one made even sorrier, the study suggested, because the valley boasted "a very high type of civilization," with one of the largest percentages of automobile ownership in the United States.[14]

Convinced of the gravity of the situation, President Franklin Roosevelt allocated $20 million of emergency relief funds in September 1935, and the Bureau speedily moved in to begin construction. Two years later the Rivers and Harbors Act authorized the Central Valley Project, which would transform the State Water Plan into a federal salvage scheme. The CVP would be the biggest project in Bureau history, and it would all be undertaken within the borders of a single state—a spectacularly rich state, with some of the wealthiest agricultural counties in the nation, not an Appalachia or a dust bowl but John Steinbeck's land of plenty. The CVP also marked the virtual abandonment by the Bureau of its original self-justification, the myth that it was set up mainly to be a builder of homes for the homeless urban masses. That justification had always been largely a propaganda device to get eastern support for western reclamation. Henceforth it would hardly be mentioned at all. From this point on, the Bureau was in the more pressing business of saving a big, multi-billion-dollar private agricultural investment.

The Central Valley Project threw a little water and a great deal of electrical power at many consumers to enlist their support, but primarily it was, in design and rationale, a faucet for irrigation farmers. Its chief feature was Shasta Dam, begun in 1938 and completed in 1944: a 602-foot-high structure, containing 6 million cubic yards of concrete and the largest hydroelectric plant in California. Part of the power from Shasta lifted the Sacramento River, down in the delta area at the massive Tracy pumping plant, into two canals. The shorter of them, the Contra Costa Channel, ran westward toward San Francisco Bay, furnishing fresh water to farms and factories threatened by saline intrusion. The other, the Delta-Mendota Canal, ran southward, paralleling the San Joaquin River. Improving on nature, the water in that canal ran uphill for 120 miles before being dumped into the river and allowed to run back toward the sea. The point to that exercise in technical virtuosity was to re-create the river that farmers and the Bureau were elsewhere destroying, to restore irrigation supplies to districts left dry by upvalley withdrawals. Now the upper San Joaquin could be consumed without stint. Forthwith the Bureau proceeded to capture that river behind a world-class dam, Friant, lying to the northwest of Fresno. From that dam, the Friant-Kern Canal, the longest man-made channel in the CVP, snaked over 150 miles south toward Delano, toward Bakersfield, toward men like Joseph DiGiorgio. And those were only the initial features. The Bureau projected an eventual plumbing system of forty dams and reservoirs, twenty-eight hydroelectric plants, and eleven main canals, the whole contraption to cost $2 billion at a minimum, or an amount roughly equal to the total value of all the farms in the state in 1930. That was how the Bureau of Reclamation defined salvage in Depression America—and how it made more rational an irrational nature.[15]

To be credible and sell its projects to Congress, the reborn, businesslike Bureau claimed to follow a rigorous system of cost-benefit accounting. The old Bureau had undertaken too many projects of marginal economic worth, projects that could never hope to recapture their costs. For the CVP, in contrast, the calculations were advertised as more methodical and hard-nosed. When completed, one Bureau study claimed, the project would produce benefits of $296 million a year. These would be set over against an annual cost and maintenance expense of $210 million—a positive ratio of almost 1.5 to 1. However, on closer inspection those benefits, so firmly arithmetical in the charts, had a disconcerting tendency to vaporize. Forty percent of them, according to the study, would accrue to the nation as a whole, in the airy form of flood control and navigation improvement (tradi-tionally considered national responsibilities), increased agricultural and industrial production, gains in "social stability," provision for future farm settlements that could remove people from relief rolls, and the like. Another 10 percent would be equally nebulous statewide benefits. Local nonfarm interests would get 11 percent of the project value. The rest of the benefits —the hard facts in the case—would go to the actual water users, including a few municipalities as well as the irrigated farms. And the bill for all that plumbing—who would pay it? Not the irrigating farmers, by and large; they would be asked to cover only 33 percent of the project costs. The greater share by far would come from the sale of power generated at Shasta Dam, in effect collecting a subsidy for valley agriculture from electricity consum-ers in the city.[16]

All but lost in the general cost-benefit statistics were those actual farms supposedly in need of salvage, suffering from groundwater depletion. The Bureau determined that there were from 200,000 to 250,000 acres in the Great Valley seriously in danger of reverting to desert—and that was all. The golden faucet would water those acres, to be sure, but its chief benefit, it began to be clear, would be that it would irrigate *three million new acres,* land that was in private hands, land that would make many gambling investors very well-to-do. Twelve years after CVP authorization, the Secre-tary of the Interior explained, "Without additional utilization of its water resources, the economic development of the Central Valley will be limited to its present level."[17] In other words, the mission of salvage turned out to be predominantly a mission of irrigation expansion. The Bureau was unabashedly undertaking, at enormous cost, with subsidies from public power and interest-free loans, the reclamation of private land—and this in

241

a valley notorious for its pick handles and tear gas, its filthy labor camps and overpriced company stores.

Strange to say, hardly anyone in the state of California in 1935, or for a long time thereafter, found anything wrong in that arrangement. A ready acquiescence indicated that the Bureau was extraordinarily adept at identifying the collective human good in California with its centralized, coordinated manipulation of nature. It came into the state as a jolly giant bearing gifts, enough gifts for all, and few people were inclined either to turn them down or to complain about their distribution or even to question the power dispensing them. One exception was J. Rupert Mason, a idiosyncratic banker who was a follower of the radical land reformer Henry George. "I never favored getting federal gifts," Mason recalled late in his life; "I believed that would have a poisonous effect on the project from the beginning." It would, he feared, undermine home rule and local control, leading to a Hitler-like concentration of power in America.[18] The typical valley farmer would have scoffed at such fears, as would their irrigation-district staffs. Harry Barnes, manager of the Madera Irrigation District, wrote this to his congressman in 1936:

> The federal government . . . has back of it the legal powers of the government which could be used to coordinate and bring into line discordant elements which under state management and subject to State laws only, might hold back the building of the project for years, through petty litigation.

His congressman, B. W. Gearhart, urged the approval of the CVP too, but on rather different grounds: "We are asking not so much for the improvement of California for Californians alone, as for its development for the benefit of all the people of the United States, for the tens of thousands of people—yes; the hundreds of thousands of people from all over the Union that are coming to California to establish their homes in its Great Central Valley."[19] And Carey McWilliams, ten years after his book attacking valley farmers appeared, was enthusiastically on the side of valley federalization: "The full and early realization of this project is absolutely vital to the future well-being of the people of California."[20] A strong wind was rising along the Potomac, gusting all the way to the West Coast, carrying a heavy load of moisture, and Californians of every persuasion were pleading that the moisture fall on them.

That near-unanimity of support did not last long. Within seven years after its full authorization in 1937, the Central Valley Project was tangled in the most serious controversy in the Bureau's history, one that once more endangered the agency's very life. How it came about and why is a story that has been told before, but the essential point of that story remains obscure. The controversy was not sought by the Bureau but happened to it, as outside forces tried to shift the direction its wind was blowing. Those outside forces were a handful of New Deal liberals on the West Coast who were new to the game of bureaucratic power enhancement and misunderstood how it must be played to succeed. They also too readily assumed that an agency whose first responsibility was the domination of nature could go on fulfilling that duty and still promote their plans for redemocratizing the West. What the controversy about the CVP revealed in the most unmistakable terms was that an institution like the Bureau of Reclamation was an improbable source of fundamental social change. As a bureaucracy, it wanted first to survive and then to augment its own power. Its natural ally was whoever already held power in rural California, and that meant the farm owners, not the laborers. Serving those owners in their hour of need was the surest formula for Bureau success. As an agency of conquest, the Bureau was inevitably going to be on the side of whoever was already committed to, and engaged in, that conquest—again, the established, successful growers. Failing to grasp those realities, the western liberals succeeded in bringing the project to a slowdown, but committed as they themselves were to its completion, to the idea of engineering a grandiose plumbing system, they finally had to relent and give up their program of social reform to get the job done.

The issue that cracked the unanimity and almost shattered the Bureau's new strategy was the small provision in the 1902 reclamation law on acreage limitation. That law, as indicated earlier, read that no single landowner could get federal water for more than 160 acres of irrigable land. Generally, the provision had been interpreted by the Bureau to mean that no owner in a federal project could hang on to more than 160 acres, though the law was explicitly a limit on water, not land. Other cloudy interpretations plagued the law, and the Bureau tended to let them go unresolved, exercising its own discretion in specific cases, avoiding sending a request to Congress for clarification of the rules. The Bureau, it was plain to see, was more eager to construct dams than to insist on a rigorous enforcement of the law. Hence it had not complained when the Imperial Valley had secured an exemption from any acreage limitation. In 1939 and 1940, it supported exemption for farmers in Nevada and Colorado. Over all, a survey revealed in 1946 that 3.4 percent of all ownerships on Bureau projects exceeded 160 acres—and those owners held 30.5 percent of all project land.[21] Such was the record of enforcement after more than four decades. Even then the Bureau concealed the real number of noncomplying owners by allowing in common-property states, including California, a farm of 320 acres, 160 acres for the wife, 160 acres for the husband, though that was not specifically allowed in the 1902 law.

Despite the Bureau's easy ways, Californians had long been leery of the reclamation law and, for fear of it, had allowed few federal projects within their borders before the 1930s, preferring as they did to go along on their own. Desire for the CVP changed their thinking, but the old leeriness was still there. The law authorizing the project (and giving farmers fifty years to repay the costs assigned to them, at no interest during that time) pointedly stated that the reclamation law would apply in the case. Californians did not want to believe it, and Bureau officials, eager to get to work, assured them there was no reason to worry. Harry Barnes, the manager of the Madera Irrigation District, in a memorandum to his board of directors, expressed a common assumption that they would be let off. The acreage limitation, he wrote, was

> wholly impracticable for a settled area such as will be served by the Central Valley Project. It is so inapplicable that no one ever considered it seriously in connection with the Central Valley, as it was realized that the Bureau would have to find a way around those provisions if the project was to operate.

On 16 September 1940, Barnes wrote to Mead's replacement as commissioner of the Bureau, John C. Page, and to the Secretary of the Interior, Harold Ickes, to find out what that way around the law was going to be. Page's answer was that Interior's legal staff was still pondering the matter —it had been a mere ten years now since federal participation in the project had first been suggested—but he was personally in favor of exempting the valley. Reassured by the commissioner himself, Barnes told his board that there would not be much difficulty in getting, if necessary, "remedial legislation."[22]

It was not going to be that simple. Late in the day, after construction was well begun on Shasta Dam and the other structures, the federal government began to scrutinize more closely the valley it was helping. Prior to that point Secretary Ickes had given the reclamation program scant consideration except to say he thought there was enough agricultural land in the United States already and that he would like to swap the the Bureau of Reclamation for the Forest Service over in the Department of Agriculture. However, when he understood that reclamation could also be about dams and electricity, Ickes came around to a more supportive position. Building concrete monoliths like Shasta and generating cheap public power were ideas he warmed to fast; the Bureau, he decided, could become his weapon against the monopolistic private utilities he disliked.[23] Ickes' yawning disinterest in agriculture and reclamation remained nonetheless and was compounded by the Bureau's complacency. His first reclamation commissioner, Elwood Mead, though a professed social reformer, did not bother to tell him about the acreage limitation or to advocate its enforcement, nor did Page. Up to the very end of the decade, both the Bureau and the Department of the Interior were placidly moving forward with their engineering schemes, avoiding any cause for alarm on the part of the growers in California, seeking a way around the acreage limitation. What changed all that undoubtedly was a jolt from the West Coast: the publication in 1939 of *The Grapes of Wrath* and *Factories in the Field*. Suddenly, it became rather difficult for a liberal government in Washington to give subsidized, unrestricted water to groups like the reactionary Associated Farmers, to underwrite their labor policies and their concentration of wealth. At least somebody would have to do some homework first.

In the fall of 1942, the water technicians contracted with several other agencies, mainly the Bureau of Agricultural Economics, to carry out a series of Central Valley Project studies. The charge was to discover what consequences the project would have for California, which in turn entailed knowing more about its existing social structure. None of the studies dealt much with the system of class division promoted by advanced irrigation, and their authors took for granted that the CVP would be finished one way or another, so that it was "no longer profitable to speculate on the wisdom of building or not building." Nor was it useful to waste time on dreaming up genuinely radical alternatives, for "the development of the project must be planned under our democratic and capitalistic system." All the same, taken together, the studies made a fairly strong case for using the Bureau's leverage over farmers to reform the valley, whether that reform were to be restricted to acreage limitation or expanded to some more ambitious program.[24]

One of the best of the studies, Problem 24, "Economic Effects," came out of the BAE's office in Berkeley. Among its authors were Marion Clawson, Walter Goldschmidt, J. Karl Lee, and Mary Montgomery—all bright, young, devoted New Deal liberals who had a knack for following every strong statement in their report with a milder one, lest any critic accuse them of being obstructionist. For all that waffling, their report threw an unflattering light on the farm scene in California. The average farm in the state, they discovered, was worth three times the value of the average American farm, putting it well out of the reach of the aspiring poor. A farm laborer who wanted to buy land there and set himself up as a grower needed at least $2,000, a virtually hopeless expectation. With the delivery of CVP water, which even under public subsidy would be expensive water, the costs of farming would go up further. Specialization of cropping made the social order even more restrictive. Carey McWilliams to the contrary notwithstanding, there were few genuine corporate farms in the state, but there was a corporatized farm economy, specialized and organized around the marketing cooperatives and their packing sheds: a tightly interwoven fabric of control made up growers, bankers, and city businessmen. The president of the California Fruit Growers Exchange, to cite but one example from the study, was also president of the Walnut Growers Association, vice-president of a bank, president of the Agricultural Council of California, a director of the State Chamber of Commerce, and president of his water district. To sluice water into this man's fields was to irrigate a near-monopolistic agriculture. The Bureau of Reclamation therefore had now to decide whether or not it was going to prop up and protect that closed society. "It is impossible," the Berkeley staff insisted, "to be neutral on this question." Yet they themselves had some difficulty deciding on a forthright stance that would be at once "practical" and reformist.[25]

The best they could offer under the late-moment circumstances was a program of enforcing acreage limitation combined with a movement away from intensive irrigation in the direction of general farming. Instead of setting up grape and lettuce factories, farmers should diversify by adding livestock to their operations. That way they would require fewer migrant laborers at harvest time and be more free of the monopolistic agribusiness pressures. In that fashion, farm ownership might become a possibility once again for the landless. Would such an economy be less efficient? The Berkeley researchers denied it, but they added, "efficiency may also be a false god, the worship of which leads to a denial of important social values." All well and good to say, but there was a practical wrinkle that the researchers could not quite get ironed out. Water costing $5 an acre-foot was not going to be paid for by letting more beef cattle lunch on irrigated pastures. The very scale of the CVP vastly overshadowed the old-fashioned diversified farm economy the researchers advocated; they were expecting a twelve-cylinder Dusenberg engine to run a Model T. Only if the American public were to pick up even more of the cost of the project could it happen, and the study did not venture that recommendation.

Other CVP studies documented the grossly unequal distribution of land in the southern reaches of the Great Valley. Although three out of four owners in Tulare, Madera, and Kern counties had only eighty acres or less, they did not dominate farming there. A mere 3 percent of the owners controlled 41 percent of all cropland, 52 percent of all land. Put another way, 60 percent of all irrigable land there was in holdings that exceeded the federal acreage limit. "This degree of concentration of land ownership," Edwin Wilson and Marion Clawson wrote, "is rarely encountered in the United States."[26] If these large growers were to get interest-free money from the government to pay for their irrigation facilities, they would be royally enriched. One study indicated that the reclamation subsidy, calculated at a noncommercial interest rate of 3 percent, would in fifty years amount to 57 percent of water development costs. Figured at 5 percent interest, the subsidy would be 78 percent of cost. Add in the subsidy on operating costs derived from power sales, and Santa Claus had arrived in the Great Central Valley, showering more than a billion dollars on the growers there.[27] In the light of such gifts, the liberals ventured to say, the American public ought to have a right to say how and by whom the water would be used. Institutionally speaking, that argument meant, of course, that the Bureau of Reclamation ought to have the right and ought to exercise it.

The liberal authors of the project studies were not a group of remote, Washington-based bureaucrats, nor were they rank outsiders to the state, unfamiliar with California, seeking to impose their social values on local people. Mostly they were Californians, many of them recent graduates of the university in Berkeley, who only recently had been given jobs in the lower echelons of the federal establishment. With Steinbeck and McWilliams, they were homegrown critics and reformers. Two of their circle, Walter Goldschmidt and Walter Packard, deserve special mention because their work, though carried out independently of the studies, was representative of an emergent leftist critique and because for a short while it had a discernible impact on federal policymakers.

Walter Goldschmidt was an anthropology student at the University of California at Berkeley when the Central Valley Project was under construction. He had been twenty-four years old when it was authorized. For a brief interlude, he got caught up in the winds blowing across the Great Valley, became in fact a gust himself, stirring up a swirl of controversy by suggesting that the big growers were an antidemocratic influence, for which he was in turn accused of cranking out biased social science, even of harboring communist sentiments. Later he would go on to a long, distinguished teaching career in anthropology at UCLA: a scholar of high standing and hardly a "radical," even in the sweeping, indiscriminate sense of that epithet as commonly used among Americans.

While still a student, Goldschmidt was hired by the Bureau of Agricultural Economics's Division of Farm Population and Rural Welfare. Among his assignments was to carry out a study of the Kern County town of Wasco, which he patterned after Robert and Helen Lynd's *Middletown* and submitted as his doctoral dissertation. He conceived it as a study of the social order of "industrial farming," or as he put it in a later reprint, of "agribusiness." Then in 1944 came his more influential work, a brilliantly conceived comparative examination of two valley towns: Dinuba, an older, smaller-scale irrigation community near Fresno; and Arvin, home of Joseph DiGiorgio's grape domain. By now the word had spread to the larger growers that here was another "pest" invading their fields, intent on proving that they were a threat to American rural traditions. Quickly they mobilized again, this time with book-burning rather than pick handles in mind. Goldschmidt, though the target of constant attacks in the press, of name-calling in Congress, and of harassment in the field, nevertheless completed the first installment of his investigation, only to have the BAE pigeonhole it as "one-sided" and refuse to continue his funding. Not until 1946 was the Dinuba-Arvin work published by a United States Senate committee under the title *Small Business and the Community*. That the study aroused so much hostility is astonishing when one realizes it was essentially a defense of petit-bourgeois values against the corporatized farm economy of California. This censored, much-feared work was only a mildly liberal critique after all.[28]

The comparison between Goldschmidt's two towns demonstrated conclusively that there were important social differences. Dinuba boasted far more local businesses, greater retail trade, a higher average standard of living, better distribution of income, fewer farm laborers, more community facilities, more newspapers and churches. Where the analysis failed was in Goldschmidt's conclusion that these social differences could be explained simply by the contrasting scale of landownership in the two communities. Though their populations were roughly the same, Dinuba counted 722 farms, averaging 57 acres each, while Arvin had only 133 farms, averaging 497 acres.[29] Ergo, it was implied that if the federal government enforced the 160-acre limit when it delivered water to Arvin, that town would be transformed into a middle-class democracy like Dinuba. But there were two flaws in the reasoning, both of which cast a shadow upon the efficacy of enforcing the acreage limit. In the first place, as Goldschmidt's own data demonstrated, the scale of landownership in the two towns was not a wholly independent variable; it was deeply conditioned by the kind of irrigation practiced. Organized in 1888, the Dinuba Irrigation District drew its water from the Kings River by using a low-scale, inexpensive technology. Arvin, in contrast, was a more recent settlement based on groundwater irrigation and plagued by depletion and high pumping costs.[30] Those contrasting ecological conditions not only could have explained to a large extent the community differences—why there was a DiGiorgio in one town and not the other—but also should have led Goldschmidt to ask whether merely controlling the distribution of land was an adequate means of democratizing the valley. His was a solution appropriate perhaps in a humid country, but not in the land of irrigation, hydraulic intensification, and the CVP.

A second weakness in the study, also virtually unnoticed by those who would cite Goldschmidt again and again over the next three or four decades, was that enforcing the acreage limitation would not have much diminished the class division in California agriculture. The farmers of Dinuba, small though they were, still depended on hired laborers to get their harvest in; fewer laborers, to be sure, but laborers all the same. That was part of the irrigation legacy even before the DiGiorgios of the valley appeared. Goldschmidt gives the following work requirements: Arvin needed 132,000 man-hours of labor in the low season and 525,000 in the peak season, while Dinuba's needs ranged from 124,000 to 669,000. Though Dinuba had more farm owners and their families on hand to help fill those needs, it also demanded more itinerants when September rolled around.[31] Because of their smaller incomes the Dinubans could keep fewer workers on the farm throughout the year, and their workers were less likely to remain in town when harvest was over. They drifted on. They became invisible. For Goldschmidt, eager to restore an entrepreneurial openness to the Great Valley, that fact apparently did not matter much. But for an Okie or a Mexican forced to tramp the state, living along the road or on welfare much of the year, the social differences between Dinuba and Arvin might understandably have appeared less compelling.

Walter Packard, in contrast, did take the unsettled conditions of the migrants seriously and proposed a more thoroughgoing alternative to the valley's rural order. The son of a successful Chicago lawyer of New England Protestant extraction and of a woman of strong moral leadership who had been active in unionization and woman's suffrage campaigns, Walter took the family conscience into agriculture and irrigation engineering. From 1909 to 1917 he was a farm extension agent in Imperial Valley, and later he assisted Elwood Mead in the Durham experimental settlement. Then the writer Lincoln Steffens along with Packard's brother and sister, all active in radical causes, directed his attention to the Russian Revolution as the wave of the future. Though never a Marxist, he found himself in perfect accord with the Russian Communist ideal of large-scale mechanized farming and planned production—that is, so long as all the people received the benefits. For him, agribusiness was an unacceptable basis for California life.

> Capitalism and democracy are not synonymous terms. Democracy, in principle, envisages a social order in which both sovereignty and the ownership and control of the common sources of supply and means of livelihood are the prerogatives of "We the people."[32]

In 1936, Packard was given his best chance ever to bring about that more democratic order in western irrigated farming. He was named director of the ninth region of the Resettlement Administration and given the job of finding lands on which he could move migrants and poor tenants into farm ownerships. His most ambitious venture was the Casa Grande Project in south-central Arizona, where he provided homes for eighty resettled farm families and tried to make them over into communitarians. Like the experiments at Durham and Delhi, this one failed.[33] But despite his mishaps in community planning, Packard had some arresting ideas to offer. No one among the California leftists illustrated more clearly than he what the historian Clayton Koppes has called the "community" New Dealer, who was interested in creating in America "a planned, ideal cooperative commonwealth."[34]

Packard's privately conducted study, *The Economic Implications of the Central Valley Project* (1942), was one of the most thorough investigations made at the time into the social structure of rural California. It was illustrated with Dorothea Lange's riveting photographs of the migrant workers' shabby world, but also with photos of the neat, white-trimmed cottages and tree-lined streets provided for DiGiorgio's employees. That juxtaposition pointed up the main question in the study: how the benefits of large-scale irrigated farming could be equitably distributed to everyone in the valley. A new and better society could not be achieved, Packard was sure, merely by enforcing arbitrary, antiquated acreage limitations; those were not "the best provisions which could be established." His own idea was to have the federal government buy the excess land from big growers and establish on it some form of collective or communal farming by the landless. "If government is to increase its services constantly as an enterpriser," he wrote, "it might go one step farther and own the land so that the benefits from government activity will be returned to the people rather than to private owners of land in enhanced land values." He would have a manager appointed for each government farm who would organize the farmers into work brigades and pay them wages, "with the normal democratic machinery for protest." The federal government should also own the new irrigation systems, rather than build them for local districts and turn them over at the end of the fifty-year repayment period. On the great farms to be established, each of them fitted out with the most advanced machinery, so Packard promised, all the modern economies of scale could be realized. What he was proposing then, though with more details, was Carey McWilliams's world of socialized factory farms. And unlike the acreage-limitation liberals, who tried to pour from the immense CVP cup into the small old bottles of traditional homestead agrarianism, Packard believed that those bottles had to be thrown away and new ones put in their place. What he did not question was whether the CVP was needed in the first place, or whether his socialized farms, designed as they were to match industrial efficiency, would be truly democratic or whether they would merely substitute a new set of bureaucratic masters for the old capitalistic ones.[35]

The objections that could be raised to Packard's scheme were in any case irrelevant. No one in the higher ranks of the Washington bureaucracy was open to his advice; instead they decided to industrialize the water and, paradoxically, try to restore the rural society using that water to a more traditional agrarian form. They decided, that is, to follow the lead of the majority of the California liberals and apply the acreage limit, or some modified version of it, in the Great Valley. That strategy became public policy in the latter part of 1943, and hearing it, the growers were stunned and outraged. Their spokesmen raged up and down the state, denouncing the government, the reclamation law, the insidious forces gathering around the farmers' fields, the communistic conspiracies bent on seizing their land and setting up tyranny.

Among the irate spokesmen was Sidney Harding, a prominent civil engineer of prim, scowling mien, who was alarmed by the way the wind was now blowing. In December 1942 he spoke before the State Chamber of Commerce, warning that the CVP studies were going in an ominous direction. Prominent engineers were being pushed aside, their opinions set at naught, and social theorists were taking over, disregarding the laws of economics. "Farm sizes," he pointed out, "are the result of economic factors that have been operating for long periods. . . . To accept indigent settlers on high cost land with expensive improvements means permanent indebtedness and the loss of an incentive for individual success." His plea for freedom from government interference and land redistribution pleased the big growers, of course, but also their friends in the state university and the Bureau of Reclamation. The dean of agriculture at the Berkeley campus mimeographed the speech and had it distributed to all of his staff members participating in the CVP studies. The Bureau's chief engineer, S. O. Harper, wrote to say, "Your statement is realistic, sound and courageous. When I see you I will be glad to pass some thoughts on, which I can't include in official correspondence." And another engineer in the Denver office, F. E.

Schmidt, sent a note reading, "A very good piece of writing. Congratulations!"[36] Clearly there were well-placed academicians and bureaucrats who were not ready to agree with the young liberals on enforcing the acreage limitation, who wanted the large growers to be unmolested in their accumulation of wealth. Unfortunately for them, the reigning powers in Washington, notably Secretary Ickes and his commissioner of reclamation from 1943 to 1945, Harry Bashore, were not listening to Harding and did intend to interfere and molest.

Even before the studies were all in, Congressman Alfred Elliott, a Tulare, California grower, introduced a rider to exempt his state from acreage limits. He got his colleagues' approval in the House, but the rider failed to carry the Senate, thanks to the determined opposition of Robert La Follette, Jr., of Wisconsin. In the Senate hearings, Elliott himself came under a blistering attack by another California farmer, Frank Swett, owner of 170 acres and director of the Contra Costa Farm Bureau. Swett called the senator an "absentee farmer," "a Junker landlord," who did not represent the views of the rank-and-file agriculturists.

> Vast haciendas, great plantations, land baronies, latifundia, may provide caviar and champagne for the barons, their associates, and their knights in legal armor, but their men who do the work on the acres, in the past, have had rather meager fare and rather meager wages. . . . We hope [the Senators] will not be seduced by the powerful few who aspire to the domination of the "agricultural empire" that they would create in the Central Valley. Do we need more emperors or dictators of empires? Don't we need, for the safety of California, agricultural commonwealths, with family farms?[37]

Convinced by the testimony of Swett and others that the acreage limit was not so severely restrictive, that in fact a 160-acre farm under irrigation in California produced considerably more wealth than the average American farm, the Senate held fast to the 1902 law.

Failing with one tack, the big growers tried another, and this one was more successful, at least for a handful of them. They got inserted in the Flood Control Act of 1944 a small clause authorizing the Army Corps of Engineers to construct a dam at Pine Flat on California's Kings River, which would furnish flood protection and irrigation improvement to farms as far downstream as the Tulare Lake area. Normally the Corps dealt exclusively in flood control and harbor work; its sudden entrance into valley irrigation was an unexpected challenge to the Bureau of Reclamation's territorial claims. Here was a dreaded rival's nose appearing in the door. Quickly the Bureau growled, warning the Corps off. Efficient, rational, coordinated, maximized water development—all the positive words it could find in its vocabulary—were now endangered, for only a single federal agency operating without competition could do the job well. Secretary Ickes bellowed: "The unjustifiable trespass by the Corps of Engineers upon this project merely means the addition of another cook when the crew was already in the hands of an expert chef."[38] However, in the view of the Kings River irrigation districts, it was time for a new chef, and this one, they were happy to see, would impose no acreage limitations on them. To the chagrin of Ickes and the Bureau, they got the chef of their choice in the 1944 act. True, President Roosevelt had seen to it that the authorization for the dam specified that reclamation law would apply here as elsewhere. It was one thing to say that in the law, however, and quite another to get the Corps actually to follow the President's wishes, the possibilities for bureaucratic evasion being so numerous. In fact, acreage limitation would never be enforced on the lands watered by the Pine Flat Dam.

A small victory by recalcitrant growers, though much has been made of it. More gratifying to them by far was that the commitment among the New Deal liberals to the excess-land provision had never been very firm. Soon, despite official pronouncements to the contrary, it began to collapse. Some few months after the 1944 Senate hearings (where the provision had been successfully defended), Marion Clawson and his associates brought out their CVP study of Problem 19, a report on the policy of acreage limitation. In it, while Elliott's defeat was still hanging in the air, they surrendered. For the sake of progress and amicability, they now recommended that the Bureau of Reclamation use the 160-acre standard only as a floor, not as ceiling (under the law the Bureau had the authority to set farm size as low as 40 acres). All farms irrigated prior to 1945, they recommended, should be allowed a maximum size of *640 acres* so long as their owners were willing to pay the interest on the construction costs, which should not exceed a minuscule 3 percent. Given the Bureau's policy of doubling the land allowance for husband-wife farms, which would raise the effective limit to 1,280 acres, this was liberal thinking indeed. It would mean that less than one in a hundred owners in the southern San Joaquin area would have to divest themselves of any land: so minimal a gesture toward redistribution of agricultural wealth as to be meaningless. Had it not been for less generous souls, like Senator La Follette, standing guard over the limit that revised policy might well have been speedily adopted.[39]

Then, only a few months after offering that deep concession the liberal

New Dealers went into wholesale retreat, abandoning the problem of California agriculture to a set of more compliant successors. In 1945, within months of Franklin Roosevelt's death, Harold Ickes left office, as did Commissioner of Reclamation Bashore. The Truman administration put Michael Straus, formerly a Chicago newspaperman, in the commissioner's seat. Despite a set of formidable eyebrows that ought to have intimidated any valley grower, Straus was a weak and expedient man, a commissioner in the old Bureau tradition of preferring, when the chips were down, technological triumphs over social justice. To be charitable, he inherited a very hot seat. On one side of him were the big farmers and their organizations, thundering and moaning that their rights were being trampled on, that any acreage limitation was impractical and unenforceable—not to mention an affront to the laws of God—that the feds were trying to ram some kind of centralized authority scheme down their dry, parched throats, that alien communists were marching on their homes. On the other side were a less organized group of eastern taxpayers and social reformers, roused by novels and reports and congressional debates, unable to fathom why they should subsidize distant and wealthy agribusinessmen with cheap water. For Straus, the danger was that the latter group might very well decide that the growers were dictating to the government and begin working to cut off funds for the whole Central Valley Project. His overriding objective had to be the securing of Bureau funds for water control, without which it was nothing. Yet he would have no program to fund if the California growers refused to participate in it. Somehow, he must give agribusiness what it wanted without appearing to do so.[40]

Making Straus's life even more difficult was a relentless bulldog, Senator Sheridan Downey from Sacramento, nipping and growling at his heels. A man of limited intelligence but strong loyalty to those with money, Downey intended to make the absolute exemption of the big growers from any acreage limitation whatsoever his chief contribution to the Republic. In 1947 he published a book, *They Would Rule the Valley,* which was mainly an attack on Straus and other so-called government revolutionaries and a defense of the unfortunate Joseph DiGiorgio, whose character, Downey feared, had been terribly maligned, throwing his prospects for federal water into jeopardy.[41] That same year the senator introduced Bill 912, which would exempt growers in California, Texas, and Colorado from the Bureau's land limit. In the hearings the bulldog snarled and barked at opposing witnesses from the American Legion, the National Catholic Rural Life Conference, the American Federation of Labor, the National Farmers Union, all testifying in favor of acreage limitation. He nearly succeeded in getting his way—and in destroying federal reclamation—until Commis-

sioner Straus outmaneuvered him. In his remarks before the Senate committee considering the bill, Straus allowed that "technical compliance" with
the law was possible and was fully acceptable to him. A corporate farmer,
for example, could deed his land to his employees, then lease it back and
go on getting subsidized water for it. Anything that would give the appearance of compliance to easterners was fine by the commissioner. And that
was fine by Congress too; the law was not changed. Downey and his effort
to discredit the Bureau, to diminish its power, were defeated, and yet the
big growers had found their way out of danger. Though the bulldog persisted in snapping away at Straus, even getting his pay stopped for a while,
he was biting at a shadow. The formula of technical compliance with the
reclamation law, which is to say no compliance at all, moved to official
status.[42] The five years of Bureau self-reassessment were over. The California liberals and those they had reached in Washington had faded away,
after first giving ground, after failing to settle on a firm policy, after
displaying considerable uncertainty about how to pour big water into the
hands of little people. Despite winning some temporary attention, they had
not been able to prevent the Bureau's own historic power structure, its logic
and priorities, from recovering control. The one solution that could have
had the most impact on the social structure of California farming—simply
not building the CVP—was never seriously contemplated.

Who, by the late 1940s, ruled the Great Valley of California? Obviously
the farm laborers did not. Did the growers rule, then, or did the bureaucrats: the men owning land or the men bringing water? Two political
scientists, Arthur Maass and Raymond Anderson, in their detailed chapters
on the valley, chapters that on balance are sympathetic toward agribusiness
and its values, maintain that the water users—that is, the growers—still
ruled, that they had managed to fend off the bureaucrats and retain control
of their destinies. They successfully played the rival government agencies
off against one another, so that local control was not preempted by some
centralized authority.[43] That is not quite so. Admittedly, there was no
revolution in California's vineyards, no socialization of agriculture as Packard or McWilliams wanted, not even a genuine enforcement of the reclamation law. Thus the big growers could congratulate themselves and relax in
their wealth; no one was going to take it away from them. But it is a mistake
to assume that an intruding power must be revolutionary or it is no power
at all. Though the growers maintained their position over the laborers, they
did not have the same freedom, the same self-reliance, the same independence they had had before the CVP. Local elite control, the growers'
autonomy, had been severely compromised in the valley.[44]

255

Consider the Bureau of Reclamation's new position in the valley and in the West. It had transcended its dreary, failed past and now could boast that it was, with minor exceptions, the technical master of water in the richest agricultural region on earth. In the early 1930s, it had been an agency tottering on the edge of extinction. With the Central Valley Project it had gained a new lease on life, a new role to play. No longer was it the wet nurse of failing project farmers on marginal lands; it had become the indispensable partner of western industrial farming. Its name was blazoned from one end of the Great Valley to the other, and in Imperial Valley as well. Surely that was not a defeat. That was a glorious success. The Bureau was now indisputably a power to reckon with, as the California farmers had discovered, and a power that had to be won over, accommodated, and incorporated into the structure of their world.

The Bureau had not won that power by taking up the role of social reformer or revolutionary. It had never been comfortable with that role, and soon saw how counterproductive it would be. A better strategy, one more suited to an agency devoted to instrumental reason, was to insinuate itself into existing valley agriculture as a "service" bureaucracy. To question the ends or challenge the values controlling that agriculture was to call into question the ends of the Bureau itself. People might begin asking why the Central Valley Project was being built at all, when crops were in surplus, when there was not enough money to eliminate poverty and hardship elsewhere. Power in a society dedicated to the absolute conquest of nature does not belong to those who try to think rationally and systematically about the ends of domination or who challenge the unexamined, unspoken ends. Nor does it rest exclusively in the hands of those who profit by a general social failure to define the ends of environmental domination. It also can be wielded by those who possess the means: the agents of instrumentalism.

Who ruled the Great Valley? No one person or group did. The hydraulic society emerging there by the forties was commanded by a convergence of instrumental forces. There were the growers harvesting crops in a profusion that was unadjusted to American need, raking in great sums of wealth that had little purpose other than mere accumulation itself. And there were the federal technicians, indefatigable in their reorganization of natural watersheds, in sending the flow up and down hill, in making reasonable what they saw as irrational. Together these groups could proudly say that they had forced the earth to obey their wishes, that they had turned "waste" into wealth, and never mind what or whom that wealth was for.

E M P I R E

Water and the Modern

West

Touch water [in the West], and you touch every-thing.

　　　—John Gunther, Inside U.S.A. *(1947)*

There is no lack of water here, unless you try to establish a city where no city should be.

　　　—Edward Abbey, Desert Solitaire *(1968)*

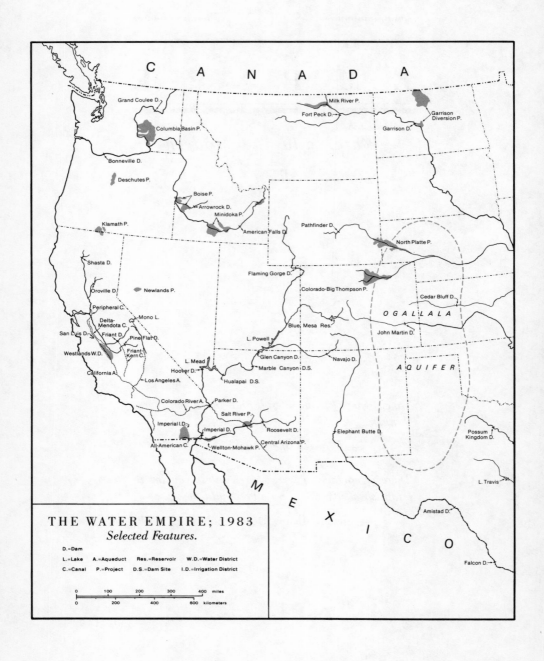

THE WATER EMPIRE; 1983
Selected Features.

D.=Dam

L.=Lake   A.=Aqueduct   Res.=Reservoir   W.D.=Water District

C.=Canal   P.=Project   D.S.=Dam Site   I.D.=Irrigation District

Standing on a green Appalachian ridge and scanning west, with their backs to the crowded, constrained world of the past, early Americans found it easy to dream extravagantly of power and glory. Below them, thrown down at their feet as it were, lay an endless stretch of hardwood and pine forests, immense open parklands with deep black soils inviting a plow, a rich lacing of brooks, seeps, springs, creeks, lakes as large as seas, and in the hazy blue distance the mighty Father of Waters. They took it as self-evident that personal wealth and national power must follow such natural abundance. What they were completely oblivious of was a precisely contradictory and more plausible proposition: that power is more likely to be strenuously sought and won under the pressure of continuing environmental scarcity than of ready-to-hand abundance. The pursuit of power may go on in any setting, of course, but it generally loses impetus without the constant goad of deprivation, whether real or imagined. The experience of overwhelming bounty can blunt the drive for technological conquest, can diminish the urgency of survival, of acquisitiveness, and say to people: relax, take it easy, why worry, the future will look out for itself, already you are in paradise.

Beyond the hundredth meridian the necessary goad was more starkly, emphatically present—a dry throat, a daily uncertainty, always the danger, the anxiety, of life in a desert or near-desert. Travelers found themselves in an even more awesome space, grander by far than any Appalachian vista, one big enough for dreaming, all right, but a land too empty, barren, dusty, and austere to invite the soul to loaf and take its ease. This landscape, in its elemental scarcity of life-supporting resources, was more clearly suited to driving people on and on to power than any part of the humid, vegetative East. Though it took a while to discover the fact, the West was the natural home of the American Empire.

How could deprivation be translated into wealth and power and influence? That was the problem posed to the arid region from the beginning. The answer, as tracked in the preceding pages, was that its people had to bend themselves to the discipline of conquest, had to accept the rule of hierarchy and concentrated force. That acceptance they seldom acknowledged, at least publicly. Again and again they told themselves and others that they were the earth's last free, wild, untrammeled people. Wearing no man's yoke, they were eternal cowboys on an open range. But that was myth and rhetoric. In reality, they ran along in straight, fixed lines: organized, regimented, incorporated men and women, the true denizens of the emergent West. It might have been otherwise, but then they would not have made an empire.

After World War Two, the western empire came at last into its own. It reigned from the 1940s on as the undisputed agricultural leader, supplying food and fiber for the nation, for the world. It took on the outlines of a new industrial behemoth, with steel mills, coal and uranium mines, assembly plants for aircraft and armaments, a scattering of scientific research institutes. Mass entertainment radiated from its cities, from Hollywood, Disneyland, the streets of San Francisco, Las Vegas, Aspen, and Dallas, radiated out over most of the globe, shaping the mass urban mind in Minneapolis and Louisville, in Manila and Rio. Out of the region came too a new generation of influential national political leaders, from Richard Nixon and Lyndon Johnson to Henry Jackson, Barry Goldwater, and Ronald Reagan, leaders whose prime instinct in many cases was to assume that America's good was the good of the American West. Accompanying that shift of economic, cultural, and political weight came a steady current of moving Americans, going West to live in unprecedented numbers. In 1965, California replaced New York as the most heavily populated state in the union— as the new empire state—counting 18.6 million inhabitants, a state richer as well as more populous than any of its eastern counterparts. And as California filled and filled, it spilled over into Oregon, Washington, Nevada, Arizona, and Colorado, buttressing its preeminence with a ring of satellites and clones. All that is not to say the West came to dominate the country in every respect. The eastern seaboard still had its Wall Street and Pennsylvania Avenue, its universities and publishing firms, and the Midwest its automobile manufacturers and Corn Belt. But the flow of power westward was unmistakable. And not to put too fine a point on it, the command over water in the region was, more than any other single factor, what made that flow possible.

The traditional notion of empire, as characterized, say, in the Old World regimes of Charlemagne or Kublai Khan or King George the Third, was of an extensive dominion ruled by a single, despotic head of state. In the hands of the Americans, empire has always been a more impersonal and indefinite notion. Emperors have not been wanted, empire has been: a condition of absolute sway, supreme command, undisputed control over nature that would give front rank, not to any one individual, but to an entire people, their values, and their institutions. They professed to seek a technological empire, a money empire, one built on and devoted to the principles of liberal democracy, one opposed to despotism and coercion. From the beginning, however, it was a notion shot through with illusion. Imperial ambitions, whatever shape they take, must at last create imperial societies, bearing a family resemblance one to another. The empire of liberal democracy, for all its contrary promises, made that fact irresistibly clear in the postwar American West. As it came to maturity there, its structure was revealed to be one of a small power elite reigning over a large, anonymous, dependent population. That elite had both a public and a private face, the double-sided face of the modern capitalist state. It ruled in the West, as it did elsewhere, through an oligopolistic hold on capital and on expertise, but here it had the special advantage of water scarcity to justify its rule, to enhance its authority, to give it the imprimatur of necessity.

If history teaches us anything unequivocally about empires, it is that sooner or later they begin to falter. The illusions on which they are constructed eventually begin to lose their hold over the minds of people. The promises they have made are simply too grand to be delivered. Contradictions begin to mount, legitimacy to crack and flake away. The unanticipated social and ecological consequences of empire become increasingly unmanageable, just as they always have, and Leviathan starts to wobble, clutching more and more frantically at panaceas. All of those patterns began to appear in the western water empire at the very moment it neared its final triumph over a recalcitrant nature.

For all its seeming motion toward some grander destiny, nature is mainly a set of cycles, a tireless repetition of old ideas. A trickle in the highlands becomes a broad watery highway coursing through lower alluvial valleys, past dense ambitious cities, and then the river disappears, at least for a while, though beginning somewhere else as a trickle once again. History is a kind of river too, returning over and over to beginnings, completing cycles, if one stands and watches long enough. How long is hard to be precise about; the time required to complete the cycle of empire cannot be predicted with any confidence. But nothing is more certain in the modern West than that the next stage after empire will be decline.

261

``TOTAL USE FOR
GREATER WEALTH''

Whatever its geography, its ethnic complexion, its degree of affluence or impoverishment, the colony's complaint is poignantly the same everywhere: that its fate is not in its own hands, that its wealth is being drained away to a distant metropolis, that it is made poorer so that others can be rich. The familiar remedy for the complaint among colonies of every sort is economic liberation, securing the freedom to make their own decisions and control their own destinies. For every colony which genuinely attains that liberation, several others fail. Hard as that freedom has been to achieve, however, it has not been so hard as another kind of liberation —freeing the colonists' minds to imagine fundamental alternatives to the old power relationship. The colony, in its pursuit of freedom, dreams of empire. It will throw off its chains by forging new ones, fastening them either on its own people or on its neighbors or, it may be, on the metropolis. So the eighteenth-century American colonies successfully struggled to be emancipated from the mother country and then proceeded to replicate the very institutions and drives they had despised as corrupt and exploitative. The ways of power are more easily learned and aped and improved upon than they are transcended or put aside.

No colony ever exhibited that fact more forcefully than the American West in its long, fierce quest to get out from under and on top. The expatriate Bernard DeVoto, looking again at his old home region on a visit in the summer of 1946, reassessing the region he had once called "the plundered province," saw that in pain and outrage, saw the West beginning to be caught in the coils of its own liberation. By that year the region was emerging at last from its long colonial status, he believed, thanks mainly to the New Deal and the water investments (like the Central Valley Project) it had made in the region. Those efforts at redistribution of national wealth had not been received by westerners with much grace, demanding as they did more and more of them, "demanding," wrote DeVoto, "further government help in taking advantage of them, furiously denouncing the government for paternalism, and trying to avoid all regulation." But for all the churlishness with which they were gathered in, the federal investments had "begun to make possible what had not been possible before"—an expanded resource base for the region that could raise it from its colonial dependency. All of that went down in Benny DeVoto's column as success, a thumping, rousing, emphatic success, for he wanted to see the region realize its dream of "adult economic development and local ownership and control." What he did not like to see, what had driven him away from the West originally, was the region's slavish adherence to the imperial mentality, to what he had once termed the "desire of growth and domination." The West, he understood even in his enthusiasm for dam building, "does not want to be liberated from the system of exploitation that it has always violently resented. It only wants to buy into it, cumulative preference stock if possible."[1]

DeVoto went back to Massachusetts disillusioned and contentious, worried mainly about what western stockmen, lumber companies, and other public-land raiders were fixing to do to the West. What he did not mention was what the water-hustlers out there were lining up to do. In the next two decades or so they would lay their hands on virtually every river and tributary in the region, obliterating entire watersheds in a rage for "comprehensive, multipurpose water development." They would insist, with a sincere, breathless urgency, a frantic, intense will to believe in which was mixed the crassest self-interest and patriotic promotion, that without more and more water, death itself was stalking the land. Their anxious need to get more water, to expand their manipulation of nature, was so intense it became a kind of totalitarian impulse—a drive to capture and hold on to every single drop that fell on the West, allowing nothing to elude their tight control or stand as a challenge to their supremacy. And in their anxiety, most of it self-induced and contrived, in their unquenchable thirst for control, they would make their final push to empire.

Nowhere was the postwar mania for water engineering more pronounced than on the southern plains. Here a generation of leaders that had gone through the double trauma of depression and dust storms in the thirties, that had been looking poverty in the face for a long time, came into office advocating a program of dams, canals, and wells as their states' salvation. Perhaps no part of the West was more insecure than this one, and none more ready to place public faith in technological formulas to overcome that insecurity. They were quick also to generalize their formulas to the rest of the globe, especially the underdeveloped countries of Asia, Latin America, and Africa, where water control, they believed, would be needed, as it was at home, to save the world for democracy. Not only were droughts and dust bowls and hunger threatening humanity abroad as they were on the American plains, but there were also communists infiltrating all those places, undermining the foundations of prosperity and progress. Massive dams on the Mekong and Indus, counterparts to those on the Brazos and Platte, would drown all the enemies at once. Senator Lyndon Johnson, clawing his way out of the obscurity of backcountry Texas, expressed that enlarging, generalizing anxiety when he wrote that "water management is . . . a decisive tool in our mighty struggle for national security and world peace." So did his colleague Robert Kerr, oilman and former governor of Oklahoma who, as the head of the Senate's Select Committee on National Water Resources, argued that river development was part of "a greater conflict," the international struggle of free peoples against godless Marxists. Whoever controlled water controlled the world's destiny.

> Can a pagan Communist nation [he asked], by enslaving
> and regimenting its people, make more efficient use of soil
> and water resources than the most advanced and enlight-
> ened nation in the world? Can ruthless atheists mobilize
> and harness their treasures of God-given wealth to defeat
> and stifle freedom-loving peoples everywhere?[2]

The answer, of course, was no—that is, it would be if Congress appropriated the money for the Kerr Plan, which would bring the Red, the White, and the Arkansas rivers under strict management, providing irrigation for the plains farmer and making Tulsa an international seaport. Thus did local ambition and global ideological conflict, a fear of deprivation and of the loss of control, all fuse and run together toward the single potent symbol of a dam.

As an exemplar of the southern plains water craze, the Texas professor Walter Prescott Webb was one of the more ironic figures. Two decades earlier he had been the man who had awakened the West to its colonial subservience and who had urged it to seek its own unique destiny in its arid condition. But by the 1950s it was clear that what he had in mind was not acceptance of and adaptation to but technological mastery over that ecology. A bigger and better industrial order than the one in the East should be created, this one to be founded on water control, making the West supreme and unassailable. In the midst of the 1953 drought, recalling earlier days when he had watched cattle dying of thirst and when his family had had to dip their water from a single scum-covered pond, he urged Texans to support Lyndon Johnson's grandiose program of federal river development. A canal, he explained, could be dug two hundred feet wide and hundreds of miles long, diverting surplus flow from the state's eastern rivers to the drier west, all the way from the Sabine to the upper Rio Grande. Such a scheme would bring "a complete revolution" to the state, he promised. It would ensure the "future growth of population, industry, and agriculture," would avert "a social and economic stagnation if not disaster," and by the end of the century would bring as much as $8.5 billion to the Gulf Coast. There was nothing uniquely western in Webb's dream of the future. Essentially it amounted to a vision of replication of the East, where Texans would earnestly make the fullest use of their limited water in the pursuit of money and industrial giantism. In that process, he hoped, they would be able to drain power away from the old imperial centers to the rising new one.[3]

Few Westerners were as candid about their sectional rivalry as Webb, nor could they risk being so if they wanted the East's cooperation. Throughout the region, from its plains and mountains to its far coast, from the 1940s onward was heard the more politic claim that completing the West's hydraulic regime was important because it would secure for the entire country an enhanced international power. Give us more water, the promise went out year after year, help us build up the region, and we will put America in command of the earth, will keep it in that position against all threats. From the western slope of Colorado came a warning from Congressman Wayne Aspinall that without a stepped-up reclamation effort the nation would not be able to meet "increasingly severe challenges from abroad," either the Soviet bloc or capitalist competitors. A University of Arizona economist pointed out that the "creation of additional wealth-producing properties" by watering arid places had created "a new empire" in the West, and that without that empire "America would not be the world-dominating America we know at the midpoint of this twentieth century." And from the halls of the Bureau of Reclamation came a supporting chorus, insisting that the size of its budget, all lavished on the West, was a measure of national resolve. Bureau Commissioner Michael Straus threw down the challenge, "Why not survive," implying that anyone who questioned the reclamation program was in favor of American cultural suicide. The Bureau's director of project planning, J. W. Dixon, lauded the water engineer in the West as "a tool for world peace." And the burly, squareheaded, cigar-chomping Floyd Dominy, son of Nebraska homesteaders, commissioner of reclamation and perhaps the most influential agency head in the postwar era, tirelessly asserted that "achieving national goals for a stronger and more prosperous America" was what was at stake in the western plains and deserts. In all these minds, the dream of domination was powerfully compelling despite its loose and rigorless logic: the West is America, money is peace, control is freedom, survival is domination.[4]

Westerners could count not only on the Bureau for support in their grand designs. There were also such influential eastern opinion-makers as Henry Luce, a strident, unblushing ideologue through the fifties for the American Empire and Pax Americana. His *Time* magazine trumpeted the West as "the endless frontier" made possible by advanced water technology. "Irrigation experts," the Luce establishment announced, "are now convinced that the rapidly growing U.S. can expand almost indefinitely within its present boundaries." Across the Rockies lay 50 million undeveloped acres waiting to be "watered into life," holding the promise of an agricultural productivity equal to that of France or Germany. *Time* noted they were capable of feeding 75 million people. Then there was the still untapped Mississippi, which could be pumped uphill to the high dry country, and the Columbia, which could be sent down south to the hot deserts—feats capable, the magazine promised, of inspiring "engineering ecstasy." And poised, eager, itching to lay hold on those possibilities, were the professional water managers, men who readily confessed with a grin to an awestruck reporter, "We enjoy pushing rivers around." Apparently enough Americans in every region took such brassy journalism to heart, enjoyed watching the river-pushers go to work, and were willing to pay something for the privilege. Federal money for western water development rose from $33 million in 1939 to $230 million in 1949 and stayed on that higher plateau thereafter.[5]

With popular enthusiasm stirred up by men like Henry Luce, with generous postwar appropriations from Congress, and with a dithery, ecstatic army of river improvers at its service, the West set itself the target of achieving nothing less than total control, total management, total power, or as the Bureau's own slogan, emblazoned on the covers of reports and project summaries and public relations material, put it, "total use for greater wealth." The war against European fascism and Asian militarism was over, a war waged for "unconditional surrender." Another war, the Cold War, pitting two superpowers armed with nuclear weapons against each other, had begun. And still a third war was now under way in earnest, this one to be waged against the western American landscape of scarcity, and it too would not stop short of total victory.

It drips endlessly from the roof of North America, from the cordillera of the Rockies, down from its eaves and gables and ridges, its mossy slates and piney shingles, running this way and that, running whichever way offers the least resistance. Put a barrel where it drips, and a second next to that one, and so on until the yard is full of barrels. Call part of that dripping the Rio Grande and give the barrels names too: Road Canyon, Sanchez, La Jara, Abiquiu, El Vado, Jemez, Elephant Butte, Caballo, Two Rivers, McMillan, Red Bluff, Amistad, and Falcon. Skip north across the plains with more barrels, putting them down right and left: Conchas, Possum Kingdom, Texhoma, Stillhouse Hollow, Fort Gibson, Cheny, John Martin, Kanopolis, Waconda, McConaughty, Pathfinder, Seminoe, Buffalo Bill, Glendo, Oahe, Sakakawea, Fort Peck, Yellowtail, Canyon Ferry,

Tiber. Barrel after barrel, each with a colorful name but all looking alike, quickly becoming an industry in their manufacture, with industrial sameness in their idea and use. The big ones must all be made to federal specifications and paid for by federal funding, but a thousand little private kegs and rusty pots can be deployed too. Run to the other side of the roof and put down more of them. Jackson, Blackfoot, American Falls, Dworshak, Cascade, Deadwood, Franklin Roosevelt, Potholes, McNary, Flaming Gorge, Blue Mesa, Navajo, San Carlos, Lake Powell, Lake Mead, Havasu, Laguna. Everywhere barrels filling in the spring, barrels emptying out again in the dry season. Plink, plink, save, save. It would have been a crime simply to stand by and watch it drip and run away. Waste not, want not. So the rooftop of the Rockies, in a matter of thirty or so frantic years, was ringed about with the means to capture and hoard all the falling, dripping mountain waters.

In the northern latitudes of the western United States, the two great challenges of the postwar period were the Missouri and the Columbia, along with their major branches. Neither river had been truly harnessed before World War Two, mainly because they were too much of a handful for the available money and technology and because the returns were too marginal to justify the effort anyway. So 150 years after Lewis and Clark had poled their way up its banks, the Missouri, longest river in the West, remained a treacherous, unpredictable force. Wide and shallow and filled with sandbars in the low season, a dark brown boiling of energy in spring floods, year after year it took lives and property and gave little back in profit. In its lower reaches were vulnerable floodplain settlements like Kansas City and Omaha that would have been happy simply to be protected from the river, though they would take wealth too. Upstream in Nebraska, the Dakotas, and eastern Montana were thousands of farmers who, like the southern plainsmen, had tasted a lot of blowing dust in the dirty thirties and now demanded some help in the form of irrigation from the river to stay in business. Both groups were prepared to accept some new, outside, central authority if it could tame the Missouri and deliver them from tribulation.[6]

The first agency to take on the Missouri was the Army Corps of Engineers as part of its mission to defend America against floods and improve inland navigation. For a long time that work had meant pulling snags out of the lower river, throwing up levees, and dredging deeper channels so that steamboats and barges could be safe. In 1933 Congress directed a somewhat reluctant Corps to undertake a new venture, the construction of a massive earthen dam, four miles wide, at Fort Peck in the Montana shortgrass country. This dam was to stabilize downstream navigation and store meltwater, but in 1942 and 1943 devastating floods gave more ambitious

267

heads in the Corps an opportunity to enlarge that role. To the forefront came Colonel Lewis Pick, a shrewd, ambitious bureaucrat-soldier, who in a terse, brief report proposed the complete dismantling of the natural river. Twenty-two dams were projected, the largest of them, Garrison in North Dakota, to be constructed on a site earlier rejected by the Corps as unsafe. Together they would cost the nation $661 million, would require the evacuation of 20,000 people (including a large Indian population from their reservations), and would cover a considerable amount of farmland with reservoirs. All this to realize what the colonel casually assumed to be self-evident benefits, not worth specifying in detail. "I mean," said Pick, "to control the water of the Missouri River."[7]

Meanwhile the Bureau of Reclamation was moving with matching fervor from an opposite direction, from headwaters and upstream reclamation possibilities toward the Corps's downriver domain. Out of their Billings office in 1944 came a proposal, drawn up by a lower functionary, W. Glenn Sloan, to construct ninety new reservoirs on the river system which would furnish irrigation water for 4.7 million acres of dry land, doubling the basin's existing reclaimed total and extending the Bureau's reach into the Dakota dust bowl. The cost was estimated at $1.3 billion, only a small part of it to be paid by farmers. If adopted independently, the plan might seriously interfere with the Corps's work, for one agency wanted to spread the river over fields while the other insisted on letting it flow in deep, steady currents in order to float commercial traffic. For two days at the Stevens Hotel in Omaha the rivals Pick and Sloan met to thrash out a compromise and save a role for both their bureaucracies. Their solution was a "Pick-Sloan" scheme in which "all the engineering features of both plans were agreed upon." Though nothing more than a paste-together job, their new, combined blueprint was a happy *modus vivendi* for each group. Together, in a cooperative spirit of river-pushing, they promised to construct an ornate hydraulic regime on the Missouri with a combined storage capacity of 83 million acre-feet, enough to give the shippers all the water they wanted and still allow irrigation diversions from Garrison and Oahe dams to open farm production east of the hundredth meridian to compensate for lands elsewhere lost in the scheme. If at points their program seemed somewhat self-defeating and irrational, a vicious circle of cost chasing cost, well, compromises can be like that. The river and the public treasury could wash over all the problems. Despite a lack of specifics on how the benefits compared with the costs involved, despite the Hoover Commission's conclusion in 1949 that Pick-Sloan was "in no sense an integrated development plan," Congress bought it. The basin subsequently fell under complex, multiheaded federal regulation, and the grand Missouri became a series of deadwater lakes.[8]

Over on the other side of the Rocky Mountain rooftop, in the Pacific Northwest, the Army Corps of Engineers and Bureau of Reclamation were again competing, this time for the chance to manage the Columbia. Here, however, they had to deal with a river that was more a wild, cold gush than a dripping. But otherwise there were marked similarities. As in the Great Plains, water development in the Northwest subsection had lagged behind the more southerly parts of the region. The state of Washington, for example, had in 1939 only one-fifth as much irrigated acreage as California, and most of it was confined to the narrow Yakima valley—yet the mightiest river in the West looped through its territory.[9] By the forties, that retarded condition began to change quickly, as one in every four federal water dollars came to be spent in the state. And where there was an influx of money there was also the occasion for bureaucratic squabbling, for a new alignment of authority, for unbounded expectations.

The Columbia was for a long while exclusively the Army's river. Getting ocean vessels as far upstream as possible, over its many rapids, was the chief idea, and that was Army work. The Rivers and Harbors Act of 1927 gave the agency an expanded mandate to survey and build a chain of dams on the river, which it was hoped would provide smooth sailing deep into the interior. The first of those dams was Bonneville, begun in 1933 and topped off in 1938, a multipurpose structure designed to generate electricity as well as navigation. The American people heard about its virtues mainly through Woody Guthrie, who was hired to write and sing songs in praise of Bonneville. They were nasal and folksy and full of downhome spunk. "Your power is turning our darkness to dawn," one of the more familiar of them went, "roll on, Columbia, roll on." The songs were, in their way, rather more impressive than the dam itself, and the Army soon looked farther upstream to the Grand Coulee site, where there was more reason for excitement.

The main stem of the Columbia charges down from the Canadian Rockies into the United States, now running north, now south, then west, then south again, struggling to find its way through the Cascades, finally turning westward to the sea. In the Pleistocene a massive block of ice forced the river up and out of its twisty canyons, compelling it to carve a new path for itself—the Grand Coulee, a detour fifty miles long and as much as a thousand feet deep—until it could regain its established course. When the ice melted, the river reverted to the old way, leaving the Coulee a dry, abandoned trench. Falling away from that ancient, disused gash in the earth was an immense stretch of eminently arable land, sagebrushy and cloudless, a land standing in a rain shadow, but a land that might, so local boosters believed, be transformed into an "inland empire" of agriculture, the Great Columbia Plain.[10]

A local newspaper editor, Rufus Woods of the Wenatchee *Daily World*, publicized in 1918 the notion of building a dam where the ice block had been in order to force the Columbia once more into the Coulee and, this time, to make it pay. He got nowhere with the idea. More prosaic minds had decided that the most practical strategy was to divert the Pend Oreille River somewhere east in Idaho and bring its water via a gravity canal downhill to the plain. The state hired General George Goethals, commander of the Panama Canal excavation, to advise it on the matter, and he too recommended the Pend Oreille alternative. That more than likely would have been the choice, had it not been for Idaho's determination to keep its water at home. In 1931 the Army engineers, impatient with interstate quarreling between Washington and Idaho, with the lack of resolution, threw their considerable prestige behind the Woods notion. So too did the Bureau of Reclamation, now rushing into the scene with New Deal backing. So also did President Franklin Roosevelt, who came out in 1934 to see the prospects for himself and, in the spirit of the old reclamation movement, pledged this to the gathered throngs:

> You have acreage capable of supporting a much larger population than you now have. And we believe that by proceeding with these great projects it will not only develop the well-being of the far West and the Coast, but will also give an opportunity to many individuals and many families back in the older, settled parts of the nation to come out here and distribute some of the burdens which fall on them more heavily than fall on the West. . . . You shall have the opportunity of still going West.

Senator Richard Neuberger of Oregon echoed that assurance when he predicted that a dam at Grand Coulee would make rural homes for "people in the slums and tenements of the East and the dust-bowl of the Middle-West," homes where they might "settle and cultivate a great chunk of fertile soil almost a continent removed" from their poverty. Now with humanitarianism and welfare-state largesse on its side, joined to the demands from local button-busting merchants and agriculturists, the dam soon materialized, reaching completion in 1941.[11]

Neuberger touted Grand Coulee Dam as "the biggest thing on earth," a boast that took in a lot of territory—the Pacific Ocean, Mount Everest, Antarctica, and the like. As human contrivances go, it was indeed elephantine, a concrete plug standing in the midst of nowhere, 550 feet high and 4,200 feet long, with fully three times the mass of Hoover Dam. An artificial lake backed up behind it for 150 miles, all the way to Canada. And inside, down in the cool depths of the structure, a pack of dynamos hummed endlessly, capable of adding 50 percent to the nation's existing hydroelectric capacity, dynamos that would soon be furnishing enough energy to lift a portion of the river into the Coulee for irrigation and still have enough left over to make the Northwest the major postwar producer of military and commercial jet airplanes, a new center for the atomic bomb industry (at nearby Hanford, Washington), and the most important supplier of aluminum. Finally, there was water to provide 1,029,000 acres with irrigation, enough water to make 17,150 new farms. And that would be only the beginning, for already both the Bureau and the Army were drawing up their separate lists of future dams along the river, 142 of them from the Bureau alone, strung out along tributaries all the way to Wyoming, supplying water to 238 projects, benefitting over 5 million acres, and so the numbers went on and on. To bring all of the glittering statistics to reality, the two agencies would once more have to put their rivalries aside and share a river system with each other, share the credit for virtuosity in domination.[12]

The Columbia Basin Project, authorized in 1944 to become the main recipient of Grand Coulee water, was one of the Bureau of Reclamation's own enterprises, and the largest and most carefully planned agricultural settlement it had ever attempted. In contrast to the Great Central Valley of California, this one was explicitly to be a program in the redistribution of wealth. Virtually all of the project area was in private hands, as was also the case in California, but on the Columbia, the federal authorities were dealing with scattered, disorganized, often marginal and hardluck wheat growers and ranchers, not the likes of Joseph DiGiorgio and the Associated Farmers. Thus the Bureau could announce, without much fear of resistance, that in exchange for the cheap water it would furnish—electricity consumers would pick up 90 percent of the dam and project costs—existing owners would have to follow the Bureau's rules. They would be allowed to keep a maximum of 160 acres per farm. They must sell excess land to the government at prewater prices, eschewing speculation and windfall profits. The government, in turn, would find new buyers for it, usually in 40-, 60-, and 80-acre farm sizes. Teams of federal planners would come into the country and, in the spirit of Elwood Mead, lay out new town settlements in the project, new farm-management models, and new transportation facilities. "We were planning *for* a group about whom we knew very little," one

271

of them, Marion Clawson, admitted at the time, "and were not planning *with* them." It was a serious flaw in his view, but because the majority of the settlers had not yet arrived, because the Bureau's experts had to prepare the ground for them to occupy, what else, he wondered, could be done? The great advantage for the planners in that situation, of course, was that they were free to make the project, in the words of Bureau official William Warne, "not Utopian, but as near the ideal American farming community as can be."[13]

Dust-bowlers and tenement dwellers were, it must said, only a small fraction of the intended beneficiaries of the remade Columbia River, not important enough in themselves to justify the effort and expense, particularly in light of the parallel development going on to the east of the Rockies, which aimed at keeping many of them at home. No, the principal goal in the Northwest was something else, something not so very different from what it was in the southern latitudes, in California, Arizona, and Texas: to repeat from the Bureau's own mouth, total use for greater wealth. According to that agency, "we have not yet produced enough . . . to sustain a desirable and reasonable standard of living, even if goods were equitably distributed; and . . . there is no limit to the human appetite for the products of industry."[14] By that thinking the overriding goal of western water development was simple and unambiguous—the goal of making more—and yet it was an elusive goal, impossible to define or achieve, for what was "desirable" and "reasonable" was confessed at the outset to be an idea without shape or limit or the means of satisfaction.

The third of the great streams running from the roof of the Rockies was the Colorado, and in the postwar era it too came in for "total use." So total, in fact, that by the early 1960s it no longer reached the sea. Much of its annual flow had come to be lost in reservoirs, soaking away into porous sandstone or evaporating into the air. Some of it passed by a tunnel under Rocky Mountain National Park into the Platte River basin for irrigation. The largest portion was diverted into California, into its agriculture and urban settlements, through the All-American Canal and through the California Aqueduct, which sucked up water from behind Parker Dam and carried it to the Metropolitan Water District on the coast. More commitments would follow, but those were sufficient to reduce the lowest reaches of the river to a mere drainage ditch, lined and edged, carrying only runoff and local floods now and then. Down in the delta the Colorado completely dried up and disappeared.

The death of the Colorado River began with Hoover Dam but was completed by a new round of demands coming from parties that had gotten nothing out of the Boulder Canyon Project Act and were now, by the 1940s, ready to be dealt into the game. The first claimant was Mexico, and that country threatened to make a great deal of noise in international circles unless the Americans guaranteed it a large, steady supply. Granted, Mexico contributed little precipitation to the river—virtually none, in fact—but then neither did California. Furthermore, the Mexican farmers had been drawing from the river for a long time too, and they were often poor, struggling folk meriting some help. The problem was to decide how much was Mexico's fair share and who should be obliged to give it. In 1944 a treaty between the two nations was signed, granting a minimum of 1.5 million acre-feet a year to the Mexicans, secured and delivered by the American reclamation investment. Californians, the most vociferous critics of the treaty, condemned it as "a first mortgage" on the river, as unfair competition in dry years for their heavy users, as an imposed modification of the western water-law principle of prior appropriation—and they were right. But the neighboring states, eager to get their own claims satisfied and some development under way, supported the State Department's treaty, and for a while the matter was settled.[15]

After Mexico got its share secured, the upper-basin states began lining up with buckets and barrels. By the Compact of 1922, those states (Wyoming, Colorado, Utah, and New Mexico) were reserved the rights to 7.5 million acre-feet, *after* they had made sure the lower-basin states (Arizona, Nevada, and California) got an equal amount. In truth, there would not be that much left over; more like 6.6 million acre-feet was all they could realistically expect in normal years. In a 1948 compact the upper-basin states agreed to divide whatever there was by the following formula, based on each state's contribution to the river: Colorado, 51.75 percent; Utah, 23 percent; Wyoming, 14 percent; and New Mexico, 11.25 percent; with 50,000 acre-feet set aside each year for northern Arizona. And then they went to work on Congress and the Bureau of Reclamation to build them a few dams and canals. First they would get a giant reservoir at Echo Park on the Green River, flooding Dinosaur National Monument, in order to be ensure enough water for the south. That would open irrigation development galore, up and down the western slope.[16]

For the men who wanted to flood Dinosaur, men like Senator Arthur Watkins of Utah, Bureau Commissioners Michael Straus and, later, Wilbur Dexheimer, and Secretary of the Interior Douglas McKay, an artificial lake would brighten up the dull, drab (and unvisited) canyons, would make good use of a wilderness containing nothing more valuable than a few old reptilian bones and scraggly piñons. Another group, however, with different values, suddenly appeared to battle the reclamationists, vowing to stop the Echo Park dam. They included Bernard DeVoto, who in a letter to Senator

John F. Kennedy declared, "The entire concept of reclamation needs a thorough overhauling."[17] There was also the writer Wallace Stegner, who depicted the virtues of an unflooded wild monument in *This Is Dinosaur*, along with David Brower of the Sierra Club, perhaps the most effective leader of the opposition, Howard Zahniser of the Wilderness Society, Arthur Carhart, a Denver conservationist, the New York publisher Alfred Knopf, and thousands of others in the West and East, all of them remembering with some bitterness that not three decades earlier they had lost a similar battle when San Francisco took over Hetch Hetchy Valley in Yosemite National Park for its water supply. This time they were determined to win, and win they did. The Echo Park dam proposal was scratched in March 1956, and Secretary McKay, stung by the defeat, resigned from the Eisenhower cabinet. Some other way would have to be found to get the upper Colorado harnessed.[18]

In the place of Echo Park, the Colorado River Storage Project Act of 1956 authorized a tremendous structure at Glen Canyon, just south of the Arizona-Utah border. To save Echo, Brower and the others supported a dam at this new site, much to their later regret, for it would drown some of the most spectacular canyons in the West. In its Lake Powell, named after explorer John Wesley Powell, Glen Canyon Dam would hold back two years' flow of Colorado water—as much as Hoover, its downstream mate. More than that, it would be what the Bureau called a "cash register," a generator of electrical power that would pay for all the other upper-basin features. There was to be Navajo Dam, dedicated in 1962, followed by Flaming Gorge in 1964, Blue Mesa and Curecanti on the Gunnison, the Central Utah Project, Seedskadee, San Juan–Chama, Paonia, and others. Glen Canyon Dam itself was completed in 1963. It was a plain chalk-white arch 710 feet high, wedged tightly between dark red stone walls, imposing in its clean, pure utilitarianism, impressive for its bulk if not grace; and running nonstop down in its turbine chamber was a cash register, counting up for tourists the dollars constantly being earned by the sale of electricity.[19]

And finally among the claimants seeking the death of the Colorado there was Arizona, a poor stepchild, left to the last and unhappy with its plight. What could be done for Arizona? Not much until it gave in to the federalization of the Colorado and ratified the 1922 compact, which, under pressure from the Mexican treaty, it got around to doing in 1944. Having done that, Arizona, rallying around the leadership of its aging but persistent United States Senator Carl Hayden, immediately began agitating for a federal program to bring the river into its dry interior. The water, it was said, was desperately needed, for Phoenix and Tucson were beginning a population explosion that in the postwar decades would take them to metropolitan status. Competing against them for local supplies were the irrigators of the Salt and Gila valleys, using 95 percent of the water and still coming up short. In 1940, the state pumped 1.5 million acre-feet from its ancient underground deposits dating from as far back as the Ice Age. In 1953, it pumped 4.8 million acre-feet. Unable to agree on state legislation to control that unrestrained pumping, Arizonans looked off to the Colorado for their salvation. Repeatedly, from 1947 on, Hayden got the Senate to approve a billion-dollar Central Arizona Project under the auspices of the Bureau of Reclamation, only to have the California delegation in the House of Representatives stop it, claiming as they did that there was not enough river left for any large new diversions. Indeed there was not, for California was by then using 5.2 million acre-feet, not the 4.4 suggested as a fair share by Congress in the Boulder Canyon Project Act. Arizona, more angered and impatient with its big thirsty neighbor than ever, filed suit in 1952 to settle once and for all its rights and those of California. "The subsequent trial," writes Norris Hundley, "proved to be among the most complicated and hotly debated in Supreme Court history."[20] When it was settled in 1964, after fifty lawyers and a court-appointed special master had worked on it, Arizona emerged smiling and triumphant. It could lay claim, the court agreed, to a full 2.8 million acre-feet of the Colorado, plus the full flow of its own tributaries—though Arizona had to give a million of its allotment to several Indian tribes, which had suffered even more than white Arizonans had as mere stepchildren of the river.

With the competing claims settled, Congress was now ready to pass the last major water-development legislation for the Southwest, the Colorado River Basin Project Act of 1968, featuring the Central Arizona Project and a handful of little gifts tacked on for its friends and supporters. The CAP would begin on the eastern shore of Lake Havasu, created by Parker Dam, where a pump would slurp 1.2 million acre-feet a year up through a pipe and tunnel, through the Buckskin Mountains, into the Granite Reef Aqueduct. That great concrete channel would transport the water eastward across the state, 307 miles in all, first to Orme Dam northeast of Phoenix, then on south in the Tucson Aqueduct, through and over and past more pumps, mountains, deserts, Indian lands, suburban sprawl, until there was nothing left in the ditch. The first water began running in 1985. Total cost of the CAP, mounting higher and higher as the years went on, was in the billions of dollars, a sum that exceeded, so a couple of the state university economists admitted, the direct benefits from the project. Thankfully all of it was federal money or it would not have been there to spend. The energy bill was staggering too. Originally the plan had been to run the pumps on hydroelectricity generated by two more Colorado River dams, one at Marble and the other at Bridge Canyon, the latter creating a reservoir that would bury a portion of the Grand Canyon National Park.[21] Once more the environmentalists buckled down to battle to save a last piece of the natural river, and once more—for the second time in the century—they were victorious. Once more, however, they lost something as well, for the energy to make the CAP go would be derived instead from coal strip-mined on Hopi sacred lands at Black Mesa in northern Arizona and burned in the Navajo Generating Station near Page, polluting the crystalline desert air with ash and poison gas.[22]

The Central Arizona Project was authorized exactly one hundred years after Powell led his small party down the unknown Colorado and exactly fifty years after the Boulder Canyon Project was passed. In the span of that century, even more so of that second half-century, the southwestern desert had been replaced over much of its extent by an astonishing urban and agribusiness complex, while the Colorado itself had been transmogrified into an industrial artifact, an almost perfectly realized expression of the new imperial West. What those northern rivers, the Missouri and Columbia, were still struggling toward, the Colorado had become—a part of nature that had died and been reborn as money.

For scale of engineering, for wealth produced, the American West had become by the 1980s the greatest hydraulic society ever built in history. It had far eclipsed not only its modern rivals but also its ancient ones, Mesopotamia, Egypt, Mohenjo-Daro, China, and the rest. It had made rivers run uphill, made them push themselves up by their own energy, and celebrated the achievement in brilliant neon colors playing over casinos, corporate offices, shopping malls, over all its new-age oases. It had turned an austere wilderness into sparkling serpentine seas where fleets of motorized houseboats circled under hot cloudless skies, where water skiers turned playfully in and out of once desolate, forbidding chasms. Then it had taken that same water and raised cotton with it, filled city pools with it, thrown it in the air with fountains and let it blow away. It had made its rivers over to produce art, learning, medicine, war, vulgarity, laughter, stinginess, and generosity. All this it had done with unmatched zeal, and most of it with the aid of the East.

To appreciate the awesome magnitude of this new hydraulic civilization, one had to start with its improbable farms, the foundations of its urban, industrial life, and they were legion and lush. The Census of Agriculture reported in 1978 that there were 45,433,535 irrigated acres in the seventeen western states: one-tenth of the world's total. California was still the leader, with 8.6 million acres; but Texas had surged into second place, with 7 million, followed by Nebraska with 5.7 million and by Idaho and Colorado with 3.5 million each. The market sales from those lands amounted to one-fourth of the nation's annual total, or $26 billion (Florida, the only eastern state with substantial irrigation, contributed a small part of that figure), roughly the value of the sum of American farm exports. Taken by counties, all but one of the top ten agricultural producers were in the irrigated West, and eight were in California alone. Of the leading 100 counties in farm-product sales, California counted 21, Texas 13. Such figures, revealing as they were of the geographical shift in agricultural preeminence, only hinted at the political brawn of these western farmers, who were in most cases gathered around their ditches and water-management needs into muscular organizations.[23]

The irrigated West, it must be added, was not yet a single coordinated monolith, for it included thousands of farmers who remained on their own, as independent entrepreneurs, continuing to pump their water from aquifers with private equipment, as well as remnant small-scale, local water cooperatives. But far and away the major force in agricultural water supply, preempting the field with its capital and expertise, drawing western ranchers and growers into a regionwide network unapproached for cohesion elsewhere, was the Bureau of Reclamation. In its seventy-fifth anniversary report, the Bureau proudly listed its accomplishments: 9.1 million acres irrigated on 146,000 farms; 322 storage reservoirs constructed, 345 diversion dams, 14,490 miles of canals, 34,990 miles of laterals, 930 miles of pipelines, 218 miles of tunnels, 15,530 miles of drains, 174 pumping plants; 49 power plants marketing more than 50 billion kilowatt-hours a year over 16,240 miles of transmission lines. It had invested nearly $7 billion for irrigation purposes alone. Most of the electricity went to the cities, and the Bureau also furnished water for 16 million municipal and industrial consumers. "Builder of the West" was the way the agency was described by one of its longtime employees, and what he might have added, but did not, was that in no other major American region had a single federal agency devoted itself so single-mindedly to so narrowly regional a mission as this one, to the responsibility, as the same writer put it, of "marshalling resources to sustain the growth of the West."[24]

In rationalizing this work, from the time of Francis Newlands on, the claim had been drummed in repeatedly that western agricultural investment benefitted every American, wherever he or she lived. For example, Congressman Aspinall, the consummate water politician to whom was due the greatest credit for the size of postwar water budgets, argued that federal reclamation made children "bigger, stronger, more alert, and healthier than

277

their parents were" by filling them up with irrigated oranges and vegetables. What's more, the farmers out there pumped money back into the national economy. By his figures, the North Platte Valley Project, to take a single case, had cost the government $22.5 million, but each year of late it had paid back $16 million in taxes and ordered as many as 20,000 boxcars of merchandise from all over the country, thereby stimulating "American business and prosperity." The Bureau too was an old hand at trotting out the justificatory data, pointing out in 1977 that eleven of its projects had, during their existence, surpassed $1 billion each in gross crop value (led by the Central Valley, Imperial Valley, Minidoka-Palisades in Idaho, Yakima, Colorado–Big Thompson, Salt River, and the relatively new Columbia Basin)—over $4 billion worth of crops grown that year from federal water, enough to feed 32 million people.[25] The figures were all true, and the economic benefits indeed substantial, as these sincere, devoted zealots believed. What was missing from their accounting, however, was any acknowledgment that the success of the West was, to a sizable extent, the failure of the East. Those boxcars of tractors and radios would, in the absence of the reclamation program, largely have gone to places like Tennessee and Ohio, especially if the government had put that $7 billion of reclamation money into helping poorer farmers there improve their skills and productivity.

Few of the crops in the West had to be grown there exclusively. Most could have been more cheaply raised in humid environments, and they would have been, had been, are raised there yet. The most common crop on federally watered farms, the Bureau itself reported, was forage to feed cows—not people—constituting 37 percent of all acres in production. Another 25 percent of reclaimed lands grew the staple cereals, mainly corn, wheat, and barley, none of them unique to the West. The southerner's traditional crop of cotton appeared on one in ten Bureau acres. Only 17 percent of Bureau-aided lands were devoted to vegetables, fruits, and nuts, and the percentage in winter-season lettuce or in citrus fruit, filling out and diversifying the American diet, was a minuscule portion of that. Clearly the West was in extensive, direct, subsidized competition with the East. The consequence of that fact, a pair of resource economists commented, was that "increased production on reclamation-served land has increased USDA payments [paid out since the New Deal, paradoxically, to reduce surpluses], stimulated regional production shifts, and reduced the incomes of nonreclamation farmers." Bureau projects, they calculated, had forced out of use at least 5 to 18 million farm acres in the East. Though there had been a net gain in national production, it had been achieved by sending thousands of rural men and women into bankruptcy, forcing them to drift to the cities looking for work, for few of them were able or willing to take up a new farm in the West.[26]

Here, then, were the outstanding achievements of the western hydraulic society—its triumphs over nature, its bright green wealth sprouting out of what had once been a dry, cracked landscape—and some of its costs entailed elsewhere. And at home, in the West, what was the structure of power associated with those triumphs? Had the region in fact become a model democracy, as forecast by a succession of promoters? Was it a society in which power and profit were broadly diffused—was it, after all, a people's Eden? Or was it instead, more or less as the earlier hydraulic societies had been, a hierarchical system of power, of unequal life-chances, of some humans dominating others? Were there concentrated, centralized forms of authority there, and did the individual and the small community stand before them in futility and impotence?

A number of observers have examined the question of power in the postwar West and its relationship to water, and virtually all of them have agreed that there has been an immense ballooning of the state, which is to say, the federal government and its bureaucratic apparatus, in the region. It would be hard to maintain otherwise—like trying to refute the setting of the sun. However, the observers have disagreed over the effects of that state apparatus on private power, over its implications for community freedom and autonomy, over its relation to festering social inequities. And, disagreeing over those matters, they have been at odds when it comes to suggesting how and by whom water should be apportioned in the future or how a genuinely democratic West would deal with its rivers.

One set of observers, and they are among the most listened-to critics of the modern hydraulic society, are the free-market advocates. What they have perceived emerging in the West is a big bruiser of a state that has shouldered private enterprise out of the water-development business, poured capital into projects that cannot meet the tests of market rationality, and played favorites when it comes to doling out the resource. The West by their account begins to look like a throwback to mercantilist England in the days before Adam Smith and laissez-faire enlightenment. Representative of this group of critics is the disillusioned New Dealer and *Newsweek* columnist Raymond Moley, who in the mid-1950s delivered a scathing attack on western reclamation, calling it a "paternalistic rainbow" and the Bureau behind it a "Napoleonic" institution in its overweening ambition. Money was being taken from the American public in the form of taxes, he charged, and redistributed according to the social values of powerful bureaucrats, and those bureaucrats favored western farmers over eastern farmers, over urban dwellers, and over industrialists who wanted water too. Three economists—Jack Hirschleifer, James DeHaven, and Jerome Milliman—made the same case a few years later when they accused the Bureau of suffering from a "monument syndrome," of building immense, costly works that were simply not good business investments. Supplying water, they complained, seems persistently to evolve into a "natural monopoly" in which prices and benefits bear little relation to costs and both freedom and reason are sacrificed. They proposed "a decentralization of authority" in making decisions about water and stated: "The cause of human liberty is best served by a minimum of government compulsion and, if compulsion is necessary, local and decentralized authority is more acceptable than dictation from a remote centralized source of power."[27] The same argument would appear in one form or another over the succeeding decades. The West, it goes, is excessively dominated, insofar as water is concerned, by the federal government, and that government is surrounded by a pack of sycophants. In the eyes of the more extreme market theorists, the region is saddled with a bureaucratic despotism not so very different from that Karl Wittfogel found in the ancient world. Only the restoration of a free, private market in water supply, investment, and pricing would bring this monster tumbling down.

A contrary critique, so dissimilar that one might well wonder whether it can possibly have been provoked by the same West, has come from another group, who might be called the "public-interest liberals." They have found the region to be a fragmented, chaotic structure of power that is incapable of working for, incapable even of perceiving, the common good: a shabby little house of private desires. In one of its rooms, the Bureau of Reclamation squabbles endlessly with the Army Corps of Engineers over who will dam what, while in an adjacent room a knot of congressmen in Stetsons and string ties are elbowing one another aside at the federal trough, diving for pieces of pork; roaming about the floor everywhere are local farmers with their hands out, their pockets open, their voices demanding and lustful. The great failing of the region from this view is that there has been too little effective central power and too weak a sense of collective purpose in the conquest of water. Rivers can never be exploited for total yield, for maximum efficiency, this critique goes, until some new superior source of authority is located that can take a broad view and do the job in a coordinated fashion. As Charles McKinley wrote in his critical study of the Columbia River schemes, "these waters are a part of a great single force which demands unified human manipulation if it is to be used to best advantage." He would have set up a National River Development and Management Administration in the Department of the Interior and under its aegis nurtured a series of river-basin commissions resembling the Tennessee Valley

Authority, beholden to no local oligarchies or old, entrenched bureaucracies.[28] Similar proposals for one or more TVA-like superagencies have been made repeatedly and for every major western stream, always with the confidence that centralization of power is not the road to serfdom, as the market ideologues fear, but a way to achieve the national welfare.

In this same vein, the writings of political scientists Theodore Lowi and Grant McConnell have been especially influential. For them, the West, particularly in its irrigated agricultural development, exemplifies a pervasive problem in American life: the capture of government power by narrow interest groups and, consequently, the subversion of democracy. Lowi, in a complex argument that cannot be done justice to here, refers to an "iron triangle" in water development that has as its three corners a handful of well-placed western congressmen, the Bureau, and organized agribusiness, together forming a closed network of power that eludes scrutiny and check. "Power goes up," he argues, "but in the form of personal plunder rather than public choice."[29] Similarly, McConnell holds that real clout in the West rests with small, cohesive private groups that have made the federal bureaucracy their servant, reduced it to an amiable, docile giant stumbling after its little master. Americans are readily fooled by this arrangement, McConnell warns. Fearing some great despotic central state that could hold life-and-death sway over their lives, they have naively trusted in the notion of "local control," all unaware that power in such a decentralized society has not been done away with but has become more firmly seated than ever, with no possibilities for challenge at the grassroots. Failing to realize the genuine threat to democracy that exists in that situation—the opportunities it opens, for instance, for rich California farmers to grab cheap water for themselves at taxpayers' expense—they have no defense. Only a strong, transcendent federal government, McConnell believes, in which a full diversity of interests are represented, can look out for the public interest.[30]

In the face of two such contradictory sets of analyses of the West, of the market men who see decisive power gathering ominously in the hands of the state and of the public-interest liberals who think it is still in the tight grasp of private elites, the cry naturally goes out: Who is right? To some extent, the answer must be that both are. The problems of the American West resemble one of those funny little pictures that, held one way, show a face with a scraggly tuft of hair on top and a bushy beard underneath, and held another way, show a very different face with a wild bush on top and a goatee. The power that has accumulated with the domination of western rivers has two faces also, one private and the other public, depending on which way one turns the picture. The most nearly adequate term for describing the composite is "capitalist state." As indicated in an earlier chapter, this will not do finally as a full or adequate description of the West, will not capture all its pecularities of history and ecology, but it comes closer than either of the accounts above to suggesting the complex but unified structure of power there.

The theory of the capitalist state, it will be remembered, denies that power in modern societies is democratically diffused, competitive, or pluralistic. It also denies that the immense bureaucratic apparatus of today is a benign force, or even a neutral one standing ready to do the bidding of whatever organized group can get into office, the good as well as the bad folks. Instead, the state has become a Leviathan in whose shadow ordinary men and women live. This large, hovering creature is not all-powerful, for the contemporary world is too complex, too diverse, too full of struggling, contending parties for any entity to rule unchallenged. Moreover, it is restrained by the purpose on which it has fattened. Depart from that purpose and Leviathan will sicken and die. In the main, that purpose is to promote the economic culture of capitalism, the core ethos of which is the rational, calculating, unlimited accumulation of private wealth. The state has come to be the single most important agency for the preservation of that culture. In the work of preserving, it finds at once the end of its being and the means to enhance its own prospects. As conservator, the state exercises military power abroad, facilitates commerce at home, educates the young, encourages investment, safeguards profit, absorbs the social and environmental costs of capitalism, and regulates the chaos of the marketplace. Above all, the state has the responsibility, not alone but finally, whenever lesser agencies fail, of dominating nature. Only through such mastery can resources be made available in infinite quantities and can the process of private accumulation continue.

The Moleys, Lowis, and McConnells see only a limited aspect of this picture, and that is where they go wrong. All of them, however, are right to a point. As the market purists accurately complain, freedom of enterprise tends to shrivel in the shadow of the modern state, but not because that shadow is thrown by a hostile form of power. Capitalism is, after all, aimed primarily at the acquiring of individual wealth; free markets are only one of its strategies for doing that, and one that has historically been quickly discarded when others, the contrived market of the state in particular, have become available. The public-interest liberals are likewise perspicacious about several details. In the capitalist state, private good does in fact become identified with the general welfare. However, removing power from local elites to some national center does not change that identification but only enlarges it, making power more concentrated than ever, more difficult to escape or overturn.

But it is not only those observers discussed above who have been unable to turn the picture around and around to get all its faces in view. The Marxists, too, have had their lapses of perception. Though they have written almost nothing on the American West specifically, they have been among the most clear-minded generally about the capitalist state and its mission. They have seen its coherence, its logic, its connections, better than almost any one else around. Too quickly, however, they have assumed that the state is merely a tool of a single elite group who own the means of production—that it is, in other words, first and last a coercive instrument of a well-defined ruling class. That kind of mechanical analysis reduces the endless conundrum of historical cause and effect to a pat formula. Is the entire culture of capitalism along with its protective, conserving state the invention of a particular economic class, the bourgeoisie? Or rather has the rise and hegemony of the bourgeoisie been an inevitable outcome of that culture? Has the class been called into existence, thrust into a position of leadership, by the culture's values and beliefs, shared more or less spontaneously by a wide spectrum of the population, as well as by its evolving relationship with nature through technology? The latter way of thinking, though admittedly messier, seems finally to be the more satisfactory, for it rightly emphasizes that a culture is not simply the invention of a handful of people at the top, something that they alone create and impose on everyone else, but that a culture, including that of capitalism, grows amorphously, anonymously, out of particular historical circumstances, out of particular environments, and in that process of growing sets up its own distinguishing structure of power.

The American West is an ecological variant on the modern world-circling culture of capitalism: a pattern of culture and society that has branched off, diversified somewhat from the parent that sent it out to find a new home for itself. It was created by the movement of that capitalist culture into an arid environment, into a land where scarcity of the vital resource of water was the prevailing environmental reality. Where there was an abundance of natural wealth lying about, waiting to be easily gathered up and made use of, capitalism as a culture and as a social order got along without much centralization of its energies. But when it encountered the raw edge of scarcity (it can create scarcity through depletion, of course, as well as come into it) that culture began to shift about. It found itself saying and accepting things it would not have accepted before. It felt the need to fabricate, or invite in, powerful organizations, above all the state, to help carry out its drives. In the West, the single most important function of that state has been, in the words of Roy Huffman, "to provide a constantly expanding resource base upon which private enterprise can build."[31] Making abundant what was scarce, putting an elusive, stingy nature within private reach where before it was unattainable: this has been the fundamental, underlying ecological role of the capitalist state, and in the West, this has been its role to a degree unmatched anywhere else in America.

The naked accumulation of wealth has, for most people, never been a wholly agreeable idea or an adequate explanation of life. Consequently, it has needed dressing up from time to time in more lofty ideals, more noble, transcendent rhetoric, even in actual garb. As Ralph Miliband shows, one of the most appealing wardrobes has been that of nationalism. For a long time now, the capitalist state has resorted to nationalistic appeals to furnish disguises for the self-enriching behavior it seeks to protect. Nationalism or patriotism has also served to muffle internal protest and dissent. "For the good of the nation"—by that appeal men and women are persuaded to go quietly along with their state apparatus and its projects, subordinating themselves, as Miliband puts it, to "a larger, more comprehensive concern which unites in a supreme allegiance rich and poor, the comfortable and the deprived, the givers of orders and their recipients."[32] There are other garments in the wardrobe besides nationalism. The grand cause of the domination of nature is one of them, perhaps the one most often brought out and worn, though it may be called by other names like "progress." Another garment used to cover the embarrassment of unconcealed self-seeking—and a capacious, well-handled one it has been in the United States —is regional pride, regional ambition. Nowhere is this more so than in the American West, where talk of making an empire, of conquering the desert, of overtaking the East, has served to distract attention from the less attractive realities of hierarchy, power elites, and the insatiability of an acquisitive culture. Finally, put the water-controlling men into a costume of oversized belt buckles, narrow-heeled boots, and big white hats, and their disguise is complete. They have fully appropriated the heroic, freedom-loving cowboy past of the West to justify their modern acquisitiveness.

Here then are the mature lineaments of the newfangled hydraulic society which, by the 1980s, had taken form in the trans-Mississippi landscape, up and down the plains, over the Rocky Mountain rooftop, across the desert basins to the coast. Not radically different in its cultural imperatives from the rest of America, or from France or Japan for that matter, it presented nonetheless a few distinctive features. On its environmental base of aridity, it had erected a closely integrated system of power that included both the state and private capitalist enterprise. Neither could survive in the harsh land without the other. Working together, however, the vision of total use could be dreamed and realized: the management of every river, every obscure remote creek, for the sake of greater wealth, for the sake of America and a greater West, for the sake of domination.

ACCUMULATION AND LEGITIMATION

Holding an empire together is a more difficult task than creating one. With success come new threats from within and without, requiring a level of vigilance that would have been inconceivable at some more primitive stage of development. In the postwar western water regime, those threats took two forms. First, there was a swelling of social criticism that the empire could not answer. Dissension over the grand project of river domination arose as its human results became difficult to reconcile with some of its original promises. That dissension, as it grew more bitter and unresolved, left in its wake a dark deposit of disillusionment, a loss of faith. The entire project began, for many, to seem morally bankrupt. Second, with all the engineering triumphs came a set of adverse ecological consequences, and they began to plague the river-pushers, defying their expertise and endangering their magnificent artifice. The first of those threats to the empire, the decline of its moral legitimacy, was the outcome of a hard-fought, impassioned controversy, lasting more than three decades, over the 160-acre limit in the national reclamation law. The fate of the limit was finally settled by Congress in 1982—but not before a fatal crack had appeared in the traditional, broad-based political alliance for arid-land reclamation.

Ironically, the threat of a lost legitimacy came precisely and inevitably through the very success of the water empire. All along in its rise to power it had been marked by latent contradictions, and those contradictions, deriving chiefly from the capitalist state mode of environmental exploitation, had always carried the potential for self-destruction. Most treacherous of them was the contradiction in purpose: the state had in the West the dual role of promoting the accumulation of private wealth through the increase of available water while maintaining social harmony in its distribution.[1] Promoting accumulation was always the more essential job, for time and instrumental reason had proved it to be the most efficacious strategy for generating economic growth, bringing in revenues, and keeping the bu-

285

reaucracy employed. It was also what the Bureau of Reclamation did best, and as the years passed, it became more narrowly focused. As some individuals got richer, they clearly came to deserve, by the rules of the Bureau's work, the fullest attention. Which is another way of saying that the accumulative function by its nature tolerated, even produced, economic inequalities. On the other hand, many of those citizens who, for one reason or another, failed to keep pace with the elite were sooner or later likely to resent their situation and feel that the state was not performing its distributive job in good conscience. They could readily accept the idea that the state apparatus ought to help individuals acquire more water, more capital, and more income—but accept only to the extent they themselves were assured that such help was fairly distributed to all. The controlling American definition of justice, as many have observed, has been one of open opportunities and plenty of them. Restrict those opportunities to a privileged handful, smaller and smaller in number, and in many people's eyes the state and its efforts began to appear less legitimate, less supportable.

Everywhere modern capitalist culture faces such a contradiction, and faces, if it cannot resolve the tension, its own death. So at least Jürgen Habermas, the German social philosopher and heir of the Frankfurt School, has argued. What he calls *Steuerungsproblemen,* or unresolved steering problems, abound in this culture and its various societies, engendering from country to country a sense of crisis that so far no state has quite been able to relieve. Apathy, alienation, a decline in mass loyalty toward institutions and traditions, a growing sense of a world gone irrational: these are some of the symptoms of the general legitimacy crisis. Can the state steer away from the rock of elite accumulation and back toward popular support? Can it revive the heroic collective spirit that once animated the drive to conquer nature? If not, a crash is coming, Habermas warns, and some new culture, some new economy, with new social arrangements and modes of production, will emerge from the wreckage.[2]

The American West, running for so long on an ascending curve of optimism, came at last to be drawn into that same general malaise. So abrupt was the reversal in mood that it left a lot of westerners bewildered and angry, determined to insist on the old clichés more stridently than ever. They began to sense but not really understand that former symbols of success like Hoover Dam no longer stirred the same old enthusiasm nationwide. Nor did Henry Luce's ebullient vision of an "endless frontier" for reclamation raise its former fervor. Too many critical questions faced the empire. But western leaders and state apparatchiks proved unable, as we will see, to respond creatively to the crisis, and so at last undermined their project of river domination.

Steering a successful course for reclamation had always required the whole-hearted support of agrarian democrats. More than any other group, it was they who gave the effort its moral legitimacy. They earnestly believed and worked to convince the public that irrigating the West was the way to open up opportunities for millions of poor Americans and to keep faith with the ideals of men like Thomas Jefferson. In the postwar period, that role of legitimation belonged preeminently to the University of California econo-mist Paul Taylor. He would never have described his part that way. On the contrary, he would have said he was a gadfly, an outsider, an outraged man fighting against the power elite, denying them legitimacy. And he was all that too: for forty years he had struggled against them to save the 160-acre limit in the reclamation law. But so long as he was successful in his struggle, and for a while he was that, Taylor added an unintended credibility to the over-all program. For he sincerely felt that the idea of water domination was a noble one, if it could be kept joined to the idea of distributive justice. That was exactly what the cause of reclamation legitimacy needed: someone to fight tirelessly for its tradition. The empire also needed to let a man like Taylor win a little. That did not happen, and that was why it irretrievably weakened its case.

Taylor first learned about the reclamation program, including the provi-sion on acreage limitation, at the feet of Walter Packard in the early forties.[3] He was then a professor at Berkeley, had been since 1922, and would stay there till his retirement and beyond. Born in 1895 in Iowa, he had studied at the University of Wisconsin with John R. Commons before coming West for graduate work. His first scholarly commitment was to labor policy, especially regarding Mexican farm workers in California. In 1939, he and his photographer wife, Dorothea Lange, collaborated on an eloquent essay, *American Exodus,* depicting the plight of the Okie migrants. Once he had heard from Packard about the acreage limit, however, he had the driving motive of his mature years: to bring about the breakup of the large agribusiness interests in California and put land in the hands of as many people as possible. A democratic West, he began to insist in a spate of articles and congressional testimony, would require the prevention of land and water monopoly and the proliferation of the small family farmstead.

Originally the acreage limit on federal water projects, as has been dis-cussed, had been set at 160 acres per family. That was a maximum, a ceiling, not a suggested optimum. Far less land than that, it was generally acknowledged, would be adequate to support a family wherever irrigation was available. Consequently, farms in the West ought to be smaller than those elsewhere, smaller than the quarter-section norm that had guided earlier, humid-land settlement. Families, the law went on, must reside in the "neighborhood" of their land—must be real farmers, that is, not speculators or landlords living in some distant city. By midcentury, however, the law had been significantly altered by Bureau "interpretation." The residency requirement was completely ignored (under the unconvincing claim that Congress had omitted it in the 1926 Omnibus Adjustment Act).[4] The 160-acre allotment had been extended to every adult member of a farm household, and it could be held in as many separate irrigation districts as one liked. Exemptions had been granted to a lengthening string of projects all over the West, though not, despite the best efforts of Sheridan Downey and Alfred Elliott, to the Central Valley of California. Luckily, Michael Straus's "technical compliance" formula allowed large landowners there to sell their excess land to friends, relatives, employees, anyone who would let them go on using it. And the Bureau everywhere allowed the unlimited leasing of land, so that a single operator could farm five or ten or fifteen thousand acres with ridiculously cheap public water. Still, for all the bureaucratic loosening, there remained a specified limit on the books and enough show of enforcement to rile the bigger accumulators. It was Paul Taylor's intention to hold fast to that limit, or some near facsimile of it, and to toughen the Bureau's adherence to it.[5]

He had his work cut out for him. During the first term of the Eisenhower presidency, Secretary of the Interior Douglas McKay, formerly an Oregon automobile dealer, now a powerfully placed official determined to remove all federal roadblocks to private enterprise, came up with a method to get around the acreage law. He offered to accept a lump-sum payment of $14 million for the Army-built dam at Pine Flat on California's Kings River (it had cost $40 million—the rest would be charged off to flood control), allowing excess owners along the river and in the old Tulare Lake basin to buy their way out of conformity. Fifty-two of the owners held among them 196,466 excess acres, and they were delighted with the McKay bargain; it was exactly what they had sought since prevailing upon the Army (instead of the Bureau) to do the work.[6] Unfortunately for them, McKay's successor, Fred Seaton, felt compelled to take that offer back as a possible violation of the reclamation law, and not until 1982 would they get their way. Meanwhile, Congressman Clair Engle of California introduced a more successful evasive strategy, the so-called Engle formula, which allowed exemption through payment of interest charges, set at very low rates, on federal water projects. This was enacted in the Small Reclamation Projects Act of 1956.[7] Still another assault on the limit came through the courts, when an excess owner in the Ivanhoe Irrigation District (Tulare County again) sued to stop the district from accepting the limit in its Bureau of Reclamation contracts. The California Supreme Court agreed with him, declaring in *Ivanhoe Irrigation District* v. *All Parties* (1957) that the acreage provision violated state law, which must take precedence in water matters. The limit was "unlawful discrimination" against the well-to-do, the court complained, a piece of "class legislation." The following year, the United States Supreme Court unanimously struck down that decision, thereby asserting not only the validity of the limit itself but the primacy of federal authority as well.[8] In all these skirmishes, Paul Taylor was at the forefront, advising and consulting with liberal senatorial allies Paul Douglas and Wayne Morse, bristling tall and angry at hearings, his keen eyes searching out any bureaucrat who would dare to empty sacred words of their meaning. He was a strong, determined hawk of a man whom little farmers could use around the barnyard for defense.

The case against the acreage limit was what it had always been. Critics contended that in the old days it had been a nice theory of dividing up the public domain, but that it now interfered with the higher principle of accumulation. In the words of the chief counsel for the Imperial Irrigation District, "it completely offsets a man's right to work, to live, and to acquire property." That refrain ran through the 1958 hearings convened by Senator Clinton Anderson of New Mexico, who was among those seeking repeal, or at least relief. The witnesses he called in those hearings included a North Dakota farmer who resented "this business of putting ceilings over him." "America has been known and admired the world over as a land of unlimited opportunity," he went on, but "acreage ceilings set at the turn of the century certainly limit the opportunity of progressive irrigation farmers." Senator Frank Barrett of Wyoming, whose bill would have applied the Engle formula to all federally reclaimed lands, stuck in his view that it was not morally right to deprive a man of his property and give it to another. And Floyd Dominy, then the Bureau's associate commissioner, confessed that he was at heart an accumulator too. He owned 380 acres as a gentleman farmer in Virginia and was "not yet convinced that is sufficient." Dominy went on:

> I think we must cut through the fog in this [hearings] room
> that has come from many well-intentioned people as to the
> sacredness of the 160-acre limit. I want to defend it, yes,

as to its principle and as to its policy. But I think that it
needs to be adjusted to the existing circumstances in any
given area.[9]

With Chairman Anderson and other western politicians, Dominy lavishly
praised the principle of redistributing reclamation benefits widely. Such
assertions were the established method of holding on to broad funding
support. It was merely the application, the substance, of that principle he
and the others found objectionable. For them, the problem was to devise
some subtle, unobtrusive way of maintaining the husk of agrarian idealism
without preserving its kernel of meaning. For Paul Taylor, the challenge
was not letting them get away with it.

Note that though the party of accumulators was scattered over the West,
California was still by far the main and loudest source of noncompliers, with
recalcitrants in the neighboring states looking on to see which way the
federal wind blew out there. In the next round of the limit controversy, after
those generally unsuccessful trials in the fifties to get the limit removed
completely, the contest would move to California altogether. Once more, its
Central Valley would become a violent battleground, though this time words
and lawyers—not pick handles and thugs—would be used, for this was to
be a battle fought, for the most part, with professors and congressmen, not
with poor alien workers. The controversy now focused on the desolate
western side of the San Joaquin River, the Westlands district still lying high
and dry and vulnerable. With no other water than what they could pump
from deep down in the ground, with water tables falling rapidly, there was
a fierce local clamoring for government aid. Controversy was also gathering
around the latest hydraulic feat in the West, and one of the most impressive:
the State Water Project of California, which was sold to legislators by
agribusinessmen to rid them of the fearsome federal rule-makers.

The State Water Project began in the early 1940s when powerful valley
agricultural interests, backed up by merchant groups and the state engineer,
made a pass at buying out the feds. When they discovered there was not
enough money, or will, to take over the entire Central Valley Project, they
turned instead to rivalry. They would jolly well do their own plumbing from
this point on. They would not let the Bureau of Reclamation add the Feather
River, plunging off the Sierra into the Sacramento basin, to its cap, but
would claim it for the state. A dam on the river at Oroville, built to
world-class scale, plus diversion of northern coastal waters southward
would yield enough water to fill a new canal, the California Aqueduct, which
would push up from the delta along the western wall of the valley and,

reviving an old fancy, leap over the Tehachapi Mountains. That was the main idea, simple and megalomaniacal. But in their master blueprint of 1957, the planners went on to speak airily of 376 new reservoirs in all and of total capital expenditures of $11.8 billion—not bad for a single state going it alone. If carried out, the plan would be larger and more costly than the entire federal reclamation program to date. The need for it, state officials said, was desperate. Los Angeles, suppurating endlessly over the southern desert, must have that kind of investment or it would die. Even more to the point, there were land interests along the aqueduct route who needed it, who were aching with thirst, who had to have an irrigation system they could reliably control. This one, it was understood, would have no acreage limitation attached.[10]

After a lot of disputation and delay, a new governor, Edmund "Pat" Brown, took the plan firmly in hand in 1959 and coaxed it through the legislature. His special aide in the campaign was a former Bureau lawyer, Ralph Brody, a smooth man destined for wealth and notoriety. One year later, the proposition went before the California public in a referendum. Now, however, only the first phase was laid out for scrutiny and the cost presented for approval was a mere $1.75 billion. Even at that, a number of independent economists said the project was a boondoggle, returning, by one estimate, barely fifty cents on the dollar. Other critics wanted water development left to the federal bureaucracy, who had the means to go after the big supplies farther north, the Columbia in particular.[11] The opposition almost prevailed, but four days before the election the Metropolitan Water District of southern California signed a contract with the state for 1.5 million acre-feet, and the southern voters now swung over to support the plan. The project passed by 170,000 votes out of almost 6 million cast. Only sixteen out of forty-four counties, and all but one of them was in the southland, gave it a majority.[12] Late in 1971, the first water crossed the mountains.

City people paid the largest part of the bill for the State Water Project, though in some cases they used none of the water. Land developers and agribusiness, on the other hand, took the largest profit. The Metropolitan Water District directors, who ostensibly represented urban consumers, could hardly have been unaware of that outcome. Perhaps because nearly half of those directors were real-estate developers or big landholders, they were not manifestly bothered. In the Great Valley, the leading beneficiaries were a few horny-handed plowmen toiling in Kern and Kings counties: Chevron USA (owner of 37,793 acres in the SWP service area), Tejon Ranch (part of the Los Angeles *Times* holdings, owner of 35,897 acres), Getty Oil (35,384), Shell Oil (31,995), McCarthy Joint Venture A (a partnership including Prudential Insurance, 25,105), Blackwell, Tenneco, and Southern Pacific. They got their water at discount and used it, not to salvage a fading economy as promised, but to put in a quarter of a million new acres of cotton, olives, pistachios, almonds, and wheat.[13]

That the *ur*-motive of the State Water Project, however overlaid it became with later justifications, was to circumvent the federal acreage limit was well understood by Paul Taylor and his associates. Their attention, though, was riveted elsewhere, on the Bureau of Reclamation and its latest round of maneuvers in the valley. Not one to be shut out of any field of budding enterprise, the Bureau was now hurrying its own schemes along to fetch more water and find more customers in the California interior. Already it had spent more money on the valley than on any other single project. Yet still there were lands unredeemed. There was, for instance, west of Fresno above the low-lying sloughs, an undeveloped flattish area the size of Rhode Island. In 1952, landowners there formed the Westlands Water District, which eventually would cover more than 600,000 acres, replacing Imperial as the largest district in the nation.[14] Directly thereafter, the Bureau began looking into the prospects of hooking up a faucet for them. The most feasible solution appeared to be a dam on San Luis Creek coming out of the Diablo Range—precisely where the State Water Project engineers also wanted to build. Handsomely, they agreed to share the facility, and San Luis Dam was budgeted by Congress in 1960. Water taken from its reservoir for federal use would carry the acreage-limit proviso; water for state use would not. The trickiness of distinguishing one water molecule from another did not trouble President John F. Kennedy, who was present to preside over the ground-breaking ceremony, quipping to the thousands sitting on folding chairs, "It's a pleasure to me to come and help blow up this valley in the name of progress." When completed in 1968, San Luis Dam was one of the half-dozen largest structures of its kind ever made, worthy enough, exclaimed Interior Secretary Stewart Udall, to bear a sign reading "Man was here!"[15] What kind of man, what kind of progress, had yet to be discovered.

Long before the Bureau and its know-how came to the rescue, Westlands had been the private fiefdom of a few exceptionally big owners. Though by cross-valley standards they earned a skimpy per acre return from the land, they were hardly poor, for they counted among their numbers the likes of Southern Pacific Railroad, Boston Ranch, Southlake Farms, Bangor Punta, and Standard Oil. You needed many acres there, it was said, to eke out a bare, marginal corporate living, many more to be really comfortable. Federal water, however, was supposed to change all that: farms would be broken into much smaller units, it was promised, new settlers would flock in by the thousands, crop yields would shoot out of sight, the economy would boom, money would blossom along every ditch. In fact, only the last of those promises turned out to be true. After the project was finished, most of the same growers were hiring the same men to ride the same tractors around the same fields. There was no new settlement and little genuine or practical opportunity for the landless—but there was indeed a great gob of money rolling in at last. Why that was the outcome is a revealing study in bureaucratic handling of the reclamation law.

By a strict interpretation of the law, the Bureau was obliged to sign contracts before any construction could begin, and the contracts had to commit landowners to sell their excess lands within ten years of receiving water and at preproject prices to prevent windfall profiteering. Commissioner Dominy saw his duty differently. He would build first, get contracts later. Eventually, under public pressure, they were indeed signed, all under the watchful eye of Ralph Brody, formerly of the governor's office and before that of the Bureau, now counsel for Westlands and the highest paid official in California. By 1976, Brody could boast that 350,000 acres in the district were under contract and of that sum 109,000 excess acres had been disposed of to 928 individuals. All in all, it was "an outstanding record of compliance."[16] Not so, said a group of U.S. senators who came out in 1975 and again in 1976 to see for themselves what had been wrought. The Bureau had no idea, charged the senators, what a family farmer was, how many of them were originally in the district, how many had been added. It had accepted sale prices that were too high, and worse yet, had not made sure that the land really went on the market. Senator Gaylord Nelson reported:

> I have witnessed few hearings in my career that have been more moving than those held in Fresno when literally hundreds of would-be family farmers appeared just to be represented by one California family farmer—a man who told their story of repeated efforts to buy reclamation land sold as excess, only to be told that it was not available in small parcels for family sized farms. These people were experienced family farmers with credit available to them from private sources. All they were asking was what the law promised.[17]

Who, then, was getting the land, if in fact it was being sold as Brody claimed, and how were they doing it?

The would-be farmers who had been excluded from buying formed the

National Land for People organization under the leadership of George Ballis, a sharp, crusty ex–labor journalist. Their investigation uncovered that, despite strenuous denials, project-aided lands were being reorganized into ever more intricate corporate holdings, with the investors typically residing in such farm neighborhoods as San Francisco, the Caribbean, Japan, and Mexico. For instance, Russell Giffen, once described as the largest farmer of irrigated land in the United States, had sold out to a hand-picked circle of cronies and "partnerships," many of them giving the same last name and the same address, which also happened to be the office of one John Bonadelle, a Fresno land speculator. All in the family, as it were. Bonadelle soon after pleaded guilty to a fraud conspiracy charge, but the Westlands shell game went on, confusing the most alert observer with its deft movements, its successive sales and resales, its shuffling of names on the door. Combined with unrestrained leasing, the game was played as a way to prevent any change whatever in the personnel or scale of farm operation. "It is like a club atmosphere," said a representative of the National Farmers Union who had personally tracked down one of the purchasers, the so-called Jubil Farms, to its New York office. "If you are a member of the club, you have access." Under this Bureau-style watchdogging of the reclamation law, there were simply no 160-acre (and precious few 320-acre) farming operations to be found in Westlands.[18]

That men and women would carry on so intricate, so demanding, even at times so flagrantly criminal a shell game as this one may require explanation. The reason, at least the indisputable part of it, had to do with the accumulative urge. Turning on a faucet for Westlands cost the American taxpayer more than $3 billion dollars. (This figure includes construction and interest charges, calculated at 6.75 percent over forty years.) The water came to growers at a measly $7.50 an acre-foot, well below the price charged on the nearby State Water Project lands—a figure so low that they were actually paying off only the yearly operation and maintenance costs. Pumping water uphill from San Luis Dam was done with cheap electricity supplied by the Bureau. The total subsidy, according to economists Philip LeVeen and George Goldman, was a whopping $2,200 per acre. Figure it out: an investor who got one of those interlocking quarter-sections received a gift from the public of $352,000.[19] In exchange, the public got more cotton, sugar beets, and tomatoes—more of them, yes, but not enough to justify their huge capital investment. It was ridiculously expensive food and fiber.

Why the Bureau or Congress would underwrite such extravagant welfare for a rich elite should by now not require any explanation. What none of the parties involved quite expected was the hullabaloo, the demands for investigation, raised over the Westlands project. People wanting an opportunity to farm, resenting their government's indifference toward them and now more effectively organized than ever, were not going to accept this outcome in silence. In 1976, National Land for People filed suit against the Department of the Interior to prevent any further approval of excess-land sales in the district. One year later, Secretary Cecil Andrus, acting under a court injunction, suspended sales approvals not only there but throughout the West, pending a general review of the reclamation law and the adoption of new rules for its enforcement.[20] And Paul Taylor up in Berkeley thought maybe the tide was turning at last, bringing in a people's program of water control.

"All around him were oaths, moans, bellowed complaints, the brief tableaux of upright wincing men, hoes dangling, their hands on the small of their backs, who were going on under the same torment." That is the world of the washed-up prizefighter Billy Tully in Leonard Gardner's novel *Fat City*. [21] It is the California agricultural worker's world, populated by winos toting along their bottles in paper bags, by street derelicts trying to pick up a little change, by old experienced hands knowing no other life, a few of them white, many more of them black, Filipino, and Mexican, in every case seasonal workers who get ninety cents an hour to thin tomatoes or top onions and who spend much of it evenings in Central Valley bars. In the postwar period, they were still around, as they had been since the nineteenth century, and they were no closer to escaping that hard lot than before, no nearer to owning their own farms or receiving public-funded water for them. The entire federal and state investment in irrigation expansion had not been made for them, did not improve their condition. It had been for the accumulative class, who were overwhelmingly white, Anglo men already owning property.[22] Even the hundreds of aspiring farmers who showed up before Gaylord Nelson wanting to buy a piece of the Westlands were well removed from the ranks of seasonal laborers. Granted, with the right kind of reclamation program it was at least conceivable that some of the Billy Tullys along with the Sanchezes and the Villanuevas of the fields could become small-time owners, bending and sweating for themselves. But that had not been the program pursued, though it had always been the promise held forth. The result was a glaring gap between the claim of wide redistribution and the bleak reality of a permanent underclass who did the brute work in western reclamation. Legitimacy slipped down into the gap and could not be pulled out.

The elaboration of irrigated agriculture, as demonstrated earlier, required a rural proletariat. For a long while Asian immigrants made up that proletariat, then Mexicans and Okies. When the Okies moved out of farm work during World War Two and into coastal defense industries, the growers fell back once more on Mexican nationals to serve. A presidential executive order in 1942 allowed them to recruit workers across the border (the so-called *braceros,* or strong-armed ones) on temporary work permits. The policy was extended in 1951, as Public Law 78, a further example of the state's promotion of the water empire. Growers claimed, in agitating for the law, that they could not find enough domestic hands to get their crops in. "We tried to bring labor from the Southern states," explained J. Earl Coke, a prominent California agricultural leader, "and the colored people just can't bend over that far."[23] In the peak year of 1959, California imported 136,012 Mexicans, and Texas used 205,959. Put more accurately, it was a tightly organized group of 50,000 growers in five key western states, assembled, for instance, as the Imperial Valley Farmers Association, who employed virtually all the *braceros.* Stories of laborers being herded north (packed like cattle into rickety old trucks by unscrupulous, exploiting contractors), of squalid housing conditions, and of starvation wages led to the termination of the import program in 1964. Still open were the possibilities of applying for permanent alien resident status— becoming a "green card" worker—or of crawling illegally under the fence at the international border.[24]

Then began, with that grudging restriction of the labor pool, a fierce race along the western ditches between the forces of unionization and of mechanization. Americans of Hispanic ancestry, the largest remaining source of workers, undertook to organize themselves, as they had tried to do in the 1920s and 1930s, into agricultural unions. Marching under the flag of the National Farm Workers Union, which bore a black Aztec eagle on a red-and-white field, and led by a cotton picker from Arizona, César Chavez, they tasted real success for the first time. In 1965, they announced a work stoppage against the grape farms of the Delano, California area. In the next year, they went on strike in the vineyards of two of the state's biggest growers, Schenley (who became the first to recognize the union) and DiGiorgio (who fought them bitterly). Those actions were followed in 1968 by a national boycott against the table-grape industry. Despite the open hostility of Governor Ronald Reagan and the entire agribusiness establishment, the NFWU persisted, winning through the seventies a series of victories in contracts, minimum-wage guarantees, and state-supervised elections.[25]

And then they began to lose. With every success, growers had an added incentive to invest in the new farming machines appearing on the scene. The weird, ingenious, and expensive technology was designed, for the most part, at public-funded universities and aided the accumulators by lowering their labor costs. One harvester clattered along the cotton rows, stripping the bolls and blowing them into wheeled bins that carted them to the gins. Another ripped grapes from their vines. Still others grabbed walnut trees by their trunks and shook the crop down. With increasing frequency it was machines that dug potatoes and beets and carrots and dumped them onto conveyor belts. By 1966, there were 460 machines in California fields alone harvesting tomatoes, and farmers were bringing in millions of tons of a new "square", thick-skinned variety of the fruit, specially created to withstand mechanical handling. "The machine won't strike," noted the chairman of an engineering department at the University of California at Davis, where much of the inventing went on; "it will work when [the growers] want it to work."[26] His words hinted of the vision that had animated the empire from the beginning—of extending its technological control as far as possible, to the total domination of the earth. If one could make water run uphill for hundreds of miles, one could do more, much more. One could turn over the whole job of irrigated cropping to genetics, to electronics, to robotics, doing away with the need for almost all field labor, completing man's triumph over the desert. No more stooping in the hot sun, no more threats to strike, no more workers, no more work.

From its very beginning, the federal reclamation bureaucracy had studiously ignored this rural proletariat toiling on its assisted lands. All of its promises of creating new farms and farmers in the West were proffered, however vaguely, to some set of noble husbandmen or yearning city people elsewhere, usually a good deal farther off. And there was another community in the West who were ignored, closed out, not regarded as the stuff from which accumulators and imperialists are made: the Indians. Outside of a few of its judges, the government did not acknowledge that the Indians might need or want water too. Yet three out of four Indians living on reservations in the United States were located in the West, and because they had for so long been disregarded, the tribes found themselves by the postwar years in a parlous situation. Reservation lands had been taken from them and sold to white irrigators or flooded behind dams. Their groundwater had been pumped away to adjacent interests. The Paiute of Nevada watched their Pyramid Lake, once an abundant fishery for cutthroat trout and cui-ui, recede lower and lower, as farmers upstream on the Newlands Irrigation Project diverted the Truckee River to raise cattle feed. The Bureau of Reclamation consigned other flows, like the Yellowstone River in Montana, to invading coal companies, despite the protests of the Crow, Cheyenne, Arapaho, and Shoshone. Some Indians wanted to secure water for their own industrial schemes, while others had the laying out of large-scale irrigation farms in mind—or merely the retaining of a right to future

297

development. But everywhere they were standing at the tail end of a long, long ditch.[27]

The Indians pinned their hopes for a fairer distribution on some principles enunciated in a Supreme Court case back in 1908, *Winters* v. *United States.* The case was over who was entitled to the Milk River of Montana: a white settler named Henry Winters and his neighbors, who were drawing off the river to their fields, or, downstream from them, the Gros Ventre on their Fort Belknap reservation. The Court concluded that the Indians had priority of claim, had in fact a special, unique right to water based on their treaty with the American government. When they came to terms with their conquerors, the tribe reserved enough water for all their future needs. Whether that right had ever been claimed or not was immaterial; the water must be there waiting for the Indians whenever they decided to use it. The white man's laws of appropriation, which gave a water right to whoever first put a river to use, could not affect those reserved native rights. Furthermore, the English tradition of riparian rights, granted to any and all streamside dwellers, could not prevail against the Indian priority. The Winters doctrine was potentially a bombshell that could blow the entire structure of western water rights, and the hydraulic society resting on it, to ruins. One Indian sympathizer, William Veeder of the Department of Justice, maintained that the Winters decision gave the tribes an unlimited claim on their watersheds, on all the streams "which rise upon, traverse or border upon Indian reservations," and that white users there, no matter how old their own claims, must now buy the right to divert or must give way. Others hotly denied so sweeping a claim.[28] A fundamental moral issue was at stake, a question of justice. Did the fact that a people had arrived in a country first give them an eternal and superior hold on its natural resources? Or did a higher right belong to the man or woman who first saw the economic promise in a resource, who first put it to use and made a profit from it? Neither the courts nor Congress managed to settle the issue. Indeed, they left it in total confusion. No one could say, would say, where or how far the Winters doctrine applied. And in that state of ambiguity the white appropriators had an uneasy but clear edge: they were already in possession.[29]

The predicament of the farm workers in the western hydraulic order was radically unlike that of the Indians. But there were some similarities. In the first place, neither group had been cut in on the benefits from water development. Now, in their new militancy, both groups could seriously embarrass the region nationally and internationally. They could testify that technological prowess and private accumulative success were not the only outcomes worth noting. There was also poverty, despair, and discrimination in the West. The instrumental reason by which the empire functioned had long ignored those darker truths, for they were about matters of morality, justice, ultimate intrinsic values, and the instrumentalists, whether public or private men, were not skilled or interested in such matters. Another parallel was that neither the field workers nor the Indians could expect much from the traditional reclamation law, regardless of how vigorously it was enforced. In particular, the acreage limit was not meaningful if one had the land, as the Indians did, but needed water or if one did not have the funds, as workers did not, to buy excess lands that came on the market. The theory of justice embodied in the limit, taken alone, was too narrow to produce a genuinely egalitarian society in the region. Moreover, it could conceivably work against these poorest, excluded groups by adding to the number of white farmers competing against the Indians' reservations or pushing for mechanization of the laborers' jobs. Finally, for both groups the danger in the controversy over the 160-acre law was that it could preempt the broader moral debate over water and its distribution, reducing to a formula, and an old-fashioned Jeffersonian agrarian formula at that, the more complex issues they wanted addressed.

By the decade of the 1970s, then, the water empire was ringed about, more than at any other time in its rise to power, by loud, angry, protesting voices. Among them were the voices of Indians and field workers. There was also a vitriolic newcomer down in Imperial Valley, Dr. Ben Yellen, fighting with broadsides and lawsuits to get the acreage limitation and residency clause enforced.[30] There was George Ballis and National Land for People agitating for the same thing in the Westlands district and across the region. Even the growers, those securely on the side of empire, were not altogether happy. They resented any semblance of federal control, especially over their acquisitive ambitions, and demanded the removal of all acreage limits whatsoever. What all of the voices were wrangling over was the legitimacy of the empire itself and how that legitimacy would be defined—what cultural values, traditions, and standards of judgment would predominate.

In August 1977 the Bureau of Reclamation, obeying the court injunction to review acreage enforcement, issued a new set of rules interpreting and applying the 1902 law. Any single individual (or any corporation) would still be limited to 160 acres, as the law said, though a family could own up to 640 acres. Through additional leasing, the operational limits could be expanded to 480 acres per person, or 960 acres per family. The time allowed for disposal of excess lands would be lowered from ten to five years, and the federal government would set up a lottery to sell lands that owners could not sell among their family, neighbors, or employees. And no owner or lessee of federally watered lands would be allowed to live more than fifty miles from them—a requirement that would be "phased in so that no undue hardship would occur." Would the enforcement of those rules make much of a difference across the West? In most places, the answer was no. Only 2 percent of all reclamation landowners had more than 320 acres; the average size of ownership units was a piddling 70 acres. A mere 0.8 percent of the units exceeded 640 acres, the family standard (though they owned 16.8 percent of irrigable acres). But there were a few places over which the rules would roll like an earthquake, shaking and knocking about the social order, and those places happened to be precisely where the Bureau had lavished its best efforts, notably the Central Valley of California. Under the proposed methods of calculating, Californians would own almost a million acres of excess lands, or 89.3 percent of the total in the seventeen-state Bureau service area. New Mexico, Texas, Nebraska, and Montana would add enough to account, with California, for 96 percent of acreage excess. In those states, the Bureau was admitting at last that there "was a very high degree of inequality" in the distribution of benefits for which it was partly responsible, and that a new, serious round of enforcement could rectify that inequality. Something like a thousand new farms could be created, the government ventured, most of them to be found in the Westlands district. That was, after all, not many farms, not enough to erase most of the lines of class and hierarchy, but it was enough to seem wildly, dangerously revolutionary to a grower named Standard Oil or J. G. Boswell, Inc., and thus it was enough to doom the new rules.[31]

The Interior Department officials dutifully took their proposed rules into western towns and cities where they hoped to hear the grassroots reaction. What they mainly heard, and it came from a choleric brigade who could not claim to represent the large, unaffected, complacent majority of reclamation farmers, was that enforcement would be catastrophic. An even smaller knot of dissidents appeared at hearings to say that the rules did not go far enough, that far stricter ceilings on family ownership and on leasing—say, a maximum of 320 acres on all operations of every kind—would make many more opportunities for new farms than the Interior scheme, but their voices were shouted down in the general organized clamor set up by the rural elite. Among those taking the elite's side was liberal Governor Jerry Brown of California, who sent his state director of food and agriculture, Richard Rominger, to protest that the 160-acre limit was "unrealistic." He had support from men like the Westlands Water District manager and the spokesman from the Pacific Legal Foundation, who charged that Interior was trying to force "a social change by attempting to create an 'agrarian' form of agriculture." The foundation subsequently got the courts to issue an injunction against the rules until an environmental-impact statement was prepared.[32] While that was in process, western congressmen and senators rushed off to Washington with a slew of proposals in their attaché cases to bury the proposed rules and amend the 1902 law.

By 1979, it was clear that the only bill that had much chance of passage was the Reclamation Reform Act, Senate Bill 14, proposed by Frank Church of Idaho to give "relief to real family farmers." It would repeal all residency requirements, make 1,280 acres the absolute maximum for operations, leased or owned or a combination thereof, but expand that limit where climate or altitude put farmers at a competitive disadvantage. Church would also free any district from those limits once it had paid out its forty-year contract with the Bureau. Hearings on the bill were held in Washington in March 1979. After drawn-out statements from state secretaries of agriculture, from the well-heeled Farm/Water Alliance, the National Cotton Council, and so forth, after twenty-three witnesses in all testified in favor of liberalizing or abolishing the old law, when the hour was late and the senators were eager to go home, George Ballis of National Land for People was allowed to come forth and speak alone in opposition. Some months later the full Senate considered the Church bill and voted in favor of it, 47 to 23. No action was taken by the House of Representatives, however, leaving the issue moot.[33]

With the new Interior rules still hanging threateningly in the air, with a string of failures to get the law rewritten by Congress, the western elite was frustrated and worried that they would again fail to get reform as they had in the 1940s and 1950s. Then, the inauguration of Ronald Reagan as President in January 1981, a man who as California's governor had sharply condemned the general idea of an acreage limit, along with the seating of a strongly conservative, Republican-controlled Senate, brightened their prospects considerably.[34] Once more a rush of new bills appeared in Capitol Hill committees. Senator James McClure of Idaho, with support from Armstrong of Colorado and DeConcini of Arizona, sponsored S. 1867, which would set the limit at a munificent 2,080 acres owned and leased. For a while it was the Senate's favored child. This time, however, the bill that was destined to succeed where all others had failed was one slipped into the House hopper by Morris Udall of Arizona. H.R. 5539 would abolish residency requirements completely. The western reclamation farmer could live in Taiwan or Palm Springs if he liked, plowing and watering at long distance. Udall's bill would set the combined ceiling for a family at 960 acres, or its equivalent in areas of lesser productivity, but at 320 acres for a corporation. It would let the Secretary of the Interior decide how long (up to a period of five years) an owner had to dispose of his excess lands. No

301

lottery was required to see that the excluded, the outsider, got a chance at the sale. The bill would allow unlimited leasing above 960 acres, so long as the lessee reimbursed in full the interest paid out by the government on the reclamation funds it borrowed. And it would exempt all Army Corps of Engineers projects from any acreage limit. On 6 May 1982, the House voted in favor of the Udall bill (228 ayes, 117 nays). In July of that year the senators agreed to shelve their own McClure bill and put Udall's in its place. The vote was 49 in favor of that move, with only 13 opposed. Thus, the Reclamation Reform Act of 1982 became law. After eight decades of dispute, loose attention, and the persistent hopes of social reformers the old 160-acre homestead principle was dumped for a new standard, one six times larger than its predecessor. For those growers whom George Ballis called the "biggies," those men who were huge in ambition but mighty few in number, constituting less than 2 percent of the reclamation owners, the way was now open to unlimited aggrandizing. Without embarrassment or danger they could openly set up truly massive operations, if they paid "full cost." What was meant by paying "full cost" turned out to be not so very onerous either: getting an interest rate, through long-term government borrowing, that was about half the going market figure, paying something like 6 or 8 percent above the water rates charged the smaller operators, with all those subsidies from urban water and electricity consumers left pleasantly intact. The power structure of the hydraulic empire was not altogether satisfied with the outcome—it wanted more liberality than it got. But, on balance, it was happy, for it was safe at last from the tattered hordes of wild-eyed agrarians, farm workers, revolutionaries, populists, and redistributionists.[35]

During these years of turmoil from the mid-1970s to 1982, much was said about the principles, the moral values, that should henceforth govern the development and use of water in the West. Little that was said was new or profoundly thought out, but what was said was strongly, passionately, and thanks to the changed political climate of the Reagan era, unabashedly urged. The debates in Congress produced especially revealing articulations of the region's public values on the matter. Judging by the frequency of their iteration, the most compelling of those principles were the following:

1. The proper role of the state should be to promote the private accumulation of wealth, not seek its dispersal into as many hands as possible; it should be to reward the successful, not the failures.
2. The laws of the marketplace are reason exemplified,

and they should be allowed to dictate what size of farm operation is most desirable, what will work best, what will be viewed as efficient.

3. The hydraulic apparatus of the West, an imposing technological triumph, should not be flawed and compromised by an antiquated agrarian ideal that belongs to the horse-and-buggy days.

Although evidence could be rustled together in support of any of the three principles, they were all more in the way of preachments than demonstrable or logical truths. Defenders of the 1902 law flailed away at them with their own statistics and preachments, but finally they could not prevail—could not crack the imperial ideology.

By the first of the principles, the federal government was to be regarded as a welcome partner in developing western water when it confined its mission to the domination of nature and left private enterprise alone. When it acted, that is, in Senator Malcolm Wallop of Wyoming's words, as "a public-investment-making entity," and in the words of his senior colleague, as "an engine of economic growth." Then, so the reasoning went, no matter how large its budget or how far-flung its tentacles, no matter how subtle or powerful its influence, no matter how deeply dependent on it westerners had become, government was not yet become that dreaded monster Bureaucracy. It was not yet an overarching authority repressing and restraining the rights of individuals. When the state took to redistributing land and water, on the other hand, the West would become, in the rumbling phrases of McClure of Idaho, a "centrally controlled, rigidly enforced egalitarian society in which excellence is not virtue and liberty no prize." In the 1979 hearings, Orrin Hatch, a prominent member of the New Right, denounced this "continuing process of bureaucratic domination" that the acreage limit imposed on his constituents in Utah (Bureau figures showed that only 0.1 percent of irrigable acres there were excess). On the same occasion John Puchen, director of California Westside Farmers, demanded to know, "Who is the Government of the United States to say that because you want to be a farmer, your income should be limited to a subsistence level?" And Bernice Wolf of California Women in Agriculture echoed many senatorial sentiments when she said, "We must preserve the sacred right of property owners to do as they wish with their property." Big government, then, was not *ipso facto* incompatible with the western way of thinking, only government, whatever its size, that attempted to mess about with the single sacred right of accumulation. The region's elite were attacking a government that said, as Wallop put it, "You're going to be frozen in place."[36]

The second principle had less visceral appeal than that of defending the raw accumulative passion, but it had the great advantage of seeming to be more scientific, more disinterested, even more humanitarian. A large body of technical literature could be brought to its defense, all of it demonstrating, so it was said, that a mere 160 acres was irrational and inefficient by the standards of contemporary marketplace agriculture. Among such studies frequently cited were those by California farm economists Gerald Dean, Harold Carter, and Warren Johnston. In their view, the economies of scale in irrigated farming all began well above the quarter-section farm unit level: at 600 to 640 acres for most of the crops they studied. Modern machinery, their studies and a few others suggested, had made the old nineteenth-century standard in farm size completely outmoded. Rigidly imposing that standard today would raise the cost of food and, as some went on to claim, threaten the hungry of the world with starvation. However simplistic, that argument provided grist for the empire's mills. Not mentioned were the other implications in the studies. Once achieved, those economies of scale typically did not go on and on upward but reached a plateau where they leveled off, or even declined, as they encountered some inefficiencies associated with overblown size. Yet no one in the agribusiness world or the United States Senate suggested that a *lid* be placed on western farm size right where those diseconomies began to show up. Taking off every lid possible was the great and only desideratum, for it was accumulation, not efficiency, that was their real, leading motive.[37]

The identification of an optimum scale in agriculture mainly reflected, of course, the cost and design of the machinery currently being invented and deployed on farms, as well as the desire of every operator to own his own full panoply of such equipment rather than to share with his neighbors; the growing dependence on a battery of chemicals; and the ability or inability to get a contract with some giant food processor. Any such optimum was best understood, not as a "law," specifying what had to be, but rather as a description of what was, of what had been devised, of what had been sought. In the agricultural engineering schools, efficiency had been persistently defined as whatever was most profitable for big operators. Therefore, the search for a so-called scientific definition of ideal scale was something of a self-fulfilling prophecy. Believe that big is better and you will work to make it so.[38]

Those who wanted to hold on to the old 160-acre acreage limit, or at least on to some lower ceiling than the one pushed by Udall or McClure, had their own studies to cite, casting the entire matter of scale and profitability into some confusion. For example, a study by two agricultural economists at Washington State University demonstrated that a 160-acre farm in the

Columbia basin could earn a family $15,590 in after-tax income, a 320-acre farm, $27,360, sums they described as respectively "quite adequate" and "quite generous" by national standards. Corroboration came from the Bureau of Reclamation's environmental-impact statement on its proposed rules, which determined that in the vast majority of irrigation districts a 160-acre farm could produce as much as or more income than the national farm average of $10,037. Quadrupling that size, as the Bureau proposed to allow for families, would have made it possible for a western farmer with subsidized water to make far more money than his counterpart in the East: as much, it was calculated, as $101,480 in net operator income in the Westlands Water District, $124,600 in Imperial Valley.[39]

The third principle may have been the most subtly persuasive of all, though it was more of an oblique presence than a well-articulated argument. The 160-acre standard, argued senators, congressmen, editorialists, and farm groups, came from another century, when dams were simply piles of brush or stones placed across a stream, when a plow or a mule-drawn fresno was sufficient to scratch out a ditch. In the shadow of a San Luis Dam or the Central Arizona Project, it seemed a hopeless anachronism. Moreover, the standard came from another, fading region. For farmers back East so small a farm and the income it provided might be all right, but not for farmers in the West, where men lived by larger expectations. Enforcing an old, outmoded social ideal of small farming in that big land of big engineering triumphs was a gross incongruity. It would create a region of "serfs" and "peasants," warned western leaders.[40] Never mind for the moment that those serfs, according to the economic studies, were making on average as much as or more than those in any other region of the world. The point was that they were men who had a spectacular hydraulic achievement to live up to and therefore could not be confined to the ambitions of lesser men elsewhere. That general, diffuse feeling of incompatibility between traditional, eastern social ideals and modern, western technological miracles was independent of any personal, self-interested acquisitiveness or any loyalty to the most accumulative class. It was unsentimental, commonsensical thinking, an honest acknowledgment that if the West had ever really wanted to establish in its valleys a more decentralized, agrarian life, where a large portion of its people would live directly on the land and make their own decisions locally, it would never have pursued the water system it got. Now it was time, westerners were insisting, that the society be conformed to its infrastructure.

Whatever the validity of these ways of thinking, they carried the day. A long-standing agrarian tradition and its powerful mystique were abandoned in 1982. For almost a century, it had been attached—granted, as rhetoric more than reality—to the western reclamation program. Now at last that program was revealed to be unequivocally an imperial one, aimed at the massing of wealth and power, using the concentrated force of the capitalist state to further that work. The next question was whether, without the cover of the agrarian tradition, such a program could still hold on to its legitimacy among Americans, even among westerners. Would they continue to finance it, as they had always done, once they had an unambiguous view of what it was after?

"The great barbecue is over," announced Senator Daniel Moynihan of New York during consideration of the McClure bill. While the taxpayers in his own home city were forced to spend over a billion dollars of their own money to improve their water supply, westerners were still asking for more federal aid. They were asking, he acknowledged, but they were not going to get it. Not a single major water-authorization bill, he pointed out, had been passed by Congress in the decade after 1972. The Corps of Engineers was without work, and the Bureau was merely finishing up old projects. The national majority that had once supported those authorizations had now disintegrated. Moynihan recounted how the governor of Arizona, flying with him in a helicopter over the Colorado River reservoirs, had joked that the water was destined for "the swimming pools of my more affluent constituents." Moynihan was incensed by such profligacy, such flagrant abuse of New York charity. What he was saying should have been taken as a warning to the western bloc in Congress that the legitimacy of their program was hanging in the balance. They did not pay him any attention, however, and ignored similar warning signals from Senators Proxmire of Wisconsin, Metzenbaum of Ohio, and Lugar of Indiana. All indicated that the Midwest, like the East, was not likely to go on financing the water empire in years to come. Nor did they heed one of their own, Congressman Jim Weaver of Oregon, who denounced the Udall bill as "the product of a well-financed campaign of a small but very wealthy group of agribusiness interests, multimillionaires and corporations. It is a bald-faced antifamily farm package of direct subsidies to the richest of America's agribusiness interests." Outside the West, and even here and there within it, the legitimacy of the program was slipping away.[41]

The irony of the situation was that, in making their case for reforming the acreage limit, the western elite had forged a tool that now could be turned against them with devastating effectiveness. They had claimed to want to live and grow by the principles of the marketplace. Very well, let them pay market prices for their water. If the West was not interested in opening new homestead opportunities for the disadvantaged, then the old justification for furnishing cheap irrigation was gone. Two Colorado State University economists, David Seckler and Robert A. Young, wrote in 1978, "We find there is no compelling rationale for anything like the amount of subsidies now being provided under federal water programs."[42] That was an old conclusion, now spreading rapidly through both professional and lay circles, and the 1982 legislation could only confirm it. In fact, the new law reflected that thinking to some degree when it spoke of "full cost" pricing for larger operations and when it required districts to agree to annual renegotiations of contracts and prices if they wanted to enjoy the new acreage liberality. Since it had been taken over by the state, reclamation had never been asked to meet the familiar market tests: Would this expenditure bring the highest possible return? Would the benefits be greater than the costs? Would private capital have undertaken this or that project? Would the water go to those willing to pay the most for it? Now, suddenly, caught in the backlash of their own reasoning, the western ideologists might have to face those tests at last.

If the empire had now to meet, and meet rigorously, the pure marketplace tests of economic success, then there might be significant shifts ahead in its structure of power. Agriculture might eventually have to give way, might be forced to migrate back eastward where its costs were lower, its western water going to a new set of customers—the industrialists, the mining and energy companies, the desert megalopolises. Moreover, under strict marketplace accounting, no new projects might be undertaken for quite some time. There might be too many other demands on capital, pressing demands from all over the world, competing against the water developers. Their dream of total use, total domination of the western landscape, might then never be fully realized. That was a distinct possibility lurking in the triumph of 1982. In winning its long battle to lift the lid on accumulation, the empire might have lost the means to finance its continuing war on the desert. And lost too its ability to command the moral capital of the nation.

For a man like Paul Taylor, however, a man who had given so much of his life to defending the agrarian tradition in the reclamation law, that sudden, unforeseen vulnerability of an empire overreaching itself was not apparent in the summer of 1982. Now eighty-seven years old, he shuffled down the corridors of Barrows Hall on the Berkeley campus where he had his office, dressed in a plaid shirt and a blue nylon padded jacket, walking slowly and gingerly with a cane in one hand. Once in his office he sat among the scholarly debris of a lifetime, sorting out his papers for the archivists. His eyesight was weakening, his sagging eyelids held in place by tape. On his desk lay an appeal from Morris Udall for a campaign contribution, and for a moment it brought the fire back into those eyes. "Should I send him money?" he asked—send money to a man who at that moment was gutting the law Taylor had worked so hard, so long, to hold on to? He had before him too the beginnings of an article for a law journal, arguing that the Metropolitan Water District had been violating the Warren Act of 1911 by selling its Colorado supplies to excess-land owners. On that and other matters he answered questions with a slow, thoughtful precision. His mind was alert and tenacious while the body gave way. Yet that alertness was tinged with melancholy, for he knew that he had failed in what he had set out to achieve. He understood and must accept that the West, or at least the elite West, had rejected a future he had wanted to see for it, a future where small farmers of many races could live harmoniously and comfortably in that dry land, with a powerful benevolent state building for them, looking out for their welfare, bringing them water. Now that was a vision that had been put aside, once and for all. It was a quaint notion left to the historians. "Well," was all Taylor could say at the end, glancing at the floor, then out the window toward the Sather Tower, "it was a good fight."

LEVIATHAN AILING

In the winter of 1975, the Bureau of Reclamation began filling the reservoir behind one of its newest dams, Teton in southeastern Idaho, at the base of the glorious mountains of the same name. There had been no end of headaches in its construction. Incredibly, the dirt-and-rock dam had been sited on one of the most active earthquake zones in the country, and the canyon walls around it were cracked and fragile, leaking water like a corroded bathtub. Scientists at the U.S. Geological Survey had questioned the wisdom of putting a structure in so treacherous a place. Economists had worried about the cost overruns. Environmentalists criticized the destruction of seventeen miles of canyon wildlife habitat. The Bureau answered by pouring more grout into the cracks. Within six months after its completion Teton Dam sprang a leak, then another. On the fifth of June 1976, its entire north end collapsed, and 80 billion gallons of water came thundering downstream, taking everything in its path: eleven people, 13,000 head of cattle, many ranchers' homes, a billion tons of topsoil, and no small part of the pride and esteem of the river controllers.[1]

A tragedy like Teton Dam could give no one satisfaction, but it could usefully suggest that the hydraulic society had a misplaced, dangerous confidence in its mastery, through concrete, steel, and earth, over nature. The best designs of the best engineers (though Teton was hardly that) could fail, not only all at once, with thunderous impact as in Idaho, but slowly too, wearing out, falling into disrepair, becoming impossible to salvage. Steel penstocks and headgates must someday rust and collapse. Concrete, so permanent-seeming in its youth, must turn soft and crumble. Heavy banks of earth, thrown up to trap a flood, must eventually, under the most favorable circumstances, erode away. After all, nothing nature could throw in the way of even so small a river as the Teton—whether blocks of lava, andesite, sandstone, granite, or gneiss, no matter how many thousands of feet thick and miles and miles across—could contain it forever; how much less likely was it that the human contrivances of the water empire could permanently withstand the force of flowing water. The message of the Teton disaster was that the days of the empire were numbered, on stream after stream, river after river. It was a signal of impending mortality, of human imperfection, of transient, elusive command. The end might not come soon, might come when it did with a whimper more than a bang, but it would come.

Teton was not the first big American dam to collapse. There was the Johnstown, Pennsylvania, disaster of 1889, which had brought John Wesley Powell to a ringing defense, despite the more than two thousand casualties. There was the St. Francis Dam catastrophe of 1928, some forty miles north of Los Angeles, which drowned more than four hundred persons and destroyed the career of the formidable William Mulholland of the Los Angeles Water and Power Department. There was the Walnut Creek washout in Arizona, Austin Dam in Texas—and how many nameless others? In 1965, Fontenelle Dam in Wyoming began leaking and had to be drained, and Navajo in New Mexico narrowly averted a similar fate; while in 1981, a large section of the Westlands irrigation facility, San Luis Dam, slid off into the water, threatening not drownings but drought from diminished reservoir capacity. And there were a few more potential disasters looming in the future: Auburn and San Fernando dams in California and Wolf Creek in Colorado had all been built in unstable seismic zones like Teton's. One study in the aftermath of the Idaho collapse argued that America's dams were ten thousand times more likely to cause a major disaster than all of the nuclear power plants. Even if the federal government could learn to put safety ahead of pork-barrel politics and guarantee its own structures, there remained the grim fact that twenty-four out of twenty-five dams around the country were in private hands, and those were often loose, bungling hands.[2]

More serious for the empire's future than any botched design or isolated disaster were the inevitable problems associated with the aging of the hydraulic system. Yet those problems were seldom confronted. In proposing dams and canals the practice had never been to include the costs of decommissioning or replacing them, for the designers had always assumed that their works were made to last, if not forever, then for a very, very long time. In 1985 Hoover Dam would be a half-century old, and no one really knew what its life-span was. Each day sediment backed up behind it, reducing its capacity, foreshadowing its end. Would it last a full century? Two? The answer would depend in part on the durability of its materials, exposed year after year to a hard climate yet expected to withstand the unrelenting pressures of a mammoth lake, and upon the vagaries of land-use management in its basin, for too much grazing or deforestation upstream could accelerate erosion and add to the sediment. Pointed warnings came from the bad experiences of other countries, for example, from Pakistan's much touted Tarbela Dam, whose life expectancy the designers had overestimated by a factor of three or four.[3] One thing was certain over the long term: whatever their span of service, the Hoovers and Grand Coulees of the West must some day hold back not water but a vast sludge drying in the sun. Eventually engineers would be forced to look for new sites, and they were not going to find any, for the good ones had already been taken, used, and rendered useless.

The failures associated with aging and carelessness of design were part of a larger environmental vulnerability that the water lords began to encounter in the postwar period. They had to contend, in ways their predecessors had never contemplated, with the limits imposed by nature, limits to what humans can do in the pursuit of domination. Hydraulic technology held out for a long time the illusion that it could bring natural forces under absolute, tight, efficient control, but in truth it multiplied the ways it could work its own demise. Each new project, grander than the last, demanded increasingly intricate supervision, greater managerial sophistication—greater, it sometimes seemed, than people could summon. There was more to go wrong, and it did go wrong, on a scale commensurate with the technology involved. In addition to the problems with the apparatus itself, three sets of environmental vulnerabilities appeared: a water-quantity problem, a decline in water quality under ever more intensive use, and a potentially irreversible degradation of the pristine ecological communities of the West. These were not mere casual or minor nuisances. They were deep systemic problems, growing out of the very program of large-scale, intensifying water control, associated with it wherever it had been pursued in history, and quite possibly without remedy. In that case, they might also prove to be fatal.

The old Incas used to say, "The frog does not drink up the pond in which he lives." They did not know the frogs or the ponds of the American West. Into that dry region had migrated the thirstiest frogs on the planet, and by the 1970s they were in fact drinking up their supplies at an alarming rate. Thousands of potholes, sloughs, and entire lakes from North Dakota to southern California had by that date been drained completely dry. Major rivers like the Colorado, the upper Rio Grande, the Arkansas, the Red, and the Platte were totally consumed or nearly so; even the copious Columbia was flowing uncommonly low at times. Despite more than a century of herculean efforts to make more water available, the thirst was still there, and it was a thirst that grew larger and more diverse with time. These frogs needed not only a little water on their tongues, in the way of all flesh, but a lot of water on their lawns, in their coal-slurry pipelines, in their manufacturing plants, and above all on their farms. They simply could not be satisfied. Scarcity for them was not merely an objective condition of nature but the product of, the rationale for, the force behind, their culture. Wherever they perceived scarcity they would drive themselves to create abundance. When and where there was abundance they would make scarcity anew. In that unceasing escalation of want they constantly ran the risk of consuming the very last drop, of becoming frogs with no ponds left.

Here were the dimensions of western thirst in the mature stage of empire. In its 1975 Westwide study of eleven states, omitting the plains tier, the Bureau of Reclamation determined that water withdrawals for all uses amounted to 136,778,000 acre-feet a year, or 45 trillion gallons. Of that sum, irrigation alone accounted for 100,717,000 acre-feet, or 74 percent. Some of that water made its way back into streams, but most of it did not. California's was the worst case in this respect: three out of every four gallons it used were considered "consumed"—that is, made unavailable for further use because of evaporation or seepage into the ground. California also made the largest withdrawals (39 million acre-feet), followed by Idaho (26 million), and Oregon (11 million). These figures must be put, of course, against the total runoff available, some 427 million acre-feet in all. That might seem like a plentitude of water, four times the quantity consumed, leaving no cause for alarm. And then one remembered where that runoff occurred and how difficult it would be to reach what was still untapped. Two states, Washington and Oregon, and their coastal ranges in particular, contributed 183 million acre-feet alone to the runoff, and that water was a far and expensive way off from most of the thirst.[4]

Americans of all regions had habitually been, as though it were their birthright, big water users, profligate users even, but westerners had become the biggest by far. In 1900, the total amount of water used across the country for all purposes was 40 billion gallons a day; by 1975, the amount was 393 billion gallons, ten times more, though the population had only tripled in size. By that later date Americans were indisputably the thirstiest people on earth, withdrawing three times as much as the world average, a considerably higher rate than in other industrial societies and enough to make an African villager, carrying a water pot home on her head, stagger in unbelief. Beyond the hundredth meridian, per capita rates of withdrawal and consumption much exceeded even those extravagant American levels. The national average withdrawal from all sources was 1,600 gallons per person per day. In Idaho it was, thanks to irrigation, 21,000 gallons. It was equally striking that not only farmers but urban westerners too, in their direct use about the house and yard, drank great draughts of water. The national average for direct personal use was 90 gallons a day, but in Tucson, it was 140 gallons, in Denver, 230, and in Sacramento, 280.[5] This was letting water slop from the cup, run freely down the chin, thoughtlessly spill on the ground, making the world stare in amazement. By 1980, resource experts were predicting a planetwide water crisis that could be a greater threat to human life than the energy shortages of the seventies. If that was to be the future, Americans would be much troubled to adjust and struggle through—and Americans in the West, drinking, bathing, guzzling, swimming, mining, watering with a loose freedom in the face of strict limits, would be the most troubled of all.

Survival, to be sure, is an elastic idea, and a crisis of survival means different things to different people. For a Punjabi farmer the lack of water might mean a nightmare of crop failure and famine, but in the modern West the immediate, foreseeable threat was not so dire. It was a threat to an established standard of living, to a margin of wastefulness, and to a future of unrestrained economic growth. That last may have been the most culturally serious. As Theodore Schad, director of the National Commission on Natural Resources, saw the problem, "Some method must be found to meet the demands in order to prevent stagnation of the economy of the West due to lack of water in the twenty-first century."[6] But even though they were less desperate than some in the world, the prospects for the West could be fearful all the same. Where would the future supplies come from to satisfy those expanding demands? Therein lay the region's challenge, a more compelling one in the late postwar period than ever before, and the acceptable, practical answers were getting harder and harder to come by.

The ground itself had always held the largest promise of water. Subsurface deposits often require little social organization to exploit, though it was a long while before people realized that and even longer before they could begin to tap them. Even the starkest desert could offer, down in its depths, a reservoir for the thirsty. Through the permeable aquifers, the water crept seaward, sometimes moving no faster than a mile per century, rising to the surface now and then in artesian wells, springs, and oases. Hydrologists calculated that there was thirty-seven times more water underground than there was on the surface, some of it billions of years old, some of it last winter's snow. A serious difficulty was that the larger portion of the underground supply lay more than a half-mile down, too deep to retrieve. Most of the rest became available only with the invention of powerful centrifugal pumps using electricity or fossil fuels. A second difficulty was that underground water was replenished at a far slower rate than the pumps could take it out. Hence, falling water tables, "cones of depression" around active wells, land subsidence, and increasingly intrusive government regulation were everywhere the outcome.[7] That pattern of expansion and overpumping, as discussed earlier, was what led farmers and urbanites alike in central Arizona and California to demand that distant rivers be brought to their doorsteps.

A similar plight came to the Great Plains in the postwar period, stirring up a similar demand. Underlying what had once been unbroken grasslands, so sparsely watered on the surface, was the paradox of the largest freshwater aquifer in the world, the Ogallala, containing 2 to 3 billion acre-feet, more water than the Mississippi had carried to the Gulf in two hundred years. The Ogallala extended from the southernmost parts of Texas northward into Nebraska. In the aftermath of the dust-bowl years, farmers around Lubbock and Plainview discovered it and with its aid raised a series of phenomenal harvests of cotton and corn. A boost to the plains farmers' efforts came in 1949 when Frank Zybach of Strasbourg, Colorado, invented the ingenious center-pivot irrigation system: a row of sprinklers mounted on a wheeled frame that rotated in a great circle around a well. The system could ride over sandy hillocks, requiring no land leveling or ditchdigging, throwing water over a field like light rain falling from the sky. By 1979, there were more than 15,000 of these units in use in Nebraska alone, and they had transformed the plains landscape from a giant checkerboard to rows and rows of bright green checkers. They had also opened up fragile lands to cropping, encouraged farmers to cut down their shelterbelts (rows of trees planted along the edges of fields to diminish the wind), and in-

313

creased the incidence of wind erosion. And they were rapidly depleting the Ogallala. By the late seventies, farmers were mining the aquifer at ten times its recharge rate, taking out an amount over the rate of replenishment equivalent to the entire Colorado River flow. Consequently, the underground water table quickly began to recede, six inches a year in some places, six feet in others. At those rates of fall, the Ogallala would be altogether depleted within thirty to forty years, by the first or second decade of the next century—and then there would have to be a devastating retrenchment in plains agriculture and the society it supported.[8]

Clearly, the cheapest way to bring supply and demand into balance was by reducing demand. That meant a program of conservation, and in every part of the West much could be done. There were thousands of miles of ditches that could be lined with concrete to prevent seepage, and there were hundreds of thousands of farmers who might be persuaded (and quickly would have been if their water were not so cheap) to pour less on their crops. However, the region was good at going after every possible molecule but exceedingly careless about putting what was captured to use. Conservation had always had about it an air of restraint, self or other, and the expansionary, accumulative culture was in its marrow opposed to restraint. Far more acceptable were the technological panaceas that had substituted for conservation—and there were still a few of them to grow ecstatic about. One group of wizards proposed towing Arctic icebergs or collapsible bladders filled with Columbia water down to the California coast. The Bureau of Reclamation undertook, in its ballyhooed Project Skywater, to make more snow fall on the Rockies by cloud seeding, thereby augmenting the spring runoff. Several other experts suggested that atomic bombs could be set off underground, fracturing rocks and enlarging the carrying capacity of aquifers. Still others wanted nuclear power plants to take the salt out of the ocean and pipe the water inland. None of those panaceas ever quite materialized. All were too costly, it seemed, or presented complicated dangers that could not be escaped.[9]

That left, as always, the traditional remedy of interbasin transfers. Find a river so far left alone and push it out of its course, push it wherever there was thirst. But in the mature days of the empire that once-popular remedy was encountering resistance from the public will and pocketbook. For example, anticipating the depletion of the Ogallala, state and federal water planners looked hopefully toward the Missouri and Mississippi, even the Great Lakes, as replacement sources, but the residents along those waters eastward were not eager to let them go. Even if they could be persuaded, the cost would be sizable: many billions of dollars, money that the western farmers could not scratch together on their own, money that other taxpayers were not eager to provide. In 1969, the voters of Texas vetoed a state water plan to pump the Mississippi River across the state to the High Plains. That left them, like their northern neighbors, with no foreseeable options but to wait for the decline. Farther west, the Columbia was still the established favorite to be everybody's savior, but here too there was a sudden resistance against any interbasin transfers. Senator Henry Jackson of Washington, working to protect his constituents from their fellow westerners, got included in the Colorado Basin Project Act of 1968, as the price of his consent to it, a moratorium on studies to bring any outside water (the Columbia was what he particularly had in mind) into the Southwest. Whether his death in 1983 would make possible the resumption of such studies and the eventual diversion of Northwest waters to the southern latitudes remained to be seen.[10] Meanwhile, as the Columbia became more closely guarded, an even more spectacular transfer, the North American Water and Power Alliance, was being debated.

NAWAPA: the water scheme to beat all schemes, or end them. If empires are at bottom feats of imagination as much as of strength or greed, then this was the western water empire's finest hour, for never had imagination conceived anything like it in the way of river manipulation. Its audacity was breathtaking. The plan came to the public in 1964 from the Ralph Parsons engineering firm in Pasadena, California, an outfit where several former Bureau of Reclamation engineers had assembled to make money consulting and designing resource projects for countries around the world. These Parsons people thought in terms of entire continents. Far to the north in Alaska, they realized, could be found almost half of the United States' fresh-water supply, stored in lakes and glaciers, flowing down the Tanana, the Susitna, and the Yukon to the Bering Sea. There also were the Canadian rivers—the Churchill, the Blackstone, the Slave, the Coppermine, the Peace, the Mackenzie—spending themselves uselessly in the Arctic Ocean or Hudson Bay. Could they made to serve the new race of pharaohs raising their pyramids in the south? Assuredly yes, if the nerve was there, along with something like $100–200 billion (the estimates varied) to pay for the apparatus. According to the plan, an array of reservoirs, tunnels, and pumping stations would divert the northern surplus into the nine-hundred-mile depression known as the Rocky Mountain Trench that runs the length of British Columbia. From the upper end of this deep trough a canal would angle southeastward across the Prairie Provinces to Lake Superior and the Mississippi, making inland barge navigation possible from the Alaska wilderness to Montreal and New Orleans. At the southern end of the Trench, electricity generated by the project would send water off into the Columbia basin, relaxing jealousies there, and into the high border country of Idaho

315

and Montana. From that latter point, the plumbing would branch in two directions, toward the east slope of the Rockies, the depleting plains lands, and toward the southwestern deserts, crossing the Snake valley, the Bonneville Flats, on and on to golden prosperity. Even Mexico, at the very end of the system, would get enough water to irrigate eight times more land than the Egyptians were reclaiming from their new Aswan High Dam. Surely men who could dream such dreams and carry them out need never fear privation, stagnation, or the closing in of restraint. They could engorge the very oceans, they could cut up the polar ice pack into cubes for their drinks, could, if they desired, master anything in their view. NAWAPA was, simply put, "feasible," and it had about it the irresistible logic of an imperial history.[11]

In the awed hush that followed the unveiling of the Parsons scheme, western leaders lined up to embrace it, though with dignified caution, as though they feared giving way too easily to their own enthusiasm. Senator Frank Moss, for instance, who had served as chairman of the Subcommittee on Irrigation and Reclamation and on the Senate Select Committee on National Water Resources, gave it his careful endorsement. It was, he wrote with an air of studied understatement, an "encouraging" proposal because it suggested that "if we are wise, and if we apply the technical knowledge we have to the problem, the whole of the North American continent can be assured of an adequate supply of good water for as long as we want to live here."[12] But alas for those seeking encouragement, the scheme proved to be at once too premature—for there were still other, more accessible streams to be mastered—and too late, for gathering across the country was the beginnings of a mood of rejection. Wallace Stegner was a prophet of that mood when he wrote in 1965 that the plan would be "a boondoggle visible from Mars."[13] What would be the ecological consequences of so grandiose a transfer, a new generation began to ask? Would the diversion cause the polar cap to melt, elevating the level of the seas around the planet, submerging coastal cities? Would the gargantuan reservoirs to be constructed trigger a series of devastating earthquakes, releasing massive floods? Could the nation afford so huge an expense? And then there was the matter of agency: who was available to carry out the project, and who could be entrusted with the power it entailed? It would take the combined managerial authority of three sovereign nations, or of some centralized, supernational force, and the American-based Bureau of Reclamation was not likely to be handed that role. Who then? Unresolved, those imponderables generated doubt, then opposition, then apathy. Thus, though the NAWAPA project had started off brightly toward realization, as so many others before it had done, in the twenty years following its publication it

316

slipped slowly from public consciousness, fading away as dreams do when they have gone too far to be credible.

By the early 1980s, the empire had reached a plateau of water development and did not know how to climb on up from there. Its existing supplies, its prospects for growth, were running out, yet no new possibilities offered themselves convincingly to a scrutinizing, distrusting people. Once before when the water developers had reached a plateau and were milling about in frustration, the federal government had thrown them down a rope. Now there was no superior agency standing ready to pull the West another notch upward, no one in a position to furnish the necessary capital and expertise, no one powerful enough to overcome all the regional and international political differences, no one able to command a continent.

The second set of environmental vulnerabilities had to do with deteriorating water quality. Reclamation, it began to be clear, was capable of taking good water and making it bad. Indeed, at some advanced point in its intensification, it could hardly do otherwise. Water quality, of course, was a problem that concerned more than the West. In fact, for a long time it seemed to be more of an eastern malady, the result of too many people flushing their body wastes and toxic chemicals into waterways and, more seriously yet, into aquifers, polluting them for the indeterminate future. Eventually, as its population and industry swelled, those problems became the West's too. In addition, the region had a few water-spoilers that were all its own: the corruption draining from densely packed, dreary cattle feedlots and their mountains of manure, as well as that from a hundred million tons of radioactive uranium tailings left lying about on the banks of the Colorado River. Then there were those threats to water quality from irrigated agriculture, perhaps the most discouraging of all because they were the bitter fruit of some very proud achievements.

The warm, moist environments created by reclamation, as noted elsewhere, have in land after land offered ideal breeding grounds for a host of pests, some of them pathogens preying on humans, others of them insects, fungi, and nematodes that damage crops. This predicament appeared in the West early on, and farmers there quickly became avid technicians of pest control. In 1872, California citrus groves were besieged by an imported scale insect that fed on the trees' sap. That threat was defeated by biological control methods—the clever introduction of an Australian lady beetle that attacked the scale insects. Later, however, irrigation farmers turned almost exclusively to a series of deadly chemicals. They were among the first and most heavy users of DDT in the post–World War Two years. From 1962 to 1974, pesticide use nationally doubled, then doubled again in the next eight years. In that escalation, the West set the pace. California was consistently the leading user among the states, spending in 1978 the sum of $1 billion a year on chemical pesticides (insecticides, rodenticides, herbicides, fungicides) and their application, about one-fifth the American total. Some of those poisons were the chlorinated hydrocarbons, such as DDT—until it was banned for use in the United States in 1972—heptachlor, aldrin, dieldrin, chlordane, and endrin. Others were the organic phosphates, including parathion, malathion, DBCP, EDB, benzine, hexachloride, and toxaphene. They were sprayed on codling moths in the apple orchards of the Yakima valley, on pink bollworms infesting cotton in Arizona and Imperial, on aphids crawling on cantaloupes near Rocky Ford, Colorado, on spider mites raging through San Joaquin alfalfa fields. Each application, it soon was apparent, made necessary another and stronger dose, as the pests quickly developed genetic resistance or as the poisons killed off useful, nontarget species that had kept the pests in some kind of check. Western farmers, with sizable and profitable investments in their system of irrigated agriculture to protect, found they could not live without the expensive pesticides. But neither could they live with them.[14]

Rachel Carson, in her book *Silent Spring,* told the story of the Tule and Upper Klamath Lake area of Oregon, where DDT from surrounding reclamation lands drained into wildlife refuges, killing herons, pelicans, grebes, and gulls.[15] That was in 1960. Subsequently, water contamination by pesticides and its lethal effects on the food chains in nature became a familiar tale. Consumers began to worry about dangerous residues on the fruits and vegetables they ate, with good reason, for virtually all Americans were carrying detectable amounts of the poisons in their fatty tissues, and those residues were linked to ailments ranging from liver and blood disease to, possibly, cancer. Western farm workers had to live with some of the most serious consequences: it was they who were hired to do the actual spraying and dusting of cauliflower, peaches, lettuce, strawberries, and other crops. Reentering the sprayed field even as late as a month afterward, they would suffer from blisters, inflamed skin, and reddened eyes. Nor was that the worst of it. Between 1950 and 1961, more than 3,000 farm workers were poisoned in California by pesticides and other farm chemicals, and of that number 22 adults and 63 children died. A biophysicist at the University of California reported that "the severity of pesticide-related illnesses to farmworkers is probably greater than that attributed to all occupational causes in any other type of work in California."[16] This was a consequence of the water empire that no one in earlier stages had had any premonition of, that no one more recently involved in it had intended, yet one that nobody knew quite how to shake off. The unintended costs in lives and money were high and tragic, but without those pesticides, even when used in a more restrained and integrated program of pest management, the irrigation economy might very well collapse.

The degradation of the precious water on which the West depended had further ominous aspects. A regimen of intensive cropping must soon deplete the soil, necessitating the application of chemical fertilizer. The fertilizer in turn, under continual artificial watering, must leach into the groundwater or streams, contaminating drinking sources. Nitrates in the fertilizer, where sufficiently concentrated in an aquifer, could produce methemoglobinemia, or "blue-baby syndrome," a condition of inadequate oxygenation of the blood, and such concentrations were indeed found and found frequently in places like the irrigated Platte River valley.[17] And then there was the oldest and most endemic form of water decline associated with all hydraulic societies: salinization, the poisoning of water and soil alike by salt buildup.

Salt is a generic term covering not only the familiar sodium chloride in the kitchen shaker but also a range of chemical compounds that are reactions between bases and acids. These include calcium carbonate (chalk), zinc sulfate, barium chloride, sodium bicarbonate, various phosphates, nitrates, and hydrates. Typically they have a whitish or grayish color, and their structures are crystalline. They readily dissolve in water, making it "hard," or alkaline, leaving in teakettles and pipes a scaly deposit. Clustered heavily around the roots of plants, salts interfere with moisture take-up, causing stress, diminished productivity, and even death.[18] Fortunately for living things, the salts, though originally scattered through the earth, have been diminished in the upper soil layers by the steady rainfall of billions of years and have washed into the sea, allowing vegetation to flourish. Everywhere, that is, except in the arid lands. There the salts remain abundant and omnipresent. A desert torrent, violent but soon over, may bring them to the surface, leaving them behind as a glittering crust, or they may collect in stagnant pools. Whichever, the climate there is too dry to greatly diminish them. Desert plants therefore must be highly salt-tolerant to thrive.

What nature has taken geological eons to achieve, the leaching of salts from the root zone of plants, the irrigator undertakes to do in a matter of decades. Covering the arid soil with artificial rain, two or three feet deep over each acre in a year's time, has several effects on the salts. First, the water table may rise, bringing with it dissolved salts, until it intrudes into the root zone, saturating the ground with dangerously saline water just where the farmer's crops are trying to grow. The only remedy then, other than decreasing the irrigation, is to lay down an expensive network of drains, which will remove the salt, but only by pouring it in concentrated form into streams and rivers. Another effect, and a more obvious one to the casual passer-by, is for the salt to come to the surface and, as the water evaporates in the dry air, to be left behind there—an acceleration of a natural process. Then the irrigator must use more, not less, water to flush away the white crusting, washing it off downstream for someone else to deal with. The use and reuse of that water makes it more and more saline, until the last man on the last ditch might as well be dipping from the ocean. This is a discouraging predicament coming from the attempt to transform, over-night as it were, a desert environment into a humid one. What seems at first to be an easy, and miraculous, achievement turns out to be a Sisyphean labor.

Salinization, the process of concentrating what had been diffused, be-came in the postwar years a worldwide environmental disaster. Agricultural expansion into dry, marginal lands led to salt buildup, led to man-made wastelands, led to impoverishment and hunger in country after country. Pakistan at one point was losing 60,000 acres of fertile cropland a year to salinization, and Peru had 10 percent of its agricultural area similarly degraded. In the Helmud Valley of Afghanistan, in the Punjab and Indus valleys of the Indian subcontinent, in northern Mexico, in the Euphrates and Tigris basin of Syria and Iraq, salinity was a severe problem dogging the developers' plans.[19] Gradually it became clear that the same problem had damaged early irrigation civilizations, perhaps had even destroyed them. An American traveler to Iraq in the late 1940s, Frank Eaton, saw from his train window miles and miles of salt lying white on the surface, shining in the night like snow. It was the insidious force, he argued, that had brought ancient desert societies to their destruction. "Compared to the magnitude of this slow-moving event," he added, "our dust bowl was but a passing incident." Some years later, two archaeologists, Thorkild Jacob-sen and Robert Adams, supported that historical hypothesis, arguing as they did that "growing soil salinity played an important part in the breakup of Sumerian civilization." So long as there had been "a powerful and highly centralized state," they went on, a state that could keep strong vigilance over the side-effects of irrigation, Sumer thrived; but the eventual weaken-ing of that state, its distraction and failure to command obedience, allowed the problems of salt and silt to pile up to the point of hopelessness.[20] The lesson drawn by these observers for modern irrigators was that salinization was a trouble that might be managed, but only by furthering the concentra-ting, power-accreting tendencies of the hydraulic society.

In the American West, too, salinization became a more and more serious ailment, producing loud cries that the federal government step in and save the irrigators. Especially in the most intensively developed parts of the water empire, the Colorado basin and the southern half of the Great Central Valley, conditions reminiscent of Pakistan or Sumer could be found. It took, nonetheless, an international confrontation to make the situation there dramatic and compelling. Late in 1961, the government of Mexico made a formal protest to Washington that its agreement with this country over the Colorado River was being violated. In the treaty of 1944 Mexico had been guaranteed, so it claimed, not only 1.5 million acre-feet of water a year, but water of good quality, suitable for irrigation. Instead, it was receiving highly saline water. The protest riveted attention on the mounting environmental crisis along the Colorado, one never mentioned in all the authorizations for more dams and aqueducts. In 1962, the State Department established an advisory Committee of Fourteen (made up of two representatives from each of the seven basin states) to prepare recommendations on how to respond to Mexico. Mainly, they proposed to let Washington handle it, and while it was doing that, to give the western Americans some aid too. Ten years later, President Richard Nixon agreed with President Echeverría of Mexico to work toward a permanent solution, and Herbert Brownell was named to head a task force on the matter. Minute 242, which fixed a limit on the salt content of the water delivered across the border, was signed in 1973.[21]

The cause of Mexico's ire lay, of course, in heavy river use north of the border, but nothing in the Minute directly addressed that. The river itself, as noted earlier, was drying up. During the fifties, the flow at the international boundary averaged 4.24 million acre-feet a year; in the sixties, it fell to 1.52. This drop meant that there was less fresh current to dilute the polluted water seeping back from agricultural users. The Bureau of Reclamation made the situation worse in 1952 when it completed a new irrigation project, Wellton-Mohawk, using Colorado water on some 60,000 acres east of Yuma, Arizona. Soon the project was producing cotton and citrus crops valued at over $1,000 an acre. It was also soaking a great deal of water into those crops—more than five times as much, one report claimed, as the Israelis, employing an advanced, economizing system of drip irrigation, were using on similar crops in Israel. An impermeable substratum under the project lands kept the irrigation water from draining downward, so farmers had to find other methods to get rid of it. Their solution was to drain the used water, and now it was very salty water, back into the Colorado—and out of their concern. Immediately thereafter Mexico found its supplies jumping to a salinity level of 1,500 parts per million (ppm), double the norm. Did the Bureau then (or the State Department or basin users) propose to shut down this project and clean up the Colorado? They did not. Instead, the federal government built, at public expense, a bypass channel that would void the saline excretions farther south, where they would not pollute Mexico's fields. And it undertook to construct, again with public monies, a desalting plant, costing $178 million, to reduce the salt level in the Wellton-Mohawk backflow. That plant was authorized in the Colorado River Basin Salinity Control Act of 1974.[22]

In the case of Wellton-Mohawk, the salinity threat had an easily defined local source, but that was not usually so. The degradation of water and land had in most instances no clear single perpetrator. Scientists speak of "salt loading," the dissolving of salts into the drainage, and "salt concentrating," the loss of diluting water from a solution through evaporation. Both these phenomena are spread widely around, and controlling them is as hard as keeping dust out of the air. American irrigators in the Colorado basin came to that frustrating realization as, in the wake of the Mexican wrangle, they themselves had to contend with the problem. With the onward march of their empire, the river became a bit saltier each year. Before any diverters had appeared, the Colorado at Lees Ferry, its halfway point, was carrying a salt load of 5.1 million tons a year, or about 250 ppm. That was nature's own leachings from shale formations, mineral springs, and salt domes upcountry. By 1972 that natural level had been raised by human activities to 606 ppm. One study showed that Grand Valley farmers in western Colorado were alone adding 8 tons of salt to the river from each acre they farmed, while in Uncompaghre Valley the pickup was 6.7 tons. Those were areas that had been continuously irrigated since the latter decades of the nineteenth century—yet the salt was still there, still washing out, in quantity. Two engineers for the Colorado River Board of California estimated that by the year 2000, the current at Lees Ferry would be 800 ppm saline. Downstream the condition worsened. The water at Imperial Dam near the border read 785 ppm on average from 1941 to 1969, then 850 ppm from 1963 to 1967, and was predicted to reach 1,340 ppm by the end of the century.[23]

The economic implications for the growers of Imperial Valley were grim, for they, with the Mexicans, were the last to drink. Lying low as they did —below sea level, in fact—growers there had been forced from the time of first settlement to spend hugely on a system of drainage. By the early seventies, they had put out more than $66 million on tile drains and canal linings, discharging the runoff into the sump of the Salton Sea. But once the water coming through the headgates began to deteriorate, the growers were in a new and more serious sort of trouble. They must then shift to salt-tolerant crops, and with them they would earn less cash, be able to hire fewer workers, be strapped to maintain their hydraulic apparatus. Or they must consume more water—if they could get it—to rinse away the poisonous deposits, and that would mean needing more fertilizers, pesticides, and pump energy too. A single point increase in ppm, said the Bureau of Reclamation, cost those irrigators $108,400, directly and indirectly, and that amount would leap, by the year 2000, to $240,000.[24]

Anticipating these calamities, the Colorado River Board of California, with support from Governor Reagan, called in 1970 for federal assistance to the agribusiness valley. They wanted fresh water brought in from their state's northern coastal rivers. They wanted someone to find a cheap way to take the salt out of the Pacific Ocean, with the resulting brine to be injected safely out of the way in deep geological formations. They wanted weather modification to get more snowfall and runoff. They demanded control of salinization at its sources in the upper Colorado basin. Some of those demands were delivered by the Colorado River Basin Salinity Control Act of 1974. It instructed the Bureau, in addition to building the desalting plant, to spend $125 million on containing the salt dribbling out of the Crystal Geyser in Utah, the Las Vegas Wash, and other natural sources up north. Here once again were structural or engineering solutions, aimed at controlling nature, not man. What was needed, in the opinion of critics, was a forthright facing of the main issue, an overextended reclamation program that was neither economically rational nor ecologically sustainable. Until that was done, salinization would continue to be a stalking danger.[25]

In the San Joaquin Valley, grappling with the salt threat was quite as ineffectual. By 1981, there were 400,000 acres affected there by high (or "perched") brackish water tables, located mainly in Kern, Kings, and Fresno counties. To salvage those farms and their owners, as they had been salvaged so many times before, the government set about to dig a master drain, the cost to be partly repaid by the irrigators. The drain was to draw off the saline water and dump it three hundred miles away near San Francisco. Without the drain, one reporter wrote, "more than 1 million acres in the San Joaquin could undergo desertification during the next 100 years."[26] Saving those lands was not, however, to be the end of the problem. There was also the question who or what would be sacrificed in that salvation. One hint of an answer came late in 1983. Scientists at the Kesterson National Wildlife Refuge, lying below the Westlands, discovered a pathetic cohort of fledglings in their nests: coots, stilts, grebes, and ducks born with stumps for feet, missing eyes and beaks, dying soon after birth, reminiscent of the human thalidomide deformities of a previous decade. The birds were the victims of selenium compounds and other salts leaching from nearby irrigated fields. The drain, when completed, might save the refuge and its waterfowl, along with the growers, but only to pour the same poison into the environment elsewhere. Congressman George Miller, representing Californians living where the drain would vent, vowed to stop it, calling it "nothing short of a dagger pointed at the heart of San Francisco Bay and the delta."[27]

Could the lowering specter of salinization ever really be exorcised from the western water empire? Some of its engineers and agriculturists had no doubt that it could be, that it was a temporary nuisance which a little time and expense could banish. Others were much less confident. Throughout history, wherever irrigation has been carried on intensively, they pointed out, salinization has come in its wake, like dust following the wind. It is the way of empires to believe they will be forever impregnable, that they will give the law to nature, not vice versa, that their power and expertise will conquer all. But from the vantage of 1983, that confidence was falling apart.

Salinity, sedimentation, pesticide contamination, diminishing hopes of replenishment, the dangers of aging, collapsing dams: all these were the hydraulic society's worsening headaches. But there was another peril, altogether different in kind from these and even less manageable because it had to do with faith, not technique. A sense of irreparable loss began to settle about the water empire by the late twentieth century, a remembrance of things past. Once, men and women recollected, the West had been a land of canyons leading on to canyons where tamarisk and cottonwoods rustled in a slight breeze blowing up at twilight, a region of broad flatlands where sandhill cranes alighted during their migrations to spear at frogs and crayfish. Deer came out in that lost time to browse in the bottomlands, finding shelter there in winter, encountering, it might be, a mountain lion lying hungrily in wait. Then was a time too of wrens singing a bright, bubbling melody that echoed from the canyon walls, of swallows wheeling and dipping over a stream for mayflies. In the spring run, salmon came fighting their way upstream from the ocean, seeking their birthing place. Beaver chewed down aspen logs, dragging them into midstream for a dam, a lodge, a home for their kits. And everywhere the water purled on, free and uninhibited, racing and slackening, curling back on itself, rippling over hidden rocks, meandering under empty skies, a thing always alive, voracious, unpredictable and full of mystery. Not all of that older time had been lost, but most of it had, and there were many who were not pleased to see it go. Good riddance, had always been the response of the water manipulators; let nature give way to a greater, man-made West. Only the sentimental, the misguided, would mourn that loss or criticize the gain. Leave the elegies to poets, therefore, and get on with constructing the future. What the proponents of empire did not anticipate was that there would come a day when such advice would be rejected. Nor did they appreciate that the nostalgia they scorned might turn out to be more than a silliness. It might transform itself into a profoundly subversive force, one that could bring an empire low. Nostalgia for what has been lost might lead people to the discovery of new, radically disturbing moral principles, in this case the idea that pristine nature in the West has its own intrinsic value, one that humans ought to understand and learn to respect. In that event, to save what remained of that lost natural world from the imperialists, the instrumentalists, the accumulators, could appear to be a struggle worth making. Conceivably, too, nostalgia might serve as a basis for imagining an alternative future society quite different from the reigning imperial order.

By the 1970s, impassioned friends of the western river past could be found, to the consternation of the empire, in all parts of the region and across the country, sorting out their loyalties, moving from private elegies to the politics of preservation. In one dramatic instance, a young man named Mark Dubois chained himself to a rock in the middle of California's Stanislaus River, protesting the flooding of its wildness behind New Melones Dam.[28] Others challenged the reclamation men armed with chainsaws who were cutting out along thousands of streamside acres the so-called phreatophytes—the trees and other plants that grew along the waterways, pumping moisture through transpiration into the air, wasting what should have gone to a farmer.[29] Other nay-sayers canvassed to save estuaries like San Francisco Bay from poisoning and from eutrophication through diminished inflow.[30] Or to rescue Mono Lake and its rookeries, even its brine shrimp, from Los Angeles's increasing megalopolitan thirst.[31] Still others, in the tradition of Mary Austin and John Van Dyke, went out to fight for a remnant of desert, a place that might have been unredeemed and gaunt but was made more precious than ever by its rarity. The instances of such conflict multiplied in the newspapers, engendering after a while a kind of glazed boredom in readers. So many court appeals, so much repetitious testimony, so familiar the main story, so unending the details. But it would be a mistake to let that feeling of familiarity obscure the historical novelty of what was happening. Never before had a great water-dominating civilization encountered so informed, relentless, determined, and successful an internal opposition. Not Egypt, not the China of the Han dynasty, not the Aztecs or the Sumerians. It was as though the American water empire had created, against its will, a dissidence precisely commensurate with its unparalleled technological success. And now it found itself embattled, losing, unable to hold on to its credibility. It was caught in a dialectic that Karl Marx had never predicted, one pitting not merely rival classes pursuing their competing self-interest but rival ways of valuing nature.[32]

325

The most sensational success of the emergent party of protest came in 1977 when they managed to persuade a new President, Jimmy Carter of Georgia, to veto a slew of environmentally damaging and economically questionable water projects, nine of them in the West, up for reauthorization. Those projects included Fruitland Mesa in Colorado, which would spend $70 million to benefit fifty-six farmers; the Garrison Diversion in North and South Dakota, which would destroy prairie wetlands wholesale and send salty irrigation return flows into Canada; and the Central Arizona and Central Utah projects. Nothing like that presidential veto had ever happened before to the region, not in seventy-five years of extracting money from the public treasury, and its leaders and elite reacted with shocked, spluttering wrath. Shortly, they succeeded in getting the veto overridden. But in their triumph over a clumsy, uncertain President Carter, the empire leaders might have seen that their success was written on the water, dissolving before their eyes. Those would be the last projects authorized by Congress—for how long no one could yet say, perhaps a short while, perhaps forever. As Senator Moynihan pointed out, not one new project had made it through Congress after 1972. Even when westerner Ronald Reagan, a darling of the empire, defeated Carter in 1980 and moved into the White House, that situation would not change. Much would be proposed in the way of new schemes—$10 billion worth, in fact—but as late as 1985 none of them had managed to run the gauntlet.[33]

The party of preservation and protest, however, had more success in stopping the expansion of the hydraulic society than it had in dismantling it. In 1983 the apparatus was still in place, still pumping the rivers dry, as was the capitalist state that oversaw its operation. Millions of acres of farmland remained in subsidized, profitable production, though besieged by difficulties, and millions of city dwellers had moved into the region to keep the empire busy and in control. Nonetheless, something important had changed, to what effect it remained to be seen. Now, as at no other point in its history, the water-control apparatus (including its managers and its chief profiteers) was coming to be seen, not as a crowning, self-justifying achievement of a world-beating people, but as a necessary evil. The domination of nature had been achieved, and it would not be easy to undo, perhaps could not be. But at the same time domination was no longer a language that westerners or other Americans spoke with much enthusiasm. Somewhere an old river god might be listening to such talk and might exact a retribution.

S E V E N

CONCLUSION

Nature, Freedom, and the
West

Water taken in a little moderation can do no harm.

—*Mark Twain*

The ancient water-controlling civilizations of Asia were all stagnant and fearful of change. The elaborate infrastructures they created in their drive for technological dominance over nature became an obstacle to new possibilities, to creativity. Marvin Harris calls this inflexibility the predicament of the "hydraulic trap." Today that sense of being trapped by our own inventions pervades industrial societies everywhere. In this respect, the situation of the American West is hardly unique. It especially claims our attention because it is a modern variant on the oldest form of infrastructure rigidity and because it exemplifies, as its predecessors did, the problem of the trap in the crystalline clarity of desert light.

The essential question facing the region today, and the question that this study has been leading up to, is this: Does stagnation have to be the future of the West, as in other hydraulic societies, or can the trap be pried open and people walk free from their history? Now, confronting that question directly, I confess there is no unequivocal answer to be given.

History is always easier to understand than it is to change or escape. In the case of the West, a reversal of past trends must be regarded as a small possibility—and nothing more than that. Long the mythic land of new beginnings, it is now a region heavily encased in its past. What has been done there with the water and land over the past century and a half has had consequences for the people as well. It has handed them a fate, and there will be no quick release from it. For some time to come, the region will likely be ruled over by concentrated power and hierarchy based on the command of scarce water. There are, after all, many people living there these days who are dependent on the hydraulic apparatus, along with many vested interests, protective of their position. Despite the empire's loss of legitimacy and ecological sustainability, they will resist any substantial changes in it.

Much depends, of course, on the willingness of western Americans to yield to the rule of authority over them. If they accept those dominating powers as indispensable to their welfare, then the hydraulic trap will not be escaped, at least by rational, humane methods. No one will make the effort to find alternative ways of organizing institutions and using rivers, and the power elite will go on appropriating every available drop of water for its canals and pipelines, while providing the masses with a few dribbles to support them in their managed oasis life. And the masses will, in gratitude, agree to make no trouble. They will not feel secure enough to go and meet the desert on their own, nor be willing to take the trouble to do so when the rewards of acquiescence are so high. For the pessimist, that scenario is the most plausible one for the future. All through history, he will insist, the masses have tolerated one elite after another, and they will go on doing so now in the American West. Their lethargy, their conformity, their lack of self-confidence, and their thirst will outweigh any resentments they may feel toward those in power. The historical record gives plenty of reasons for accepting this pessimistic analysis.

But then again, perhaps the future may not turn out quite that way after all. In the broader contemporary world, there is some evidence that the old obedience to established authority has begun to crack somewhat. A new spirit of restlessness and challenge may be gathering, and it may acquire sufficient momentum to force radical changes in the western water empire. Beginning in the 1960s, a generation of protesters came on the scene, and their questioning mood spread to the larger, older population. Many ordinary citizens learned to speak out against the principles and powers governing the modern industrial apparatus, to dispute the creed of unending growth, larger and larger units of organization and domination, and the reign of expertise and profit. So clamorous have the protests been at times that the hierarchists have become deeply worried, gloomily warning of impending catastrophe if people do not settle down. Among the high-placed Jeremiahs is the Harvard professor of government Samuel Huntington, who fears that there has been of late a dangerous upsurge of popular unrest and that it threatens the survivability of modern complex societies. To avoid chaos there must be, in his opinion,

> a realistic appreciation that we can't go back to a simpler world—that we're going to live in a world of big organizations, of specialization and of hierarchy. Also, there has to be an acceptance of the need for authority in various institutions in the society.

Elsewhere Huntington describes the disease he believes is infecting the industrial world as "an excess of democracy". It is sapping the vitality of the economy, spreading distrust of those in power, and raising hopes (misguided ones, he insists) that people can once more manage their own lives.[1] If he is right about the strength of the democratic rebellion, then the implications for the hydraulic order in the American West could be very grave. After moving for so long in the direction of empire, the region may be about to join the rest of industrial civilization in trying to make an about-face, seeking a freer, more human scale in its relationship with nature. Such a turning, to reiterate, would not be easy to effect, but, conceivably it could happen. The historian has no doubt that big changes are always possible, even in the most stagnant circumstances. Indeed, they are at some point inevitable. Furthermore, the new turn toward freedom might be far less grim than Huntington fears—unless one is sitting high up on the pyramid.

Let us assume that the next stage in the West will not be a mere continuation of the present. What then might we expect? What should we work for? Now no one could reliably prepare a detailed blueprint for a posthydraulic society. To do so would be to indulge in fantasy or utopianism, neither of which is much to be trusted. And it would be to substitute for the combined searchings of millions of people, generation following generation, the schemes and predictions of a single individual, which is not the way history is made. But one can confidently say that there are certain general strategies the West is going to have to pursue if it wants to find its way toward a more open, free, and democratic society. Those strategies must begin with a new relation to nature and a new technics.

Humans have been drinking, directly and indirectly, from the rivers of the West for a very long time now, and they will go on doing so, as they have a right to do, for the indefinite future. That is incontestable. The problem is how to do that drinking in ways that are not destructive to the integrity of the natural order. A river, to be sure, is a means to economic production, but before that it is an entity unto itself, with its own processes, dynamics, and values. In a sense it is a sacred being, something we have not created, and therefore worthy of our respect and understanding. To use a river without violating its intrinsic qualities will require much of us. It will require our learning to think like a river, our trying to become a river-adaptive people. In the past, groups as diverse as the Papago Indians and the Chinese Taoists seem to have met that requirement successfully, and there is much we can learn from them. If we could cultivate a consciousness more like theirs, the effects would be immense. We would start thinking about creating a very different kind of water-exploiting technology than the one we have been designing and putting into play. We would come to agree that henceforth no river should be appropriated in its entirety, nor be constrained to flow against its nature in some rigid, utilitarian straitjacket, nor be abstracted ruthlessly from its dense ecological pattern to become a single abstract commodity having nothing but a cash value. Such a change in thinking, from nature domination to nature accommodation, will be difficult to achieve anywhere in American culture, but nowhere more so than in the parched reaches of the West. Yet without such a shift in perception and valuing, such a freeing of our minds from the tyranny of instrumentalist reasoning about nature, there can be no basis for a more democratic social order.

One of the most compelling intuitions of the last few decades has been that the unprecedented environmental destructiveness of our time is largely the result of those "big organizations" Samuel Huntington defends as necessary and inevitable. Whatever they may accomplish in the manufacture of wealth, they are innately anti-ecological. Immense centralized institutions, with complicated hierarchies, they tend to impose their outlook and their demands on nature, as they do on the individual and the small human community, and they do so with great destructiveness. They are too insulated from the results of their actions to learn, to adjust, to harmonize. That is another way of saying that a social condition of diffused power is more likely to be ecologically sensitive and preserving. In contrast to the big organization, whether it be a state or a corporation, the small community simply cannot afford massive intervention in the environment. Moreover, it lacks the technical hubris common to concentrated power. When it does undertake to make use of an entity like a river, that effort is more easily undone if it goes awry, and the damage is more readily perceived and repaired. In short, the promotion of democracy, defined as the dispersal of power into as many hands as possible, is a direct and necessary, though perhaps not sufficient, means to achieve ecological stability.[2]

In the years to come, practical men and women looking to create a new West along these lines might reexamine the social and environmental ideals of John Wesley Powell, distilling out of them their democratic essence. He proposed, it will be remembered, a West divided into hundreds of watershed-defined communities. Each of them was to be left responsible for its own development and for the conservation of its own lands and waters, reaching from streambeds to the natural divides separating one community from another. Much of that territory was to be owned in common and managed for the public good. Power was to be seated within and limited to the boundaries of these communities. They would have to generate much of their own capital, through their own labor, just as the Mormons initially did in Utah. They would have to use their own heads instead of those of outside experts, though science and technology might, if carefully controlled and kept open to popular participation, be put to their service. This scheme of Powell's, if worked out in modern terms unencumbered by his urge to dominate nature, would bring a radical devolution of power to the ordinary people of the West. The resulting communities, relying on their own capital and their own knowledge, could free themselves from the distant, impersonal structures of power that have made democracy little more than a ritual of ratifying choices already made by others—of acquiescing in what has been done to us.

In no way could such self-managing communities maintain their independence by pursuing all-out the large-scale, commercially oriented agriculture of today. To be free of outside control means not participating to any great extent in the national or world marketplace, concentrating instead on producing food and fiber for local use. Independence also means a significant cutback in irrigation dependency and intense water consumption. When so much is taken from the river that the flow is severely diminished or exhausted, downstream communities complain and seek redress. Inevitably water rivalry leads to the setting up of powerful state arbitrators and bureaucratic regulation. Fortunately, there are alternatives to both agribusiness and bureaucracy, though they are not so profitable and they require considerable local self-discipline. They include relearning old, discarded techniques of floodplain and dry farming, finding or creating new cultivars that require little water, shifting to a more pastoral economy based on sheep, goats, and cattle, and diversifying into a variety of craft and small industrial livelihoods.[3] Those western farmers who wanted to raise cotton or corn on an extended basis would have to migrate back East, where the rain is naturally available and the farmer does not have to rely on technological giantism.

Redesigning the West as a network of more or less discrete, self-contained watershed settlements would have another environmental benefit. It would train the widest possible number of people in the daily task of understanding and adapting to their ecological conditions. They would not be able to turn the job over to a federal agency. They would be forced to restrain their lives more closely within the limits of their immediate world, and those limits would be starkly before them, impossible to ignore or evade. They would have to bear the costs of their mistakes, not pass them on to other regions to absorb. Direct responsibility is the surest road to carefulness: that is the oldest, clearest lesson in the environmental history of the species. By and large, it has not been a road taken by Americans. Instead, we have tried constantly to evade the discipline of nature by moving on to new, virgin lands when we spoiled those in our possession, by drawing on distant sources of commodities when we exhausted local supplies, and by calling on a federal agency for help when we got in trouble.

333

A West organized more along Powell's lines would make all those options less available, leading to a more ecologically conscious people.

If this model of settlement and use were in fact to become the next stage in western history, it would have little adverse effect on the lower economic classes in the West, though conceivably it might improve their lot by giving them a better chance to participate and to share in river use. On the other hand, there can be no denying that anything like this decentralized, localized, nonhydraulic West would lower profits, require a redistribution of population eastward, and diminish the wealth as well as the power of the hierarchy. That was why they turned it down a hundred years ago. And to the extent that ordinary westerners agreed with that decision then, they were saying that they too preferred private wealth to equality of condition, personal accumulation to personal or communal autonomy, a metropolitan bourgeois style of life to an ecologically disciplined one. Having turned down the possibility once, the West may well do so again. But if it does do so, then it should at least be honest and forthright about it. The hard fact it must face up to is that, despite so much rhetoric to the contrary, one cannot have life both ways—cannot maximize wealth and empire and maximize democracy and freedom too. An unwillingness to acknowledge that fact has been a characteristic American as well as western trait, one deriving from the innocence and dreaminess of youth. Now it can no longer be evaded. A clear-minded choice has to be made. That is what the West, the last American place for dreaming and for evasion, has to tell us in the starkest possible terms.

The English iconoclast E. F. Schumacher has written that "every increase of needs tends to increase one's dependence on outside forces over which one cannot have control, and therefore increases existential fear."[4] That has been the central point of this book. What Schumacher did not say is that one of the best places to go to free oneself from both the needs and the fear is the western American desert. Deserts have long had a remarkable liberating effect on people. In the Old World one of their traditional functions, along with providing a setting for pompous, vulnerable, despotic empires, has been to show humans what their true needs were, helping them slough off their useless baggage and arrive at a sense of essentials. In the United States, that alternative use has seldom been sought or valued. When experienced, it has more often than not been a traumatic moment, not a liberation. For example, the forty-niners who had to dump out their Chippendale chests along the trail in the Humboldt Sink were being taught what was essential to living, all right, but in the unexpectedness and bitterness of that circumstance it was a hard, painful education for them, one they had not undertaken voluntarily and would quickly try to forget. Encountered more freely and rationally, however, the desert can be a means to freedom. There, one can liberate oneself from extraneous needs and in that process also rid oneself of the demands of outside powers and of the shapeless, nagging fear they instill.

Approached deliberately as an environment latent with possibilities for freedom and democracy rather than for wealth and empire, the unredeemed desert West might be an unrealized national resource. It might be valued as a place of inspiration and training for a different kind of life. Relieved from some of its burdens of growing crops, earning foreign exchange, and supporting immense cities, it might encourage a new sequence of history, an incipient America of simplicity, discipline, and spiritual exploration, an America in which people are wont to sit long hours doing nothing, earning nothing, going nowhere, on the bank of some river running through a spare, lean land. They would come then to the river to see a reflection of their own liberated minds, running free and easy. They would want little, enjoy much. Now and then they would dip their hands into the current and drink a little. They would irrigate their spirit more than their ego. In the midst of what had once been regarded as the bleakest scarcity they would find abundance. Is it a fable, this alternative, a idyll from an inaccessible yesterday, or is it a real possibility, one being pushed along to fulfillment by the currents of history? The West will let us know.

NOTES

The notes below fill a dual function. They provide documentation for the text, and they serve to a limited degree as a bibliographical guide to the literature on water and society in the American West and elsewhere. Those interested in a more elaborate guide should consult Lawrence Lee, *Reclaiming the American West* (Santa Barbara, Calif., 1980); and the bibliographies published by the Agricultural History Center, University of California, Davis.

The major abbreviations of sources employed in the notes are these:

AH—Agricultural History
Bancroft/UCB—Bancroft Library,
University of California, Berkeley
Cong. Rec.—Congressional Record
JW—Journal of the West
NA/RG—National Archives
Record Group, Washington
PHR—Pacific Historical Review

Proc. ASCE—Proceedings of the
American Society of Civil Engineers
Trans. ASCE—Transactions of the
same
WRCA/UCB—Water Resources
Center Archives, University of
California, Berkeley

I. INTRODUCTION:

Reflections in a Ditch

1. Thoreau, "Walking," in *Walden and Other Writings* (New York, 1950), 607–8.
2. A good introduction to the valley's ecology is Elna Bakker, *An Island Called California* (Berkeley, 1972), 110–57. The native vegetation of the prairies, which she describes as "California's Kansas," has been almost wholly replaced by invading species, so that "no other plant community in western North America has changed so much, over such large areas, and in so short a period of time" (p. 149). Also, Hans Jenny et al., "Exploring the Soils of California," in Claude Hutchison, ed., *California Agriculture* (Berkeley, 1946), 318–50. A splendid environmental history of a characteristic part of the valley is William

Preston's *Vanishing Landscapes* (Berkeley, 1981), on which I have drawn at numerous points.

3. Robert Heizer and Albert Elsasser, *The Natural World of the California Indians* (Berkeley, 1980), 16, 37–45, 71–72, 91–101. See also A. H. Gayton, "Culture-Environment Integration," *Southwestern J. of Anthropology*, 2 (1946): 252–68; and A. L. Kroeber, *Cultural and Natural Areas of Native North America* (Berkeley, 1963), 53–55. Sherburne Cook calculates the native population in the Great Central Valley at the time of contact to have been 160,000, or about half the state's total. *The Population of the California Indians, 1769–1970* (Berkeley, 1976), 42–43. By the middle of the nineteenth century the Indians had been reduced, mainly by epidemics, to one-fourth of their original numbers.

4. Francis Farquhar, ed., "The Topographical Reports of Lieutenant George H. Derby," *California Historical Society Q.*, 11 (1932): 103, 252, 255.

5. Muir, *The Mountains of California* (Garden City, N.Y., 1961), 260–68.

6. Dasmann, *The Destruction of California* (New York, 1965), 48.

7. A recent effort to achieve this reorientation is Gerald Nash, *The American West in the Twentieth Century* (Englewood Cliffs, N.J., 1973), esp. 1–7. Nash's telling phrase for the region is "an urban oasis," which suggests something of the hydraulic theme I emphasize here. See also the essays in "Water and the West," *JW*, 22 (1983): 3–68.

8. Among the many writings on Turner the best place to start for a sympathetic insight into his ideas and background is Ray Billington's *America's Frontier Heritage* (New York, 1966), 1–22, and his *Frederick Jackson Turner* (New York, 1973), 444–71.

9. Turner, "Contributions of the West to American Democracy," reprinted in *The Frontier in American History*, ed. Ray Billington (New York, 1962), 258, 260, 279.

10. Webb, *The Great Plains* (Boston, 1931), 8. Leland Brandhorst points out that irrigation, unlike Webb's other innovations, moved from the west eastward. "The North Platte Oasis," *AH*, 51 (1977): 166. A work inspired by Webb and providing useful background for this present study is W. Eugene Hollon, *The Great American Desert*, rev. ed. (Lincoln, Neb., 1975).

11. Webb, 271–72.

12. DeVoto, "The West: A Plundered Province," *Harper's*, 169 (Aug. 1934): 355–64. Echoing Webb, DeVoto suggests that "the West . . . was born of industrialism" (p. 358) and that it has been dependent on those forces, mainly in the form of financial organizations, ever since.

13. Lamm and McCarthy, *The Angry West* (Boston, 1982), 324 and passim.

II. TAXONOMY:

The Flow of Power in History

Wittfogel, Marx, and the Ecology of Power

1. See my "History as Natural History," *PHR*, 53 (1984): 1–19.
2. These details are taken from G. L. Ulmen's massive intellectual biography of Wittfogel, *The Science of Society* (The Hague, 1978). See also Ulmen, "Wittfogel's Science of Society," *Telos*, 24 (1975): 81–114.
3. The sources of the idea are traced by Anne Bailey and Josep Llobera in *The Asiatic Mode of Production* (London, 1981), 13–45.
4. Wittfogel, "The Hydraulic Approach to Pre-Spanish Mesoamerica," in Frederick Johnson, ed., *The Prehistory of the Tehuacan Valley*, vol. 4, *Chronology and Irrigation* (Austin, 1972), 65.
5. Marx, *Capital*, trans. Samuel Moore and Edward Aveling (New York, 1906), 197–99, 562, 662.
6. See Alfred Schmidt, *The Concept of Nature in Marx* (London, 1971), for an excellent discussion of this subject. He sums up Marx's mature view thus: "Nature is to be mastered with gigantic technological aids, and the smallest expenditure of time and labour. It is to serve all men as the material substratum for all conceivable consumption goods" (p. 55). *Marx and Engels on Ecology*, ed. Howard Parsons (Westport, Conn., 1977), is a useful, though excessively worshipful, compendium of their writings on nature.
7. Marx, *Grundrisse*, trans. Martin Nicolaus (New York, 1973), 410.
8. Quoted in Ulmen, *Science of Society*, 105.
9. This argument also informs the new discipline of cultural ecology. For that field's development, see Robert Netting, *Cultural Ecology* (Menlo Park, Calif., 1977), 1–7; and Marvin Harris, *The Rise of Anthropological Theory* (New York, 1968), 654–87.
10. Wittfogel, "The Theory of Oriental Society," reprinted in Morton Fried, ed., *Readings in Anthropology*, 2nd ed. (New York, 1968), 2: 180.
11. Wittfogel, *Oriental Despotism* (New York, 1981), 2–3, 20 ff.
12. "Theory of Oriental Society," 198. Marvin Harris describes this phenomenon as the "hydraulic trap" in his *Cannibals and Kings* (New York, 1977), 233–47.
13. The chapter in *Oriental Despotism* entitled "Total Terror—Total Submission —Total Loneliness" gives an especially poignant statement (in the light of Wittfogel's own imprisonment) of this theme. It is "the distant past" as imagined and distorted by a historian who knew modern prisons and concentrations camps from the inside.

14. *Oriental Despotism*, 10, 179–81, 219–25, 427–29, 438–41. According to Wittfogel, the Soviet system is the culmination of hydraulic society in the same way that capitalism is the outgrowth of feudalism.
15. Wittfogel, "Ideas and the Power Structure," in William de Bary and Ainslie Embree, eds., *Approaches to Asian Civilizations* (New York, 1964), 87.
16. This criticism was also made by Arnold Toynbee in a review of *Oriental Despotism* in *American Historical Rev.*, 52 (1958): 197.
17. For the results of that symposium, see Julian Steward, ed., *Irrigation Civilizations* (Washington, 1955). Included are papers by Robert Adams on Mesopotamia, Donald Collier on Peru, and Angel Palerm on Mesoamerica, and Wittfogel's "Developmental Aspects of Hydraulic Societies."
18. Steward, *Theory of Culture Change* (Urbana, Ill., 1963), 37.
19. Other symposia that have dealt with the Wittfogel thesis include Richard Woodbury, ed., *Civilizations in Desert Lands*, U. of Utah Anthropology Paper 62 (Salt Lake City, 1962); and Theodore Downing and McGuire Gibson, eds., *Irrigation's Impact on Society* (Tucson, 1974). See also William Mitchell, "The Hydraulic Hypothesis," *Current Anthropology*, 14 (1973): 532–34.

The Local Subsistence Mode

1. The foregoing description has been influenced at many points by Karl Polanyi's *The Great Transformation* (Boston, 1944), 43–55.
2. Homer Aschmann, "Evaluations of Dryland Environments by Societies at Various Levels of Technical Competence," in Woodbury, *Desert Lands*, 4; Kent Flannery, "The Ecology of Early Food Production in Mesopotamia," *Science*, 147 (1965): 1247–56.
3. Steward, *Ethnography of the Owens Valley Paiute*, U. of California Pub. in American Archaeology and Ethnology, no. 33 (Berkeley, 1933), 233–50.
4. E. Richard Hart, "Zuni Agriculture," paper read at Laurier Conference on Ethnohistory and Ethnology, 30 Oct. 1980, pp. 3–4. I am indebted to the author for furnishing a copy of this text.
5. Dozier, *The Pueblo Indians of North America* (New York, 1970), 131–33.
6. The destruction of Papago agricultural ecology is the theme of Charles Bowden's excellent book, *Killing the Hidden Waters* (Austin, 1977), pt. 1. I am also indebted to Gary Nabhan of the Office of Arid Lands Studies, U. of Arizona, for providing a draft of his unpublished paper "Papago Indian Desert Agriculture and Water Control, 1697–1934." The same author's book *The Desert Smells Like Rain* (Berkeley, 1982), is an eloquent account of Papago ways. See also Alice Joseph, Rosamond Spicer, and Jane Chesky, *The Desert People* (Chicago, 1949), 28–39; and Amadeo Rea, *Once a River* (Tucson, 1983), chap. 1.
7. This account is based on Gary Nabhan, "Living with a River," *J. of Arizona*

History, 19 (1978): 1–16; and Nabhan, "The Ecology of Floodwater Farming in Arid Southwestern North America," *Agro-Ecosystems,* 5 (1979): 245–55.

8. McGee, "The Beginning of Agriculture," *American Anthropologist,* 8 (1895): 366.

9. Emil W. Haury, *The Hohokam* (Tucson, 1976), 120–51.

10. James Ayres, "Use and Abuse of Southwestern Rivers—The Desert Farmer," *Hydrology and Water Resources in Arizona and the Southwest,* vol. 1, Proc. of Arizona Academy of Science (Tempe, 1971), 378.

11. Haury, 149; Woodbury, "A Reappraisal of Hohokam Irrigation," *American Anthropologist,* 63 (1961): 557.

12. Masse, "Prehistoric Irrigation Systems in the Salt River Valley, Arizona," *Science,* 214 (1981): 414–15; Doyel, *American Scientist,* 67 (1979): 544.

13. Geertz, "The Wet and the Dry," *Human Ecology,* 1 (1972): 37. His *Agricultural Involution* (Berkeley, 1963) describes the hydraulic-trap phenomenon in irrigated Indonesia.

14. John Eyre, "Water Controls in a Japanese Irrigation System," *Geographical Rev.,* 45 (1955): 197–216.

15. Thomas Glick, *Irrigation and Society in Medieval Valencia* (Cambridge, Mass., 1970). Glick corrects Wittfogel's miscategorization of this Spanish system as a hydraulic society (pp. 172–74), but is less convincing when he rejects Wittfogel altogether. See also Norman Smith, *Man and Water* (New York, 1975), 20–21.

16. John Bennett, "Anthropological Contributions to the Cultural Ecology and Management of Water Resources," in L. Douglas James, ed., *Man and Water* (Lexington, Ky., 1974), 43.

The Agrarian State Mode

1. Lao-tse, *Tao te Ching,* trans. Gia-fu Feng and Jane English (New York, 1972), no. 80. I am indebted to Wes Jackson for the "patch" notion of early agricultural ecology; it is a model, he points out, that has great potential for reforming modern industrial farming toward more diversity and sustainability.

2. McNeill, *Plagues and Peoples* (Garden City, N.Y., 1976), 40. See also E. L. Jones, *The European Miracle* (Cambridge, 1981), 6–7; Mark Elvin, *The Pattern of the Chinese Past* (London, 1973), 186; Ivan Poulinin, "Disease, Morbidity, and Mortality in China, India, and the Arab World," in Charles Leslie, ed., *Asian Medical Systems* (Berkeley, 1976), 127; and George Borgstrom, *The Hungry Planet,* 2nd ed. (New York, 1972), 108.

3. Through the agency of the state, however, the bureaucrats did exercise considerable control over private property where it existed. See Wittfogel, *Oriental Despotism,* 228–29.

4. *Ibid.,* 29–30, 90–100.

5. I have been unable to locate the source for this much-quoted statement; it may be apocryphal. Semiramis was the Greek name for Sammuramat, who ruled during the minority of her son Adad-Nirari III. See George Roux, *Ancient Iraq* (London, 1964), 250.

6. Even those who give the state priority commonly admit that the cause-and-effect equation is not simple. For example, Eric Wolf and Angel Palerm, writing on the Valley of Mexico, one of most disputed areas for the Wittfogel thesis, argue that the state there "did not grow out of irrigation, but preceded it." They go on, nevertheless, to add that, "once established . . . irrigation probably operated in turn to centralize and intensify political controls." "Irrigation in the Old Acolhua Domain, Mexico," *Southwestern J. of Anthropology*, 11 (1955): 274. And Eva Hunt, who has studied the nearby Tehuacan Valley archaeology, describes irrigation as a necessary, if not sufficient, cause for the appearance there of a large centralized state: "No single variable," she writes, "can produce complex socio-cultural developments on its own impetus." "Irrigation and the Socio-political Organization of the Cuicatec Cacicazgos," in Johnson, *Chronology and Irrigation*, 245. See also Robert and Eva Hunt, "Canal Irrigation and Local Social Organization," *Current Anthropology*, 17 (Sept. 1976): 389–411. Robert Adams, a student of ancient Mesopotamian cities, has made the most concerted attack on the hydraulic society argument. Great irrigation works were, he insists, "more a 'consequence' than a 'cause' of the appearance of dynastic state organization." Unfortunately, what that other cause really was, if not irrigation, he leaves muddled and uncertain. "Early Civilizations, Subsistence, and Environment," in Carl Kraeling and Robert Adams, eds., *City Invincible* (Chicago, 1960), 280.

7. *Oriental Depotism*, 27.

8. *Ibid.*, 108–9, 114.

9. *Ibid.*, 25–27.

10. Barois, *Irrigation in Egypt*, trans. Major A. M. Miller, 50th Cong., 2nd sess., House Doc. 134 (Washington, 1889), 64–68.

11. *Oriental Despotism*, 30–45. Those monuments, writes Wittfogel, achieved their aesthetic effect with "a minimum of ideas and a maximum of material" (p. 44).

.12. *Ibid.*, 165–67; "The Hydraulic Approach to Pre-Spanish Mesoamerica," 65–66.

13. On the Tigris-Euphrates area, consult: Robert Adams, "A Synopsis of the Historical Demography and Ecology of the Diyala River Basin, Central Iraq," in Woodbury, 15–29; Adams, "Agriculture and Urban Life in Early Southwestern Iran," *Science*, 136 (1962): 109–22; R. D. Whyte, "Evolution of Land Use in Southwestern Asia," in L. Dudley Stamp, ed., *A History of Land Use in Arid Regions* (Paris, 1961), 57–118; Jacob Gruber, "Irrigation and Land Use in Ancient Mesopotamia," *AH*, 22 (1948): 19–77; Samuel Kramer, *The Sumerians* (Chicago, 1963), 5, 104–5; Stanley Butler, "Irrigation Systems of the Tigris and Euphrates Valleys," *J. of Irrigation and Drainage Div., Proc. ASCE*, 86 (Dec. 1960): 56–79.

14. Among other works on South Asia, see George Taylor, Jr., "Water, History, and the Indus River," *Natural History*, 74 (May 1965): 40–49; A. L. Basham, *The Wonder That Was India*, 3rd ed. (New York, 1967), 194–95; Edmund Leach, "Hydraulic Society in Ceylon," *Past and Present*, 15 (April 1959): 2–26; and Leach, *Pul Eliya* (Cambridge, 1961), 16–17. Leach argues that the hydraulic thesis is overgeneralized; in South Asia, he believes, small-scale, localized systems predominated, creating a more feudal than bureaucratic or totalitarian order. Mainly, however, he succeeds in muddying the water, not refuting Wittfogel. His own evidence suggests that Ceylon was not really a hydraulic society, therefore can offer no case against the thesis.

15. Robert Gray, *The Sonjo of Tanganyika* (London, 1963); Joseph Buttinger, *The Smaller Dragon* (New York, 1958); Marshall Sahlins, *Moala* (Ann Arbor, Mich., 1962); Paul Kosok, *Life, Land, and Water in Peru* (New York, 1965); and Ellen Semple, *The Geography of the Mediterranean Region* (New York, 1931), chap. 16.

16. Karl Butzer, *Early Hydraulic Civilization in Egypt* (Chicago, 1976), 91. See also his "Civilizations: Dynamisms or Systems?" *American Scientist*, 68 (1980): 517–23; and Jean-Philippe Lévy, *The Economic Life of the Ancient World*, trans. John Biram (Chicago, 1967), 8–9.

17. John Waterbury, *Hydropolitics of the Nile Valley* (Syracuse, N.Y., 1979); and Desmond Hammerton, "The Nile River—A Case History," in Ray Oglesby, Clarence Carlson, and James McCann, eds., *River Ecology and Man* (New York, 1972), 171–214.

18. M. S. Drower, "Water Supply, Irrigation, and Agriculture," in Charles Singer, E. J. Holmyard, and A. R. Hall, eds., *A History of Technology*, vol. 1 (Oxford, 1954), 523–25, 535–39.

19. Hamdan, "Evolution of Irrigation Agriculture in Egypt," in Stamp, 125.

20. See Robert Tignor, "British Agricultural and Hydraulic Policy in Egypt, 1882–1892," *AH*, 37 (1963): 63–74.

21. Willcocks and Craig, *Egyptian Irrigation*, 3rd ed. (London, 1913), 796; Hamdan, 121.

22. Butzer, *Early Hydraulic Civilization in Egypt*, 110–11.

23. It is in the nature of scholars to defend their own turf from being invaded by the large ideas of others, while pointing to their application elsewhere. Thus, O. H. K. Spate thinks the Wittfogel thesis fits China better than India (in *Annals of Assoc. of American Geographers*, 49 [1959]: 93), while Maurice Meissner maintains that India furnishes a better example than China ("The Despotism of Concepts: Wittfogel and Marx on China," *China Quarterly*, 16 [1963]: 99–111).

24. Needham, *Science and Civilization in China*, vol. 4, pt. 3 (Cambridge, 1971), 212.

25. Charles Greer, *Water Management in the Yellow River Basin of China* (Austin, 1979), 23–30.

26. Needham, 235, 247–49. On the contrast between Taoist and Confucian water thought, see his vol. 2 (Cambridge, 1956), 57–61.

27. Eisenstadt, review of *Oriental Despotism*, in *J. of Asian Studies*, 17 (1958): 440–44. See also Wolfram Eberhard's review in *American Sociological Rev.*, 13 (1958): 446–48. Some scholars, like Eberhard, tend to ignore China's irrigation and argue that it was a feudal society dominated by a rural gentry, much like western Europe. Joseph Needham, however, accepts the Wittfogel characterization: water control, he writes, "invariably tended to concentrate power at the centre, i.e., in the bureaucratic apparatus arched above the granular man of 'tribal' clan villages." But he defends that bureaucracy as "a magnificent instrument of human social organization"—precisely the defense one might expect from an ardent but conventional socialist. See his "Science and Society in East and West," *Centaurus*, 10 (1964–65): 182–83. Wu Ta-k'un agrees to a point that China's "despotic character was accentuated by the development of artificial irrigation works," in his article "An Interpretation of Chinese Economic History," *Past and Present*, 1 (Feb. 1952): 3.

28. Ch'ao-ting Chi, *Key Economic Areas in Chinese History* (New York, 1970), 2, 5.

29. This is the argument made by Lewis Mumford in *Technics and Human Development* (New York, 1967), 168–75.

The Capitalist State Mode

1. Wittfogel, "Agriculture: A Key to the Understanding of Chinese Society, Past and Present," Morrison lecture (Canberra, 1970), 6. See also Ulmen, *Science of Society*, 241–42, 457.

2. Lon Fuller, "Irrigation and Tyranny," *Stanford Law Rev.*, 17 (1965): 1021–42. According to Wittfogel, the industrial revolution in Europe led to an open, democratic society based on "the advance of the mechanical arts," and it ought to be promoted abroad to save the world from totalitarianism. "The Hydraulic Civilizations," in William Thomas, Jr., ed., *Man's Role in Changing the Face of the Earth*, vol. 1 (Chicago, 1956), 161–62.

3. Lewis, *The Abolition of Man* (New York, 1947), 35; Gorz, *Ecology as Politics* (Boston, 1980), 20.

4. Mumford, 207.

5. The best study of this group of social philosophers is Martin Jay, *The Dialectical Imagination* (Boston, 1973). Other useful guides are: David Held, *Introduction to Critical Theory* (Berkeley, 1980); Zoltan Tar, *The Frankfurt School* (New York, 1977); H. Stuart Hughes, *The Sea Change* (New York, 1977), 134–88; and Trent Schroyer, *The Critique of Domination* (Boston, 1973). On Wittfogel's relationship to them, see Ulmen, *Science of Society*, 134–35, 211, 476–78.

6. Max Horkheimer and Theodor Adorno, *Dialectic of Enlightenment*, trans. John Cumming (New York, 1972), ix.

7. Horkheimer, *Critique of Instrumental Reason*, trans. Matthew O'Connell et al. (New York, 1974), vii.

8. This "unreason" of reason is also a theme in the writings of Herbert Marcuse, who prefers to attribute it to the rise of "technological rationality." See, for example, his *One-Dimensional Man* (Boston, 1964). And Jürgen Habermas likewise distinguishes between reason as a liberating force and the "means-end rationality" of contemporary society, which calls on science and technology to give it legitimacy. "Technology and Science as 'Ideology,' " in his *Toward a Rational Society*, trans. Jeremy Shapiro (Boston, 1970). All of these Frankfurt philosophers owe much to Max Weber and his studies of modern consciousness. See also Michael Zimmerman, "Marx and Heidegger on the Technological Domination of Nature," *Philosophy Today*, 23 (1979): 99–112.

9. Horkheimer, *Eclipse of Reason*, 21.

10. *Ibid.*, 97, 108.

11. A fine study of the theme is William Leiss's book *The Domination of Nature* (Boston, 1974). Leiss argues that the modern crusade to dominate nature has had the effect of concealing, perhaps deliberately, "newly developing forms of domination in human relationships" associated with industrial mass production (p. xiv).

12. Horkheimer and Adorno, *Dialectic of Enlightenment*, 3–4. Also, Horkheimer, *Eclipse of Reason*, 63, 104. The seventeenth-century English philosopher of scientific method, Francis Bacon, is one of the most important sources of the domination idea. See Leiss, 45–71; Donald Worster, *Nature's Economy* (San Francisco, 1977), 30–31; and Carolyn Merchant, *The Death of Nature* (San Francisco, 1980), 164–90.

13. Martin Jay argues, on the basis of Institute criticisms of Marx's philosophical assumptions, that they "presented a revision of Marxism so substantial that it forfeited the right to be included among its many offshoots." *Dialectical Imagination*, 296.

14. Horkheimer, *Eclipse of Reason*, 151, 197; *Critique of Instrumental Reason*, 49; Horkheimer and Adorno, *Dialectic of Enlightenment*, xiv. Influenced by Freud and his theories of psychological repression, Horkheimer wrote in *The Eclipse of Reason:* "The human being, in the process of his emancipation, shares the fate of the rest of his world. Domination of nature involves domination of man. Each subject not only has to take part in the subjugation of external nature, human and nonhuman, but in order to do so must subjugate nature in himself. Domination becomes 'internalized' for domination's sake." (p. 93).

15. Frank W. Blackman, "Mastery of the Desert," *Western America*, 1906.

16. Finch, "Some Modern Wonders Named," *Civil Engineering*, 25 (Nov. 1955): 33, 40.

III. INCIPIENCE:

A Poor Man's Paradise

Confronting the Desert: Death and Life

1. *Audubon's Western Journal: 1849–1850* (Cleveland, 1906), 158–60.
2. Nelson, "Desert Passages" (Ph.D. diss., Yale U., 1980), xlii.
3. Manly, *Death Valley in '49*, ed. Milo Milton Quaife (Chicago, 1927), 155.
4. *Ibid.*, 272–73.
5. The health rush began about 1870. See Carey McWilliams, *Southern California Country* (New York, 1946), 96–101.
6. Frederick Vernon Colville and Daniel Trembly MacDougal, *Desert Botanical Laboratory of the Carnegie Institution*, Carnegie Inst. Pub. 6 (Washington, 1903), 1. Major desert research seems to have begun in the period 1880–1900, when European scientists like Paul Maury, Georg Volkens, and Eugenius Warming began to publish articles on Algeria and the Middle East. See also Colville's "Sketch of the Flora of Death Valley, California," *Science*, 20 (1892): 342.
7. MacDougal, *Botanical Features of North American Deserts*, Carnegie Inst. Pub. 99 (Washington, 1908); Shreve, *Vegetation of the Sonoran Desert*, Carnegie Inst. Pub. 591, 2 vols. (Washington, 1951), 1: v–vii; Clements, "The Origin of the Desert Climax and Climate," in T. H. Goodspeed, ed., *Essays in Geobotany in Honor of William Albert Setchell* (Berkeley, 1936), 87–140. On Clements's ecological theory, see Ronald Tobey, *Saving the Prairies* (Berkeley, 1981), 76–99; and Donald Worster, *Nature's Economy* (San Francisco, 1977), 208–22.
8. Shreve, "The Problems of the Desert," *Scientific Monthly*, 38 (1934): 199.
9. *The Expeditions of Zebulon Montgomery Pike*, 2 vols., ed. Elliott Coues (Minneapolis, 1965), 2:525; Irving, *Astoria*, ed. Edgeley Todd (Norman, Okla., 1964), 210.
10. Early in the twentieth century one writer promised: "Only a few years will elipse before the term 'desert' will cease to be used in connection with any part of the territory of the United States." "The Mastery of the Desert," *North American Rev.*, 182 (1906): 684. He was a little optimistic, but he has left successors. When Walter Prescott Webb tried, a half-century later, to extend the desert to its earlier broad sweep, he ran into a blistering fire from regional defenders. See his essay "The American West," *Harper's*, 214 (May 1957): 25–31.
11. Colville and MacDougal, 34.
12. Austin, *Earth Horizon* (Boston, 1932), 157. Austin died in 1934 in New Mexico.

13. For general background on her life and writing, see Thomas Pearce, *Mary Hunter Austin* (New York, 1966); and Augusta Fink, *I-Mary: A Biography of Mary Austin* (Tucson, 1983).

14. Austin, *The Land of Little Rain* (New York, 1971), 8, 16–18, 45–46.

15. Austin, *Earth Horizon*, 234. The best account of the episode, especially of the Austins' role in it, is William Kahrl, *Water and Power* (Berkeley, 1982), 104–47.

16. Van Dyke, *The Desert* (Salt Lake City, 1980), ix. The introduction to this edition by Richard Shelton is useful for biographical details. See also *National Cyclopedia of American Biography* (New York, 1930), C, 489–90. Despite his illness, Van Dyke lived until 1932.

17. Van Dyke, 171.

18. *Ibid.*, 21–22.

19. *Ibid.*, 143.

20. *Ibid.*, 57–62. Another protest came from the the popular desert writer George James: "It would be a tremendous pity to reclaim all the desert. We need it for other and better things than growing melons and corn. It is required for the expansion of the soul, the enlargement of vision of perhaps only a few men, but those few will help influence and benefit the world." *The Wonders of the Colorado Desert*, 2 vols. (Boston, 1906), 1: 353.

The Lord's Beavers

1. Wells Hutchins, "The Community Acequia," *Southwestern Historical Q.*, 31 (1928): 275. See also Thomas Glick, *The Old World Background of the Irrigation System of San Antonio, Texas*, Southwestern Studies Monograph 35 (El Paso, 1972); Paul Horgan, *Great River: The Rio Grande*, 2 vols. (New York, 1954), I:60, 212, 347, 368–69; and Michael Meyer, *Water in the Hispanic Southwest* (Tucson, 1984).

2. W. W. H. Davis, cit. Alvin Sunseri, "Agricultural Techniques in New Mexico at the Time of the Anglo-American Conquest," *AH*, 47 (1973): 334. Sunseri notes (p. 332) how the need for massed labor on New Mexico's irrigation works led to "a social-political organization that was oppressive in nature."

3. Richard Jackson, "Righteousness and Environmental Change," in Thomas Alexander, ed., *Essays on the American West, 1973–1974* (Provo, Utah, 1975), 31–36.

4. John Widtsoe, "A Century of Irrigation," *Reclamation Era*, 33 (1947): 99.

5. Charles Hillman Brough, *Irrigation in Utah* (Baltimore, 1898), 7–12; George Clyde, "History of Irrigation in Utah," *Utah Historical Q.*, 27 (1959): 27–36.

6. George Thomas, *The Development of Institutions Under Irrigation* (New York, 1920), 16; Brough, 75.

7. Thomas, 33–35.

8. The devolution to the county courts is discussed, from a different perspective,

in Thomas, 57–91. See also James Allen, "The Unusual Jurisdiction of County Probate Courts in the Territory of Utah," *Utah Historical Q.*, 36 (1968): 132–42.

9. Thomas, 117–37; Brough, 36–44.

10. Brough, 36.

11. Cit. Gordon Bakken, "The English Common Law in the Rocky Mountain West," *Arizona and the West*, 11 (1969): 127.

12. Mark Leone, *Roots of Modern Mormonism* (Cambridge, Mass., 1979), 86–110. See also Charles Peterson, *Take Up Your Mission* (Tucson, 1973).

13. Arrington, "Taming the Turbulent Sevier," *Western Humanities Rev.*, 5 (1951): 396.

14. For the influence of irrigation on the Church's organization, see George Strebel, "Irrigation as a Factor in Western History, 1847–1890" (Ph.D. diss., U. of California, Berkeley, 1965), 139–73. Leonard Arrington and Dean May see Mormonism supporting a Jeffersonian rural democracy—an interpretation that works only if one ignores the strong centralized church-state fusion in the religion and Jefferson's antagonism toward such fusion. Arrington and May, "A Different Mode of Life," in James Shideler, ed., *Agriculture in the Development of the Far West* (Washington, 1975), 3–20.

15. Widtsoe, *In a Sunlit Land* (Salt Lake City, 1952), 74. Editorial on Widtsoe, cit. Leonard Arrington and Davis Bitton, *The Mormon Experience* (New York, 1979), 312. Arrington and Bitton are especially useful on Mormon contributions to irrigation and agricultural science.

16. Lamar, *The Far Southwest, 1846–1912* (New York, 1970), 309–12.

17. Brough, 45–46. The first Utah sugar beet factory was set up at Lehi in 1890. See Leonard Arrington, *Great Basin Kingdom* (Lincoln, Neb., 1958), 240–44. Arrington maintains that Young opposed the railroad and that "Mormon economic policy, in 1869 and immediately thereafter, was devoted almost fanatically to the tightly-reined independent theocratic commonwealth" (p. 244).

18. Arrington, 203–18; Brough, 63–69. The latter offers evidence of "the favorable attitude of the Mormon Church toward capitalist irrigation" (p. 69). On English irrigation investments elsewhere, see Roger Clements, "British-Controlled Enterprise in the West Between 1870 and 1900, and Some Agrarian Reactions," *AH*, 27 (1953): 132–41.

In the Shadow of the Rockies

1. The standard sources remain David Boyd, *A History: Greeley and the Union Colony of Colorado* (Greeley, 1890); and James Willard, ed., *The Union Colony at Greeley, Colorado, 1869–1871* (Boulder, 1918). Also see James Willard and Colin Goodykoontz, eds., *Experiments in Colorado Colonization, 1869–1872* (Boulder, 1926).

2. Greeley, cit. Albert Brisbane, *A Concise Exposition of the Doctrine of Association*, 2nd ed. (New York, 1843), frontispiece. For general background on Fourierism, see Alice Felt Tyler, *Freedom's Ferment* (New York, 1944), 217–20; and Frank and Fritzie Manuel, *Utopian Thought in the Western World* (Cambridge, Mass., 1979), 641–75.

3. Meeker's career as a communitarian, poet, novelist, religious convert, Civil War correspondent, and agricultural writer is described in Boyd, *A History*, 15.

4. Bestor, *Backwoods Utopias*, 2nd ed. (Philadelphia, 1970), 249–52.

5. For an example of this utopian spirit, see Donald Mercer, "The Colorado Co-operative Company, 1894–1904," *Colorado Mag.*, 44 (Fall 1967): 293–306.

6. Boyd, *A History*, 52–54.

7. Clark, *Colonial Days* (Denver, 1912), 138.

8. *Ibid.*, 68. Boyd says of Meeker: "We found that he could write better about farming than farm" (*A History*, 58).

9. Hayden, *Seven American Utopias* (Cambridge, Mass., 1976), 284.

10. Boyd, *Irrigation near Greeley, Colorado*, U.S. Geological Survey, Water Supply and Irrigation Papers, no. 9 (Washington, 1897), 61.

11. The literature on western water law is vast. A good recent survey is Robert Emmet Clark, ed., *Waters and Water Rights* (Indianapolis, 1972), vol. 5. Also useful are Samuel Wiel, *Water Rights in the Western States*, 3rd ed., 2 vols. (San Francisco, 1911); Wells Hutchins, *Water Rights Laws in Nineteen Western States*, USDA Misc. Pub. 1206 (Washington, 1971–); and Ralph Hess, "Arid-Land Water Rights in the United States," *Columbia Law Rev.*, 16 (1916): 480–95.

12. Webb, *The Great Plains* (Boston, 1931), 431–52.

13. Samuel Wiel argued that the riparian doctrine was not part of English common law but was taken by Americans from the French civil code. "Waters: American Law and French Authority," *Harvard Law Rev.*, 33 (1919): 133–67. See also Wiel, "Origins and Comparative Development of the Law of Watercourses in the Common Law and in the Civil Law," *California Law Rev.*, 6 (1918): 245–67; (July): 342–71. The American jurist James Kent, he argues, introduced the riparian idea into Anglo-American law in this statement from his *Commentaries on American Law:* "Every proprietor of lands on the banks of a river has naturally an equal right to the use of the water which flows in the stream adjacent to his lands, as it was wont to run . . . without diminution or alteration." It was indeed a clear statement of riparianism, but I have not found any modern authority who accepts Wiel's argument as to its source. See also Arthur Maass and Hiller Zobel, "Anglo-American Water Law," *Public Policy*, 10 (1960): 109–56.

14. Horwitz, *The Transformation of American Law 1780–1860* (Cambridge, Mass., 1977), 31. One source of the language and resource thinking in the appropriation doctrine may have been the English philosopher John Locke, who speaks

351

repeatedly of "appropriating" from a state of nature. See Locke, *Two Treatises of Government*, ed. Peter Laslett (Cambridge, 1967), 304–20.

15. See, for instance, Chennat Gopalakrishnan, "The Doctrine of Prior Appropriation and Its Impact on Water Development," *American J. of Economics and Sociology*, 32 (1973): 61–72.

16. See Robert Clark, *Waters and Water Rights*, 5: 40–222, on the "Colorado doctrine." Colorado first adopted prior appropriation in territorial legislation, later adding it to its first state constitution. In the 1882 case, *Coffin* v. *Left Hand Ditch Company*, the state supreme court declared that the riparian principle was inapplicable to the state. See Robert Dunbar, "The Significance of the Colorado Agricultural Frontier," *AH*, 34 (1960): 119–25. Also, Harry Scheiber, "Property Law, Expropriation, and Resource Allocation by Government," *J. of Economic History*, 33 (1973): 244. Scheiber argues that Colorado "blazed the way for the West" in extending the use of eminent-domain law to private uses.

17. C. B. Macpherson, *The Political Theory of Possessive Individualism* (Oxford, 1962), 24–25, 54–55.

18. Cit. Boyd, *A History*, 93.

19. *Ibid.*, 127. Also, Robert Dunbar, "Water Conflicts and Controls in Colorado," *AH*, 22 (1948): 180–86; and Moses Lasky, "From Prior Appropriation to Economic Distribution of Water by the State—Via Irrigation Administration," *Rocky Mountain Law Rev.* 1 (1929): 161–216, 248–70, (Nov.): 35–58.

20. Art. VIII, sec. 1, of the Wyoming Constitution reads: "The water of all natural streams, springs, lakes, or other collections of still water, within the boundaries of the State, are hereby declared to be the property of the State." Wyoming set up a state board, along with a state engineer, to grant water rights and adjudicate them.

21. Mead, *Irrigation Institutions* (New York, 1910), 50.

22. F. H. Newell, *Report on Agriculture by Irrigation in the Western Part of the United States, 11th Census: 1890*, 52nd Cong., 1st sess., House Misc. Doc. 340 (Washington, 1894), 1. That census also reported that Colorado had the highest percentage of land surface under irrigation—1.34%—and the leading single county, Boulder, with 14.04% of its area irrigated (p. 2).

23. Mead, *Irrigation Institutions*, 327.

The Redemption of California

1. Kevin Starr describes King's career in *Americans and the California Dream, 1850–1915* (New York, 1973), 97–105.

2. King, "Annual Address," *California Farmer*, 18 (19 Sept. 1862): 10.

3. Robert Kelley, *Gold vs. Grain* (Glendale, Calif. 1959), 56–57, 154–56, 203–4. Hydraulic mining, at the same time that it devastated farmland and waterways, developed engineering skills that, in the 1880s, after the mining stopped, were

applied to irrigation and municipal waterworks. See Walter Huber, "An Engineering Century in California," *Trans. ASCE* (Centennial Transaction, 1953): 99–101.

4. King, 10–11. For similar effusions see James and John Warren, "Memorial to Congress on an Agricultural College for California," *AH*, 40 (1966): 53–56.

5. George, "What the Railroads Will Bring Us," *Overland Monthly*, 1 (1868): 298.

6. R. H. Allen, "The Spanish Land Grant System as an Influence in the Agricultural Development of California," *AH*, 9 (1935): 128.

7. Gates, "Public Land Disposal in California," in Shideler, 176. See also Gates, "California Land Policy in Its Historical Context," in *Four Persistent Issues* (Berkeley, 1978), 19. The present-day pattern of concentrated land ownership in California is largely the result of those early accumulations.

8. Marx, *Capital*, trans. Samuel Moore and Edward Aveling (New York, 1906), 785. By "primitive accumulation" Marx meant the stage before factories and factory profits, when, as in the case of England, the peasants were expropriated and the land gathered into a few large estates.

9. One writer tells of seeing 430,000 acres of wheat growing in a wide belt along both sides of the San Joaquin River, in farms as large as 36,000 acres. Ezra Carr, *The Patrons of Husbandry on the Pacific Coast* (San Francisco, 1875), 66. See also Rodman Paul, "The Beginnings of Agriculture in California," *California Historical Q.*, 52 (1973): 20–26; Frank Adams, "The Historical Background of California Agriculture," in Claude Hutchison, ed., *California Agriculture*, (Berkeley, 1946), 35–36; Howard Reed, "Major Trends in California Agriculture," *AH*, 20 (1946): 252–53; Lawrence Jellinek, *Harvest Empire* (San Francisco, 1980), 47–60; Reynold Wik, "Some Interpretations of the Mechanization of Agriculture in the Far West," in Shideler, 73–83; and William Preston, *Vanishing Landscapes* (Berkeley, 1981), 130–35.

10. Gilbert Fite, *The Farmer's Frontier, 1865–1900* (New York, 1966), 163, 166–68.

11. John Ganoe, "The Beginnings of Irrigation in the United States," *Mississippi Valley Historical Rev.*, 25 (1935): 65.

12. T. S. Van Dyke, "Irrigation in Southern California," *Independent*, 45 (4 May 1893): 8; R. Louis Gentilcore, "Ontario, California and the Agricultural Boom of the 1880s," *AH*, 34 (1960): 77–87. In 1880 William Hammond Hall counted 82,485 irrigated acres in Los Angeles and San Bernardino counties, with about one-third in citrus fruits, olives, and grapes. *Report of the State Engineer* (Sacramento, 1880), pt. 4, 59.

13. *Report of the Commissioner of Agriculture for the Year 1873* (Washington, 1874), 283. The common experience, in the United States and abroad, was that irrigation increased land values by 500% or more. See Edward Bates Dorsey, "Irrigation," *Trans. ASCE*, 16 (1887): 98.

14. Gates, "California Land Policy," 19; Gerald Nash, "Henry George Reexamined," *AH*, 33 (1959): 133–37.

353

15. Virginia Thickens, "Pioneer Agricultural Colonies of Fresno County," *California Historical Society Q.*, 25 (1946): 17–38, 169–77. On Tulare County colonies, see Preston, 149–54.

16. Thickens, 31–32. Lilibourne Winchell, *History of Fresno County and the San Joaquin Valley* (Fresno, 1933), 137.

17. George Freeman, "Among the Irrigators of Fresno," *Overland Monthly*, 9 (1887): 624. Freeman adds: "The colony life, neighbors being so near, gives great satisfaction to women and children, especially those used to the lonely life of stock farms, or frontier ranches" (p. 628).

18. Frank Norris, *The Octopus* (Garden City, N.Y., 1928), I, 48.

19. Richard Orsi, *"The Octopus* Reconsidered," *California Historical Q.*, 54 (1975): 200–1; 210–12.

20. M. B. Levick, *Fresno County California* (San Francisco, n.d.).

21. San Joaquin and King's River Canal and Irrigation Company, *Agricultural Lands and Waters in the San Joaquin and Tulare Valleys*, prospectus (San Francisco, 1873), 7.

22. Gates, "Public Land Disposal," 172–73; Gates, "California Land Policy," 19; Edward Treadwell, *The Cattle King*, rev. ed. (Boston, 1950), 63, 66.

23. Gates, "California Land Policy," 19. Eventually the Kern County Land Company was acquired by Tenneco, an oil corporation; in 1973 the parcel amounted to 362,843 acres in California, plus over 1 million acres in other states. See Robert Fellmuth, *Politics of Land* (New York, 1973), 515.

24. John Ganoe, "The Desert Land Act in Operation," *AH*, 11 (1937): 142–57; Paul Gates, *History of Public Land Law Development* (Washington, 1968), 638–41.

25. Haggin, *The Desert Lands of Kern County, Cal.* (San Francisco, 1877), vii. This document is mainly a set of affidavits from several hundred individuals testifying to the desert condition of the Haggin lands.

26. William Smythe, *The Greatest Irrigated Farm in the World*, pamphlet (San Francisco, 1893).

27. Visalia *Delta*, 8 November 1878, cit. Margaret Cooper, *Land, Water, and Settlement in Kern County, California, 1850–1890* (New York, 1979), 252.

28. Gordon Miller, "Shaping California Water Law, 1781 to 1928," *Southern California Q.*, 55 (1973): 13–22.

29. Legislative Irrigation Committee of State Irrigation Convention, *Address to the Legislature of the State of California, Twenty-sixth Session*, pamphlet (Fresno, 1884), 3–5.

30. The distinction, a familiar one in western American history, is widespread elsewhere too. See Robert Edgerton, " 'Cultural' vs. 'Ecological' Factors in the Expression of Values, Attitudes, and Personality Characteristics," *American Anthropologist*, 67 (1965): 442–47.

31. Treadwell, 80–94.

32. This "California doctrine" is discussed in Robert Clark, 5: 232–384. Something like it is followed by other West Coast states and the Great Plains states.

On Washington's similar riparian-appropriation compromise, see Emmett Vandervere, "History of Irrigation in Washington" (Ph.D. diss., U. of Washington, 1948), 96–102.

33. In *Miller and Lux* v. *Madera Canal and Irrigation Company* (1909), the California court held that the riparian proprietor "is not limited by any measure of reasonableness" in restraining an appropriator—another victory for Henry Miller. That decision was reaffirmed in *Herminghaus* v. *Southern California Edison Company* (1926). Then in 1928 Californians passed a constitutional amendment that made the doctrine of "reasonable and beneficial use" the state's law; it did not abolish riparian rights, but henceforth they had to be exercised in a way that was both reasonable and economically beneficial. See Miller, 32–33.

34. The instrumentalist bias in western American resource law, which favors exploitation and development over nonuse, is ably discussed by Harry Scheiber and Charles McCurdy, "Eminent-Domain Law and Western Agriculture, 1849–1900," in Shideler, 112–30.

35. Malone, "The California Irrigation Crisis of 1886: Origins of the Wright Act" (Ph.D. diss., Stanford U., 1965), 13; Benjamin Rhodes, "Thirsty Land: The Modesto Irrigation District" (Ph.D. diss., U. of California, Berkeley, 1943), 51–52.

36. John Bennett, "The District Irrigation Movement in California," *Overland Monthly*, 29 (1897): 252–57. In light of the many lawsuits brought by large landowners against irrigation districts, Elwood Mead called the Wright Act "a disgrace to any self-governing people," meaning that it was unwise not to have put district voting on a property basis. Mead, *Irrigation Institutions*, 213.

37. Because it authorized districts to issue bonds, the Wright Act, rather than the Utah Act of 1865, became the model for other western states. In 1917 North and South Dakota and Texas became the last of the seventeen states in the region to enact irrigation-district acts. Voting qualifications varied widely from state to state, but fourteen states required property ownership, and Colorado, Wyoming, and Montana calculated votes on the basis of acreage owned. See Wells Hutchins, *Irrigation Districts*, USDA Technical Bull. 254 (1931).

38. *11th Census: 1890*, 1; Grunsky, "The Material Progress of California," *Overland Monthly*, 29 (1897): 516.

39. Mead, *Report of Irrigation Investigations in California*, USDA Office of Experiment Stations, Irrigation Investigations Bull. 100 (Washington, 1901), 32.

40. These difficulties are discussed district by district in Frank Adams, *Irrigation Districts in California, 1887–1915*, California State Dept. of Engineering Bull. 2 (Sacramento, 1916). Due to overbonding, the Wright Act was amended in 1897 to give the large landowners a veto over district policies.

41. Hall, "Irrigation in California," *National Geographic*, 1 (April 1889): 7. Hall served as state engineer from 1878 to 1891, when the office was abolished. See Charles Korr, "William Hammond Hall: The Failure of Attempts at State

355

Water Planning in California, 1878–1888," *Southern California Q.*, 45 (1963): 305–22; and Gerald Nash, *State Government and Economic Development* (Berkeley, 1964), 189–94.

The Ideology of Democratic Conquest

1. Emory, *Notes of a Military Reconnoissance*, 30th Cong., 1st sess., House Exec. Doc. 7 (Washington, 1846), 98.
2. Marsh, *Irrigation: Its Evils, the Remedies, and the Compensations*, 43rd Cong, 1st sess., Senate Misc. Doc. 55 (Washington, 1874), 4–5. The paper was prepared at the request of the U.S. commissioner of agriculture and, writes Marsh's biographer, "made considerable breeze in Congress" with its advocacy of the public ownership of water. David Lowenthal, *George Perkins Marsh* (New York, 1958), 308. See also Marsh, *Man and Nature* (Cambridge, Mass., 1965), 313, 321–22.
3. Marsh, *Irrigation*, 6–7. Considerable opposition to irrigation developed in California among medical men, who believed that malaria was caused by marshes, stagnant water, and their "effluvia." See Kenneth Thompson, "Irrigation as a Menace to Health in California," *Geographical Rev.*, 59 (1969): 198–214.
4. Marsh, *Irrigation*, 22.
5. Weber, *Economy and Society*, ed. Guenther Roth and Claus Wittich, 4th ed., 3 vols. (New York, 1968), 1: 31–38, 212–15.
6. Useful for understanding the process, particularly as it has worked (and failed) under advanced capitalism, is Jürgen Habermas, *Legitimation Crisis*, trans. Thomas McCarthy (Boston, 1975).
7. Brough, 109.
8. Reeve, "Irrigation and Agriculture," *Independent*, 45 (16 Feb. 1893): 35. This author predicted that someday 350 million acres would be irrigated in the West. "The possible agricultural population which can find room here," he went on, "is simply incalculable" (p. 34).
9. *Ibid.*
10. *Ibid.;* Nimmo, "Uncle Sam's Farm," *Frank Leslie's Illus. Newspaper* (7 Dec. 1889), 322. Nimmo spoke too of "a mighty empire" arising out of arid-land reclamation, "the last, and perhaps the most important chapter in the history of the subjugation of wild lands to the uses of civilized man upon this continent." *Ibid.* (16 Nov.), 258–59.
11. Estee, "The Irrigation Problem," annual address before the State Agricultural Society of California (Sacramento, 1874), 23; *Reclamation of Arid Lands by Irrigation*, Report of Committee on Arid Lands of California State Board of Trade (San Francisco, 1889), 46–47.
12. *Reclamation of Arid Lands*, 48–50.
13. Hall, "Irrigation in California," 12–13; Seattle *Sunday Times*, 8 Feb. 1903.

14. In some cases the breaking up of large estates was a passing phenomenon. R. H. Allen tells of a Spanish land grant where the poorest lands were sold to colonists; after they failed, the estate was reassembled. "Often the large holdings," he writes, "remained intact and were leased in parcels" to a tenant class ("Spanish Land Grant System," p. 142).

15. Hall, *Report of the State Engineer* (1880), pt. 4, 125. See also Hall, "The Irrigation Question. Memorandum No. 2: California and Australia" (Sacramento, 1886), 14.

16. Stewart to Nelson Thomasson, 12 Dec. 1891, William M. Stewart Papers, Nevada Historical Society, Reno.

17. See Lawrence Lee, "William Ellsworth Smythe and the Irrigation Movement," *PHR*, 41 (1972): 289–311; Martin Carlson, "William E. Smythe," *JW*, 7 (1968): 41–47; and "William Ellsworth Smythe," *National Cyclopaedia of American Biography* (New York, 1927), 17: 443–44. On his colonization efforts see Lawrence Lee, "The Little Landers' Colony of San Ysidro," *J. of San Diego History*, 21 (1975): 26–51; and Henry Anderson, "The Little Landers' Land Colonies," *AH*, 5 (1921): 139–50.

18. Cit. Martin Carlson, "The Development of Irrigation in Nebraska, 1854–1910" (Ph.D. diss., U. of Nebraska, 1963), 201–2.

19. Smythe, *The Conquest of Arid America* (Seattle, 1969), 43. Advertisements for the book carried the endorsement of Buffalo Bill Cody, who had given up the Wild West Show for a Wyoming irrigation scheme: "In my opinion, it will prove the greatest benefit to mankind of any book ever published outside of the Bible."

20. *Ibid.*, 11. The prefatory quotation to Smythe's Part First is from Andrew Carnegie's book and is a good example of how men of great wealth propagated the notion that democracy is the result of economic and geographical expansion. Carnegie concludes with satisfaction: "The capitalist and property owner is more secure in the enjoyment of his property in the new [i.e., the United States] than in the old country" (p. 477).

21. Smythe, *Constructive Democracy* (New York, 1905), 246.

22. *Ibid.*, 327.

23. Lee, Introduction to Smythe, *Conquest*, xxxv.

24. Smythe, *Conquest*, 32–33.

25. *Ibid.*, 64. Smythe advocated a program of government-financed reclamation, which will be discussed in the next chapter. Even in this, his thinking was couched in corporate capitalist terms: the government was described as "the public capitalist" and as "the United States of America, Unlimited," as though it were a super-Carnegie, putting its money into smaller entrepreneurial ventures. Smythe, *Conquest*, xxvii–xxviii.

IV. FLORESCENCE:

The State and the Desert

"A Commonwealth Within Itself"

1. Sparks, "Irrigation and the American Frontier," *Chautauquan*, 35 (1902): 568, 570.
2. Powell, cit. William Culp Darrah, *Powell of the Colorado* (Princeton, 1951), 312. See also A. Bower Sageser, "Los Angeles Hosts an International Congress," *JW*, 4 (1965): 411–24.
3. The standard biographies are Darrah, *Powell*, and Wallace Stegner, *Beyond the Hundredth Meridian* (Boston, 1954). The latter is an especially fine study of Powell's career, though it glosses over the technocratic side of the man.
4. Powell, *Geographical and Geological Surveys West of the Mississippi*, 43rd Cong., 1st sess., House Report 612 (Washington, 1874), 10.
5. Powell, *Report on the Lands of the Arid Region of the United States*, ed. Wallace Stegner (Cambridge, Mass., 1962), 56.
6. Powell, "Institutions for the Arid Lands," *Century*, 40 (1890): 111. See also his "History of Irrigation," *Independent*, 45 (1893): 1–3. This essay is remarkable for its failure to mention the despotic features of ancient hydraulic societies; instead, Powell dwells on the more flattering argument that "civilization sprang from [irrigated] agriculture" in the Old World deserts.
7. Everett Sterling, "The Powell Irrigation Survey, 1888–1893," *Mississippi Valley Historical Rev.*, 27 (1940): 421–34. Cf. Darrah, chap. 19; and Arthur Frazier and Wilbur Heckler, *Embudo, New Mexico: Birthplace of Systematic Stream Gaging*, U.S. Geological Survey, Professional Paper 778 (Washington, 1970).
8. George Rothwell Brown, in *Reminiscences of Senator William M. Stewart of Nevada* (New York, 1908), 17.
9. The congressional debate over the irrigation survey is well laid out in Thomas Manning, *Government in Science* (Lexington, Ky., 1967), chap. 9.
10. *Report of the Special Committee on the Irrigation and Reclamation of Arid Lands*, 51st Cong., 1st sess., Senate Report 928 (Washington, 1890), pt. 1, 15. Stewart's majority report includes a summary of the tour and his proposals (pp. 1–94). The minority members criticized those proposals as being "in the interest of the great cattle companies" and "the great irrigation companies rapidly developing in the West, turning over all water rights for irrigation to these and practically excluding the poor settler wishing to obtain a homestead on the land" (p. 98).
11. Stewart to John Conness, cit. John Townley, "Reclamation in Nevada, 1850–1904" (Ph.D. diss., U. of Nevada, Reno, 1976), 171–72. Stewart finds a lone

scholarly defender in Thomas Alexander, *A Clash of Interests* (Provo, Utah, 1977), 146–55. According to this writer, Stewart was a beleaguered westerner fighting against outside powers that wanted to "lock up" his region's resources.

12. *Report of the Special Committee,* pt. 5, 23; F. H. Newell, *Report on Agriculture by Irrigation in the Western Part of the United States, at the Eleventh Census: 1890,* 52nd Cong., 1st sess., House Misc. Doc. 340 (Washington, 1894), pt. 20, 1. Cf. Richard Hinton, *Irrigation in the United States,* 49th Cong., 2nd sess., Senate Misc. Doc. 15 (Washington, 1887).

13. *Report of the Special Committee,* pt. 5, 17–23; Powell, "The Irrigable Lands of the Arid Region," *Century,* 39 (1890): 671–72.

14. Stegner, 338. Powell's general approach to social problems, Stegner suggests, anticipated the New Deal of the 1930s and the modern welfare state, but "the myth-bound West . . . insisted on running into the future like a streetcar on a gravel road" (p. 338).

15. *Report of the Special Committee,* pt. 5, 66.

16. Miles, "Our Unwatered Empire," *North American Rev.,* 150 (1890): 376.

17. Powell, "Institutions for the Arid Lands," 113. For Powell's populist position versus Mead's state-control scheme, see Robert Dunbar, "The Search for a Stable Water Right in Montana," *AH,* 28 (1954): 145.

18. *Report of the Special Committee,* pt. 5, 201.

19. *Ibid.,* 95, 200.

20. Powell, "Institutions for the Arid Lands," 68.

21. *Report of the Special Committee,* pt. 5, 17.

22. For the subsequent expansion of federal control over the basin, see Ira Clark, "The Elephant Butte Controversy," *J. of American History,* 61 (1975): 1006–33. Cf. Donald Pisani, "Federal Reclamation and Water Rights in Nevada," *AH,* 51 (1977): 540–58; and "State vs. Nation: Federal Reclamation and Water Rights in the Progressive Era," *PHR,* 51 (1982): 265–82.

23. Powell, "The Lesson of Conemaugh," *North American Rev.,* 149 (1889): 156. That disaster is described in more detail in David McCullough, *The Great Flood* (New York, 1968); see esp. pp. 262–63, on the irresponsibility of experts there.

Passages to India

1. Mary Hallock Foote, *A Victorian Gentlewoman in the Far West,* ed. Rodman Paul (San Marino, Calif., 1972), 269–329. Also, Rodman Paul, *When Culture Came to Boise: Mary Hallock Foote in Idaho,* Idaho Historical Series, no. 19 (1977); and Paul Murphy, "Early Irrigation in the Boise Valley," *Pacific Northwest Q.,* 44 (1953): 177–84. Wallace Stegner's novel *Angle of Repose* (1971) is based on Mary Foote's life in the West.

2. Foote, *Victorian Gentlewoman,* 265.

3. The drawing accompanied her article "Pictures of the Far West—VII," *Century*, 38 (1889): 299–300.

4. Foote, *The Chosen Valley* (Boston, 1892), 52–53, 314.

5. Wegmann's book, when it first appeared in 1888, had only 106 pages; the seventh edition (1922) had 553 pages, plus more than 100 pages of plates— evidence of the rapid maturation of American hydraulic engineering. On Arthur Foote's library, see *Victorian Gentlewoman*, 296–97. A result of his reading may have been his scheme to introduce the Nile's basin-irrigation system into California. See Foote, "The Redemption of the Great Valley of California," *ASCE Trans.*, 66 (1910): 229–79.

6. Deakin, *Irrigation in Western America* (Melbourne, 1885), 12, 36–38, 94.

7. Robert Hill, "Irrigation in the Texas-New Mexico Region," *Independent*, 45 (1893): 11.

8. See Oscar Lewis, *George Davidson* (Berkeley, 1954). Davidson's main interest, this biographer writes, "was always the practical application of advances in science to the problems of commerce and industry" (p. 49). For two decades he hired out to survey and promote private irrigation schemes, including that of James Haggin of Kern County.

9. *Report of the Board of Commissioners on the Irrigation of the San Joaquin, Tulare, and Sacramento Valleys of the State of California*, 43rd Cong., 1st sess., House Exec. Doc. 290 (Washington, 1874), 25, 39, 40.

10. Davidson, "The Application of Irrigation to California" (1879), in Alonzo Phelps, ed., *Contemporary Biography of California's Representative Men* (San Francisco, 1881), 123; Davidson, *Irrigation and Reclamation of Lands for Agricultural Purposes as Now Practiced in India, Egypt, Italy, etc.*, 44th Cong., 1st sess., Senate Exec. Doc. 94 (Washington, 1875). Cf. Robert Burton Buckley, *The Irrigation Works of India*, 2nd ed. (London, 1905).

11. Wilson, "The Irrigation Problem in Montana," *National Geographic*, 2 (1889): 212–29.

12. Wilson, "Irrigation in India," U.S. Geological Survey, *12th Annual Report, 1890–91* (Washington, 1891), pt. 2, 369; Wilson, "American Irrigation Engineering," *Trans. ASCE.*, 25 (1891): 161. See also his "Irrigation in India," *Trans. ASCE.*, 23 (1890): 217–53; and "Irrigation Engineering," *Independent*, 45 (1893): 3.

13. U.S. Geological Survey, *13th Annual Report, 1891–92* (Washington, 1893), pt. 3, 120.

14. Wilson, *Manual of Irrigation* (New York, 1893), 40–41. Cf. Franklin King, *Irrigation and Drainage*, 5th ed. (New York, 1907), 208–17; and John Widtsoe, *The Principles of Irrigation Practice* (New York, 1920), 331–47.

15. Willcocks, *Sixty Years in the East* (Edinburgh, 1935), 266. This autobiography is a revealing portrait of the morally zealous British irrigation brigade. "The white man's real burden," Willcocks writes, "lies in replenishing the earth and subduing it" (pp. 72–73).

16. Deakin, *Irrigated India* (London, 1893), 20, 21, 26, 234.
17. *Ibid.*, 237.
18. Whitcombe, *Agrarian Conditions in Northern India*, vol. 1 (Berkeley, 1972), 119. For a parallel in economic dislocation see Robert Tignor, *Modernization and British Rule in Egypt, 1882–1914* (Princeton, 1966), 214–48. Under British engineering Egypt went from being self-sufficient to being a food-importing country.
19. Tignor, 71, 76–78.
20. See Hilgard, T. C. Jones, and R. W. Furnas, *Report on the Climatic and Agricultural Features of the Arid Region of the Pacific Slope* (Washington, 1882), 29–44; Hilgard, *Report on the Physical and Agricultural Features of the State of California* (San Francisco, 1884), 99; and especially Hilgard, "Alkali Lands, Irrigation and Drainage in Their Mutual Relations," appendix to *California State Experiment Station Report, 1890* (Sacramento, 1892). Hilgard's life and work are discussed in *Science*, 43 (1916): 447–53.
21. Mead, *The Arid Public Lands—Their Reclamation, Management, and Disposal*, 55th Cong., 1st sess., House Doc. 130 (Washington, 1897), 18.
22. John Stow, cit. Keith Thomas, *Man and the Natural World* (New York, 1983), 276.
23. Newell, "Discussion," *ASCE Trans.*, 62 (1909): 10–11; Newell, *Water Resources* (New Haven, Conn., 1920), 191.
24. "The Colorado River" (1912), Lippincott Papers, WRCA/UCB. Cf. this statement by R. H. Forbes, *The River-Irrigating Waters of Arizona*, U. of Arizona Agricultural Experiment Station Bull. 44 (1902), 206: "When the Colorado is understood and utilized as successfully as is its greater and better known parallel, it will be recognized as the American Nile, the creator of a new country for the irrigator, and Mother of an Occidental Egypt."

A Long, Strong Rope

1. *Cong. Rec.*, 11 Aug. 1894, 8422–23.
2. Paul Gates, *History of Public Land Law Development* (Washington, 1968), 650–51; William Smythe, *The Conquest of Arid America* (Seattle, 1969), 193–94, 270–71; and Benjamin Hibbard, *A History of Public Land Policies* (Madison, Wis., 1965), 437.
3. Lewis Gould, *Wyoming* (New Haven, Conn., 1968), 131–33.
4. Mead, "Arid Public Lands," 4–5.
5. See Mary Ellen Glass, *Water for Nevada* (Reno, 1964), on that state's agricultural situation through the 1890s. On its controversies with California, there is Donald Pisani, "Storm over the Sierra: A Study in Western Water Use" (Ph.D. diss., U. of California, Davis, 1975).
6. Lilley and Gould, "The Western Irrigation Movement, 1878–1902," in Gene

Gressley, ed., *The American West*, (Laramie, Wyo., 1966), 72–74. Like the engineers, they equate a "rational" with a national program of water development. A contrasting view is presented by Stanley Davidson, "The Leadership of the Reclamation Movement, 1875–1902" (Ph.D. diss., U. of California, Berkeley, 1951). Davidson believes the federal program was the work of irrational, sentimental reformers and crusaders who imposed it on the West. The truth is that federalization was the product of an imperialist, expansionary culture and that reformers, rationalizers, and western economic interests alike gave it their enthusiastic support.

7. Chittenden, *Preliminary Examination of Reservoir Sites in Wyoming and Colorado*, 55th Cong., 2nd sess., House Exec. Doc. 141 (Washington, 1897), 55. See Gordon Dodds, *Hiram Martin Chittenden* (Lexington, Ky., 1973), 31–41. "The Chittenden report," wrote William Smythe, "represents the break of day" (*Conquest*, 271).

8. Mead, "Arid Public Lands," 7. He moved a step closer to federalization in his "Rise and Future of Irrigation in the United States," *Yearbook of the U.S. Dept. of Agriculture, 1899* (Washington, 1900), 609.

9. Warren to William Stapleton, Warren Papers, U. of Wyoming. Stapleton was editor of the Denver *Republican* newspaper, which vehemently fought against federalization. Warren, however, did an about-face and supported it. On Maxwell, see Andrew Hudanick, Jr., "George Hebard Maxwell," *JW*, 14 (1975): 108–21; and John Ganoe, "The Origin of a National Reclamation Policy," *Mississippi Valley Historical Rev.*, 18 (1931): 39–40.

10. Smythe, 273–74. The Silver Republicans explicitly called for a national government construction program, while the Republicans spoke more vaguely of "adequate national legislation" that would leave water distribution in the hands of the states. The Democratic platform spoke only of the need for "an intelligent system" of water development.

11. *The Public Papers of Francis G. Newlands,* ed. Arthur Darling, 2 vols. (Boston, 1932), 2: 65. Newlands apparently relied heavily on F. H. Newell's advice in drafting his bill. Townley (p. 304) argues that Newlands was motivated mainly by a desire to recoup on some bad personal irrigation investments and by political considerations.

12. 32 Stat. 388.

13. *Cong. Rec.,* 13 June 1902, 6778. Eastern and midwestern opposition was hardly intense or widespread. Seven of the 10 Massachusetts representatives failed to vote at all, 2 voted in favor. Illinois's representatives voted 13 in favor, 1 opposed, 8 not voting. The largest number of nays came from Pennsylvania (13), then New York (8), and Ohio (7). There was not a single nay from west of the Mississippi.

14. On Roosevelt's active support, see Smythe, 281–93. Roosevelt fiercely resented Newlands's hogging all the credit for the legislation, even claiming the Nevadan "had nothing to do with getting the bill through." Roosevelt to

Charles Fletcher Lummis, *The Letters of Theodore Roosevelt*, ed. Elting Morison, vol. 3 (Cambridge, Mass., 1951), 317.

15. J. Leonard Bates, "Fulfilling American Democracy: The Conservation Movement, 1907 to 1921," *Mississippi Valley Historical Rev.*, 44 (1957): 29–57; Roy Robbins, *Our Landed Heritage*, rev. ed. (Lincoln, Neb., 1976), esp. 330–33. More recently, Richard Alston has made somewhat the same case in his "Commercial Irrigation Enterprise: The Fear of Water Monopoly and the Genesis of Market Distortion" (Ph.D. diss., Cornell U., 1970). Alston criticizes reclamation leaders for being so afraid of monopoly that they destroyed the market-allocation mechanism in water development, which would have led to more "productive" use of the resource. Although he overstates the antimonopoly fear, Alston has a point: from its beginning federal reclamation was exempted from the dicta of Adam Smith.

16. Hays, *Conservation and the Gospel of Efficiency* (New York, 1969), preface. Hays declares: "The modern American conservation movement grew out of the firsthand experience of federal administrators and political leaders with problems of Western economic growth, and more precisely with Western water development" (p. 5).

17. The latest and most successful effort to clear away the confusion surrounding Progressivism is Daniel Rodgers's essay in *Reviews in American History*, 10 (1982): 113–32. He describes three distinct "languages" among the Progressives: that of antimonopolism, that of social bondedness, and that of technical efficiency. All of them were indubitably found among the proponents of federal reclamation, with all the internal contradictions that Rodgers indicates.

18. *Cong. Rec.*, 21 Jan. 1902, 836–37.

19. *Ibid.*, 27 March 1902, 6723–24, 6726.

20. *Ibid.*, 6742. George Ray et al., "Views of the Minority," *Irrigation and Reclamation of Arid Lands*, 57th Cong., 1st sess., House Report 794 (Washington, 1902), pt. 2.

21. *Cong. Rec.*, 1 March 1902, 2278, 2282, 2283; 27 March, 6730, 6743, 6747.

22. *Ibid.*, 27 March 1902, 6740.

23. *Ibid.*, 6 February 1902, 1383.

24. *Ibid.*, 1 March 1902, 2283; 27 March, 6755.

25. *Ibid.*, 27 March 1902, 6734. Newlands persisted in claiming that the 1902 act aimed mainly at social reform. In a California address he maintained that the act's purpose was "to destroy land monopoly; not only to prevent the monopoly of the public land, but to break up the existing land monopolies throughout the arid region." *Sacramento Valley Development Assoc. Bull.* 23 (1905): 15. He was surely speaking for himself, not for the William Stewarts and other conservatives in Congress, who also readily voted for it.

26. Lampen, *Economic and Social Aspects of Federal Reclamation* (Baltimore, 1930).

Failure

1. F. H. Newell, "The Reclamation of the West," *Smithsonian Institution Annual Report, 1903* (Washington, 1904), 827–41; Alfred Golzé, *Reclamation in the United States* (Caldwell, Idaho, 1961), 26–28.

2. F. H. Newell, "The Work of the Reclamation Service," *Smithsonian Institution Annual Report, 1904* (Washington, 1905), 328. The total amount in the fund when the first projects were authorized in 1904 was $23 million.

3. *Cong. Rec.*, 21 June 1910, 8684–89. One of the largest of those projects was the one in Yakima Valley, Washington, which had started out as a private venture organized around the Sunnyside Canal. See Calvin Coulter, "The New Settlers on the Yakima Project, 1880–1910," *Pacific Northwest Q.*, 61 (1970): 10–21; and "The Victory of National Irrigation in the Yakima Valley, 1902–1906," *ibid.*, 42 (1951): 99–122. Also, Emmet Vandervere, "History of Irrigation in Washington" (Ph.D. diss., U. of Washington, 1948), 142–91.

4. Arthur P. Davis, "Investigations in Arizona," *Proceedings of the First Conference of Engineers of the Reclamation Service*, U.S. Geological Survey, Water-Supply and Irrigation Paper (Washington, 1904), 129–30; H. L. Meredith, "Reclamation in the Salt River Valley, 1902–1917," *JW*, 7 (1968): 76–83; Christine Lewis, "The Early History of the Tempe Canal Company," *Arizona and the West*, 7 (1965): 227–38.

5. George Wharton James, *Reclaiming the Arid West* (New York, 1917), 65–85.

6. U.S. Bureau of Reclamation, *Landownership Survey on Federal Reclamation Projects* (Washington, 1946), tables 2, 3, and 6.

7. *Official Proceedings of the Thirteenth National Irrigation Congress* (Portland, 1905), 28–30. Calls for amending the 1902 law to exempt established owners from acreage limitation were never voted on at the congress; the issue was considered too disruptive of the reclamation cause.

8. Lampen, *Federal Reclamation*, 60.

9. Tucker, *First Conference of Engineers*, 124.

10. Gillette, "Reclamation from the Viewpoint of the Settler," *Irrigation Age*, 31 (1916): 120; Means, "Discussion of Irrigation," *Trans. ASCE*, 62 (1909): 44.

11. See Richard Beidleman, "The Gunnison River Diversion Project," *Colorado Mag.*, 36 (1959): 187–201, 266–85; M. F. Cunningham, "Cashing in on Natural Wealth," *Harper's Weekly*, 61 (1915): 369; Newell, *Water Resources*, 160–61.

12. Ray Teele, *Irrigation in the United States* (New York, 1915), 219, 227, 234–35. Lampen (pp. 67–68) calculates that the average cost overrun on federal projects was 176%. On the Idaho cases see Charles Coate, "Federal-Local Relationships on the Boise and Minidoka Projects, 1904–1926," *Idaho Yesterdays*, 25 (1981): 7–8; H. H. Caldwell and M. Wells, *Economic and Ecological History Support Study*, Idaho Water Resource Board (Moscow, Idaho, 1974), 45–50.

13. Francis Tracy, *Private Irrigation Enterprise Compared with Government Reclamation*, 62nd Cong., 2nd sess., Senate Doc. 869 (Washington, 1912), 19, 21.

14. Layton, *The Revolt of the Engineers* (Cleveland, 1971), vii, 117–27. The "engineer-technocrat" who replaced Newell is discussed in Gene Gressley, "Reclamation and the West via Arthur Powell Davis," *The Twentieth-Century American West* (Columbia, Mo., 1977), 78–101; and "Arthur Powell Davis, Reclamation and the West," *AH*, 42 (1968): 241–58. Gressley finds no inconsistency between Davis's "Jeffersonian" values and his technocratic drive to plan and manage. It makes more sense, I think, to see the democratic rhetoric of such a man as a species of self-deception and nostalgia rather than as a serious political program.

15. James, xv. This book is a clear example of the effort to legitimate modern bureaucratic and technical power as a democratizing force. Editorial, *Irrigation Age*, 30 (1915): 69.

16. *Cong. Rec.*, 28 Fed. 1922, 3174; Committee of Special Advisors on Reclamation, *Federal Reclamation by Irrigation*, 68th Cong., 1st sess., Senate Doc. 92 (Washington, 1924), xi.

17. Committee of Special Advisors, 26, 80; Samuel Fortier, *Trans. ASCE*, 90 (1927): 688. Alvin Johnson found a "forbidding squalor" on many projects. "Economic Aspects of Certain Reclamation Projects," in U.S. Bureau of Reclamation, *Economic Problems of Reclamation* (Washington, 1929), 16.

18. George Kreutzer, *Conference on Reclamation and Land Settlement, 14–15 December, 1925* (Washington, 1925), 15.

19. Committee of Special Advisors, xii, xvi.

20. Teele, "The Federal Subsidy in Land Reclamation," *J. of Land and Public Utility Economics*, 3 (1927): 339–40; Newell, *ASCE Trans.*, 90 (1927): 705–6. "This subsidy," declared the secretary of agriculture, "seems inconsistent with the efforts now being made by the Federal Government to restrict agricultural production." *Report of the Secretary of Agriculture, 1930* (Washington, 1930), 40–41. Cf. Ray Teele, *Economics of Land Reclamation in the United States* (London, 1927), 54; and Joseph Sax, "Selling Reclamation Water Rights," *Michigan Law Rev.*, 64 (1965): 13–46.

21. Smith and Padfield, "Land, Water, and Social Institutions," in William McGinnies and Bram Goldman, eds., *Arid Lands in Perspective* (Tucson, 1969), 327–28.

22. One of the few scholars who has noted the impact of reclamation federalization on local western communities is Michael Robinson in his *Water for the West* (Chicago, 1979), 32–33.

23. A good but excessively enthusiastic account, which exaggerates Mead's "humanitarianism," is Paul Conkin, "The Vision of Elwood Mead," *AH*, 34 (1960): 88–97. A different Mead, one in harmony with Coolidge's business-oriented presidency, appears in Donald Swain, *Federal Conservation Policy, 1921–1933* (Berkeley, 1963), 81–95. But Swain makes too large a distinction

between Mead and his predecessors, and he generously concludes that Mead's more businesslike policies were "sagacious" and effective.

24. Mead, *Helping Men Own Farms* (New York, 1920), 141. In large part Mead's agrarian utopia was designed to ward off radical challenges from groups like the Industrial Workers of the World; see pp. 131, 198. Donald Pisani comes to conclusions rather similar to my own in his article "Reclamation and Social Engineering in the Progressive Era," *AH,* 57 (1983): 46–63.

25. James Kluger, "Elwood Mead: Irrigation Engineer and Social Planner" (Ph.D. diss., U. of Arizona, 1970), 29n, 214. Kluger also relates (p. 63) how Mead, while inveighing against speculators, himself made a good deal of money in real-estate ventures. Mead's racial prejudices appear in *Helping Men Own Farms,* where he laments the entry of the Japanese into California agriculture (p. 5); and in "Making the Desert Bloom," *Current History,* 31 (1929), where he proudly announces that 96% of federal project settlers are either old-stock Americans or European immigrants (p. 129).

26. Mead, *Helping Men Own Farms,* 40–96; and "Federal Reclamation—What Should It Include?" 6–7, 10–12; Kluger, 71–86.

27. Kluger, 86.

28. Mead, *Helping Men Own Farms,* 203.

29. Roy Smith, "The California Land Settlements at Durham and Delhi," *Hilgardia,* 15 (1943): 463–66, 478.

30. Kreutzer, cit. Lampen, 117. Cf. Ignatius O'Donnell's settler guidebook published by the Reclamation Service, *Better Business: Better Farming: Better Living* (Washington, 1918). Every irrigated farm, he instructs, should be planned as "a manufacturing plant" and farmers should learn the "community spirit . . . in a businesslike manner because it is good business" (p. 7).

31. Widtsoe, *Success on Irrigation Projects* (New York, 1928), 138.

V. FLORESCENCE:

The Grapes of Wealth

A Place Named Imperial

1. The historical geology of the Colorado River is described in E. Blackwelder, "Origin of the Colorado River," *Bull. of the Geological Society of America,* 36 (1934): 551–66; Godfrey Sykes, *The Colorado Delta,* Carnegie Inst. Pub. 460 (Washington, 1937), 37–107; Henry James, "The Salient Geographical Factors of the Colorado River and Basin," *Annals,* 135 (Jan. 1928): 97–107; Israel Russell, *Rivers of North America* (New York, 1898), 271–75; Clarence Dutton, *Tertiary History of the Grand Canyon District,* U.S. Geological Survey

Monograph 2 (Washington, 1882); Fred Kniffen, "The Natural Landscape of the Colorado Delta," *U. of California Pub. in Geography*, 5 (1931–32): 149–244. On the ecology of the Grand Canyon itself, see James Hastings and Raymond Turner, *The Changing Mile* (Tucson, 1965); and Joseph Wood Krutch, *Grand Canyon* (New York, 1958).

2. H. T. Cory, *The Imperial Valley and Salton Sink* (San Francisco, 1915); Daniel MacDougal, *The Salton Sea* (Washington, 1914); C. E. Grunsky, "The Lower Colorado River and the Salton Basin," *Trans. ASCE*, 59 (1907): 1–62.

3. Helen Hosmer, "Triumph and Failure in the Imperial Valley," in T. H. Watkins, ed., *The Grand Canyon* (Palo Alto, Calif., 1969), 206–7; Frank Waters, *The Colorado* (New York, 1974), 296–7; Donald Pisani, *From the Family Farm to Agribusiness* (Berkeley, 1984), chap. 4.

4. J. A. Alexander, *The Life of George Chaffey* (Melbourne, 1928), 292. See also Frederick Kershner, Jr., "George Chaffey and the Irrigation Frontier," *AH*, 27 (1953): 115–23.

5. John Ganoe, "The Desert Land Act Since 1891," *AH*, 11 (1937): 276.

6. George Kennan, *E. H. Harriman* (Boston, 1922), II, 132–35. See also Charles Rockwood, "Born of the Desert," Calexico *Chronicle* (May 1909); Robert Schonfield, "The Early Development of California's Imperial Valley," *Southern California Q.*, 50 (1968): 279–307, 395–426; Allen Day, "The Inundation of the Salton Sea by the Colorado River and How It Was Caused," *Scientific American*, 94 (1906): 310–12.

7. H. T. Cory describes this battle in his paper "Irrigation and River Control in the Colorado River Delta," *Trans. ASCE*, 76 (1913): 1204–1453. See also Kennan, II, 136–73; Remi Nadeau, *The Water Seekers* (Santa Barbara, Calif., 1974), 148–65; and "The Salton Sea," *Scientific American*, 116 (1917): 415.

8. Harold Bell Wright, *The Winning of Barbara Worth* (New York, 1966), 58–59, 98.

9. *Ibid.*, 290.

10. J. Smeaton Chase, *California Desert Trails* (Boston, 1919), 358.

11. *Ibid.*, 286–87.

12. Frank Adams, *Irrigation Districts in California*, California State Div. of Engineering and Irrigation Bull. 21 (Sacramento, 1929), 338.

13. *Ibid.*, 337–43. See also Carl Grunsky, *The Colorado River in Its Relation to the Imperial Valley, California*, 65th Cong., 1st sess., Senate Doc. 103 (Washington, 1917).

14. Adams, 345. Albert Chandler, "Irrigation in California," in Zoeth Eldredge, ed., *History of California*, vol. 3 (New York, 1915), 309–11.

15. Ernest Leonard, "The Imperial Irrigation District" (Ph.D. diss., Claremont Graduate School, 1972), 63, 80–85, 153.

16. *Ibid.*, 83–91, 98–110.

17. Alexander, 306.

18. Newell, cit. M. L. Requa and H. T. Cory, *The California Irrigated Farm Problem* (Washington, 1919), 157–74.

19. Requa and Cory, 22, 59–60, 114–15.

20. Leonard, 8–9.

21. *Problems of Imperial Valley and Vicinity*, 67th Cong., 2nd sess., Senate Doc. 142 (Washington, 1922); Norris Hundley, "The Politics of Reclamation," *California Historical Q.*, 52 (1973): 305–8; Beverley Moeller, *Phil Swing and Boulder Dam* (Berkeley, 1971), 11–12. Hiram Johnson, "The Boulder Canyon Project," *Annals*, 135 (1928): 153, 156.

22. L. M. Holt, "The Reclamation Service and the Imperial valley," *Overland Monthly*, 51 (1908): 72. Also, L. M. Holt, "How the Reclamation Service Is Robbing the Settler," *ibid.* (1907): 510–12; Andrew Chaffey, discussion, *Trans. ASCE*, 75 (1913): 1527–28; Alexander, 317–33.

23. Hundley, "Politics of Reclamation," 297, 310–15; Moeller, 16–24.

24. Norris Hundley, *Water and the West* (Berkeley, 1975), 184–85, 192–93, 308–10. Also see Reuel Olson, "The Colorado River Compact" (Ph.D. diss., Harvard U., 1926). Mexico was allotted 1.5 million acre-feet a year under the compact.

25. Mary Austin, "The Colorado River Controversy," *Nation*, 125 (1927): 512.

26. The standard account of the dam's construction is Paul Kleinsorge, *The Boulder Canyon Project* (Stanford, Calif., 1941), 185–230. See also Imre Sutton, "Geographical Aspects of Construction Planning: Hoover Dam Revisited," *JW*, 7 (1968): 301–44. The American Society of Civil Engineers criticized the dam as speculative and promotional; Elwood Mead replied to their charge in "Economic Justification for Reclamation Activities," *Reclamation Era*, 21 (1930): 18–21. His main arguments had to do with saving Imperial Valley from floods and guaranteeing the growth of coastal cities.

27. Hundley, *Water and the West*, 333. For an excellent account of the Six Companies and their role in the new West, see Peter Wiley and Robert Gottlieb, *Empires in the Sun* (New York, 1982), 15–23, 30–35.

28. *Ninth Annual Report of the Reclamation Service, 1908–1910* (Washington, 1911).

29. Robert Findley, "An Economic History of the Imperial Valley of California to 1971" (Ph.D. diss., U. of Oklahoma, 1974), 689–72. Findley reprints the Wilbur letter and believes it is a reasonable reading of the law. More convincing is Paul Taylor, "Water, Land, and Environment in Imperial Valley," *Natural Resources J.*, 13 (Jan. 1973): 1–35. Taylor discusses the more recent ruling, in 1964, against Imperial exemption by Solicitor of the Interior Frank Barry and the subsequent court cases on the matter: *U.S.* v. *Imperial Irrigation District* (1970–71), *Yellen* v. *Hickel* (1971–72). In 1980 a conservative Supreme Court upheld the Wilbur exemption.

"I Never Knowed They Was Anything Like Her"

1. See page 47.
2. *Fourteenth Census of the U.S.: 1920, vol. 7, Irrigation and Drainage* (Washington, 1922), 15, 69ff.
3. Elwood Mead, *Irrigation Institutions* (New York, 1910), 380–81.
4. Albert Henley, "Land Value Taxation by California Irrigation Districts," *American J. of Economics and Sociology,* 27 (1968): 380. Also see Hendrick Teilmann, "The Role of Irrigation Districts in California's Water Development," *ibid.,* 22 (1963): 409–15; Wells Hutchins, *Irrigation Districts,* USDA Technical Bull. 254 (1931). Hutchins counted 407 active districts in the West by 1928, 73 of them in California, ranging in size from 288 acres to 557,000. The other major form of local organization was the mutual water company, which was a private utility in which farmers were at once the stockholders and consumers.
5. Sidney Harding, "Preliminary Office Report on the Possibilities of Forming an Irrigation District in Madera County, California," 11 Jan. 1916, WRCA /UCB. Richard Adams and W. W. Bedford, *The Marvel of Irrigation* (San Francisco, 1921), 18–20. The role of irrigation in creating advanced business farming is touched on by Lawrence Jelinek, *Harvest Empire* (San Francisco, 1980), 55; and M. R. Benedict, "The Economic and Social Structure of California Agriculture," in C. B. Hutchison, ed., *California Agriculture* (Berkeley, 1946), 401–2.
6. R. E. Hodges and E. J. Wickson, *Farming in California* (San Francisco, 1928), 34, 38. E. J. Wickson, *Rural California* (New York, 1923), 383–85; "The California Fruit Industry," in Eldredge, vol. 5 (New York, 1915), 321–42; H. E. Erdman, "The Development and Significance of California Cooperatives, 1900–1915," *AH,* 33 (1958): 179–84; Erich Kraemer and H. E. Erdman, *History of Cooperation in the Marketing of California Fresh Deciduous Fruits,* U. of California Agricultural Experiment Station Bull. 557 (1933), 117–20. One of the largest of these cooperatives was the California Packing Company, organized in 1916 by an Italian immigrant, Mark Fontana; later it became Del Monte, the largest cannery operation in the world (Jelinek, 64).
7. Cross, "Cooperation in California," *American Economic Rev.,* 1 (1911): 543–44. On the influence of business values in western agriculture, see Gerald Nash, "Rural Society in the Far West," in James Shideler, ed., *Agriculture in the Development of the Far West* (Washington, 1975), 53–54; Elvin Hatch, *Biography of a Small Town* (New York, 1979), 267–71.
8. Karl Marx, *Capital,* trans. Samuel Moore and Edward Aveling (New York, 1906), 366–68.
9. Linda Majka and Theo Majka, *Farm Workers, Agribusiness, and the State* (Philadelphia, 1982), 9.
10. Jefferson Davis, "Slavery in the Territories," *Congressional Globe,* 14 Feb.

1850, app. 1, 154. Blacks, of course, did become part of the labor pool of the irrigated West, especially in Texas.

11. *California Farmer*, 26 May 1854, 164.

12. Charles Nordhoff, *California: For Health, Pleasure, and Residence* (New York, 1872), 90; Lloyd Fisher, *The Harvest Labor Market in California* (Cambridge, Mass., 1953), 4; Ping Chiu, *Chinese Labor in California, 1850–1880* (Madison, Wis., 1963), chap. 5.

13. Masakazu Iwata, "The Japanese Immigrants in California Agriculture," *AH*, 36 (1962): 25–37; Robert Higgs, "The Wealth of Japanese Tenant Farmers in California, 1909," *ibid.*, 53 (1979): 488–93; Adon Poli and Warren Engstrand, "Japanese Agriculture on the Pacific Coast," *J. of Land and Public Utility Economics*, 21 (1945): 352–64; Emil Bunje, *The Story of Japanese Farming in California* (Berkeley, 1957).

14. Dhan Mukerji, *Caste and Outcast* (New York, 1923), 269–70.

15. Carey McWilliams, *Factories in the Field* (Santa Barbara, Calif., 1971), 130–33.

16. Leo Grebler, Joan Moore, and Ralph Guzman, *The Mexican-American People* (New York, 1970), 61–66; Paul Taylor, "The Desert Shall Rejoice, and Blossom as the Rose," in T. H. Watkins, ed., *The Grand Colorado* (Palo Alto, Calif., 1969), 158; Ernesto Galarza, *Merchants of Labor* (Charlotte, N.C., 1964), chaps. 1–3. Carey McWilliams, *North from Mexico* (New York, 1968), provides useful background, as do Manuel Gamio's *Mexican Immigration to the United States* (Chicago, 1930), and Paul Taylor's multivolume series *Mexican Labor in the United States* (Berkeley, 1928–32).

17. 78th Cong., 1st sess., Senate Report 1150, (Washington, 1942), pt. 4, 522–23; Edwin Pendleton, "History of Labor in Arizona Irrigated Agriculture" (Ph.D. diss., U. of California, Berkeley, 1950), 597–98, 618, 629–30.

18. Pendleton, 68, 123–25; Paul Taylor, "Power Farming and Labor Displacement in the Cotton Belt," *Monthly Labor Rev.*, 44 (1938): 27–28.

19. A good account of this movement is Walter Stein, *California and the Dust Bowl Migration* (Westport, Conn., 1973), esp. 3–27.

20. Paul Taylor and Tom Vasey, "Drought Refugee and Labor Migration to California, June–December 1935," *Monthly Labor Rev.*, 42 (1936): 312–18; Edward Rowell, "Drought Refugee and Labor Migration to California in 1936," *ibid.*, 43 (1936): 1355–63. See also David McEntire, "Migrants and Resettlement in the Pacific Coast States," *Land Policy Rev.*, 1 (1938): 1–7; Paul Taylor, "Again the Covered Wagon," *Survey Graphic*, 24 (1935): 348–51, 368.

21. Pendleton, 47–49.

22. "I Wonder Where We Can Go Now," *Fortune*, 19 (1939), 91–92; U.S. Dept. of Labor, Bureau of Labor Statistics, *Three Decades of Labor* (Washington, n.d.), 28–30.

23. Walter Stein, "The 'Okie' as Farm Laborer," in Shideler, 214–15.

24. McWilliams, *Factories*, 230–32, 260–63.
25. Cletus Daniel, *Bitter Harvest* (Ithaca, N.Y., 1981), 108–9, 141–66.
26. *Pacific Rural Press*, 16 Dec. 1939, reports on the annual convention of Associated Farmers in Stockton. One attendee charged McWilliams with being a rouser of class hatred and a teacher of "communistic doctrines, of which neither a Lenin or a Stalin need feel ashamed." And the leader of the "wives' group" complained that radicals like McWilliams were turning California into "a sort of bird refuge for cuckoos, scolding jays, and sharp-billed butcher birds."
27. Carey McWilliams, *The Education of Carey McWilliams* (New York, 1979), 27–38; McWilliams, "A Man, a Place, and a Time," *American West*, 7 (1970), 4–5, 7.
28. Robert Benton, "The Ecological Nature of *Cannery Row*," in Richard Astro and Tetsumaro Hayashi, eds., *Steinbeck: The Man and His Work* (Corvallis, Ore., 1971), 131–39.
29. John Steinbeck, *The Grapes of Wrath* (New York, 1939), 126. Page references are to the Viking Compass edition.
30. *Ibid.*, 310.
31. *Ibid.*, 279.
32. McWilliams, *Factories*, 234–35.
33. *Ibid.*, 5.
34. *Ibid.*, 325.
35. See R. W. Davies, *The Socialist Offensive* (Cambridge, Mass., 1980); and *The Soviet Collective Farm, 1929–1930* (Cambridge, Mass., 1980). Also Moshé Lewin, *Russian Peasants and Soviet Power* (Evanston, Ill., 1968), 446–513.

Who Rules the Great Valley?

1. William Brown and S. B. Show, *California Rural Land Use and Management* (Washington, 1944), 2: 371.
2. Frank Adams, David Morgan, and Walter Packard, "Economic Report on San Joaquin Valley Acres Being Considered for Water Supply Relief Under Proposed California State Water Plan," 12 Nov. 1930, typescript, NA/RG 115, 8; F. E. Schmidt, "Report on Value of Central Valley Project Irrigation Supply to the Upper San Joaquin Valley in California," March 1942, typescript, NA/RG 115, 13. Schmidt notes that "insufficiency of water supply did not compel curtailment of acreage"; in fact, farmers there, responding to good markets, upped their acreage by 21% in the 1930s (p. 20). See also California Division of Water Resources, *San Joaquin River Basin Bull.* 29 (Sacramento, 1931), 33, 127–34. Also see S. T. Harding, *Water in California* (Palo Alto, Calif., 1960), 83.
3. Adams, Morgan, and Packard, 98.

4. Cecil Dunn and Philip Neff, *The Arvin Area of Kern County* (Bakersfield, 1947), 44; Sheridan Downey, *They Would Rule the Valley* (San Francisco, 1947), 171–81.

5. Resolutions Adopted at Water Users Conference, American Farm Bureau Federation, Los Angeles, 25–27 Feb. 1935, WRCA/UCB. See too Robert Dunbar, "Pioneering Groundwater Legislation in the United States" *PHR*, 47 (1978): 565–84; and Dunbar, *Forging New Rights in Western Waters* (Lincoln, Neb., 1983), 162–91.

6. Caughey, "The Californian and His Environment," *California Historical Q.*, 51 (1972): 199.

7. Marshall, *Irrigation of Twelve Million Acres in the Valley of California*, 16 March 1919, 3, 7. One story has it that Marshall came on his grand idea while sitting in his office on the Berkeley campus, looking out at the water flowing wastefully through the Golden Gate. See the transcribed oral history "Frank Adams, University of California, on Irrigation, Reclamation, and Water Administration," Bancroft/UCB, 1959, 299.

8. Donald Pisani, "Water Law Reform in California, 1900–1913," *AH*, 54 (1980): 316. The Water Commission Act of 1914 was the key legislative basis for a new centralized state water bureaucracy. See also Pisani, *From the Family Farm to Agribusiness* (Berkeley, 1984), chaps. 11–12; and Clarke Chambers, *California Farm Organizations* (Berkeley, 1952), 147–59.

9. Mary Montgomery and Marion Clawson, *History of Legislation and Policy Formation of the Central Valley Project* (Berkeley, 1948), 21–54. Montgomery, "Central Valley Project—Highlights of Its History," *Land Policy Rev.*, 9 (1946): 18–19.

10. Donald Swain, "The Bureau of Reclamation and the New Deal, 1933–1940," *Pacific Northwest Q.*, 61 (1970), 137–141.

11. The founding of the National Reclamation Association in 1932 followed Mead's speech "Necessity for Organized Western Support for Reclamation," reprinted in *Reclamation Era*, 24 (1933): 17–18. See also Mead, "Reclamation Under the New Deal," *ibid.*, 25 (1935): 1–2, 5.

12. James Pope, "Reclamation," *Reclamation Era*, 25 (1935): 5; *National Irrigation Policy—Its Development and Significance*, 76th Cong., 1st sess., Senate Doc. 36 (Washington, 1939), 2, 23–24, 26.

13. Paul Gates, *History of Public Land Law Development* (Washington, 1968), 691. The Reclamation Project Act of 1939 made official what had been unofficial policy for a long while: that the Bureau of Reclamation should be in the business of generating electrical power as well as irrigating crops—the so-called multipurpose mission. A good account of how hydropower came to finance the agency's program is Michael Robinson, "Conservation Ideals and Bureaucratic Self-Interest," paper read at American Historical Association meeting, Washington, 1980.

14. Adams, Morgan, and Packard, 13, 91.

15. Alfred Golzé, *Reclamation in the United States* (Caldwell, Idaho, 1961), 192–95; Robert de Roos, *The Thirsty Land* (New York, 1968), 6–7.

16. Schmidt, iv–v, 105–7. Nowhere in his calculations did this investigator explain how he arrived at so large an estimate of national benefits. Bureau of Reclamation, "Allocation of Costs," CVP Studies, Problem 8 (Washington, 1947), 2. As an astute foreign observer noted, "Much of the impetus behind any large-scale irrigation scheme comes from vested business interests that stand to gain from the resultant economic activity, whether ultimately the project as a whole shows profit or loss." H. J. Wood, "Water Plan for the Great Valley of California," *Economic Geography*, 14 (1938): 362. The original CVP repayment scheme assessed irrigators only 17%, though 63% of costs were for that use; see Paul Taylor, "Water, Land, and People in the Great Valley," *American West*, 5 (1968): 71.

17. Bureau of Reclamation, *Central Valley Basin*, 81st Cong., 1st sess., Senate Doc. 113 (Washington, 1949), 3.

18. "J. Rupert Mason on Single-Tax, Irrigation Districts, and Municipal Bankruptcy," transcribed oral history, Bancroft/UCB, 1959, 296.

19. B. W. Gearhart, *Cong. Rec.*, 1 July 1937, 6704. The promise of new homes was made to war veterans and defense industry workers, and before them, to migrants from eastern poverty and land calamities. One valley woman wrote to Secretary Ickes urging that the new irrigated acreage be opened to the poor rather than be left in the hands of the Associated Farmers; "I am thoroughly in favor of giving the dust-bowl farmers some such kind of chance." Anna Holden to Ickes, 24 March 1940, NA/RG 115. But that suggestion was never acted upon.

20. McWilliams, *California: The Great Exception* (New York, 1949), 329.

21. *Landownership Survey on Federal Reclamation Projects* (Washington, 1946), 24–25. There were altogether 106,338 separate ownerships on Bureau projects, covering 4,030,167 acres; 3,485 of those owners held more than 160 acres each, and 867 owned more than 320 acres. The Nevada exemption was for the Newlands project. On the other major area exempted, see Oliver Knight, "Correcting Nature's Error," *AH*, 30 (1956): 157–69. Knight argues that the Bureau "wanted the [Colorado] project at any cost" (p. 168). Also consult Ralph Wertheimer, "Legislative and Administrative History of Acreage Limitations and Control of Speculation on Federal Reclamation Projects," appendix to CVP Studies, Problem 19 (Berkeley, 1943), 40–48.

22. Barnes, memorandum to Madera Irrigation District Board of Directors, 31 Oct. 1940, WRCA/UCB.

23. Swain, 138. Ickes endorsed reclamation for the first time at the 1936 dedication of Boulder (later Hoover) Dam, when the vision of extracting "wealth" from water seized his imagination as firmly as it did that of any western booster.

24. Marion Clawson et al., "Economic Effects," CVP Studies, Problem 24 (Washington, 1949), 22, 239.

25. *Ibid.*, 113–14, 189–90, 194, 246.

26. Wilson and Clawson, "Agricultural Land Ownership and Operation in the Southern San Joaquin Valley," mimeographed report (Berkeley, 1945), 1. That degree of concentration was also rare in California; 95% of its irrigated farms in the mid-1940s were less than 160 acres in size.

27. Marion Clawson et al., "Acreage Limitation in the Central Valley," CVP Studies, Problem 19 (Berkeley, 1944), 28.

28. For background to this controversy see Paul Taylor, "Walter Goldschmidt's Baptism in Fire," *Paths to the Symbolic Self*, in *Anthropology UCLA*, 8 (1976): 129–40; and Richard Kirkendall, "Social Sciences in the Central Valley of California," *California Historical Society Q.*, 43 (1964): 185–218.

29. Goldschmidt, "Agribusiness and the Rural Community," *As You Sow* (Montclair, N.J., 1978), 304–14.

30. *Ibid.*, 296–303.

31. *Ibid.*, 315–20.

32. Packard, "Land and Power Development in California, Greece and Latin America," transcribed oral history, Bancroft/UCB, 1970, 579–81.

33. See Edward Banfield, *Government Project* (Glencoe, Ill., 1951). In the foreword Rexford Tugwell writes: "Our simple impulse to better the economic situation of a few almost hopelessly poverty-stricken folk in the Southwest came to grief not because the conception was bad or because the technique was mistaken but because the people there could not rise to the challenge. It was character which failed" (pp. 11–12).

34. Koppes, "Public Water, Private Land," *PHR*, 47 (1978): 616–17.

35. Packard, *The Economic Implications of the Central Valley Project* (Los Angeles, 1942), 73–77, 82, 83. See also Packard, "The Central Valley Project," *New Republic*, 113 (1945): 98–100.

36. Harding, "The State's Interest in the Central Valley Project," 6; Harper to Harding, 19 Dec. 1943; undated note from Schmidt: all in WRCA/UCB. See also Harding, "A Life in Western Water Development," transcribed oral history, Bancroft/UCB, 1967, 236–41.

37. Swett, testimony before the Commerce Committee, *Hearings on H.R. 3961*, 78th Cong., 2nd sess. (Washington, 1944), 617.

38. Ickes, foreword to Arthur Maass, *Muddy Waters* (Cambridge, Mass., 1951), xii. Maass's book is an excellent account of the Pine Flat episode; see also his "Administering the CVP," *California Law Rev.*, 38 (1950): 666–95, a plea for centralized bureaucratic control along the lines of the Tennessee Valley Authority. The struggle for coordinated management is discussed further in Merrill Goodall, "Land and Power Administration of the Central Valley Project," *J. of Land and Public of Utility Economics*, 18 (1942): 299–311.

39. Clawson et al., "Acreage Limitation in the Central Valley," 30–31.

40. The 1940s acreage-limitation battle is discussed in more detail by de Roos, 73–103; Alten Davis, "The Excess Land Law in the Central Valley of California" (Ph.D. diss., U. of California, Berkeley, 1962); Paul Taylor, "Central

Valley Project: Water and Land," *Western Political Q.*, 2 (1949): 228–53; Varden Fuller, "Acreage Limitation in Federal Irrigation Projects with Particular Reference to the Central Valley of California," *J. of Farm Economics*, 31 (1949): 976–82; and the pro-and-con articles in *California Law Rev.*, 38 (1950).

41. Senator Downey writes of DiGiorgio that his life "has been copied straight from the ingenuous pages of Horatio Alger. . . . He is American folklore come to life. He is the immigrant's byword, the Ellis Island legend" (*They Would Rule the Valley*, 172). Downey was replaced in the Senate in 1948 by Richard Nixon.

42. Straus indicated how "technical compliance" might be achieved in *Hearings on S. 912*, 80th Cong., 1st sess. (Washington, 1947), 104–12. See also Koppes, 624–25; and Lawrence Lee, "California Water Politics," *AH*, 54 (1980): 404.

43. Arthur Maass and Raymond Anderson, *And the Desert Shall Rejoice* (Cambridge, Mass., 1978), 366.

44. Central Valley farmers voted overwhelmingly to join the CVP in district elections. DiGiorgio likewise signed a contract with the Bureau, though protesting what he regarded as its "illegal and dictatorial position." Later, his 4,200-acre Sierra Vista Ranch was subdivided and sold by the Bureau in thirty-one parcels, at an average price of $250,000: there was at least that much teeth in the technical-compliance formula. See "The Bureau Coerces DiGiorgio," *California Farmer*, 196 (17 May 1952): 533; and *ibid.*, 238 (2 June 1973): 17–20, 22.

VI. EMPIRE:

Water and the Modern West

"Total Use for Greater Wealth"

1. DeVoto, "The West Against Itself," *Harper's*, 194 (Jan. 1947): 2.
2. Kerr, *Land, Wood and Water* (New York, 1960), 323–24; Johnson, *ibid.*, 10. See also Theodore Schad, "Water Resources Planning—Historical Development," *J. of Water Resources Planning and Management Div., Proc. ASCE*, 105 (1979): 16–20.
3. Webb, *More Water for Texas* (Austin, 1954), 2, 4, 54, 58.
4. Aspinall, "Reclamation Pays," *Cong. Rec.*, 27 June 1961, 11466; George Barr, "Discussion," *J. of Farm Economics*, 31 (1949): 983; Straus, *Why Not Survive?* (New York, 1955), esp. 78 ff. on American engineering abroad; Dixon, "Social and Economic Implications of Irrigation Development," *Civil*

Engineering, 22 (Sept. 1952): 106; Dominy, "The Overall Importance of Irrigation and Drainage Both Nationally and Internationally," *J. of Irrigation and Drainage Div., Proc. ASCE*, 90 (1964): 17.

5. "Endless Frontier," *Time*, 58 (30 July 1951): 48–51.

6. Joseph Kinsey Howard, "Golden River," *Harper's*, 190 (1945): 511–23; Rufus Terral, *The Missouri Valley* (New Haven, Conn., 1947), chap. 2; Richard Baumhoff, *The Dammed Missouri Valley* (New York, 1951); Henry Hart, *The Dark Missouri* (Madison, Wis., 1957), 59–64.

7. Albert Williams, *The Water and the Power* (New York, 1951), 217–23; *A Review of Reports on the Missouri River, for Flood Control*, 78th Cong., 2nd sess., House Doc. 475 (Washington, 1944); Pick, cit. Hart, 154. A devastating indictment of the Corps of Engineers and its treatment of the Missouri Sioux is Michael Lawson's *Dammed Indians* (Norman, Okla., 1982). Over 200,000 acres of tribal lands were flooded by dams in North and South Dakota, causing more such damage than any other public works projects in America.

8. Alfred Golzé, *Reclamation in the United States* (Caldwell, Idaho, 1961), 210–17; Hoover Commission on the Organization of the Executive Branch, *Task Force Report on Natural Resources* (Washington, 1949), 24.

9. Emmett Vandervere, "History of Irrigation in Washington," (Ph.D. diss., U. of Washington, 1948), 240. Good general histories are Stewart Holbrook, *The Columbia* (New York, 1956); and Murray Morgan, *The Columbia* (Seattle, 1949).

10. See D. W. Meinig, *The Great Columbia Plain* (Seattle, 1968), 3–16.

11. Bruce Mitchell, "Rufus Woods and Columbia River Development," *Pacific Northwest Q.*, 52 (1961): 139–44; Bruce Harding, "Water From Pend Oreille," *ibid.*, 45 (1954): 52–60; Richard Neuberger, *Our Promised Land* (New York, 1938), 64.

12. Neuberger, "The Biggest Thing on Earth," *Harper's*, 174 (1937): 249–50; Bureau of Reclamation, "Summary of Preliminary Economic Information: Columbia Basin Project—Washington," June 1945, NA/RG 195, 53; U.S. Dept. of Interior, *The Columbia River* (Washington, 1947), 22–23.

13. Clawson, cit. Carl Taylor, "The Sociologists' Part in Planning the Columbia Basin," *American Sociological Rev.*, 11 (1945): 331; Warne, "Memorandum for the Commissioner," 28 Jan. 1941, NA/RG 115. See also Carl Hesig, "New Farms on Newly Irrigated Land," *Land Policy Rev.*, 2 (Nov.–Dec. 1939): 10–16; and Bureau of Reclamation, *Settlement of the Columbia Basin Reclamation Project*, pamphlet (Washington, 1944). According to Jay Franklin, the paternalism of the Columbia project was "technical rather than political" and would lead, he predicted, to "a culture which will be both as stable as that of Egypt under the Pharaohs and as dynamic as a Detroit assembly line." *Remaking America* (Boston, 1942), 138.

14. Bureau of Reclamation, "Preliminary Economic Information," 8. See also Marion Clawson, "Post-War Irrigation Developments and the National and

Regional Economy," *J. of Farm Economics*, 27 (1945): 152, on the "growth complex" behind reclamation.

15. A thorough account of this episode is Norris Hundley's *Dividing the Waters* (Berkeley, 1966). The treaty also settled rival American and Mexican claims to the lower Rio Grande (pp. 131–32). On the conflict between Arizona and California, see John Terrell, *The War for the Colorado River*, 2 vols. (Glendale, Calif., 1965).

16. Dean Mann et al., *Legal-Political History of Water Resource Development in the Upper Colorado River Basin*, Lake Powell Research Project Bull. 4 (Los Angeles, 1974).

17. DeVoto to Kennedy, cit. Elmo Richardson, *Dams, Parks and Politics* (Lexington, Ky., 1973), 139.

18. For the dispute over Dinosaur see Richardson, 129–52; and Roderick Nash, *Wilderness and the American Mind*, 3rd ed. (New Haven, Conn., 1983), 209–20.

19. Later David Brower came to regret Glen Canyon Dam as the greatest failure of his environmentalist career. See John McPhee, *Encounters with the Archdruid* (New York, 1971), 143. For other environmentalists' reaction to the dam and the canyons it flooded see Eliot Porter, *The Place No One Knew* (San Francisco, 1963); and Edward Abbey, *Desert Solitaire* (New York, 1968), 151–52.

20. Hundley, *Water and the West* (Berkeley, 1975), 302. Arizona's groundwater-supply problems are discussed in Dean Mann, *The Politics of Water in Arizona* (Tucson, 1963), 43–66; Maurice Kelso, William Martin, and Lawrence Mack, *Water Supplies and Economic Growth in an Arid Environment* (Tucson, 1973); Lawrence McBride, "Arizona's Coming Dilemma," *Ecology Law Q.*, 2 (1972): 357–84; Robert Dunbar, "The Arizona Groundwater Controversy at Mid-Century," *Arizona and the West*, 19 (1977): 5–24.

21. Mann, 138–43; "Central Arizona Project," Bureau of Reclamation leaflet (Washington, n.d.); Rich Johnson, *The Central Arizona Project* (Tucson, 1977). Helen Ingram, "Politics of Water Allocation," in Dean Peterson and A. Berry Crawford, eds., *Values and Choices in the Development of the Colorado River Basin* (Tucson, 1978), 61–74, is excellent on the silencing of debate over CAP.

22. For the impact of energy development on this area, see Robert Durrenberger, "Colorado Plateau," in John Fraser Hart, ed., *Regions of the United States* (New York, 1972), 226–28; Alvin Josephy, Jr., "The Murder of the Southwest," *Audubon*, 73 (July 1971): 52–67; and Suzanne Gordon, *Black Mesa* (New York, 1973). The Indians were to be given 25 cents for each ton of coal mined on their lands. Peabody Coal Company, *Mining Coal on Black Mesa* (St. Louis, Mo., 1970), 3.

23. U.S. Dept. of Commerce, *1978 Census of Agriculture. Vol. 1, Summary and State Data* (Washington, 1981),

24. Bureau of Reclamation, *Water and Land Resource Accomplishments: 1977* (n.p., n.d.), 1–2; William Warne, *The Bureau of Reclamation* (New York, 1973), 16. See also Floyd Dominy, "The Role of Irrigation in the West's Expanding Economy," *J. of Irrigation and Drainage Div., Proc. ASCE*, 94 (1968): 401–18; and the rebuttal by William Martin, Robert Young, Maurice Kelso, and Jimmye Hillman, *ibid.*, 95 (1969): 611–16.

25. Aspinall, 11465–66; Bureau of Reclamation, *Water and Land Resource Accomplishments*, 5.

26. Bureau of Reclamation, *Water and Land Resource Accomplishments*, 8; Charles Howe and K. William Easter, *Interbasin Transfer of Water* (Baltimore, 1971), 140, 167. Other eastern attacks on the economic wisdom of western reclamation came from Otto Eckstein, *Water-Resource Development* (Cambridge, Mass., 1961), 192–236; and Vernon Ruttan, *The Economic Demand for Irrigated Acreage* (Baltimore, 1965). Ruttan pointed out (pp. 46–48) that western farmers were paying as little as $1.99 per acre for water that the government paid $66.19 to develop. See also Richard Berkman and W. Kip Viscusi, *Damming the West* (New York, 1973), 78–102; and Earl Heady, "Food and Agricultural Policies," *J. of Water Resources Planning and Management Div., Proc. ASCE*, 105 (1979), 151–59. Also, National Water Commission, *Water Policies for the Future* (Washington, 1973), 126–49, which, after surveying the achievements, recommended an end to future irrigation subsidies.

27. Moley, *What Price Federal Reclamation?* (New York, 1955), 21, 56. Hirschleifer, DeHaven, and Milliman, *Water Supply* (Chicago, 1960), 35, 358, 361. "In this country," these authors write, "water investments are typically undertaken prematurely and on an overambitious scale" (p. 359).

28. McKinley, *Uncle Sam in the Pacific Northwest* (Berkeley, 1952), 575. The Tennessee Valley Authority model was an unstable amalgam of political ideas: part centralized planning, replacing local control, and part decentralism, moving management out of the federal government. See David Lilienthal's idealizing account *TVA: Democracy on the March* (New York, 1944), esp. chap. 14.

29. Lowi, *The End of Liberalism*, 2nd ed. (New York, 1979), 279.

30. McConnell, *Private Power and American Democracy* (New York, 1966), 3–8 esp.

31. Huffman, *Irrigation Development and Public Water Policy* (New York, 1953), 5. A good example of this process is described in William Robbins, "The Willamette Valley Project of Oregon," *PHR.*, 47 (1978): 585–605, featuring in this case the Army Corps of Engineers and flood control. That centralization follows the growth of such state investments is the argument of Ian Gough in "State Expenditure in Advanced Capitalism," *New Left Rev.*, 92 (1975): 85.

32. Miliband, *The State in Capitalistic Society* (New York, 1969), 207. Despite its simplistic emphasis on class hegemony, this book is immensely illuminating for the student of western water history.

Accumulation and Legitimation

1. For a more general account of this dual role see James O'Connor, *The Fiscal Crisis of the State* (New York, 1973), 6. Also, Alan Wolfe, *The Limits of Legitimacy* (New York, 1977), 250–52.

2. Habermas, *Legitimation Crisis*, trans. Thomas McCarthy (Boston, 1975), 4.

3. "Paul Schuster Taylor, California Social Scientist," transcribed oral history, Bancroft/UCB, 1975, II, 145. Taylor was also closely associated with many of those engaged in the Central Valley Project studies, and he served as Walter Goldschmidt's dissertation adviser. Many of Taylor's pertinent writings were collected in *Essays on Land, Water, and the Law in California* (New York, 1979).

4. That act referred only generally to the provisions of the reclamation law without specifically mentioning the requirement that farmers live "in the neighborhood" of their farms. The Bureau, convinced that such a requirement was too old-fashioned, claimed a new system of joint or district liability had been set up by the act, doing away with individual liability and the need for residency; when brought to the courts, however, the Bureau's interpretation was declared false, and only an explicit act of Congress in 1982 repealed the provision.

5. As Taylor told Mary Ellen Leary, the underlying issue was the integrity of administrative bureaus in government—their willingness to obey the law. See Leary's "The Power of a Tenacious Man," *Nation*, 219 (1974): 333–38.

6. The largest of these owners was the J. G. Boswell Co., a cotton producer farming over 19,000 acres (later as much as 185,000, all with federally subsidized water); it also developed close connections with the Safeway food chain and the Los Angeles *Times* conglomerate. Paul Taylor's writings on the Pine Flat Dam and Tulare Lake include: "The Excess Land Law," *California Law Rev.*, 47 (1959): 499–541; and "Whose Dam Is Pine Flat?" *Pacific Spectator*, 8 (1954): 349–59; "The Excess Land Law," *Yale Law J.* 64 (1955): 477–514.

7. Paul Taylor, "The Excess Land Law," *Rocky Mountain Law Rev.*, 30 (1958): 499–508.

8. See Ivanhoe Irrigation District v. McCracken, 357 U.S. 275. Also, Paul Taylor, "Destruction of a Federal Reclamation Policy?" *Stanford Law Rev.*, 10 (1957): 76–111; "The Excess Land Law," *Western Political Q.*, 12 (1959): 828–33.

9. Senate Committee on Interior and Insular Affairs, *Acreage Limitation (Reclamation Law) Review: Hearings*, 85th Cong., 2nd sess. (Washington, 1958), 77–78, 88, 136, 191.

10. *The California Water Plan*, Department of Water Resources Bull. 3 (Sacramento, 1957); *The California State Water Project in 1976*, Bull. 132–67 (Sacramento, 1967); William Kahrl, ed., *The California Water Atlas* (Sacramento, 1979), 50–56; Garmulch Gill, Edward Gray, and David Seckler,

"The California Water Plan and Its Critics," in David Seckler, ed., *California Water* (Berkeley, 1971), 3–27.

11. Passage of the plan is the theme of Harvey Grody, "From North to South," *Southern California Q.*, 60 (1978): 287–326. See also *Paul Schuster Taylor*, 346–56; Keith Roberts, "The Public Role of Engineering," *Engineering Issues: J. of Professional Activities, Proc. ASCE*, 99 (1973): 21; George Ballis, *An Evaluation: The California Water Plan*, Public Affairs Institute pamphlet (Washington, 1960); Robert Fellmuth, *Politics of Land* (New York, 1973), 156–74; Richard Walker and Michael Storper, "The California Water System," *Public Affairs Report*, U. of California Inst. of Governmental Studies, 20 (1979), which is mainly on Phase II of the plan, the proposed Peripheral Canal to divert Sacramento water around the delta and south.

12. Kahrl, 53.

13. Don Villarejo, "New Lands for Agriculture: The California State Water Project," California Inst. for Rural Studies (Davis, 1981), 3, 6.

14. A "water district" in California differs from an "irrigation district" in that voting in it is weighted by property, not one person—one vote. In later decades the trend has been toward this antidemocratic form of political organization and water control; so argue Merrill Goodall, John Sullivan, and Timothy DeYoung in *California Water* (Montclair, N.J., 1978). In the Westlands, they point out (pp. 20–21), ten landowners own 43% of all the land and can control elections. In Tulare Lake Basin Water Storage District, the Boswell corporation alone has 37,845 votes, a controlling majority.

15. Udall, cit. "Goliath CVP Grows, San Luis Dedicated," *Reclamation Era*, 54 (1968): 57. On the controversy over acreage limits here, see Paul Taylor, "Excess Land Law," *UCLA Law Rev.*, 9 (1962): 1–43; "Excess Land Law," *California Law Rev.*, 52 (1964): 978–1014; and "California Water Project," *Ecology Law Q.*, 5 (1975): 1–52.

16. Brody, "What's Really Happening in Westlands?" *Western Water*, 28 (May–June 1976): 4. For the Bureau's lax record throughout the CVP, see General Accounting Office, *Congress Should Reevaluate the 160-Acre Limitation on Land Eligible to Receive Water from Federal Water Resources Projects"* (Washington, 1972), which found that systematic leasing was allowing widespread evasion of the spirit of the law. The ten largest farm operators—one of them operating over 40,000 acres in seven different districts—were collecting in 1971 a subsidy worth $3.2 million (pp. 10–11).

17. Nelson, *Cong. Rec.*, 13 Sept. 1979, S12470.

18. David Weiman, testimony before the Senate Select Committee on Small Business and Committee on Interior and Insular Affairs, "Will the Family Farm Survive in America?" *Hearings*, 94th Cong., 1st sess., (Washington, 1975), 53; Oakland *Tribune*, 10 July 1974; San Francisco *Examiner*, 27 March 1975; Fellmuth, 175–78; Bureau of Reclamation, *Special Task Force on San Luis Unit, CVP* (Washington, 1978), 193–212; George Baker, "Family Farming vs.

Land Monopoly," *California J.*, 7 (1976): 294; Mary Louise Frampton, "The Enforcement of Federal Reclamation Law in the Westlands District," *U.C. Davis Law Rev.*, 13 (1979–80): 89–122.

19. LeVeen and Goldman, "Reclamation Policy and the Water Subsidy," *American J. of Agricultural Economics*, 60 (1978): 929–30. See also LeVeen, "Looking Backwards at the San Luis Project," undated mimeographed paper, WRCA/UCB.

20. National Land for People, Inc. v. Bureau of Reclamation, 417 F. Supp. 449 (D.D.C. 1976). The injunction was subsequently lifted, then reinstated in 1979.

21. Gardner, *Fat City* (New York, 1969, Dell ed.), 78.

22. In the Westlands district, for all its immensely wealthy growers with federal subsidies, there was a great deal of poverty. The Mexican-American majority there was the poorest group; in 1970 its average family had six members and an annual income of $3,000 (Fresno *Bee*, 12 June 1980). See also Paul Barnett, *Imperial Valley*, California Inst. for Rural Studies (Davis, 1978), on class and race inequalities.

23. Coke, "Reminiscences on People and Change in California Agriculture, 1900–1975," transcribed oral history, Special Collections, U. of California, Davis, 1976, 39. Coke was director of the California State Department of Agriculture under Governor Ronald Reagan, and his interviewer describes him as "the most influential single figure on the California agriculture scene for the past fifty years" (p. iv).

24. Ellis Hawley, "The Politics of the Mexican Labor Issue, 1950–1965," *AH*, 40 (1966): 157–76. See also the works by Ernesto Galarza on this period, including *Merchants of Labor* (Charlotte, N.C., 1964) and *Farm Workers and Agri-business in California, 1947–1960* (Notre Dame, Ind., 1977). Galarza was research and education director of the National Agricultural Workers Union and was active in the campaign to end the *bracero* program. Also see Peter Kirsten, *Anglo over Bracero* (San Francisco, 1977).

25. The history of this period can be approached in part through Chavez's life and achievements. See Peter Matthiessen, *Sal Si Puedes* (New York, 1969); Joan London and Henry Anderson, *So Shall Ye Reap* (New York, 1970), esp. chaps. 7–8; and Jacques Levy, *Cesar Chavez* (New York, 1975).

26. Cit. Bernard Taper, "The Bittersweet Harvest," *Science 80*, 1 (Nov. 1980): 82. Also, Wayne Rasmussen, "Advances in American Agriculture," *Technology and Culture*, 9 (1978): 531–43; Andrew Schmitz and David Seckler, "Mechanized Agriculture and Social Welfare," *American J. of Agricultural Economics*, 52 (1970): 569–77; and Roy Bainer, "Science and Technology in Western Agriculture," in James Shideler, ed., *Agriculture in the Development of the Far West* (Washington, 1975), 56–72.

27. Alvin Josephy, Jr., "Here in Nevada a Terrible Crime," *American Heritage*, 21 (June 1970): 93–100; Paul Jones, "Reclamation and the Indian," *Utah*

Historical Q., 27 (1959): 51–56; "The Indian Water Wars," *Newsweek*, 101 (13 June 1983): 80–82; Richard Berkman and W. Kip Viscusi, *Damming the West* (New York, 1973), 151–96.

28. Veeder, "Winters Doctrine Rights," *Montana Law Rev.*, 26 (1965): 149. See also his "Water Rights in the Coal Fields of the Yellowstone River Basin," *Law and Contemporary Problems*, 49 (1976): 77–96; and "Water Rights," *Indian Historian*, 5 (Summer 1972): 4–9. See also Winters v. United States, 207 U.S. 567 (1908).

29. For an excellent overview of the matter, with thorough notes to the literature, see Norris Hundley, Jr., "The Dark and Bloody Ground of Indian Water Rights," *Western Historical Q.*, 9 (1978): 455–82.

30. Michael Kinsley, "Ben Yellen's Fine Madness," *Washington Monthly*, 2 (1971): 38–49.

31. Water and Power Resources Service [Bureau of Reclamation], *Acreage Limitation: Draft Environmental Impact Statement* (Washington, 1981), 2-1 to 2-4, 3-11, 3-12, 3-13, 3-23. The rules were announced in 1977, after which an impact statement was forced by a suit brought by Fresno County against the government. In the statement "large" and "small" farm alternatives were also considered, the latter defined by a 320-acre operation limit, which if enforced would have produced 9,138 new farms. National Land for People favored a 100-acre ceiling on ownership, 640-acre on operation: see Peter Bass and Edward Kirschner, "Demographic, Economic, and Fiscal Impacts of Alternative Westlands Reclamation Act Enforcement Scenarios," *American J. of Agricultural Economics*, 60 (1978): 935–40. Dropping out of sight was an older idea, proposed by Congressman Robert Kastenmeier of Wisconsin, that the government purchase all reclaimed lands above 160 acres and either sell or lease them. For a related and intriguing "regional land bank" idea, see Sheldon Greene, "Promised Land," *Ecology Law Q.*, 5 (1976): 748–50. Another ignored option was some system of small-scale cooperative farming, as discussed by Philip LeVeen, "Enforcing the Reclamation Act and Rural Development in California," *Rural Sociology*, 44 (1979): 685–86.

32. Don Razee et al., "The 160-Acre Limit: America Faces Agrarian Reform," *California Farmer*, 248 (7 Jan. 1978): 9, 10, 12, 16.

33. Senate Committee on Energy and Natural Resources, *Reclamation Reform Act of 1979: Hearings*, 96th Cong., 1st sess. (Washington, 1979). *Cong. Rec.*, 13 Sept. 1979, S12464-511; 14 Sept., S12553-96.

34. Reagan had opposed the acreage limit as governor of California; see State of California, *Report of the Governor's Task Force on the Acreage Limitation Problem* (Sacramento, 1968), where his appointees argued that limits "are contraincentives" and "impede growth." Reagan and his task force stood for the self-contradictory policies of a free-market approach to farm size and a subsidy for irrigation; see Harry Hogan, *The Acreage Limitation in the Federal Reclamation Program* (Arlington, Va., 1972), 270.

35. *Cong. Rec.*, 5 May 1982, H1822; 6 May, H1902; 16 July, S8495.

36. Wallop, *Cong. Rec.*, 13 Sept. 1979, S12484; Senator Alan Simpson, S12511; McClure, S12468. Hatch, *Reclamation Reform Act of 1979,* 165; Puchen, 339; Wolf, 1679; Wallop, 228.

37. Harold Carter and Gerald Dean, *Cost-Size Relationships for Cash-Crop Farms in Imperial Valley, California,* California Agricultural Experiment Station, Giannini Foundation Research Report 253 (1962); Warren Johnston, *Economies of Size and Imputed Values of Farmland in the Imperial Valley of California, ibid.,* Report 314 (1971); William Martin, "Economies of Size and the 160-Acre Limitation," *American J. of Agricultural Economics,* 60 (1978): 923–28. Martin maintains that enforcement of the old limit would lead to a 1% drop in food production, causing prices to rise $24 per capita. In contrast, Bruce Johnston and Peter Kilby argue that "almost never does land reform decrease production, occasionally it has a neutral effect, most often it has a positive effect." *Agriculture and Structural Transformation* (New York, 1975), 162.

38. A useful discussion of this question is Philip Raup's "Economies and Diseconomies of Large-Scale Agriculture," *American J. of Agricultural Economics,* 51 (1969): 1274–83. Farm economist David Holland writes, "I personally remain unconvinced that technical economies are very important in agriculture." The larger farms, he suspects, show smaller per-acre yields. Discussion, *ibid.,* 60 (1978): 941–42. See also Kevin Calandri and Susan McGowan, "Environmental, Social, and Economic Implications of the 160-Acre Limitation Law for California," paper presented at Western Economic Association meeting, Honolulu, June 1978, 12–23; and Angus McDonald, *One Hundred and Sixty Acres of Water* (Washington, 1958), 29, 36.

39. David Holland and Douglas Young, "The 160-Acre Limitation: An Examination of Economically Viable Farm Size in the Columbia Basin of Washington State," reprinted in *Reclamation Reform Act of 1979,* 907–10; David Seckler and Robert Young, "Economic and Policy Implications of the 160-Acre Limitation in Federal Reclamation Law," *American J. of Agricultural Economics,* 60 (1978): 579.

40. The requirement that reclamation farmers live on or near their farms was especially resented as "feudal" and "peasantlike." See, for example, the impassioned resistance to the idea expressed by Randall Koenig and Peter Thompson, "Acreage, Residency, and Excess Land Sales," *San Diego Law Rev.,* 15 (1978): 914–15. Also, the recommendation (in Hogan, 292) that Congress "move the Reclamation farmer into a market economy and away from the agrarian mythic family farm way of life." These writers fail to realize that business and industrial farming rely as much as agrarianism does on myths of human nature and on such nonrational passions as raw greed and unreason masquerading as reason.

41. Moynihan, *Cong. Rec.*, 16 July 1982, S8484–85; Weaver, *ibid.,* 5 May 1982, H1826. For the continuing failure to get new water projects passed, see Congressional Research Service, Library of Congress, *Major Legislation of the Congress: Summary Issue,* 97th Cong. (Jan. 1983), MLC-107.

42. Seckler and Young, "Economic and Policy Implications of the 160-Acre Limitation in Federal Reclamation Law," *American J. of Agricultural Economics* 60 (1978): 576.

Leviathan Ailing

1. Dorothy Gallagher, "The Collapse of the Great Teton Dam," *New York Times Mag.*, 19 September 1976, 16, 95–102, 108.
2. See Gaylord Shaw, "The Nationwide Search for Dams in Danger," *Smithsonian*, 9 (April 1978): 36. Also, Charles Outland, *Man-Made Disaster* (Glendale, Calif., 1963); Allen Cullen, *Rivers in Harness* (Philadelphia, 1962); and Peter Briggs, *Rampage* (New York, 1973). On the San Luis failure, see San Francisco *Examiner*, 1 October 1981.
3. Sid Gautam, "Irrigation Development in Third World Countries: Dreams and Disasters," *Irrigation and Drainage in the Nineteen-Eighties,* Irrigation and Drainage Div., ASCE, Specialty Conference (New York, 1979), 353, 355.; M. Taghi Farvar and John Milton, eds., *The Careless Technology* (Garden City, N.Y., 1972), 155–367. The Water Resources Council in the United States estimated in 1968 that the storage capacity of American reservoirs was being reduced at the rate of 1 million acre-feet a year by sedimentation; the problem is, of course, much more severe in some areas—especially in the Southwest —than in others: see Public Land Law Review Commission, *One Third of the Nation's Land* (Washington, 1970), 150.
4. Bureau of Reclamation, *Westwide Study Report on Critical Water Problems Facing the Eleven Western States* (Washington, 1975), I, 46.
5. Fred Powledge, *Water* (New York, 1982), 37–38; William Ashworth, *Nor Any Drop to Drink* (New York, 1982), 49; "War over Water," *U.S. News & World Report,* 31 Oct. 1983, 57; U.S. Water Resources Council, *The Nation's Water Resources, 1975–2000* (Washington, 1978), I, 12–13; C. Richard Murray and E. Bodette Reeves, "Estimated Use of Water in the United States in 1970," U.S. Geological Survey Circ. 676 (Washington, 1970), 22–23.
6. Schad, "Western Water Resources: Means to Augment the Supply," in *Western Water Resources* (Boulder, 1980), 117. See also "Water in the West," *The Economist,* 14 May 1983, 41–46. The problems of the region are made especially severe by periodic droughts; for example, the one of 1977–78, which devastated the entire West.
7. The Bureau of Reclamation estimates that there are 6.2 billion acre-feet of water stored at depths of 50 to 200 feet (*Westwide Study Report,* II, 4). California counts as much as a sixth of that amount, according to Erwin Cooper, in *Aqueduct Empire* (Glendale, Calif., 1968), 114. The heavy withdrawal of this water has led to severe cracking and slumping of the earth's surface as much as 30 feet in some parts of California. See J. F. Poland and

G. H. Davis, "Land Subsidence Due to Withdrawal of Fluids," *Reviews in Engineering Geology,* 2 (1969): 187–269. Robert Dunbar, in "The Adaptation of Groundwater-Control Institutions to the Arid West," *AH,* 51 (1977): 662–80, discusses California's doctrine of "correlative rights," an application of the riparian principle of equal use to all. Also, Robert Reis, "Concepts of Ground Water Production and Management—The California Experience," *Natural Resources J.,* 7 (1967): 53–87.

8. Donald Green, *The Land of the Underground Rain* (Austin, 1973), 145–64; James Aucoin, "The Irrigation Revolution and Its Environmental Consequences," *Environment,* 21 (Oct. 1979): 17–20, 38–40; U.S. Water Resources Council, I, 17–20. A comparable Idaho experience is described by David Smith, "Superfarms vs. Sagebrush," *Proc. of the Assoc. of American Geographers,* 2 (1970): 127–31.

9. David Todd, "Groundwater Utilization," in David Seckler, ed., *California Water* (Berkeley, 1971), 182; Schad, 118–32.

10. The view that such transfer is right and inevitable is taken by Charles Corker, "Save the Columbia River for Posterity, or What Has Posterity Done for You Lately?" *U. of Washington Law Rev.,* 41 (1966): 838–55. The idea to divert the Columbia began with the Bureau's United Western Investigation of 1948: see S. P. McCasland, "Water from Pacific Northwest to Deserts of Southwest," *Civil Engineering,* 22 (Feb. 1952): 45–48.

11. Ralph M. Parsons Co., *North American Water and Power Alliance Studies* (Los Angeles, 1965); and Senate Committee on Public Works, *Western Water Development* (Washington, 1966). The Soviet Union has contemplated a similarly ambitious scheme that would divert the Ob and Irtysh rivers southward toward the Caspian and Aral seas irrigation areas. See Thane Gustafson, "Technology Assessment, Soviet Style," *Science,* 208 (1980): 1343–48; and I. P. Gerasimov and A. M. Gindin, "The Problem of Transferring Runoff from Northern and Siberian Rivers to the Arid Regions of the European USSR, Soviet Central Asia, and Kazakhstan," in Gilbert White, ed. *Environmental Effects of Complex River Development,* (Boulder, 1977), 59–70.

12. Moss, *The Water Crisis* (New York, 1976), 254.

13. Stegner, "Myths of the Western Dam," *Saturday Rev.,* 23 Oct. 1965, 31.

14. Howard Reed, "Major Trends in California Agriculture," *AH,* 20 (1946): 254–55; Robert van den Bosch, *The Pesticide Conspiracy* (Garden City, N.Y., 1980), 23–24. On the banning of DDT and other compounds see Thomas Dunlap, *DDT* (Princeton, 1981), 231–45; John Perkins, *Insects, Experts, and the Insecticide Crisis* (New York, 1982). Also, J. R. Bradley, "Pesticide Effects upon the Agroecosystem," in Frank Guthrie and Jerome Perry, eds., *Introduction to Environmental Toxicology* (New York, 1980), 289–98.

15. Carson, *Silent Spring* (Boston, 1962), 49–50.

16. Joel Schwartz, "Poisoning Farmworkers," *Environment,* 17 (June 1975): 33. According to Frank Guthrie ("Pesticides and Humans," in Guthrie and Perry,

p. 302), nearly 3,000 farmers and agricultural workers are hospitalized from pesticide poisoning each year. Peter Matthiessen discussed the farm workers' reluctance to draw attention to their pesticide danger (*Sal Si Puedes*, 215). See also David Pimental et al., "Environmental and Social Costs of Pesticides," *Oikos*, 34 (1980): 126–40; and J. E. Davies, J. C. Cassady, and A. Raffonelli, "The Pesticide Problems of the Agricultural Worker," in W. B. Deichman, ed., *Pesticides and the Environment* (New York, 1973): 223–31.

17. Cit. Aucoin, 39.

18. Plants vary considerably in their sensitivity to salts, the grasses, grains, cotton, and beets having a relatively high tolerance among cultivars. See George Cox and Michael Atkins, *Agricultural Ecology* (San Francisco, 1979), 301–2.

19. Asit Biswas, "Environmental Implications of Water Development for Developing Countries," in Carl Widstrand et al., eds., *Water and Society*, pt. 1 (Oxford, 1978), 287; Biswas, "Water: A Perspective on Global Issues and Politics," *J. of Water Resources Planning and Management Div., Proc. ASCE*, 105 (1979): 216; UNESCO, *Salinity Problems in the Arid Zones*, Arid Zone Research 14 (Paris, 1961). More than a third of the world's irrigated land is plagued by salt problems: so estimates Gaylord Skogerboe, "Agricultural Impact on Water Quality in Western United States," in Hsieh Wen Shen, ed., *Environmental Impact on Rivers* (Fort Collins, Colo., 1973), 12-1.

20. Eaton, "Irrigation Agriculture along the Nile and the Euphrates," *Scientific Monthly*, 49 (1949): 41; Jacobsen and Adams, "Salt and Silt in Ancient Mesopotamian Agriculture," *Science*, 128 (1958): 1254–58. See also Erik Eckholm, *Losing Ground* (New York, 1976), 114–28.

21. Herbert Brownell and Samuel Eaton, "The Colorado River Salinity Problem with Mexico," *American J. of International Law*, 2 (1975): 255–71. See also the articles in the special issue of *Natural Resources J.*, 15 (1975): 1–239.

22. Wesley Steiner, testimony before the Senate Committee on Interior and Insular Affairs, *Hearings on S. 1897, etc.*, 93rd Cong., 2nd sess. (Washington, 1974), 207–36; Brent Blackwelder, statement before the House Committee on Interior and Insular Affairs, *Hearings* (Washington, 1974), 306–12; Norris Hundley, *Dividing the Waters* (Berkeley, 1966), 172–80; David Sheridan, "The Underwatered West," *Environment*, 23 (March 1981): 20–39.

23. Myron Holburt and Vernon Valentine, "Present and Future Salinity of Colorado River," *J. of Hydraulic Div., Proc. ASCE*, 98 (1972): 503–20; B. Delworth Gardner and Clyde Stewart, "Agriculture and Salinity," in Dean Peterson and A. Berry Crawford, eds., *Values and Choices in the Development of the Colorado River Basin* (Tucson, 1978), 127.

24. Vernon Valentine, "Impacts of Colorado River Salinity," *J. of Irrigation and Drainage Div., Proc. ASCE*, 100 (1974): 495–510; A. D. K. Laird, "Desalting Technology," in Seckler, 148–51. Skogerboe ("Agricultural Impact," 12-7) reports that the Salton Sea now has a salinity level of 40,000 ppm, higher than the ocean. It picks up 3.5 million tons of new salt each year from Imperial fields, according to Cooper, 74–75.

25. Colorado River Board of California, *Need for Controlling Salinity of the Colorado River* (Sacramento?, 1970), 68–69, 78. See also Ralph Johnson, "Our Salty Rivers," *Land and Water Rev.*, 13 (1978): 460–61, on the need for federal responsibility.

26. Sheridan, 14–18.

27. San Francisco *Chronicle*, 25 Nov. 1983. Another possibility, other than the drain, is a desalting plant. One has been planned for the Kesterston area, a $4.7 million experimental reverse-osmosis plant; the fresh water it produces will cost about $300 an acre-foot (Fresno *Bee*, 16 Oct. 1981). All desalting plants use enormous quantities of energy, nor is it clear yet how the waste brine can be safely disposed of.

28. The New Melones Dam, the second largest earthfill structure in the country, begun in 1974, was to inundate most of the Stanislaus River canyon. See John Mitchell, "Friend vs. Friend," *Audubon*, 82 (May 1980): 36–53; Thomas McHugh, "Allocation of Water from Federal Reclamation Projects?" *Ecology Law Q.*, 4 (1974): 350–51; and Tim Palmer, *The Stanislaus* (Berkeley, 1982).

29. Harry Blaney, "Consumptive Use and Water Waste by Phreatophytes," *J. of Irrigation and Drainage Div., Proc. ASCE*, 87 (1961): 37–46. These plants, which include the salt cedar, cottonwood, and juniper, cover 16 million acres in the West and annually consume—"steal" is the more common term—25 million acre-feet of water.

30. See Charles Goldman, "Biological Implications of Reduced Freshwater Flows on the San Francisco Bay–Delta System" in Seckler, 109–24, for the impact of the proposed Peripheral Canal. Also, Harry Dennis, *Water and Power* (San Francisco, 1981). The canal was turned down by the state's voters in a June 1982 referendum by a vote of 3.3 to 2.0 million. Northern counties, which feared losing their water to the south, voted as high as 97% against it; it was the first major water project to be defeated in California history (San Francisco *Examiner*, 10 June 1982).

31. This controversy is discussed by William Kahrl, *Water and Power* (Berkeley, 1982), 429–36; and "Mono Lake," *Western Law J.*, 4 (Fall 1982): 1, 14–16.

32. General discussions of the adverse environmental consequences of hydraulic engineering include: Robert Hagan and Edwin Roberts, "Ecological Impacts of Water Projects in California," *J. of Irrigation and Drainage Div., Proc. ASCE*, 98 (1972): 25–48; Lawrence Lee, "Environmental Implications of Governmental Reclamation in California," in James Shideler, ed., *Agriculture in the Development of the Far West* (Washington, 1975), 223–29; W. Frank Blair, "Ecological Aspects," in *Water, Man, and Nature* (Washington, 1972), 11–12; Philip Williams, "Damming the World," *Not Man Apart*, 13 (Oct. 1983): 10–11; Edward Goldsmith and Nicholas Hildyard, eds., *The Social and Environmental Effects of Building Large Dams* (Camelford, Cornwall, 1984).

33. Paul Gates, "Pressure Groups and Recent American Land Policies," *AH*, 55 (1981): 104; Powledge, 307–8; Philip Fradkin, *A River No More* (New York, 1981), 3–13.

VII. CONCLUSION:

Nature, Freedom, and the West

1. Huntington, "Is Democracy Dying?" *U.S. News & World Report,* 8 March 1976, 51. See also Huntington, Michel Crozier, and Joji Watanuki, *The Crisis of Democracy* (New York, 1975), 113.
2. A similar argument has been made by David Orr and Stuart Hill, "Leviathan, the Open Society, and the Crisis of Ecology," *Western Political Q.,* 31 (1978): 457–69.
3. The beginnings of a new "eco-agriculture" for the Great Central Valley of California are suggested by Isao Fijimoto in "The Movement for an Ecological Agriculture and Appropriate Technology," in Committee on the Judiciary, *Priorities in Agricultural Research of the U.S. Department of Agriculture— Appendix,* 95th Cong., 1st sess. (Washington, 1978), 1039–54. So far, however, no one has systematically addressed the problem of designing a more democratic, ecologically harmonious water technology in the West—a "soft path" for the future.
4. Schumacher, *Small Is Beautiful* (New York, 1973), 31.

INDEX